"In a book that will grip scholars of global social movements and the Middle East and policymakers, Navid Pourmokhtari deploys a nuanced reading of Foucault on power and resistance to great narrative effect in tracing the history of the 2009 Iranian Green Movement."
John Foran, University of California, USA

"In this timely and informative book, Navid Pourmokhtari addresses some of the most pressing questions about the Iranian Green Movement that emerged in 2009. This is an essential read for anyone wishing to understand the great struggle within Iranian society for democracy and social justice."
Ramin Jahanbegloo, Jindal Global University, India

"Navid Pourmokhtari enlists Michel Foucault to provide a careful and original account of Iran's 2009 Green Movement as a broad-based civil rights movement. This book gives an excellent account of the Green Movement's history and some possible futures for Iranian social and political life."
Corey McCall, Penn State University, USA

"Pourmokhtari's fascinating book presents a Foucauldian analysis of Iran's 2009 Green Movement, a 'movement of movements' which sought civic rights and democratic accountability. To do so, he also adroitly analyzes the disciplinary project of the Islamic Republic and everyday forms of resistance to it."
Jeff Goodwin, New York University, USA

"The Green Movement of 2009 in Iran introduced a new generation of popular uprisings of the 21st Century. Navid Pourmokhtari's book is a welcome addition to a growing literature on one of the most remarkable political movements in the Middle East and beyond."
Asef Bayat, University of Illinois Urbana-Champaign, USA

"More than a decade after the rise of a major civil rights movement in Iran, this book is the most mature and balanced assessment of what happened when millions of Iranians poured into their streets demanding liberation from tyranny and freedom to be integral to the democratic aspiration of their homeland. About half a dozen volumes and countless learned essays later, Pourmokhtari's seminal study is a living testimony that social uprisings and the manner of reading them for the posterity are the engine of history. A superb book and an indispensable work of scholarship."

Hamid Dabashi, Author of *The Fox and the Paradox: Iran, the Green Movement and the USA*

Iran's Green Movement

This book examines the emergence and development of the 2009 Green Movement in Iran. The approach emphasizes the context and the local and historical specificities in which mass oppositional movements arise, develop and conduct their operations. Meanwhile, it foregrounds an account of multiple modernities that work to transcend modernist assumptions.

The volume describes and analyzes the power modalities—disciplinary, biopolitical, and sovereign—employed by the Islamic Republic to governmentalize the masses. Bearing a triangular methodology, the book consists of six semi-structured interviews with authorities and activists who participated in the pivotal events of that period; discourse analysis focusing on the Iranian constitution and the relevant government policy documents and speeches; and archival analysis. These provide the historical background, perspectives and insights required to analyse and explicate the conditions responsible for the emergence of the Green Movement and to grasp how collective action was enabled and organized.

Marking a particular historical phase in the development of a home-grown democracy in post-revolutionary Iran, the Green Movement is transforming the country's political landscape. This book is a key resource to students and scholars interested in comparative politics, Iranian studies and the Middle East.

Navid Pourmokhtari (PhD) teaches Politics at the University of Alberta and Grant MacEwan University. His research interests lie in the areas of international relations and comparative politics, with a special focus on mass oppositional movements, peace studies and international security studies. His most recent publications have appeared in *Third World Quarterly, Sociology of Islam, Jadaliyya, the Journal of Human Trafficking* and *Foucault Studies*, amongst others.

Iranian Studies

Series editors: Homa Katouzian, *University of Oxford*
and Mohamad Tavakoli-Targhi, *University of Toronto.*

Since 1967 the International Society for Iranian Studies (ISIS) has been a leading learned society for the advancement of new approaches in the study of Iranian society, history, culture and literature. The new ISIS Iranian Studies series published by Routledge will provide a venue for the publication of original and innovative scholarly works in all areas of Iranian and Persianate Studies.

Persian Calligraphy
A Corpus Study of Letterforms
Mahdiyeh Meidani

Iranian National Cinema
The Interaction of Policy, Genre, Funding and Reception
Anne Démy-Geroe

Judeo-Persian Writings
A Manifestation of Intellectual and Literary Life
Edited and Compiled by Nahid Pirnazar

Foreign Policy of the Islamic Republic of Iran
Between Ideology and Pragmatism
Przemyslaw Osiewicz

Secularization of Islam in Post-Revolutionary Iran
Mahmoud Pargoo

Iran's Green Movement
Everyday Resistance, Political Contestation and Social Mobilization
Navid Pourmokhtari

For more information about this series, please visit: https://www.routledge.com/middleeaststudies/series/IRST

Iran's Green Movement
Everyday Resistance, Political Contestation and Social Mobilization

Navid Pourmokhtari

Routledge
Taylor & Francis Group
LONDON AND NEW YORK

First published 2021
by Routledge
2 Park Square, Milton Park, Abingdon, Oxon OX14 4RN

and by Routledge
605 Third Avenue, New York, NY 10158

Routledge is an imprint of the Taylor & Francis Group, an informa business

© 2021 Navid Pourmokhtari

The right of Navid Pourmokhtari to be identified as author of this work has been asserted by him in accordance with sections 77 and 78 of the Copyright, Designs and Patents Act 1988.

All rights reserved. No part of this book may be reprinted or reproduced or utilised in any form or by any electronic, mechanical, or other means, now known or hereafter invented, including photocopying and recording, or in any information storage or retrieval system, without permission in writing from the publishers.

Trademark notice: Product or corporate names may be trademarks or registered trademarks, and are used only for identification and explanation without intent to infringe.

British Library Cataloguing-in-Publication Data
A catalogue record for this book is available from the British Library

Library of Congress Cataloging-in-Publication Data
A catalog record has been requested for this book

ISBN: 978-0-367-74445-8 (hbk)
ISBN: 978-0-367-74446-5 (pbk)
ISBN: 978-1-003-15788-5 (ebk)

Typeset in Times New Roman
by SPi Global, India

This work is dedicated to the uncelebrated multitudes, especially the Baha'is of Iran, who have sacrificed so much to create a better world, and to my wife Shadan and daughter Mouness, who are the light of my world.

Contents

Introduction ... 1

1. Critical literature review ... 9

2. Theorizing the Green Movement: A Foucauldian model ... 33

3. The coming of a disciplinary society to post-revolutionary Iran: Ordinary Iranians and everyday resistance ... 61

4. Social mobilization and political contestation in Iran at the turn of the millennium: The 1999 student movement and the 2006 women's one million signature campaign ... 98

5. The Green Movement as a movement of movements and the rise of a home-grown rights-based society in post-revolutionary Iran ... 146

Conclusion: What were the Iranians dreaming about in 2009? The Green Movement of counterconduct: A history of the past, the present and the future ... 189

Bibliography ... 202
Index ... 227

Introduction

In June 2009, in the immediate aftermath of Iran's tenth presidential election, there appeared on the streets of Tehran and other major Iranian cities something unprecedented in the thirty-year history of the Islamic Republic: immense crowds, comprised mostly of students, women and youth, engaged in spontaneous forms of collective action against what was widely perceived to be election fraud. Over the course of the next nine months, urban streets and squares would echo with cries of *Ra'aye Man Kojast?*, "Where is my vote?," the signature refrain of the demonstrators (Rahe Sabz, 2010). The so-called Green Movement had emerged upon the scene. Taking their cue from the two oppositional leaders, Mir-Hossein Mousavi and Mehdi Karoubi, in particular the former who had chosen the colour green, sacred to Shi'a Islam, to symbolize his presidential campaign, demonstrators filled the streets, their green banners, posters, balloons and bracelets proclaiming their defiance. These massive demonstrations, some the largest since the 1979 revolution, took the majority of political commentators and policy makers, indeed the world at large, by surprise. The ensuing crisis gave rise to a popular oppositional movement of formidable strength, one that would challenge the status quo as nothing else had in the post-revolutionary period, dividing religious and political elites asunder and rocking the Islamic Republic to its very foundation.

The street demonstrations that erupted that June would continue in some cities for nine more months, despite the presence of powerful security forces that included the Islamic Revolutionary Guard Corps and paramilitary *basiji* militias that were sophisticated and brutal in equal measure. Bringing to bear the full machinery of state repression, which included terror and intimidation applied indiscriminately (Hashemi & Postel, 2010), the Islamic Republic had heretofore succeeded in crushing oppositional movements in their infancy—but not this time. Despite the systematic, brutal and unrelenting assault directed against them (Dabashi, 2011), the protestors, marching under the banner of the Green Movement, succeeded in maintaining a presence on the street, thereby exerting pressure on Tehran to recognize their demands—in and of itself something unprecedented in the history of post-revolutionary Iran.

The Green Movement's chief impact laid in challenging the two keystone institutions of the Islamic Republic, namely the Guardian Council and the Office of the Supreme Leader. The former was responsible for supervising elections and selecting candidates deemed fit to contest the presidency. To its credit, as early as June 16, three days after the initial uprising began, the Council announced that it had authorized a partial recount of the electoral vote, the aim being to address the concerns of those on the streets who suspected widespread electoral fraud (Raja News, 2014). This initiative was, however, firmly rejected by both Mousavi and Karoubi who, sensing the mood in the streets, demanded new elections, which, as it turned out, were never called.

Never before had the Islamic Republic and its Supreme Leader faced so daunting a challenge. Not only were the latter's demands to end the demonstrations ignored; responsibility for the massacre of activists—estimates vary from eighty to several hundred (The Guardian, 2009; Radio Farda, 2009)—was pinned on his august person in whom was invested ultimate political authority. Heretofore, this sublime figure had been held to be irreproachable—now this was no longer the case. An irresistible tide of popular defiance had repudiated all that was invested in him, including the *vilayat-e faqih*, or the Rule/Guardianship of the Jurist, one of the foundational principles of the post-revolutionary Iranian constitution and a chief source of its legitimacy. And so it came to pass that on November 4 (Aban Student Day) and later on December 26 (the Shi'ite holy day of Ashura), both marked by beatings, arrests and the deaths of several demonstrators, crowds filled the streets, chanting *Marg bar Khamenei*, "Death to Khamenei," and *Khamenei Ghatele Velayatesh Bateleh*, "Khamenei is a Murderer; His *Vilayat* (Leadership) is Invalid" (Rahe Sabz, 2009; Rahe Sabz, 2009a). This was accompanied by demands on the part of some demonstrators for the creation of an Iranian Republic that would supersede an Islamic Republic widely perceived as illegitimate (Etemadi, 2009). It was these unanticipated events that plunged the latter into an "unprecedented crisis of … legitimacy" (Bashiriyeh, 2010, p. 62), prompting some to predict "the beginning of [its] end" (Sadri, cited in Bashiriyeh, 2010, p. 66).

The Green Movement was the first of its kind in the Middle East and North Africa (MENA) to focus on winning civil rights; it was also the first instance of mass mobilization in the new millennium, at least on so immense a scale. This has led some observers, including Charles Kurzman (2012), to speculate that it may have inspired the Arab Spring, which two years later would shake the whole MENA region to its foundation. Writing in 2011, Mir-Hossein Mousavi, one of the symbolic leaders of the Green Movement, echoed this view:

> The starting point of what we are now witnessing on the streets of Tunis, Sanaa, Cairo, Alexandria and Suez can undoubtedly be traced back to the days of the 15th, 18th and 20th of June 2009 when people took to the streets of Tehran in millions shouting "Where is my vote?" and peacefully demanding a return of their … rights.
>
> (cited in Kurzman, 2012, p. 162)

Thus, the Green Movement may have influenced these more recent political upheavals, and precisely because it was the "[first] movement [of its kind, one] that most outside observers [had not] expect[ed] to see in a region such as [MENA]" (Nasri, 2009, para. 2). Mojtaba Mahdavi provides a sense of the magnitude of its impact in describing it as a watershed event that "transcend[ed] constructed dichotomies, such as tradition and modernity, faith and freedom ... [the] particular and universal, and [the] sacred and secular" that have traditionally informed much of what passes for social science scholarship on the region (2011, p. 94).

Not surprisingly, this landmark movement captured the attention of several prominent scholars who have labelled it variously as a "civil rights movement" (Dabashi, 2011), a "major non-violent movement in the Gandhian style" (Jahanbegloo, 2010), a "great emancipatory event" (Žižek, 2009), an "Iranian-style Intifada" (Fisk, 2009), a "Persian Spring" (Halliday, 2010), "something unique and new" (Javaherian, cited in Postel 2010), "something quite extraordinary" (Dabashi, 2009); indeed, a movement "ahead of our inherited politics, floating ideologies or mismatched theories" (Dabashi, 2009, para. 20).

Thus, understanding the Green Movement may offer insight into the dynamics likely to come into play in any number of MENA countries where a popular movement seeks to alter fundamentally the political status quo. It may also aid in identifying the conditions under which a people are willing to defy openly a state that appears, at least on the surface, to be unchallengeable. Lastly, it may provide insight into the nature, dynamics and attributes of oppositional movements and their techniques and tactics and particular modes of activism, as well as the various forms of social and political change now emerging in MENA.

All this is of singular importance given that the literature on MENA social movements has long been dominated by mainstream social movement theories, which, as will be argued, fall far short of elucidating adequately the conditions necessary for the emergence of oppositional movements in this part of the world, or of accounting for the experiences, trajectories, aims and aspirations of their constituents. As will be shown, this is due in large measure to the exceptionalist views, West-centric orientations, modernist assumptions and universalizing tendencies embedded in these theories that lead MENA oppositional movements to be viewed as regressive, fundamentalist and/or backward, thus explaining why they have been relegated to the margins of Social Movement Studies.

At the same time, given that the Green Movement emerged but a few short years ago and that a number of political developments in the post-Ahmadinejad period (2013–present) have fundamentally altered the Iranian social and political landscape, its genesis, history and impact are not as yet clearly discernible. In particular, more empirical work is required to elucidate the Green Movement's relationship, if any, to earlier oppositional movements—something that has received short shrift in the literature—if we are to understand the complex conditions existing between state and society during the post-revolutionary period that might account for the Green Movement's emergence and the commitment on the part of its constituents to contest the status quo.

It is precisely owing to the reasons discussed above that this book draws so heavily on the work of Michel Foucault, and especially his analysis of power and resistance and studies of the 1789 French and 1979 Iranian revolutions. The purpose here lies in applying a Foucauldian-inspired theoretical framework—to my knowledge the first time this has been done so comprehensively and on so large a scale in the case of any mass oppositional movement within the MENA region—that is sensitive to the geographical and sociohistorical context within which oppositional movements in the region have emerged and conducted their operations. At the same time, such a framework would take account of multiple modernities, vis-à-vis the exclusivist notion of a single European/Western-inspired notion of modernity that is a defining feature, as well as a chief assumption, of the leading social movement theories—a notion that carries with it the implication that Western oppositional movements represent both harbingers as well as promoters of social and political progress, while excluding other alternatives.

The research questions posed here were born of a curiosity about a people who in 1979 set in motion one of the greatest sociopolitical mobilizations of the twentieth century, and who some three decades later would once again pour onto the streets in one of the greatest mass mobilizations of the new millennium. Understanding what, in the latter case, drove Iranians to challenge the Islamic Republic requires examining the state–society relationship extant in the post-revolutionary period; the institutions and groups and organizations contesting the social and political status quo; and the dynamics, relations and processes from which would spring so many of those mundane life practices, which, as will be shown, would be governmentalized and politicized by the Islamic Republic. Such an investigation will allow me to address my principal research question: *What set of conditions, historical, economic, social, and political, gave rise to the 2009 Green Movement?* It will also prepare the ground for answering three questions that follow logically from the first: *What ends did the Green Movement seek to achieve and to what extent were they realized? And to what degree, if any, did it represent a paradigm shift in Iran's sociopolitical landscape?*

With a view to addressing the above questions, this book employs a triangular methodology consisting of interviews, discourse analysis and archival analysis of primary and secondary sources. Examining the Green Movement's genesis and the historical factors responsible for its emergence, in addition to establishing its relationship to earlier oppositional movements of the post-revolutionary period, required interviewing leaders and activists who had played a prominent role in the 1999 Student Movement, the 2006 Women's One Million Signature Campaign and the Green Movement itself: Ali Afshari, Ali Abdi, Rouzbeh Safshekan, Sabra Rezaei and Zeynab Peyghambarzadeh. Also interviewed were scholars with a special interest in Foucault's concept of governmentality vis-à-vis the power–resistance nexus, specifically Walter Williams and Corey McCall, the aim being to strengthen the book's theoretical backbone.

Discourse analysis, the second corner of the triangulation methodology employed here, is used to elucidate Iran's constitution, relevant post-revolutionary-era government policy documents and publications, speeches by members of political elites, the purpose being to reveal the underlying concepts, imperatives, attitudes, assumptions and norms informing these texts, and hence the policy initiatives aimed at disciplining and governmentalizing, as well as subordinating and marginalizing, youth, women and student groups, the principal foci of the case studies presented here.

Lastly, I draw extensively upon archival resources, both primary and secondary. The former includes the diaries and speeches of prominent activists; YouTube clips of cell-phone footage shot during the demonstrations; and manuscripts and letters published by Green Movement leaders prior to, during and following the 2009 uprising. These sources provide detailed, first-hand accounts of the social and political conditions that gave rise to the Green Movement, as well as its aims, organizational and leadership structures, and the strategies and tactics informing its various modes of collective action.

The secondary sources, both published and unpublished, including textbooks, editorial commentary, book reviews, biographies and video documentaries, offer invaluable insight into how the masses, and particularly student, youth and women's groups, came to be mobilized and conduct their operations. Together, primary and secondary sources reveal the multidimensional character of the Green Movement and how that character was shaped, at least in part, by earlier contention episodes, such as the 1999 Student Movement and the 2006 Women's One Million Signature Campaign.[1]

In this book it is argued that the Green Movement may be more profitably viewed as a movement of movements, a concept that captures its fluid and multidimensional character as an amalgam of smaller social movements or, in Foucauldian terms, a coalition of smaller movements of counterconduct, which in 2009 coalesced to defy the state. This quintessential movement of movements was, as will be seen, the product of a particular phase in the history of post-revolutionary Iran, one marked by a yearning on the part of both activists and ordinary citizens to partake of the inalienable civic rights denied them by the state. Thus, it will be argued that the emergence of the Green Movement does, indeed, represent a paradigmatic shift in terms of the aims, aspirations and demands of Iranians for social and political change.

Chapter breakdown

Chapter 1, "Critical Literature Review," has three objectives. The first is to provide an overview of the scholarly literature locating the Green Movement within various episodes of contention politics, i.e., diverse kinds of social and political struggles, the aim being to make a case that it is, in fact, a social movement. The second requires surveying major social movement theories developed in the Western world so as to establish that a social movement of this kind possess, by virtue of the political setting within which it emerges and operates, certain specificities that are inconsistent with some of the foundational assumptions of leading mainstream social movement theories. Building on this point, the final objective lies in establishing the Green Movement as a movement of movements, an analytical concept, which, it will be argued, best captures its manifold characters.

Chapter 2, "Theorizing the Green Movement: A Foucauldian Model," makes a case for applying a Foucauldian theoretical perspective to analysing oppositional movements. The chapter commences by a discussion of Foucault, and of his works broadly, to ascertain the point that a closer interrogation of his work reveals much in the way of theory that can be applied to both Political Science and Social Movement Studies. In light of the latter discussion, and to theorize the Green Movement, I will proceed by detailing what a Foucauldian account of social movements actually entails and how it can contribute to explicating cases of oppositional collective action in general and the Green Movement in particular. Drawing on Foucault's triangulation of power, discourse and the everyday resistance–governmentality nexus, I demonstrate how it might be possible to construct the broad contours of a theoretical framework capable of shedding light on the conditions giving rise to the emergence of oppositional movements, in addition to explicating various modes of solidarity building and techniques and tactics for defying state power. In particular, I show how Foucault's triangulation offers a blueprint for mapping the conditions requisite for the emergence of "episodes of contention," for understanding the process of solidarity building, and for analysing particular techniques and modes of defiance/resistance and contestation/protestation. This chapter also describes the methodology and research design used here and discusses their utility and limitations. Lastly, it introduces and explicates what I call Islamist governmentality, a concept used to exclusively reference and explain the Islamic Republic's conduct of conduct.

Chapter 3, "The Coming of a Disciplinary Society to Post-Revolutionary Iran: Ordinary Iranians and Everyday Resistance," provides a historical account of everyday forms of resistance among ordinary Iranians in the post-revolutionary period. Using a Foucauldian approach to examining power and resistance, I show how, vis-à-vis the various arts, rationales and technologies of power employed by the Islamic Republic and its project of Islamist governmentality, resistance of this kind worked to challenge the social and political status quo. This in turn will showcase how, in post-revolutionary Iran, various procedures for enforcing conduct consistent with state-defined norms have, over time, become domains of sociopolitical struggle in their own right, sites of contestation where the authorities are often compelled to relax, and on occasion even abandon, rules and regulations that broad segments of society will not, and cannot, tolerate.

What I wish to show here is that, first, far from constituting mundane practices, everyday forms of resistance represent political acts carried out at the very points at which power is applied; as such, they work to communicate to the authorities a profound disaffection with the status quo. Second, such forms of resistance reveal the ways in which power relations, conceptualized by Foucault as disciplinary, biopolitical and sovereign, are experienced, challenged and disrupted at the points of their application. All this is important because, as I argue, only by investigating acts of everyday resistance can one grasp how social mobilization and political contestation—in Foucauldian terms movements of counterconduct (those moments of singularity wherein bodies pour onto the streets to challenge the technologies of power)—might occur and make their weight felt in a particular locality or setting.

Chapter 4, "Social Mobilization and Political Contestation in Iran at the Turn of the Millennium: The 1999 Student Movement and the 2006 Women's One Million Signature Campaign," examines the two outstanding cases of social mobilization and political contestation in Iran at the turn of the millennium: the 1999 student movement and the 2006 Women's One Million Signature Campaign. Both are viewed as precursors to the Green Movement, because women, students and youth comprised the great majority of their actors, just as they would in 2009.

This will serve to elucidate, among other things, how in a semi-authoritarian[2] context social mobilization and sociopolitical contestation at the grassroots level develop and are sustained and how new subjectivities are constructed. In addition, I demonstrate how tactics and techniques of resistance come to be developed and solidarities forged among oppositional elements in political settings that are ill-disposed to mobilization and protestation.

With regard to these tactics and techniques and solidarities, I map out the historical context or, in Foucauldian terms, the conditions of possibility, for the emergence, in the aftermath of the Ayatollah Khomeini's death in 1989, of a dominant discourse, one that by way of being promoted by the state, in particular that part of the state apparatus with a monopoly over certain technologies of power, came to inform the policies and disciplinary apparatus of the Islamic Republic, hence its project of Islamist governmentality, in the process profoundly impacting the lives of ordinary Iranians. I also delineate how the emergence of this dominant discourse provided the conditions of possibility for the development of a counterdiscourse that questioned, and undermined, not only the former's legitimacy but also its particular way of constituting the world.

In the course of examining these kinds of political operations, I address three key questions: At what point, under what conditions, and in response to what kinds of sociopolitical issues did these discourses come into existence? How did they enable government policies and practices aimed at containing resistance, or, in the case of the opposition, practices directed at delegitimizing the status quo? And finally, how did the former contribute to creating the conditions of possibility for mass radical resistance? The arguments presented in this chapter also explain how the new subjectivities forged in the crucible of these two cases of collective action would influence Green Movement activists, especially with regard to inspiring their democratic orientation.

Chapter 5, "The Green Movement as a Movement of Movements and The Rise of a Home-Grown Rights-Based Society in Post-Revolutionary Iran," surveys political developments during the period 2005–2009, beginning with the inauguration of the Mahmoud Ahmadinejad government and concluding with the mass demonstrations extending from June 2009 to the capture and house arrest in February 2011 of the symbolic leaders of the Green Movement: Mir-Hossein Mousavi and Mehdi Karoubi. Referencing the trajectories of the student, youth and women's groups opposed to a neo-Islamist governmentality, I examine the underlying conditions and processes responsible for their coalescing into a united front. This chapter also provides a definition of the term movement of movements and articulates how this concept can aid in understanding the Green Movement's various dimensions, especially in relation to the earlier cases of social mobilization cited above. Lastly, the 2009 election crisis is analyzed with a view to determining whether, in providing the conditions of possibility for the emergence of a homegrown rights-based society, the Green Movement signifies a paradigm shift in the aspirations and assumptions of dissident groups operating within Iran.

The *concluding chapter, "What were the Iranians Dreaming about in 2009? The Green Movement of Counterconduct: A History of the Past, the Present and the Future,"*[3] summarizes the arguments presented in this book and highlights its

8 *Introduction*

findings, while situating the Green Movement within the broader history of post-revolutionary Iran. As the title suggests, the objective here is to explicate what Iranians have been dreaming about since 2009, that is, to examine what the Green Movement means to them and how it reflects their aspirations and demands. At the same time, I outline its prospects for informing sociopolitical trends in the post-Ahmadinejad era. I conclude by explicating how conceptualizing the Green Movement as a movement of movements may contribute to elucidating contemporary cases of collective action within MENA.

Notes

1 Note that other mass social movements would emerge during the post-revolutionary period, in particular those comprising workers. Regarding the latter, Farhad Nomani & Sohrab Behdad's (2012) "Labor Rights and the Democracy Movement in Iran: Building a Social Democracy," Saeed Rahnema's (1992) "Work Councils in Iran: The Illusion of Worker Control," and Hamid Yazdan Panah's (2015) "Iran's labor movement: Interview with labor activist Mansour Osanlou" are most insightful. These are ignored here owing to their relatively smaller role in the events of 2009 and also because of space and time constraints.
2 Daniel Brumberg and Farideh Farhi (2016, p. 5) coined the term to refer to hybrid political systems like that of Iran, i.e., part authoritarian, part democratic, that are able to do "more than merely mix mechanisms of democracy, political pluralism, and [authoritarian] rule," precisely because their "ruling elites [have at their disposal] an array of tools—constitutionally sanctioned or via informal prerogatives given to certain elements within the state—[with which] to manage, co-opt, or divide potential oppositional movements or challeng[e] elites." For a further discussion of this last point, see Daniel Brumberg and Farideh Farhi's *Power and Change in Iran* (2016).
3 The title was inspired by the curious question posed by Foucault while in Iran observing the 1979 revolution: "What are the Iranians dreaming about?" (Foucault, 2005a).

1 Critical literature review

Introduction

The aim of this literature review is to situate Iran's 2009 Green Movement within the spectrum of a contentious politics, the term used by McAdam et al. (2001 p. 5) to refer to diverse kinds of "collective [socio] political struggles." The objectives here are threefold: the first is to provide an overview of the scholarly accounts that locate this sociopolitical upheaval within various episodes of a contentious politics. With a view to making the case that the Green Movement is in effect a social movement, the second part will survey major social movement theories developed in the West, the purpose being to establish that a social movement of this kind possess, by virtue of the semi-authoritarian setting within which it emerged and operated, certain specificities that are inconsistent with some of the foundational assumptions of leading mainstream social movement theories. Building upon this latter point, the third section will reference the Green Movement as a movement of movements, an analytical concept, which, it will be argued, best captures its multiple characters, and one that I will use as a foundational framework to illuminate the potential contribution of this research project to the scholarly literature on the Green Movement and, more broadly, Middle East and North Africa region (MENA) social movements.

Characterizing the green movement

Some have characterized the Green Movement as an "establishment movement" or an elitist movement founded by political elites (Majd, 2010, p. 62). As Negin Nabavi points out, this view, which represents the "conventional wisdom," signifies the Green Movement as "a clash between conservatives and reformists" within governing circles—in other words, as a manifestation of party politics (2012, p. xii). This perspective can be challenged, however, on the grounds that it ignores the huge crowds that took to the streets seeking to bring about the kind of sociopolitical change that went far beyond mere infighting among political factions. It was these groups, among others, that risked everything to participate in protracted street demonstrations aimed at winning the civic rights and freedoms that alone might secure a brighter future (Dabashi, 2011a). To ignore this point is to fail to apprehend the motives underlying an uprising whose spontaneity, magnitude and endurance would place it outside the purview of party and/or factional politics and beyond the control of the reformist leaders in Tehran. The latter point is implicit in declarations made by Mir-Hossein Mousavi and Mehdi Karoubi, the symbolic leaders of the Green Movement, as to their positions vis-à-vis Green activists, the former professing himself to be "a humble companion of the Green Movement" (Mousavi, 2009), the latter "an ordinary clergyman who felt obliged to defend the rights of the people" (Karoubi, cited in Mostaghim & Daraghi, 2009).

For others, the Green Movement is seen as a revolution because it embodies a "shift in power away from ... corrupt elites" and toward their counterparts committed to establishing "participatory and representative government" (Fischer, 2010, p. 499). This view is too limited, however, given that the term revolution denotes either a radical change in or transfer of social and political institutions (Goldstone, 1980; Foran 1993). Jeff Goodwin (2001, p. 9) offers definitions that capture both of these concepts: a broad definition of revolution as "any and all instances in which a state or a political regime is overthrown and thereby transformed by a popular movement in an irregular, extra-constitutional and/or violent fashion" and a more "restrictive" one that entails "not only mass mobilization and regime change, but also more or less rapid and fundamental social, economic and/or cultural [transformation], during or soon after the struggle for state power."

However one chooses to define it, the Green Movement began as a broadly-based public response to allegations of election fraud, replete with a demand for a fresh election or, at the minimum, a vote recount, in addition to greater electoral transparency and accountability. Thus, what emerged was a civic movement advocating political reform. And despite the massive demonstrations, at no time did these result in sweeping political reforms aimed at ushering in revolutionary change. It is thus apparent that the Green Movement, however conceived, falls in neither of Goodwin's categories; rather, at the very most, can it be said to have constituted a "potentially revolutionary situation," one that was, however, to have no revolutionary outcomes (Bashiriyeh, 2001, p. 62).[1]

Still for others, the Green Movement is seen as a refolution (Bayat, 2013), a term coined by Timothy Garton Ash (2009, para.9) to describe the "mix of reform and revolution" that would shape the series of sociopolitical events transpiring in East European countries during the early 1990s, leading to their liberation from Soviet rule and transition to post-communist states. According to Ash, while these movements were potentially revolutionary in terms of their impact, they cannot in any strict sense be called revolutions, given that the economic, political, and legal transitions they set in motion were achieved largely by reforming existing institutions. Thus, based on this view, these kinds of mass movements are more appropriately described by the more nuanced term "refolution."

Conceptualizing the Green Movement as a refolution, as opposed to a revolution, is to capture a better sense of the character of the 2009 demonstrations—largely peaceful and reform-minded. Yet even this label does not fully capture the complex nature of the Green Movement, given that they set in motion no process that can be described as part reform, part revolution; in other words, despite their scale, there would be no transition of power or even the most modest institutional reforms.

The Green Movement can be best characterized, I would argue, as a social movement. Such movements exist to facilitate various forms of collective action aimed at advancing a specific social or political agenda, resisting or reversing government policy by mobilizing "people with common purposes and solidarity in sustained interaction with elites, opponents and authorities" (Tarrow, 1998, p. 4). According to this definition, argues Charles Tilly, a social movement is characterized by three fundamental and interconnected factors: organized and sustained demands for the authorities to respond to a call for change; a repertoire of activist-oriented events such as street marches, public meetings, and media statements; and "public representations of the cause's worthiness, unity, numbers, and commitments" (Tilly, 2004, p. 7).

Iran's Green Movement satisfies all three of these criteria: over the course of nine months the disparate oppositional groups made concerted demands upon the Islamic Republic to implement social and political reforms; staged massive public demonstrations, most notably street marches, in which tens of thousands, in some cases millions, participated; and publicized "the cause's worthiness, unity, numbers, and commitments" by displaying banners and posters exclaiming *Ra'aye Man Kojast?*, "Where is my vote?," *Ebtaale Entekhabat, Payaane Eteraazaat*, "A fresh round of elections equals an end to street demonstrations," *Age Taghallob Nabood Mellat Ke Inja Nabood*, "If there was no election fraud, we would not be here," *Ma Bishomarim*, "We are countless," *Irani Mimirad Zellat Nemipazirad*, "Iranians would rather die before accepting disgrace" (Faryaade Mardom, 2009). In this way, the disparate oppositional elements come to unite in common cause against a government that in their eyes no longer possessed legitimacy.

Mainstream social movement theories

The question to be addressed here pertains to whether leading mainstream social movement theories are capable of explaining adequately episodes of mass mobilization occurring within a MENA context. Or more precisely, if the Green Movement is best characterized as a social movement, can these theories fully explain its character and dynamics, as well as the conditions under which it emerged? Addressing these questions requires engaging the leading mainstream theories informing social movement studies. Decades after its formal articulations, social movement studies is a comprehensive field in its own right. Thus, rather than presenting a laundry list of theoretical trends in the field, this literature review will be limited to surveying some of the more influential and authoritative theories on social movements, both American and European, that have shaped the field's theoretical landscape as well as its research agenda, and which have either been applied to, or made reference to, the phenomenon of social mobilization in MENA. In what follows, during the course of delineating the historical contexts and conditions giving rise to these theories, I shall analyze their key assumptions regarding oppositional movements to gauge how far such assumptions can account for the specificities, and by implication complexities, of social movements in contemporary MENA societies.

American social movement theories

In the United States, dominant social movement theories took their inspiration chiefly from the civil rights, feminist, student liberation and anti-war movements that emerged in the 1960s. While each had a specific agenda—a legislated end to racial segregation, radical reform of the education system, withdrawal of US troops from South Vietnam, respectively—all were "self-consciously" politically oriented and looked exclusively to Washington for remedies (Davis, 1999, p. 594). All, moreover, were perceived to be "forces for progress toward democracy" (Garner & Tenuto 1997, p. 5), and on the basis of two assumptions: "democracy materializes in the context of social movement activism" (Davis, 1999, p. 599); and "social movements emerge vis-à-vis "opportunities and constraints afforded by [the liberal democratic state]" (Garner & Tenuto, 1997, p. 23).

Resource mobilization theory (RMT), one of "the dominant paradigm(s) for studying collective action in the United States," seeks to explain how, in light of political opportunities or conditions within political systems that either facilitate or inhibit collective action, actors come to recognize and seize upon opportunities to initiate collective action (Buechler, 1995, p. 441). From this perspective, the resources available to oppositional groups prior to mobilizing, and the ways in which these are pooled and employed, play a critical role in determining how they make their presence felt and the level of effort they can bring to bear to affect social and political change (Jenkins, 1983; McCarthy & Zald, 1977). In this schema, structured leadership emerges as a pivotal aspect of social mobilization; indeed, for leading RMT theorists, such as McCarthy and Zald, this factor plays a key role in identifying and defining grievances and exploiting opportunities to initiate collective action. According to these luminaries, "[o]nly after a well-defined leadership emerges do we find well-defined group action" (1973, p. 17).

RMT focuses primarily on economic factors—cost-reducing mechanisms, career benefits for cadres, the division of labour, management incentives—which speaks to the centrality of aggregated resources, chiefly money and labour, to promoting collective action (Oberschall, 1973; McCarthy & Zald, 1977). Seen in this light, the emergence, endurance and impact of a social movement organization (SMO) will hinge largely on the capacity to collectivize "what would otherwise remain individual grievances" (Wiktorowicz, 2004, p. 10)—a capacity predicated upon such factors as effective communications, the degree of professionalism among SMO staffs, and well-defined leadership. Thus, a central tenet of RMT holds that "social change requires a high level of technical expertise" (Garner & Tenuto, 1997, p. 23).

Other strands of social movement theory developed by American scholars shift the focus from the human and material resources available to SMOs to the political environment in which they operate (McAdam et al., 1996; Kitschelt, 1986). The best known of these is political process theory (PPT). Shaped by social movement theorists of the stature of the late Charles Tilly, the late Mayer Zald, Doug McAdam, and Sidney Tarrow, PPT is "currently the hegemonic paradigm among social movement analysts," informing the field's "conceptual landscape, theoretical discourse, and research agenda" (Goodwin & Jasper, 2004, pp. 3–4).

According to this model, it is the opening up of political opportunities, or the structure of political opportunities, that provides a window of opportunity for collective action. Doug McAdam (1996) identifies three "consensual" dimensions of political opportunity used to explicate the emergence of social movements: (1) access to a political system, which reflects the degree of its openness; (2) intra-elite competition and/or elite allies who encourage or facilitate collective action; and (3) a declining capability on the part of the state to repress oppositional movements. These three broad structural factors have recently been joined by an external factor, understood broadly as international/geopolitical pressures that can provide "favourable conditions" or "open[] up ... opportunit[ies]" for a movement to emerge (Markoff, 2012. p. 53; see also McAdam, 1996).

As the above suggests, PPT aims to advance a universal, causal theory of social movements predicated upon a set of structural factors, i.e., "factors that are relatively stable ... and ... outside of the control of movement actors" (Goodwin & Jasper, 2004, p. 4). For the most part, it is the susceptibility on the part of the state to popular political pressure, coinciding with the public's awareness of that susceptibility and willingness to exploit it, which triggers the mobilization of a mass movement. In this schema, the actors' wisdom and creativity, their conscious choices, i.e., their agency, and the outcome of those choices, can be understood and evaluated by referencing "the rules of the games in which those choices are made"—that is, structure (Meyer, 2004, p. 128).

European social movement theories

In Europe, the new social movement theories were directed at addressing what was deemed to be a deficiency in classical Marxism, namely the failure to recognize the potential inherent in collective action for bringing about social change. For European social movement theorists, this failure stemmed from the economic and class reductionism to which classical Marxism was prone. According to the former, all politically significant social action is to be grounded in the economic logic of capitalist production "and that all other social logics [were] secondary at best in shaping such action" (Buechler, 1995, p. 442). Class reductionism dictated that social actors are identified, for the most part, by class relations rooted in the process of production, other social identities playing at best a secondary role in constituting collective actors. Such assumptions inevitably led Marxists to ground proletarian revolution in the sphere of production, thereby dismissing, or at least downgrading, other forms of social protest.

Against this background, there emerged new social movement theories, rooted in traditions of continental European social theory and political philosophy, which could be used to reformulate the historical theory of emancipation (Cohen, 1985; Klandermans, 1991; Larana et al. 1997). With new social movements springing up in Europe in the 1960s—the student movements that erupted in 1968, in addition to the environmental, feminist, ecological and anti-nuclear movements, among others—social movement theorizing assumed a direction that was both "non-class and 'new' [in terms of] social and political logic" (Davis, 1999, p. 594). Thus, theorists began to look to "other logics of action," particularly those based upon politics, culture and ideology, with a view to locating the mainspring of collective action, while also examining "other sources of identity such as ethnicity, gender and sexuality as the definers of collective identity" (Buechler, 1995, p. 442). The term new social movements thus came to encompass a diverse array of movements that developed, in large part, "as a response to the inadequacies of classical Marxism for analyzing collective action" (Buechler, 1995, p. 442).

Two features of the new social movements stand out. First, rather than contesting political power per se, they limited themselves for the most part, so the argument goes, to challenging dominant codes. For example, on the basis of his concept of "historicity"—which is interrogated in detail below—Alain Touraine (1988) contends that new social movements "act upon themselves": they represent themselves and their actions through their cultural models, and in so doing challenge dominant cultural codes (p. 40). In the same vein, the late Alberto Melucci (1989) opines that new social movements are "self-referential," that is, "they are not just instrumental for their goals[;] they are a goal in themselves" (p. 69). Thus, for new social movements, the reference point for social struggle is not principally the political system or the state. As Paul Gilroy (1991, p. 224) writes:

> New social movements are not primarily oriented towards instrumental objectives, such as the conquest of political power or state apparatuses, but rather towards "control of a field of autonomy or independence vis-à-vis the system" and the immediate satisfaction of collective desires ... The very refusal to accept mediation [by] the existing frameworks and institutions of the political system or to allow strategy to be dominated by the task of winning power within it, provides these movements with an important focus of group identity.

Second, these movements were theorized in the context of a historically specific phase in the development of Western liberal societies, an attribute that, as Steven Buechler (1995, p. 443) observes, speaks to "the most distinctive feature of new social movement theories." While different theories prescribe clearly differentiated models—post-industrial society (Touraine 1988), post-materialist society (Inglehart, 1997), advanced capitalist society (Habermas, 1975), information society (Melucci, 1996), etc.—contingent upon the specific constituencies and issues under examination, they have one commonality: all operate based upon, and work to reference, a type of "societal totality" (Buechler, 1995, p. 442), one closely bound up with the new structural features emerging in Western Europe that were precipitating new patterns of sociopolitical action as the old order was dissolving—in the process providing a context for collective action. In investigating the post-industrial nature of this totality—an historical stage, indeed, the highest level of historicity—Touraine (1988) pits it against its industrial predecessor with a view to examining new patterns of sociopolitical actions and the conditions governing their emergence. In the same vein, in his theory of post-materialist society, Ronald Inglehart (2003; 2008) examines another account of that totality, one that focuses on the role of the so-called post-materialist values in shaping collective action—again pitting this stage against its materialist predecessor. Both theories, however, share common ground in so far as they situate new social movements in relation to a historically specific phase within democratic and technologically advanced European societies—a crucial point I shall revisit shortly when gauging the applicability of all the above theories to MENA.

Social movement theories and specificities of MENA oppositional movements: Mobilizing structures and the politics of everyday life

As the above discussion reveals, American social movement theorists view social movements as parcels of collective action that present, for the most part, an "organized, sustained, self-conscious challenge to existing authorities" (Tilly, 1984, p. 304). In the "politically open and technologically advanced Western societies" (Bayat, 2013, p. 20) in which they emerged, they would operate, more or less, as formal business-like enterprises, whose success is contingent upon resources, financial and otherwise, a centralized leadership, clearly defined division of labour, high degree of professionalization, strategic planning—factors having to do with technical expertise. It is, moreover, by acts of mobilization and protestation, chief among them petitioning and lobbying, that the actors engage and influence mainstream political institutions, such as parliaments, legislatures, and political parties, with a view to bringing about change (Bayat, 2013).

But what of those political settings where mobilizing structures such as formal organizations, professional staffs, and centralized leaderships are either non-existent, rudimentary and/or severely handicapped by (semi-)authoritarian states, where acts of mobilization, such as petitioning and lobbying, are ineffectual so far as pressuring governments unaccountable to an electorate, and /or where the political channels for effecting meaningful change are controlled by factions having, respectively, a monopoly over various levers of power?

Home to several states where in the past mobilizing structures have been effectively ruled out, the MENA region can serve as an ideal laboratory for examining such questions. Indeed, while each possesses distinctive structural/societal features and modes of governance, one can discern common approaches to dealing with oppositional movements, all of which operate under severe handicaps. Of these, Bahrain, Saudi Arabia, Syria and Iran, each with its own distinctive brand of authoritarianism, represent outstanding cases of polities that have historically, and to varying degrees, proven most adept at denying opponents opportunities to build formal organizations with clearly defined command structures.

I say "each with a distinctive brand of authoritarianism" and "to varying degrees" in order to differentiate these states in terms of the opportunities afforded oppositional movements. Thus, for example, a republican, semi-democratic Iran under the reformist government of Mohammad Khatami (1997–2005) promoted the development of a civil society in which student, youth and women's groups could operate with some degree of impunity; indeed, this was the case until Ahmadinejad's rise to power. Nothing of the kind has ever been possible in the far more authoritarian milieus of Bahrain, Syria and Saudi Arabia, where oppositional groups have historically had little or no opportunity to engage in any kind of subversive action.

This applies to Iran as well; those oppositional leaders that dared emerge from underground have variously been imprisoned for short periods, disappeared (Faeq al-Mir of Syria), been detained and then arrested repeatedly (Louay Hussein of Syria), placed under house arrest (Mohammad Mosaddegh, Mir-Hossein Mousavi and Mehdi Karoubi of Iran), sentenced to long prison terms (Mohammed Saleh Al-Bejadi of Saudi Arabia and Ibrahim Sharif of Bahrain), exiled (Sheikh Ali Salman of Bahrain), or in extreme cases executed (Sheikh Nimr Baqir Al-Nimr of Saudi Arabia) (Al-Haj, 2014; Alkarama, 2016; Independent News; 2016; Pourmokhtari, 2017a).

Even efforts on the part of civil society groups to advance reform agendas through official channels have often proven ineffectual. Such was the case even during the reform-minded Khatami administration (1997–2005), when the conservative establishment, more often than not, succeeded in obstructing or blocking the passage of reform measures through the *Majlis*, the Iranian Parliament. It was enabled in this respect by the control it wielded over the judiciary and the powerful supervisory bodies charged with approving legislation (Moslem, 2002). This explains, for example, the failure on the part of the *Majlis* in the early 2000s to ratify the Convention on the Elimination of All Forms of Discrimination against Women (CEDAW), a United Nations initiative hailed by feminists as an international bill of rights for women.[2]

If adopted, CEDAW would have directly challenged a host of laws and practices that had long worked to marginalize and subordinate women (Pourmokhtari, 2017). Following a press campaign by Iranian feminists aimed at pressuring the government to adopt CEDAW, the Khatami administration, in December 2001, drafted the requisite legislation and submitted it for ratification to a reformist-dominated *Majlis*. However, immediately prior the final vote, the enabling bill was placed on hold owing, according to the speaker Mehdi Karoubi, to concerns on the part of conservative clerics serving in the judiciary and elsewhere, regarding its compatibility with *Shari'a* law (Tohidi, 2006; Pourmokhtari, 2017).

Under pressure from activists, reformist deputies, over the course of the following two years, demanded an official enquiry, but to no avail. Finally, in August 2003, the Guardian Council, chief among the aforementioned supervisory bodies, announced that CEDAW would not be ratified (Feminist News, 2013). CEDAW's fate exemplifies how in political settings such as Iran, efforts to bring about social and political change through official channels are often frustrated by factions holding a monopoly over certain exercises of power. This does not mean, however, that oppositional groups have failed entirely in advancing and/or reclaiming their rights via this avenue. For example, as will be discussed in Chapter 4, over the course of 2008 women activists were successful in pressuring the *Majlis* to repeal two patriarchal laws and replace them with gender-neutral legislation. Specifically, women were granted the right to inherit a husband's property and to receive equal blood money in the event of an accident covered by an insurance company. Yet, such victories, however significant, were few and far between, hence the efforts on the part of oppositional groups to seek other ways to contest the status quo.

When combined, all the above factors—closed political environments, government crackdowns on opposition cadres, the absence of formal leaderships, the inefficacy of acts of mobilization to pressure the state to adopt social and political reforms—work to imbue oppositional movements in the region with certain specificities. For example, far from posing an "organized [and] sustained ... challenge to existing authorities" (Tilly, 1984, p. 304), as is often the case with oppositional movements in the Western world, collective action in MENA takes the form, more often than not, of "open and fleeting struggles [waged] without [formal] leadership ... or structured organization" (Bayat, 2013, p. 46). Furthermore, owing to the absence of these features, it is predominately the power of ordinary people (Bayat, 2013), not the efficacy of mobilization structures, that creates the potential to change the rules of the game and to bring about or at least push for social and political change and/or reform.

MENA and the politics of everyday life

Relatedly, and herein lies another specificity among those MENA states where social and political reform is likely to be blocked or at least hampered by factions with a monopoly over power, where open political channels are non-existent, and/or where oppositional groups are denied political rights, particularly where challenging government policy is concerned: mobilizing actors may seek out alternative domains, most often of a public kind, in which to voice their demands and/or express discontent, thus transforming them into loci of resistance and defiance.

In the case of MENA it is the urban streets that lend themselves most readily to contesting the status quo. Ali Mirsepassi calls this spatial phenomenon the "tradition of democracy in the streets" (2010, p. ix). A primary venue for expressing discontent in the region, it is a "consistent and powerful aspect of ... protest movements" (Mirsepassi, 2010, p. ix) across much of the Middle East and North Africa, as evinced by the 1979 Iranian revolution, the 1994 uprising in Bahrain, the so-called Uprising of Dignity, the 1999 Iranian student movement, and the mass demonstrations in Yemen, Egypt, Tunisia and Bahrain, and elsewhere in the region.

Asef Bayat defines what he calls "street politics" as the participative use of streets for the purpose of "express[ing] grievances, forg[ing] identities [and] enlarg[ing] solidarities" (Bayat, 2013, p. 13). In this way, he asserts, "a small demonstration [can] grow into a massive exhibition of solidarity" aimed at contesting and negating the status quo (Bayat, 2013, p. 13). Thus, streets have become, in effect, the locus for a tug of war between the state and the masses. And "[i]t is [owing to] this epidemic potential of street politics" that, not surprisingly, "almost every" major case of contention in MENA has ultimately "[found] expression in the urban streets" (Bayat, 2013, p. 13).

Ever mindful of Foucault's (1978, p. 93) dictum that "power is everywhere," I wish to suggest here, that in the MENA region urban public spaces often serve as a locus wherein social and political conflict and contestation play out. This means that it is not urban streets per se that are political, given the omnipresence of power, but rather the acts performed within them. Consequently, it might be more to the point to adopt what Nancy Fraser (1989, p. 18) calls the "politics of everyday life" as a point of departure for understanding and examining cases of collective action. The politics of everyday life serves as a domain wherein a people engage in everyday but cunning and contentious strategies, tactics and acts aimed at subverting and challenging rules of conduct. By examining the politics of everyday life, one can understand how rules, codes, norms, laws and regulations, the conduct of conduct in other words, come to be resisted and subverted at the point of application. Notes Nancy Fraser (1989):

> Foucault enables us to understand power very broadly, and yet very finely, as anchored in the multiplicity of what he calls "micropractices," the social practices that constitute everyday life in modern societies. This positive conception of power has the general but unmistakable implication of a call for [a] "politics of everyday life" (p. 18).

The term politics of everyday life, which will be discussed in detail in Chapters 4 and 5 with reference to Iran's 1999 Student Movement, the 2006 Women's One Million Signature Campaign and the 2009 Green Movement, refers to a strategy of defiance used by subjugated bodies, in this case protestors and demonstrators, to transform governmentalized zones into strongpoints from which to defy and contest power, and by implication the very political order it reproduces.

In this regard, what lends public spaces their significance is that while they have "increasingly becom[e] the domain of ... state power" (Bayat, 2013, p. 53)—which "regulates their use [and] mak[es] them 'orderly'" (Bayat, 2013, p. 53) through laws and regulations—they have also become, simultaneously and contingent on the will of the masses, "[loci for] "shaming" the authorities" (Mirsepassi, 2010, p. ix). In this way, such loci can be transformed into spaces of resistance, sites of political contestation and social negation of the status quo. Thus, it is hardly surprising that Tehran's Azadi Square (2009), Cairo's Tahrir Square (2011–2012) and Istanbul's Taksim Square (2013) emerged as signifiers of mass discontent during the spate of uprisings in which each figured prominently. In each case, by de-legitimizing and de-authenticating governmental regimes, immense crowds were able to showcase their counterpower by exploiting mainstream and social media. They succeeded in this regard by occupying these public spaces/governmentalized zones, in the process disrupting the normal flow of everyday life.

And indeed, as I have inferred elsewhere (Pourmokhtari, 2017), a so-called politics of everyday life directed at winning social and political rights is no longer the monopoly of MENA oppositional movements. Its counterparts that have recently sprung up in the liberal democracies of the West—the Occupy Movement, Black Lives Matter and Idle No More—also engage in an informal, spatial politics, replete with street demonstrations, such as sit-ins, as surrogate channels for a formal politics (Ancelovici et al., 2016; Idlenomore, 2017). Thus, one can argue that even liberal institutions are not always responsive to grassroots demands. This point serves to transcend the false dichotomy of East versus West, in particular the view prevailing in the social and political sciences of the former as comprised of frozen, exceptional entities bereft of human rights, human dignity, equality, and freedom. Despite these commonalities, however, the fact remains there do exist significant differences, for example, in their repertoires of contention, the historical and context-dependent grievances of their actors, modes and techniques of demonstrating and protesting, leadership structures, and specificities of power relations, reflecting the highly differentiated societies from which they have emerged (Ancelovici et al., 2016; Idlenomore, 2017; Kaulingfreks, 2015).

The politics of everyday life as played out in public spaces is by no means limited to expressing mass discontent. It also serves as a surrogate channel for demanding change and pursuing reforms where formal political institutions, such as parliaments and legislative assemblies, have failed. To show the extent to which public spaces are crucial to this project I examine in Chapter 4 the 1999 Student Movement and the 2006 Women's One Million Signature Campaign.

Such cases are not, however, confined to the Iranian context. To take but one example, in June 1994, in an effort to bring about political and socioeconomic reform, over 1,500 Bahraini activists staged a sit-in before the headquarters of the Ministry of Labor.[3] This single event sparked a series of uprisings (1994–1999) that would undermine the Al Khalifa monarchy and bring into question its very legitimacy. These manifestations of a profound discontent would also be among the first post-ideological[4] cases of collective action within the region. The point to grasp here is that the demonstrators elected to engage in a politics of everyday life only upon discovering that the formal institutional channels for effecting change were either inadequate to the task or had been blocked entirely. In the years and months leading up to the Bahraini uprising, oppositional groups had sought repeatedly to reform/democratize the political process by petitioning the government. In each instance, however, their efforts had proved fruitless (Refworld, 2006; Pourmokhtari, 2017).

Unable to work through official channels, these groups were left with no option but to appropriate urban public spaces where they could express discontent and voice demands in ways the authorities might ignore only at their peril.[5] By engaging in an everyday politics of resistance they succeeded in "mut[ing] [politics as usual] within [spaces] ... supposed to be its natural ... habitat" (Walters, 2012, p. 80), such as the Parliament, while transforming urban spaces/governmentalized zones into political loci of defiance whose very existence served to de-authenticate the status quo and de-legitimize the political system as a whole. In this way, by engaging in a politics of everyday life, that signal feature of defiance and principal strategy for conducting contention episodes, they worked to challenge and subvert the rules/norms of conduct.

Applying political process theory to Iran and other MENA countries

Political process theory (PPT) is informed by certain presuppositions that limit its efficacy for analyzing oppositional movements based in Iran and elsewhere in the MENA region. Owing to the emphasis on structural conditions, PPT theorists view mass mobilizations as a response to opportunities that reflect "the vulnerability of the state to popular political pressure" (Kurzman, 1996, p. 153), or metaphorically as "'windows' that open and close" (Kingdon, cited in Goodwin & Jasper

2004, p. 12), which means "they are either there or not there" (Goodwin & Jasper, 2004, p. 12). From this perspective, oppositional movements are assumed to be comprised of agents possessing an a priori and mechanistic essence, i.e., "potential groups with preexisting desires … who only await the opportunity to pursue them" (Goodwin & Jasper, 2012, p. 15). Not only does this dispose PPT theorists to overextend "the concept of 'political opportunities'" by equating them with the "larger 'environment' in which social movements are embedded" (Goodwin & Jasper, 2004, p. 27); it also predisposes them to focus by and large on the "state or the polity as the only field of struggle that really matters" where mobilization and collective action are concerned (Goodwin & Jasper, 2012, p. 15). However, as Jeff Goodwin and James Jasper (2004, p. 11) argue, there exists "an extraordinarily large number of processes and events, political and otherwise, [that can] potentially influence movement mobilization, and they do so in historically complex combinations and sequences."[6]

This fetishization of the state as an entity presenting social movements with opportunities to mobilize is, however, highly problematic where such opportunities are seldom, if ever, provided by polities determined to maintain the status quo at whatever cost. As will be seen, even during the reform-minded Khatami administration, oppositional groups functioned under the unrelenting scrutiny of a security apparatus directed by the conservative establishment, which included para-military groups, prepared to use whatever means necessary to ensure the survival of the state. Thus, in the Iranian context, the so-called mobilizing structures—formal leaderships, organizational structures, professional staffs—deemed by social movement theorists to be the foundational building blocks of social movements, are at best rudimentary as well as severely handicapped by state repression.

Moreover, in Iran a Ministry of Intelligence dominated by hardliners is able to exert a stranglehold on the media, whether state-owned or private, resulting in the dissemination of misinformation and the framing of events in ways that advance a conservative agenda. This also applies to the state-sponsored social media. Thus, those dissidents courageous enough to transgress the narrow limits of public discourse imposed by the state risk arrest and show trials, often resulting in long jail terms, as was the case in the wake of the 1999 Student Movement and 2009 Green Movement (Afshari, 2015; Time, 2009; Karami, 2016). It is hardly credible that oppositional movements would have open opportunities to mobilize in political environments of this kind.

With survival a chief priority, and by monopolizing the security and juridical apparatuses, the conservative establishment has succeeded over the years in perfecting what might be called the art of repression. Referring to repression as an art— something essential to understanding Tehran's formidable security apparatus and multilayered system of governance, both of which are examined in Chapter 3—is to underscore its shrewd calculations, refined skills and practical know how, macro/micro techniques and nuanced measures, and intuitive grasp of the psychology of fear, all orchestrated with a view to silencing the majority, thereby perpetuating the status quo. This explains why in Iran, as Kurzman (1996) and Pourmokhtari (2014) have shown, open opportunities for mobilization are best described as "highly restricted or uncertain" (Beinin & Vairel, 2011, p. 8) and why, more often than not, "mobilizations emerge in the[ir] absence" (Beinin & Vairel, 2011, p. 8).

These realities compel us to seek out factors other than open opportunities to mobilize extant in the political environment if we are to plumb the root causes of collective action in the MENA region. Some recent cases of mobilization are instructive in this regard. For example, in the case of the 2009 Iranian Green Movement, it was the oppositional forces—chiefly students and women's groups—that took the lead in creating opportunities to mobilize (Pourmokhtari, 2014). Both were motivated, in part by discriminatory policies implemented by the Ahmadinejad administration during its first term in office (2005–2009), in part by the widespread perception of election fraud. At no time during this period, or prior to it, did the state provide anything that might be construed as an open opportunity to mobilize. Thus, opportunity was "what [they made] of it" (Kurzman, 2004a, p. 117).[7]

Two years later, a wave of protests would sweep through Tunisia, revealing the authoritative will of disparate peoples longing for the kind of fundamental change that alone might usher in a brighter future. Again, one might argue that those who filled the Arab streets created their own opportunities—opportunities that may be viewed as attributes of the actors themselves. Perhaps nothing better illustrates this last point than a solitary act of defiance on the part of a young Tunisian street vendor named Mohammad Bou'azizi. In December 2010 Bou'azizi set himself ablaze to protest the arbitrary confiscation of his wares and the harassment and humiliation suffered at the hands of a municipal official and her aides. This single incident triggered massive demonstrations throughout the country, precipitating what would come to be called the Arab Spring.

Thus, with respect to the Green Movement and this first flowering of the Arab Spring, one might argue that the demonstrators felt compelled to put their lives on the line, spurred on by moral outrage directed at governments that had violated their sense of justice beyond the point of endurance. No longer willing to be governed by those for whom human dignity, moral rights and social justice were merely empty slogans, they took to the streets, determined to confront their tormentors. In such circumstances, a people may come to perceive themselves as agents of sociopolitical change, as actors capable of advancing their interests and possessed of a sense of authority, legitimacy, and subjectivity stemming from a certainty that the status quo is fundamentally unjust—actors determined to leave their mark on history "under circumstances they have the power to change" (Kurzman, 2004a, p. 117).

New social movement theories and their application to Iran and other MENA cases

The lived and context-based experience, trajectory and history of those who filled the streets of Iranian and Tunisian cities demanding change is nowhere reflected in the new social movement theories, and not surprisingly given that they take as their datum the technologically advanced and politically open societies of the West. For this reason, they are prone to making grand and monolithic assumptions about social movements, which make their application highly problematic in the Middle East and North Africa. Touraine's highly influential post-industrial society theory, which rests upon the assumption that history unfolds in a succession of stages— commercial, industrial and post-industrial—is a case in point. According to this luminary, post-industrial societies have attained an unparalleled level of historicity or historical development— the highest to be precise—wherein societal movements are no longer conceptualized as "dramatic events" but rather as "the work that society performs upon itself" (Touraine, 1981, p. 29). This work has as its goal the control of historicity, by which he means "the set of cultural models that rule social practices" and that provide "the symbolic capacity that enables [a society] to construct a system of knowledge together with the technological tools which it can use to intervene in its functioning" (Touraine, 1977, p. 26). Henceforth, Touraine contends, in post-industrial societies "there can be no societal movement other than the collective actions that are aimed directly at the affirmation and defense of the rights of the subject—of his freedom and equality" (Touraine, cited in Bakan & MacDonald, 2002, p. 290). For this reason, the new "societal movements have become moral movements," in contrast to their predecessors that were of a religious, political or economic character (Touraine, cited in Bakan & MacDonald, 2002, p. 290).

Touraine uses this last point to articulate the concept of levels of historicity, from which he derives the corollary that only post-industrial societies can achieve the "highest level of historicity," namely, that of self-production (1981, p. 105). In contrast, "traditional" societies still "lie within history," and for this reason, their ability to produce the cultural models that govern how they function is more limited, the reason being that the distance that historicity requires (from God, oneself and the world as object) has not been achieved (Touraine, 1981, p. 105). In terms of the opposition constructed here, i.e., between post-industrial and traditional societies, MENA societies still lie within history being too close to God and therefore too preoccupied with religious concerns. Thus, they lack the kind of moral movements that are a hallmark of the post-industrial societies of the West—not to mention the post-industrial economies that represent the means for attaining the highest level of historicity along Touraine's evolutionary continuum.

The best that may be said about such overarching theorization is that it reflects a historically specific period of Western history; at its worst, Arturo Escobar opines (1992, p. 37), it conceives Third World societies, and by implication their oppositional movements, "as lacking historical agency or ... as only having a diminished form of agency compared with the European case."

Inglehart's (2003; 2008) account of social movements, like Touraine's, is predicated on yet another variation on Western societal totality. His widely celebrated theory of post-materialist society rests on the presupposition that once a society reaches a certain level of socio-economic achievement, it turns its attention to issues and concerns that lie beyond the attainment of economic and physical security, in this case the satisfaction of purely material needs. These issues and concerns are related to values—self-expression values in his terminology—bound up in principles such as democracy, gender equality, and human rights, among others. This tendency is intrinsic to the post-material democracies of the West and is manifest in their demands for change.

Inglehart views changes in values to be the product of technological and material development. They occur, moreover, in a fixed and linear way: "economic development leads to specific mass values and belief systems" (Inglehart, 1997, p. 69) and "tends to propel societies in a roughly predictable direction; industrialization leads to occupational specialization, rising educational levels, rising income levels, and eventually brings unforeseen changes" (Inglehart & Baker, 2000, p. 21), for example, in gender roles and political participation, which in turn galvanize social movements into collective action,

According to this mono-causal theory of social change, it is no more than a pipe dream to contemplate the existence in non-Western societies of oppositional movements with progressive demands, as none of these societies has transitioned to a post-material society committed to realizing self-expression values; indeed, many remain, according to this model of social change, pre-industrial in character. Thus, concludes Inglehart, while "the younger generations in Western societies have become progressively more egalitarian than their elders ... the younger generations in Muslim societies have remained almost as traditional as their parents and grandparents, producing an expanding cultural gap" between the two societies (Inglehart & Norris, 2003, p. 68). It is the latter that "constitute[s] the ... clash between Muslim societies and the West" (Inglehart & Norris, 2003, p. 68). Moreover, because they are steeped in tradition, these younger Muslim generations are ill disposed to the gender equality, social tolerance, and political activism that are the norm in the West.

Inglehart's grand model of causation, however, ignores the "situation and the context within which [values] become relevant" (Haller 2002, p. 142), overlooking the experiences and trajectories of non-European societies, with their long struggles for progressive reforms and democratic rights, some dating back to the early decades of the twentieth century, for example, Iran's 1906 Constitutional Revolution and Egypt's 1923 Feminist Union (Afary, 1996; Al-Ali, 2008). It is the existence of these struggles, along with the contextually contingent values informing them, that calls into question Inglehart's chief determinant of social change, namely the level of technological and economic development, which he views to be a precondition for the emergence of progressive values and the kind of social change predicated upon them. In this way, Inglehart's grand model of causation works to equate Western history with progressive values. His is a "one-size-fits-all" model of social change, and by implication collective action, that is unable to account for radical social change other than that predicated upon an exclusive experience of European sociality.

Above all, what the preceding analyses reveal is that, and this is crucial to acknowledge, neither Touraine, who numbers among the Eurocentric left, nor Inglehart, a West-centric liberal, can explain the recent rise in Western Europe and North America of right-wing nationalist/populist/racialist movements that, along with being xenophobic, are anti-LGBT, for example, the Tea Party and the so-called Alt-Right (Skocpol & Williamson, 2016; Lundskow, 2012). In contrast, recent oppositional movements like Black Lives Matter and Idle No More have articulated clear and specific demands for basic social justice and political rights (Williamson et al., 2011; Lundskow, 2012), which, one can only assume, are to be realized in a post-industrial or post-materialist society, at least according to the Touraine/Inglehart view of an evolutionary continuum. Thus, one can discern that these theories fail even to explain fully the complexity of Western liberal democracy itself. They are, as the examples here clearly show, neither universal nor representative of the particularities of the West.

Social movement studies and MENA oppositional movements

The above discussion reveals that the new social movement theories as well as their Western forebears, which were formulated in light of European and North American experiences and trajectories, "coevolved with the relatively stable ... democracies of the West" (Oliver et al. 2003, p. 215), and, by implication, and despite all "claims to universality," are predicated upon a set of "historically-specific developments occurring in the United States [and] Europe" (Davis, 1999, p. 92). Thus, some theorists, in particular Americans, were disposed to understand social movements of an oppositional kind in reference to opportunities or constraints afforded by the liberal democratic state; others, especially their European counterparts, held that democratic societies had transitioned from an industrial to a post-industrial/advanced-capitalist/post-material stage of development, and, as such, it was their structural features that shaped oppositional social movements. These theories are grounded in a historically specific experience within the context of Western liberal democratic polities. It is this feature that lends them much of their analytical power and empirical underpinning, while at the same time, as Arthur Escobar points out, "greatly shap[ing] and limit[ing]" their utility with respect to other contexts (1992, p. 30).

MENA societies, social movements and essentialism

Thus, asserts Charles Kurzman, "apply[ing] contemporary social movement approaches [in a non-European or non-North American context]" presents a formidable challenge (2004b, p. 294). Despite this caveat, however, the leading social movement theories have acquired a hegemonic status predicated upon their universalizing assumptions and grand causal narratives, their efficacy in constructing general categories for social movements, and their referencing of what is assumed to be a uniquely Western phenomenon to modernity—factors that "at present," Fernando Calderon (1986) asserts, ultimately make "the theoretical analysis of social movements ... limited, [or, at best,] under construction" (p. 331). All this has profound implications for conceptualizing MENA oppositional movements, of which two in particular require elucidation.

The first has to do with the essentialist manner in which MENA oppositional movements —traditionally consigned to the margins of social movement studies—are construed as exceptionalist cases of mobilization, a view stemming from an understanding of MENA movements as rooted in a religious revivalism of a strictly fundamentalist nature and hence divorced from anything deemed to be even remotely utopian or progressive. For example, both Alberto Melucci (1996. p. 104) and Alain Touraine (cited in Bayat, 2005, p. 894) conceptualize MENA oppositional movements, for example, the 1979 Iranian Revolution, in terms of a "regressive utopianism" or as "anti-movement[s]," respectively, thereby reducing them to manifestations of Islamic fundamentalism—in effect dismissing them as reactionary, anti-democratic, and anti-modern movements instigated by traditional peoples.

Other luminaries, such as Sidney Tarrow (1998), express similar views, referring to the Middle East of the 1990s as a land of "ugly movements," "rooted in ethnic ... claims [or] in religious fanaticism and racism," and dominated by "radical Islamic fundamentalists who slit the throats of folk singers and beat up women who dare to go unveiled" (p. 194). These accounts work ultimately to relegate MENA movements to the margins of scholarly analysis where they are dismissed as exceptionalist cases.

The positions taken by Melucci and Touraine can surely be questioned given that their modernist assumptions and West-centric orientation work to consign oppositional movements in the MENA, along with the societies from which they spring and the conditions governing their emergence, to grand categories, the defining feature of which is an essentialism (Pourmokhtari, 2017a). One can discern in Touraine's (1988) thought, for example, how his normative concept of levels of historicity—according to which only social movements in the post-industrial societies of the West can achieve the highest level, a standing that lends them their progressive and modern character and which distinguishes them from all other societies, meaning those that still lie within history—leads inexorably to his dismissing the 1979 revolution as an anti-movement.

Equally intriguing are the totalizing accounts of MENA societies presented by these theorists, wherein a religio-centrism is assumed to be the defining feature of Islamist movements. The latter is understood almost exclusively as a kind of religious revivalism replete with primordial loyalties and signifying the peculiar and unique and is cast as the engine of, as well as dominant code for, social mobilization (Bayat, 2007). In other words, there exists a tendency to reify Islam as a static religion and Islamism as a monolithic sociopolitical project, overlooking the variations that occur across time and space as well as among social strata and religious sects (Bayat, 2007, 2013).

MENA social movements have therefore come to be perceived as Islamist movements: as monolithic entities with regressive, indeed backward-looking, agendas, even as historically frozen entities prone to violence, all sense of their diversity and complexity lost. In characterizing a regressive utopianism, Melucci (1996) asserts that such movements, whose defining feature is a "totalizing monism," forge their "identit(ies)" in terms of the past, drawing on a totalizing myth of rebirth" (p. 104). These cases—the Iranian Revolution of 1979 stands as a prime example—he contends, represent nothing more than "a mythical quest for the Lost Paradise ... [which in turn] crystalizes into fanatic fundamentalism" (1996, p. 105).

Such accounts are like a "god trick," to borrow Donna Haraway's epithet, offering up a vision that is "from everywhere [but in fact] nowhere" (1988, p. 584). They show little interest in uncovering the complex forces propelling MENA movements forward. And yet the historical record is clear: the Iranian Revolution of 1979 was a convulsive reaction on the part of diverse societal groups, including, but not limited to, nationalists, social democrats, leftists and other sub-variants, among them Islamists and Muslim liberals and nationalists, all of whom took to the streets. It was, in fact, the Ayatollah Khomeini's call for, and pledge to promote, pluralism in the post-Shah era—and, in particular, the statements to this effect issued during his brief period of exile in France—that rallied these diverse elements to his cause—a cause that received additional momentum by repeated claims on his part to have no interest in governing the country.[8]

At the outbreak of the Islamic Revolution, moreover, Iran possessed, contrary to popular belief, nothing remotely resembling a strong Islamist movement; rather, the latter was at an early stage of development when overtaken by the events of February 1979. Asef Bayat makes this point abundantly clear in his analysis of the social and political impact of Islamism upon Iran, which shows that in 1979 Islamists represented only one among many disaffected groups working to topple the monarchy; moreover, their subsequent seizure of the state apparatus was only made possible "by the popular mobilisation of various sectors of the population" (2005, p. 897). Indeed, only well after the revolution had been consolidated and the Islamic Republic established did Islamization proceed and state Islamization or Islamization from the top eventually prevailed.

This is not to deny that the Middle East and North Africa are home to a number of extremist movements, including the Taliban and the more recent so-called Islamic State in Iraq and Syria; rather, it is to point out that during the 1990s there emerged in the region some remarkably progressive movements. Indeed, the first "post-Islamist" movements called for a "fus[ion of] religiosity and rights, faith and freedom, Islam and liberty" as well as advocating pluralism, the rule of law, and human rights and freedoms (Bayat, 2013, p. 37).

The term "post-Islamism" is, according to Mojtaba Mahdavi (2011, p. 94), "a relatively new concept that has emerged in the past two decades to describe a new phenomenon, a stage of development, and discourse in the Muslim world." Far from constituting an all-encompassing concept, post-Islamism has been operationalized, according to Asef Bayat, who is often credited with coining the term, as "both a condition and a project" (2007, p. 10). As a condition, it is to be understood as a counterdiscourse against the political project of Islamism, and in particular its totalizing and mono-politicized calculus for governing every facet of existence—one "where[in] ... a rethink about the Islamist project takes place, leading to emphasizing rights instead of duties, plurality instead of a singular authoritative voice, historicity rather than fixed scripture, and the future instead of the past" (Bayat, 2009, p. 44). Put differently, "it strives to marry Islam with individual choice and freedom, democracy, and modernity"—all part of a quest to conceive an alternative to a single European/Western notion of modernity; or, to put it another way, it represents a longing for "alternative modernit[ies]" (Bayat, 2009, p. 44).

In this light, post-Islamism is to be understood as a critique of Islamism, and precisely "[its] internal contradictions," which explain its failure "to reinvent itself" and, above all, the failure on the part of its Islamist advocates to operationalize it as a concept, a social and political condition, and a mono-causal calculus for governing life (Bayat, 2007, p. 11). Thus, concludes Bayat, post-Islamism in this sense emerges as a critique of Islamism as a project, wherein "following a phase of experimentation, the appeal, energy and the source of its legitimacy ... are exhausted, even among its once-ardent supporters" (2007, pp. 10–11). In this way, post-Islamism can also be understood, according to Bayat (2007), as a "project" that foregrounds "a conscious attempt to conceptualize and strategize the rationale and modalities of transcending Islamism in social, political, and intellectual domains" (p. 11). Post-Islamism, however conceived, ultimately "signifies the impact of secular exigencies on a religious discourse in our post-secular age" (Mahdavi, 2011, p. 95)—a point lost amidst the exceptionalist tendencies that inform much of what passes for scholarly analysis of MENA movements, contributing to further marginalization in the field of social movement studies.

Social movement theories and their uncritical application to MENA

The second problem to do with analyzing MENA social movements through the lens of leading mainstream social movement theories lies not with the theories themselves, but rather with their uncritical application, as exemplified in Quintain Wiktorowicz's (2004) edited volume *Islamic Activism*, Mohammad Hafez's (2003) *Why Muslims Rebel?* and Janine Clark's (2004) *Islam, Charity, and Activism*. These works seek primarily to demonstrate that MENA social movements constitute normal cases of mobilization in that they confirm theoretical predictions, thus attesting to their universalistic assumptions regarding social mobilization and collective action.

To be sure, these efforts are encouraging in that they move the debate beyond the straitjacket of exceptionalist tendencies. Yet the manner in which analysis is tailored to showcase the predictive power of mainstream theories has drawn criticism owing both to the failure to elucidate the full range, character and dynamism of MENA movements and to the missed opportunities to contribute innovatively and critically to the broader social science scholarship on the region.[9]

Undeniably, some of the more recent cases of mobilization to emerge in the Middle East and North Africa raise serious doubts as to the relevancy of dominant social movement theories in this context. For example, at the time Iran's Green Movement was taking shape, there existed nothing that might be described as an open opportunity for mobilization. There existed no sign of dissension among ruling elites or of anything resembling a challenge to state institutions, most notably the Office of the Supreme Leader and the Guardian Council; no hint that the political system was willing to accept even the most modest of reform measures; no diminution in the capacity or willingness on the part of the state to crush resistance; and no indication of any geopolitical/international crisis looming on the horizon (Pourmokhtari, 2014). Thus, an

> analysis of the political environment prior to the June 2009 election reveals that on no account can a case be made for an opening or expansion of

> 'political opportunities,' which would imply weakness on the part of Tehran that might be exploited by oppositional groups to mobilize *en mass.*
>
> (Pourmokhtari, 2014, pp. 156–157)

At the same time, owing to the semi-authoritarian setting in which it took shape and operated, the Green Movement lacked the kind of mobilizing structures—most notably formal organizations, structured leadership and a clearly defined division of labour—thought to be essential to organizing and sustaining collective action. Like most of its counterparts in the region, it would manifest itself primarily in spatial, mainly street, demonstrations. The latter's spontaneity, unpredictability and dynamism, and lack of centralized leadership, all point to the Green Movement's informal organizational structure.

Nor, as some social movement studies theorists may suggest, was the Green Movement the product of religious sensibilities and tendencies; rather, characteristic of post-Islamist movements, it was grounded in demands for plurality, accountability, democratic rights and freedoms, and a general wish to rein in the political role of state-sponsored religion (Bayat, 2013). The Green Movement has also been described as post-ideological (Dabashi, 2011b) or non-ideological (Banuazizi, 1999) to connote that it had no direct relation to ideologies that have fuelled social and revolutionary movements in MENA and elsewhere in the second half of the twentieth century, among them anti-colonial nationalism, Third World socialism, Marxism and militant Islamism. Rather, its roots lie in a long struggle for political reform, democracy and rule of law—in an "indomitable will to [build] enduring democratic institutions" (Dabashi, 2011b, p. 60).

From the preceding discussion, one might conclude, at least with reference to the cases delineated above, that recent mass movements in the Middle East and North Africa are not necessarily theory-confirming in that, however generally conceived, they do not conform to the chief presuppositions underpinning dominant social movement theories; nor are they, as was shown in the Tunisian case, for example, exceptionalist, a view/position that works to dismiss nearly all MENA cases as regressive, fundamentalist and anti-modern, thus subjecting them to totalizing narratives, in the process relegating them to the margins of social movement studies.

As a corrective to this position, the work proposed here seeks to understand the Green Movement by subjecting it to detailed historical analysis that takes account of the semi-authoritarian context in which it emerged. This will reveal its specificities, characteristics and implications for sociopolitical trends in Iran and in the broader context of MENA. Such an enquiry will contribute to the scholarly literature on MENA social movements by investigating the dynamics driving Iran's Green Movement. The knowledge and insights thus gained may be applied to studying social mobilization and social change throughout the region. The investigative approach to be employed here involves bringing the Green Movement within the purview of social movement theories, a task that requires identifying the specific conditions that shaped and triggered it, the dynamics at play, the various modes of agency at work, and the movement's potential to bring about sociopolitical change notwithstanding the exceptionalist attributes routinely ascribed to oppositional movements in the region.

With a view to bringing MENA cases within the purview of social movement studies, MENA scholars have called for conceptual as well as theoretical innovation aimed at moving beyond the trans-historical, grand causal, and universalistic models that currently dominate the field. This is deemed imperative for two reasons: first, these models hold certain assumptions that make their application problematic to MENA, in particular with regard to explaining "the intricate texture and dynamics of change, [social activism], and resistance in this part of the world" (Bayat, 2013, p. 5); second, given that "sociological concepts are produced in relation to specific socio-historical contexts, they are not automatically reproducible from one case to another" (Beinin & Vairel, 2011, p. 7). Thus, Asef Bayat (2013) asserts, a "fruitful approach," one making for an authoritative and genuine contribution to the literature, involves "analytical innovation [and] rejects both "exceptionalism" and an uncritical application of conventional social science concepts, but also thinks to ... introduce fresh perspectives and ... new analytical tools [that] make sense of regional realities" (pp. 3-4). It is in this spirit that I introduce the concept of *harakat al-harakaat*,[10] or movement of movements as a framework for understanding Iran's Green Movement.

Iran's green movement as a movement of movements

The analytical concept of a movement of movements transcends exceptionalist tendencies stemming from a narrow religio-centric view of social movements in MENA as fundamentalist, anti-utopian or backward; it can also serve as a conceptual framework for understanding the Green Movement as a vehicle for social and political change. Moreover, in transcending universalizing and totalizing narratives and taking into account the semi-authoritarian setting within which the Green Movement was born, evolved and conducted operations, it can elucidate the specificities of a social movement years in the making. Thus can the concept of a movement of movements serve to illuminate the Green Movement's origins, multiple characters, diverse composition, and objectives, along with the conditions under which it emerged.

Most importantly, a movement of movements provides a framework for understanding the Green Movement as a mega social movement or coalition of smaller movements of counterconduct embracing and representing smaller oppositional movements—mainly student, youth and women's groups (Postel, 2010; Jahanbegloo & Soroush, 2010; Adelkhah, 2012; Khosrokhavar, 2012)—that independently of one another would have had little, if any, hope of success in mobilizing against the state hardliners, as evinced by the fate of earlier oppositional movements that were either crushed in their infancy or driven underground by the state security apparatus. Only the Green Movement was capable of mounting street demonstrations of a scale and duration that would rock the Islamic Republic to its foundations. This could only be achieved by weaving together these diverse and single-interest movements into a grand coalition, galvanized by a common purpose, namely to challenge and negate the Islamic Republic's rule, or in Foucauldian terms conduct of conduct, as evinced by the two most popular slogans chanted during the street demonstrations: *Ma Bishomarim,* "We are Countless," and *Natarisd Ma hame Baham Hastim,* "Do not be Afraid; We are All in This Together." In this sense, a movement of movements is to be understood as an aggregation of diverse societal groups with the common aim of mobilizing in opposition to a conservative establishment to which they have become disaffected.

At the same time, it is the very heterogeneity of a movement of movements that lends it its inclusiveness. Whereas earlier oppositional movements had been dominated by special interest groups focused on single issues—gender discrimination, academic freedom, workers' rights—the Green Movement, with its diverse constituencies and multipolar voices, set its sights on pursuing a far broader and more ambitious reform agenda, one aimed at institutionalizing political accountability and transparency, the rule of law, citizens' rights and civic freedoms, as evinced by what would become its signature refrain: "Where is my vote?" (Rahe Sabz, 2010). What this inclusivity reflects is a widening of the struggle for both a home-grown democracy and a civil society —twin phenomena that must be seen and interrogated as features of a particular historical phase in both the development of Iranian society and its tug of war with a clerical oligarchy, one marked by conflicts stemming from tensions between, on the one hand, an established religio-political order that had effectively instrumentalized, and by implication institutionalized and governmentalized, religion as a vehicle for legitimizing its rule and, on the other, an emerging grassroots movement bent on dismantling it; between religious duties and allegiances to the state and the rights and obligations of citizenship; between clerical authoritarianism and republicanism.

The inclusive demands made by the Green Movement and articulated by its disparate voices reveal the multidimensionality of the state's manifold governmental rules, making this movement of movements a site of collective social resistance, as manifest in its repertoire of collective action, such as massive street marches and the communal practice of chanting *Allahoakbar*, "God is Great," from rooftops. What would emerge immediately after the June 12 presidential election was a multilayered protest movement embodying a resistance of resistances against various modes of subordination and marginalization—gender, economic, social, political, among others—employed by a multiplicity of legal, administrative and security apparatuses orchestrated by the state in, as will be seen, areas as diverse as the family, academe, the courts, and, above all, public spaces where everyday life unfolds, and thus where governmental power comes to be exercised in ubiquitous forms. Hence, the Green Movement may be seen as a rainbow collectivity whose disparate groups would coalesce so as to resist the state program of governmentalization in its myriad forms. It was this active resistance played out on a national stage that would showcase these diverse struggles and thus the power of activists and ordinary people, who, even in the absence of a formal leadership and organizational structure, succeeded in mobilizing for the express purpose of opposing specific modalities of governmental power.

Conclusion

In this chapter I reviewed some of the central theories associated with social movement studies with a view to assessing their utility for elucidating oppositional movements operating in a MENA setting, and the Green Movement in particular. These theories, by virtue of their modernist assumptions, West-centric orientation, and at times totalizing narratives, were found to be inadequate as far as accounting for the specificities of such movements, or the conditions leading to their emergence and modes of mobilization and protestation.

As discussed earlier, moreover, the history of the Green Movement points to several factors crucial to analyzing a movement of movements or, as Hamid Dabashi puts it, elucidating its "full dimensions ... yet to be unpacked" (2009, para. 5). Particularly germane to this task is the work of both interrogating the conditions in which disparate social strata achieve unity and solidarity and examining the role of a highly decentralized leadership in inspiring mass mobilization.

Above all else, the Green Movement's history highlights the need for a greater understanding of the complex relations between state and society in contemporary Iran and of how such relations shape social movements in general. In particular, greater attention needs to be paid to the relationship between the Green Movement and earlier post-revolutionary social movements if a better understanding is to be derived of the dynamics and character of future mass mobilizations and their likely trajectories and outcomes.

At the same time, as the Green Movement emerged but a few short years ago, its strategic direction and impact, as well as its precise effects, have yet to be clearly discerned, let alone subjected to systematic analysis. As such, a more thorough examination of this movement of movements is required if the scholarly literature is to move beyond the dichotomy of victory and defeat to speculate on its long-term impact and potential. As will be shown, one thing is certain: for the immediate future, the conditions that gave rise to this phenomenon, as well as the indomitable will on the part of the great majority of Iranians to alter them, will in no way diminish.

Notes

1 Also note that, according to Charles Tilly (1978), a revolutionary situation and a revolutionary outcome must coexist for a revolution to occur.
2 The discussion on the ratification of CEDAW will be analyzed and discussed in further details and with reference to the 2006 Women's One Million Signature Campaign in chapter 4.
3 The immediate cause of the demonstration was, according to a report published by Human Rights Watch, soaring unemployment, at one point reaching 15 percent (Refworld, 2006).
4 The term post-ideological is used here to refer to instances of collective action motivated by no specific ideology, as, for example, the majority of cases of collective action transpiring in the region over the course of the twentieth century, e.g., the 1979 Iranian revolution. In the series of uprisings that would periodically shake Bahrain between 1994 and 1999, leftists, liberals and Islamists joined forces, setting aside ideological differences, to demand democratic reforms. The term was first coined by Alain Touraine to refer to what he calls the moral movements of the 1960s and '70s that erupted in Western Europe—environmental, feminist, ecological, etc. None of these, as is argued, were inspired by a specific political ideology. Hamid Dabashi (2011) borrows the term to refer to the recent cases of mobilization in MENA, including the Green Movement, given their cadres' lack of ideological commitment to collective action.

5 In the case of the Bahraini uprisings (1994–1999), a series of confrontations between state security forces and demonstrators resulted in 40 civilian deaths. In 2001, in a bid to end the turmoil, Hamad Ibn Isa Al Khalifa, King of Bahrain, agreed to adopt a National Action Charter providing for ways and means of implementing a program of progressive reform, following a 98% referendum vote in its favour. The charter was followed in 2002 by a new constitution that established a constitutional monarchy, endorsed the principle of equality between Sunnis and Shi'ites, and extended civil and property rights to all citizens, among other things (Pourmokhtari, 2017).
6 Note that in response to criticism from a number of social movement scholars, including Jeff Goodwin, James Jasper and Charles Kurzman; Doug McAdam, Sidney Tarrow and the late Charles Tilly did include in *Dynamics of Contention* (2001) a revised PPT that articulates a more "relational" model of social movements, one far better suited to the study of oppositional movements in the MENA region. However, as Beinin and Vairel (2011, p. 6) rightly opine, even this reformulated theory is overly complex in respect to the causal/empirical mechanics used to explicate oppositional movements; nor is it entirely free of structural bias in the sense that "[the authors] appear not to have completely changed their minds about the classical categories they helped to establish. They … reuse … or adjust them [, merely] modifying their meaning [or simply] reasserting them."
7 This point requires clarification. The Islamic Republic holds municipal, parliamentary and presidential elections every four years. Prior to each election cycle, the authorities invariably open up the political arena to maximize voter turnout with a view to bolstering the legitimacy of the state. The tenth presidential election, slated for June 12, 2009, proved no exception to this rule, with Tehran going so far as to tolerate public debates and discussions as well as open shows of support for oppositional candidates. The question here, however, has to do with whether this easing up, which ranks third on McAdam's (1996) list of "structural conditions" responsible for precipitating collective action, signaled a diminished capacity on the part of the state to repress political dissent. As I have shown elsewhere (Pourmokhtari, 2014), prior to the 2009 election, and even when the Green Movement was gathering steam, there was no such easing up. Were this so, we ought to have witnessed an intensification of collective action. That this failed to occur suggests the state was as strong as ever at the time the Green Movement was coalescing. However, as discussed in subsequent chapters, it is essential to acknowledge that such "liberalizing" episodes provide the opportunity for a politics of counterpower to emerge, something not unique to the 2009 election.
8 While in exile, Ayatollah Khomeini declared repeatedly that he had no interest in governing the country. Thus, for example, in a January 9, 1979 *Le Monde* interview, he vowed that "[a]fter the Shah's departure from Iran, I will not become a president nor accept any other leadership role. Just like before, I [shall] limit my activities only to guiding and directing the people." And in a November 28, 1978 *Le Journal* interview, the future Supreme Leader opined that "[i]t is the Iranian people who have to select their own capable and trustworthy individuals and give them … responsibilities. However, personally, I can't accept any special role or responsibility." In an earlier November 8 *United Press* interview he emphasized, "I have repeatedly said that neither my desire nor my age nor my position allows me to govern." For an overview of Ayatollah Khomeini's remarks on any future role he might play in a post-Pahlavi Iran, see Jalal Matini's (2003) "Democracy? I meant theocracy: The most truthful individual in recent history."
9 An analysis of these works, focusing on, among other things, a tendency to embrace uncritically key aspects of leading mainstream social movement theories is provided in details elsewhere. See, for example, Bayat (2013, pp. 3-5) and Beinin & Vairel (2011, pp. 1-5).
10 *Harakat al-harakaat* is the Arabic translation of the concept of movement of movements. Special thanks is owed Asef Bayat for providing the Arabic translation of the concept of a movement of movements.

2 Theorizing the Green Movement
A Foucauldian model

Introduction

Michel Foucault has inspired a rich body of work in a number of the fields comprising the social sciences. Yet curiously, despite his seminal work on the relationship between power and governance, few scholars working in the field of Political Science or the subfield of social movement studies have applied a Foucauldian perspective to examining the phenomenon of mass social mobilization/collective action directed at contesting the political and social status quo.[1] This may stem, in large part, from the commonly held view that Foucault had far more to say about regimes of power than about contention politics or the relationship between state and society, an understanding of which is essential to analysing great social ruptures and political upheavals.[2] However, as will be seen, a closer interrogation of his work reveals much in the way of theory that can be applied to both Political Science and social movement studies. Indeed, Foucault is at pains to show that his work transcends the boundaries of any single discipline: "I would like my books to be a kind of toolbox that people can rummage through to find a tool they can use however they wish in their own area: I don't write for an audience, I write for users, not readers" (Foucault, 1974, pp. 523–254). He later asserts, "I don't write a book so that it will be the final word; I write a book so that other books are possible, not necessarily written by me" (cited in O'Farrell, 2005, p. 9).

Taking these statements at face value, this chapter argues that a close examination of his work reveals the broad contours of a theoretical framework for analysing the complex relationship between state and society, one that provides a vantage point from which to analyse his work within the purview of social movements in general, and Iran's Green Movement in particular, and from which to understand how such episodes of contention emerge vis-à-vis governmental political power and grassroots resistance. The chief merit of such an approach lies in a sensitivity to the political context within which oppositional movements form, develop and conduct their operations. At the same time, I argue that by advancing an account of multiple modernities, a Foucauldian model transcends certain dominant social movement theories with their linear conception of social and political progress, their exclusivist understanding of social and political development and their modernist assumptions.

I begin this chapter by analysing Foucault's work vis-à-vis its potential to transcend the boundaries of certain fields within the social sciences, in particular Political Science. After first examining the utility of his work for explicating the relationship between politics, government and power, I then turn to his analysis of governmentality with a view to elucidating how, in light of his studies of the governmentality–power–resistance nexus, one might go about constructing a theoretical framework for explicating mass social and political upheavals in relation to governmental-political power. Lastly, I apply his concept of governmentality to Iran. But first, a few remarks concerning Foucault's work and its utility for the social sciences, and Political Science in particular, are in order.

Social sciences as political science: The political Foucault

Foucault's contribution to the field of Political Science has, until recently, been marginal to say the least. This observation represents a point of departure for Paul Brass' authoritative "Foucault Steals Political Science" (2000), wherein the author asserts that while Foucault's "work ought by now to have become a focal point for the resurrection of ... topics [pertaining to] ... power and government," the twin focal concepts of Political Science, in reality, and certainly "[r]regrettably, ... such a turn" is far from a full-fledged "occur[rence] in the discipline," at least in so far as anything like a systematic engagement with Foucault's work that might allow for a comprehensive application of his analyses of power and governance beyond the field of social theory (Brass, 2000, p. 305). Concludes Brass:

> The subject matter of what has been traditionally considered central to the discipline, [that is, power and government,] has been stolen [, in this case appropriated systematically] by Foucault while central trends in the discipline as a whole have departed markedly from a serious engagement with those topics.
>
> (2000, p. 305)

Such is particularly the case with the state–society relationship, that of ruler and ruled, and the complex interrelations, knowledges, rationalities and mentalities underpinning it. Brass takes on the work of "demonstrate[ing] the importance of Foucault's insights into the nature of power and governance for a discipline that calls itself political science" (2000, p. 305). To illuminate further as well as validate his viewpoint, one need look no farther than to how, in foregrounding the relationship among government, governed and power, classical Marxism, as a dominant theoretical/analytical trend in Political Science, has been used by many in the field to provide a rather narrow and limited account of power, government and society. To be precise, one can make the case that Foucault was inspired by "Marxists ... [who see social and political] conflict everywhere" (Goodwin & Jasper, 2012, p. 15). As such, his analyses, in particular those focusing on madness and sexuality, "largely adopt[] [a Marxist-inspired understanding of] economic classes as [the determinants of] ... primary political groupings" (Goodwin & Jasper, 2012, p. 15).

That said, Foucault's approach to questions of power and government transcends, and by implication problematizes, that of Marxists, which is informed by a set of analyses that "assum[es] potential groups" at both state and societal levels, have nothing more than "pre-existing desires and objective interests" where their interactions and interrelationships are concerned (Goodwin & Jasper, 2012, p. 15). This state of affairs has compelled Marxists, by and large, to "giv[e]" in their analysis of power and government "[almost] no attention to the processes that might create the appropriate subjects, dispositions and desires" (Goodwin & Jasper, 2012, p. 15). As a result, classical Marxists tend to "see the state or the polity as the only field of struggle that really matters" with respect to analysing and elucidating the analytics of power and government, and, by implication, the state–society relationship, for ultimately "their model [functions to] re-crown the sovereign state that Foucault was so insistent on decentering" (Goodwin & Jasper, 2012, p. 15).

The question that arises at this juncture is one of why Foucault should be used to explicate and analyse the phenomenon that is the state–society–government relationship beyond the classical accounts offered by Political Science. The answer lies in the multilayered and generative approach he adopts in order to elucidate power relations, one that goes beyond a simple and narrow conception of power as a prohibiting force. This approach is closely scrutinized toward the end of the chapter. Suffice it to say here, in Foucault's formulation, analysing power from the point of view of a mere sovereign modality "does not give [it] enough credit" (Allen, 1999, p. 34), for, according to the French theorist and his disciples, power "does not simply constrain or enable pre-existing projects; it entices, it creates new goals, new subjects, new streams of action, new types of knowledge" (Goodwin & Jasper, 2012, p. 15).

Drawing on the above quotation, one can identify two vantage points from which to shed light on how and why Foucault's account of power and governance represents: (a) a timely, refreshing and pivotal explication of social and political conflict in terms of the various and specific knowledges, rationalities and mentalities driving it; and (b) a lens through which can be discerned a strategic blueprint for discomfiting and de-naturalizing classical accounts of Political Science approaches such as Marxism, by which one can transcend, indeed disrupt, social, economic, intellectual and moral categories by developing ways and means of aggregating them into the broader, and by implication more encompassing, realm of the political.

Foucault's most illuminating remarks on the reciprocal relationship between power and knowledge appear in *Power/Knowledge* (1980), a collection of essays in which he questions "the entire basis for the traditional distinction between power and knowledge embodied in the phrase of resistance to the unjust use of power: 'speak truth to power'" (Brass, 2000, p. 306). Notes Brass:

> In Foucault's thought, the phrase reveals that those who speak it [often] do not know the relations among power, truth, and knowledge [, for, in effect,] [t]here is neither knowledge nor truth that can be separated from power—not only the power in politics that political scientists have traditionally studied, but the power that reveals itself in systems of knowledge and practices in

disciplines such as medicine ..., psychiatry, criminology, and the institutions associated with them: hospitals, the asylum, and the prison.

(2000, p. 306)

For Foucault, power and knowledge and their reciprocal interactions "reveal [themselves] also in talk and practice in the domain[s] of sexuality [, madness and discipline and crime and punishment]" (Brass 2000, p. 306), key areas in Foucault's examination of institutional knowledge-based power regimes. It follows then that "power, in fact, exists alongside knowledge and the 'regimes of truth' embedded in all knowledge systems, practices, and institutions in [a given] society, from the family to the school to the factory to the army to the agencies of the state" (Brass, 2000, p. 306). This is necessarily so, given that for Foucault, "nothing ... can function as a mechanism of power if it is not deployed according to procedures, instruments, means, and objectives," or specific bodies of artificial truths, "which can be validated in more or less coherent systems of knowledge" (cited in Brass, 2000, p. 306).

Lying at the intersection of power, knowledge and truth, pre-existing bodies of knowledge "contain no vantage point for a critique of power relations," as in any given society, even the most rigorous of scholars are prisoners of dominant knowledge systems (Brass, 2000, p. 307). In this intellectual solitary confinement, "[t]here is ... no place from which intellectuals, for example, can 'speak truth to power'" (Brass, 2000, p. 307), precisely because they "are themselves agents of [a] system of power" (Foucault, cited in Brass, 2000, p. 307).

This observation compels Foucault to assert, "[t]here is no power relation without the correlative constitution of a field of knowledge, nor any knowledge that does not presuppose and constitute at the same time power relations" (1979, p. 27). Herein lies a moral and political dilemma, for if "knowledge cannot function without power nor power without knowledge" (Foucault, cited in Brass, 2000, p. 307), how is power to be critiqued objectively? According to Foucault, within this knowledge–power–truth orthodoxy, the uncritical of all stripes find themselves, knowingly or un-knowingly, the prisoners of established knowledges, for while "[p]eople know what they do; frequently they know why they do what they do; but what they don't know is what what they do does" (cited in Dreyfus & Rainbow, 1982, p. 187). In this way, the uncritical or even seemingly critical of all stripes are often confined within the political boundaries of "every statement" (Brass, 2000, p. 307), that is, every established truth, economic, historical, social, political or otherwise, which constrains their imaginations, in the process conditioning them to "exert[] a certain [and accepted modality of] power," which "implies at least a *savoir-faire*" (Foucault, cited in Brass, 2000, p. 307).

Yet, this is no mere question of "*savoir-faire*," and by implication no mere "elementary form of practice" (Brass, 2000, p. 307), for, according to Foucault, such truths/knowledges that make possible and solidify certain modalities of power function to legitimize and render operable "the disciplinary practices associated with systems of knowledge emerging from and applied within societal institutions" (Clegg, 1989, p. 153). As Stewart Clegg (1989, p. 153) observes, the "'disciplinary practices' associated with all modern institutions are also discursive practices, i.e., knowledge[s] reproduced through practices made possible by the framing assumptions of [those] knowledge[s]," which means that to transcend or critique them, one must step outside the very frameworks of the formal knowledges that produce asymmetrical power relations.

Foucault is at pains, moreover, to inform his readers and disciples, in particular the academic intellectuals among them, that it is only by breaking down the traditional boundaries existing among academic disciplines, through what he calls critique, that we can effectively scrutinize power relations, thus revealing their asymmetries, contradictions, inequities and excesses. Only through critique are we properly positioned to examine critically social, psychological, criminal, economic, moral and historical phenomena. But what, for Foucault, constitutes critique? According to the great French luminary,

> critique does not consist in saying that things aren't good the way they are. It consists in seeing on just what type of assumptions, of familiar notions, of established and unexamined ways of thinking the accepted practices are based ... To do criticism is to make harder those acts which are now too easy.
> (Foucault, 1984a, p. 456)

Foucault uses the above explanation as a departure point to invite his readers to move beyond the classical, and at times orthodox, categories of the social, psychological, criminal, economic and moral by conflating them into a single, broader category: the political. "What," Foucault (2008) asks, "is politics ... in the end, if not both the interplay of different arts [, mentalities and technologies] of government with their different reference points and the debate to which these different arts of government give rise? It seems to me it is here that politics is born" and hence the category of the political emerges (p. 313).

Foucault underscores this viewpoint when scrutinizing the role of academic intellectuals in re-solidifying established forms of knowledge and truth, and above all power relations: "[i]n my opinion, today the intellectual must be inside the pit, the very pit in which the sciences are engaged, where they produce political results" (cited in Afary & Anderson, 2005, p. 184). Explains Foucault:

> [Our] role [as intellectuals] is to address problems effectively, really: and to pose them with the greatest possible rigor, with the maximum complexity and difficulty so that a solution does not arise all at once because of the thought of some reformer or even in the brain of a political party. The problems that I try to address, these perplexities of crime, madness, and sex which involve daily life, cannot be easily resolved[] [by] the thought of some reformer or even in the brain of a political party ... It takes years, decades of work carried out at the grassroots level with the people directly involved; and the right to speech and political imagination must be returned to them ... I carefully guard against making the law. Rather, I concern myself with determining problems, unleashing them, revealing them within the framework of such complexity as to shut the mouths of [not just the] legislators [, but] all those who speak for others and above others.
> (cited in Foucault & Trombadori, 1991, pp. 158–159)

Such unprovoked attacks on intellectuals and legislators are grounded in what is perhaps his overriding imperative, indeed Foucault's *fantastic passion,* namely to invite all to speak truth to political power. That in his "opinion, today the intellectual must be inside the pit, the very pit in which the sciences are engaged" is pivotal because it is there "where they produce political results, construct another political thought, another political vision, and teach a new vision of the future" (cited in Afary & Anderson, 2005, p. 184). The latter may be achieved by what he calls a critical engagement with the politics of established truths, and hence with the regimes of power that sustain them:

> "Truth" is to be understood as a system of ordered procedures for the production, regulation, distribution, circulation and operation of statements. "Truth" is linked in a circular relation with systems of power, which produce and sustain it, and to effects of power which it induces and which extend it. [Power is a] "regime" of truth [; it] is not an institution, and not a structure; neither is it a certain strength we are endowed with; it is the name that one attributes to a complex strategical situation in a particular society.
>
> (Foucault, cited in Davidson, 2001, p. 128)

Analyzing power thus requires a form/mode of strategic unorthodoxy—strategic because one is required to speak of power and government, ruler and ruled, mad and insane, normal and abnormal, from beyond the confines of formal institutions and political arenas, parliaments, legislatures, political parties, and hence beyond the established forms of knowledges that are created and disseminated, in particular in academe:

> Education may well be, as of right, the instrument whereby every individual, in a society like our own, can gain access to any kind of discourse. But we well know that in its distribution, in what it permits and in what it prevents, it follows the well-trodden battle-lines of social conflict. Every educational system is a political means of maintaining or of modifying the appropriation of discourse, with the knowledge and the powers it carries with it.
>
> (Foucault, 1972, p. 227)

That we need to treat academe as a political arena speaks to a passion on the part of the French luminary to transcend disciplinary boundaries by grouping that which is considered non-political—the social, moral, psychological, criminal, economic, historical—into the far broader category of the political. For the intellectual, this represents a pivotal task, even if as a consequence he/she is judged to be abnormal and/or branded as mad for taking it up. For Foucault, such strategic unorthodoxies constitute an imperative, not merely because "[t]he judges of normality are present everywhere," nor because "[w]e [all live] in the society of the teacher-judge, the doctor-judge, the educator-judge, the social worker–judge," but rather because while "madness" is "the false punishment of a false solution, by its own virtue ... [it] brings to light the real problem [or what is artificially considered as truth and/or given truth], which can then be truly resolved" (1977b, p. 304). In this regard, Foucault goes so far as to claim that "madness is [a form of] illusion[]" (1988, p. 26), for if we concur that "knowledge is so important in [authenticating] madness, it is not because the latter can control the secrets of knowledge; on the contrary, madness is the punishment of a disorderly and useless science" (1988, p. 25). Conceived as such, madness is not just *madness*—it is no less, and crucially no more, than a mode of "divine spectacle" (Foucault, 1988, p. 28):

> The marvellous logic of the mad which seems to mock that of the logicians because it resembles it so exactly, or rather because it is exactly the same, and because at the secret heart of madness, at the core of so many errors, so many absurdities, so many words and gestures without consequence, we discover, finally, the hidden perfection of a language.
> (Foucault, 1988, p. 95)

That Foucault pulls out all the stops to foreground such views is attributable to the existence of a veritable host of hidden dynamics, false judgements and/or normalizing rationalities that underpin modern societies, all of which can operate beyond the purview of social institutions, and so remain, by and large, invisible. The best visible examples of such invisibilities are to be found within academe:

> [O]ne of the tasks that seems urgent and immediate to me over and above anything else, is this: It is the custom ... to consider that power is localized in the hands of the government and that it is exercised through a certain number of particular institutions, such as the administration, the police or the army. One knows all these institutions are made to transmit and apply orders and to punish those who don't obey. But I believe power also exercises itself through the mediation of a certain number of institutions that appear to have nothing in common with political power and as if they are independent of it, but in fact they are not. One knows that the university and in a general way, all teaching systems, which appear simply to disseminate knowledge, are made to maintain a certain social class in power; and to exclude the instruments of power of another social class. Institutions of knowledge, of foresight and care, such as medicine, also help to support the political power. It's also obvious, even to the point of scandal, in certain cases related to psychiatry.
> (Foucault, cited in Chomsky and Foucault, 2006, p. 40)

Following this line of reasoning, Foucault views visibility as a deception: "visibility is [itself] a trap" (1977a, p. 200), and because it masks political power. This is also true of the dominant forms/modes of knowledge: "[k]nowledge is not for knowing [per se]" (Foucault, cited in Osberg, 2010, p. iii); to the contrary, knowledge, and hence truth and theory, is no more than a "struggle against power [;] a struggle to bring power to light and open up where it is most invisible and insidious" (Foucault, cited in Foucault & Deleuze, 1977, pp. 207–208). Invisibility makes visible "the hidden perfection of a language" (Foucault, 1988, p. 95).

It is at this point that we can discern how fruitless it is to scrutinize Foucault on the basis of a single exclusive category like academic or social theorist or socioeconomic theorist or (moral) philosopher; rather, he may be more appropriately and usefully consigned to the far broader category of political theorist or problem-identifier of histories of political phenomena, in which case his work can be construed more precisely as a political examination of the social, criminal, economic and historical ills plaguing contemporary societies.

Foucault's earlier remarks on the role of the intellectual—and, in particular, his observation that "today the intellectual must be inside the pit, the very pit in which the sciences are engaged, where they produce political results [, and for the express purpose of] construct[ing] another political thought, another political vision, and teach[ing] a new vision of the future" (cited in Afary & Anderson, 2005, p. 184)—suggest that "we have an entirely interwoven network" of social relations that are in effect political, hence the imperative to merge them into the category of Political Science (Foucault, cited in Brass, 2000, p. 307). This means that "[d]espite various attempts to cling tenaciously to an apolitical, objective stance that remains above the fray [, even] intellectual labor always has specific political implications," for "intellectuals are always imbricated in the political" (McCall, 2017, p. 14). For this reason, philosophy itself "ought to be understood as 'the politics of truth'" (McCall, 2017, p. 14).

The same calculus applies to academe: "[s]chools serve the same social [and political] functions as prisons and mental institutions [, which is] to define, classify, control, and regulate people" (Foucault, cited in Braungardt, 2017, para. 1), and precisely because, and Foucault's remarks bear repeating here, "knowledge cannot function without power nor power without knowledge" (cited in Brass, 2000, p. 307). This is necessarily so because knowledge and truth are "put to the service of the administrative state and become" (Brass, 2000, p. 306) themselves part of "the machinery of [political] power" (Foucault, cited in Brass, 2000, p. 306). Hence, concludes Foucault in a memorable 1971 debate with Noam Chomsky regarding the significance of the category of the political for his work: "I would have to be ideologically blind to not interest myself in that which is most substantial to human existence [, and by implication human sciences]: ... power relations" (YouTube, 2013). Once these connections are made, we can see that for Foucault, not just power relations are political; for him, the sexual is also political, the abnormal is political, the mad is political, the psychotic is political, the criminal is political, the economic is political, the social is political, the historical is political, and it goes without saying the *political* is political, in both the literal and figurative sense of the term.

Foucault, studies of governmentality and the power–resistance nexus: A constellational approach

Social movements are complex and dynamic political entities that showcase the struggle between the political power of governmental regimes and grassroots social and political resistance. Thus, one must view such struggles primarily as "[political-]historical phenomen[a] [unfolding] in a span of time" (Bayat, 2005, p. 897). This means that "the search for universally valid propositions and models, at least for anything so complex as a social movement, is bound to fail"

(Goodwin & Jasper, 2004, p. 27). It is thus imperative to acknowledge that "historical specificities [giving rise to any form of collective action] are never entirely reproducible" (Beinin & Vairel, 2011, p. 8). If Bayat, Goodwin and Jasper, and Beinin and Vairel are correct, a comprehensive analysis of social movements must take into account the particular settings in which they emerge and conduct operations—a consideration that compels us to be ever cognizant of the "situationally contingent" (Goodwin & Jasper, 2004, p. 27) mechanisms that inspire disparate forms of social movements and grassroots sociopolitical action.

Both Charles Tilly and Saba Mahmood underscore this point by cautioning against universalizing and totalizing accounts of social movements. The latter, whose outstanding work *Politics of Piety: The Islamic Revival and the Feminist Subject* (2005) owes much to Foucault, raises serious doubts regarding the possibility of "identify[ing] universal categor[ies] of acts ... outside of the ethical and political conditions within which" they acquire their relevancy (Mahmood, 2005, p. 9; emphasis added). For his part, Tilly (1997), in "History and Sociological Imagining", contends that such analyses obscure factors such as history, politics, time, and place that are pivotal to explicating diverse forms of social mobilization.

A Foucauldian perspective offers a timely and much-needed alternative to certain universalizing and totalizing accounts of social movements. Foucault (1978) was a nominalist in the sense that he rejected the presupposition that human and social phenomena have an essential, unchanging character (O'Farrell, 2005; Gallagher, 2008). For this reason, his rich and diverse contributions to historical, social and political enquiry work to problematize all that is considered absolute, eternal and universal, even, as was shown, political, in the process inviting the reader to view social phenomena as political events and processes that showcase the radical historicity of that under study (Foucault, 1991; Baker, 1994).

Given his stance on historical nominalism and aversion to grand theory, Foucault views theorization as an endeavour that is always political, tentative, contextual and socio-historically specific (O'Farrell, 2005; Gallagher, 2008). It is to be conceived, moreover, as a form of situated practice: "theory does not express, translate or serve to apply practice: it is practice," meaning that it is a "local[ized] and regional" system of struggle against political power and thus contingent upon the setting in which it is applied (Foucault, cited in Foucault & Deleuze, 1977, p. 208).

With respect to the twin phenomena of social mobilization and collective action, a Foucauldian-inspired account of social movements has, with few exceptions (Death, 2010, 2011; Wilson, 2009), and only until recently, been largely underutilized by scholars working in the field of social movement studies. Thus, in addition to examining what a Foucauldian analysis of collective action would actually entail, this chapter delineates how it might contribute to explicating Iran's Green Movement.

A constellational governmentality

Within the corpus of Foucault's work, a vantage point for analysing social movements can be found in his writings on governmentality and its relation to power and resistance. Foucault employs the concept of governmentality in different contexts and forms to investigate, for example, how individuals and groups shape their conduct and that of others or to examine empirical domains of madness and delinquency, all with a view to foregrounding a liberal conception of governmentality. Yet a common theme runs through all his work in this area, namely "governance of and by states" (Walters, 2012, p. 12). The latter is to be understood as various articulations of what Foucault (1997) calls the conduct of conduct, by which he means the arts, techniques and rationalities of government that when combined make something called the modern state "thinkable and meaningful" (Walters, 2012, p. 12).

This begs the question of just how transferable a West-centric concept like governmentality, or liberal governmentality to be precise, is to a non-Western context? Foucault devotes little time to addressing this key question, hence my reliance on the work of William Walters, an authority on Foucault's concept of governmentality, and in particular his pioneering and insightful *Governmentality: Critical Encounters* (2012).

Certainly, as both concept and blueprint for a critical analysis of state, society and institutions, governmentality has been applied across a broad range of subfields within the social sciences (Garland, 1997; Fimyar, 2008; Purewal, 2014; Topinka, 2016), giving rise to a host of social, political, psychological, cultural and economic ramifications that vary with each case study. However significant, such analyses, asserts Walters, have ultimately, and indeed paradoxically in light of their Foucauldian provenance, "done little to suggest the possibility of a distinctive research agenda that might investigate diverse arts, configurations, and experiences of power" (2012, p. 87). The reason can be traced, he argues, to a lack of critical engagement with the new areas of concern for these scholars:

> Beyond extracting from Foucault a set of crucial insights about the constitutive power of discourse in making worlds, and the imperative of pursuing a more historicized framing of world politics, proved to be only of limited help to the researcher looking for conceptual and methodological equipment for undertaking empirical investigations.
>
> (Walters, 2012, p. 87)

Thus, and somewhat curiously, asks Walters regarding the transferable nature of governmentality to alternative political and geographical contexts/polities, "[i]f travel broadens the mind, does it also expand the power of concepts?" (2012, p. 92). "Do concepts that traverse academic borders become richer than those that stay at home?" (Walters, 2012, p. 92). All he is willing to concede in response to these questions is that "[p]erhaps the formulation of a general rule here is neither possible nor advisable" (Walters, 2012, p. 92).

However, with a view to supplementing this observation, he offers up a strategic blueprint for making governmentality, both as a concept and focal point of analysis, transferable to alternative contexts and/or polities:

> [Governmentality] is not a unified body of work but a constellation ... To constellate is to engage in a conscious and purposeful act of grouping. It

is not unlike the practice of a curator or artist who selects and assembles objects or pictures in a particular way, revealing patterns, resonances and connections that would otherwise escape our perception.
(Walters, 2012, p. 84)

Thus, for Walters, a constellational approach involves "a productive act" that "seeks to increase the intelligibility of the material ... that it serializes," in this case contention politics in general and mass oppositional movements in particular (Walters, 2012, p. 84). When applied to these two fields, moreover, a constellational approach to governmentality is "not the same thing as a school, a subfield or an attempt to formalize a new specialism" (Walters, 2012, p. 84). Indeed, insists Walters, "I am not especially keen to encourage anything like that," for some "academics often find [themselves] lobbying to have this subfield or that subfield or that specialism institutionally and professionally recognized" (2012, p. 84). On the contrary, the point here is that "[t]here are often sound political and epistemological grounds for such moves [; thus, it] should also be possible to work in collaborative and interactive ways without adding more layers of permanent institutions" (Walters, 2012, p. 84). As the author notes, "[l]ike exhibitions, constellations are temporary arrangements. They come, perhaps they resonate, perhaps they assemble a public, and they go" (Walters, 2012, p. 84). This does not mean that such a strategic conceptual stretching is devoid of authenticity and/or plausibility, for "we can say, I think, that studies of governmentality [can] undoubtedly benefit[] from their journey [outside of their home turf, in this case Western Europe]" (Walters, 2012, p. 92).

The question left unaddressed at this juncture has to do with the why of making governmentality transferable to other political/geographical contexts? The answer is two-fold: first, a constellational approach to governmentality can "open[] up new angles on debates that had in some cases become somewhat predictable" (Walters, 2012, p. 92), even instrumentalized in the service of power, such as debates on power relations and power regimes and source(s) of legitimacy and power-effects of marginalizing some groups while privileging others, all of which occur in any given polity. Second, this same approach can also serve to focus attention on those arenas, social, political, economic, that have received inadequate "attention to the specificity and technicality of political [power]" (Walters, 2012, p. 92). These points are crucial for they "allow[] us to consider ... what mutations have occurred in the idea of governmentality once it crosses disciplinary boundaries" (Walters, 2012, p. 92), while helping us understand the specific phenomena under scrutiny.

It is at this contingent and intangible level that Walters concludes constellational governmentality does "exist," but "not ... in a pure form anywhere;" rather, it constitutes a "politics of combination" (2012, p. 40), and rightly so, given that, for Foucault, as will be seen, power, that lucid and relational entity underwriting processes of governmentality, involves much more than scrutinizing a complex of specific techniques in a particular locality; hence his caveat that "[i]f we want to do an analysis of power ... we must speak of powers and try to localize them in their historical and geographical specificity" (2012, para. 12). This speaks to a conviction on his part that the whole purpose of analysing governmentality, and by implication one of its core components, power, lies with the existential reality that the latter, is, again, much more than an assembly of various techniques: "the purpose of all my analyses [of governmentality or governmentalities] is that, in light of them, we find out where are the weak points of power, from which we can attack it" (Foucault, cited in Afary & Anderson, 2005, p. 189).

And so herein lies the essence of this work's position on a constellational analytic of governmentality as an intellectual and political endeavour whereby one can "find a new host amongst knowledges," in this case regarding mass oppositional movements (Walters, 2012, p. 84). This in turn allows us, as Walters remarks, "to engage in a conscious and purposeful act of grouping" disciplinary technologies and power domains, their weak points, their effects and contradictions, and also the resistance offered them with a view to identifying and exposing "patterns, resonances and connections that would otherwise escape our perception" (2012, p. 84). It is in this spirit that the chapters to follow introduce the reader to concepts relating to both the Islamic Republic's conduct of conduct and its disciplinary and repressive strategies, in addition to various modes of grassroots resistances to them, such as Islamist governmentality and repression as an art, and presence-as-resistance, respectively.

What of governmentality?

The concept of constellational governmentality, hereafter referred to as governmentality, has to do with the "encounter between the technologies of domination of others and those of the self" (Foucault, 1997, p. 225) or "the way[s] in which the conduct of individuals or groups might be directed" (Foucault, 1982, p. 790). It is the exercise of power in terms of a set of combinations and hybrids of what, methods and techniques used to "rule over individuals, groups and situations" (Walters, 2012, p. 14). Thus, for Foucault, power constitutes a way to change peoples' conduct, or as he puts it, "a mode of action upon actions of others" (Foucault, 1982, p. 789), made intelligible in terms of the specific techniques and mentalities through which it is exercised.

This definition provides the basis for his observation that in modern societies, power operates according to a triangular formulation of sovereignty, discipline and biopower, functioning in tandem to render a society governable. The point Foucault is making here is that just as governmentality is a pervasive and heterogeneous project, so too are the power relations that sustain governmental regimes: "one could say that power relations have been progressively governmentalized, that is to say, elaborated [and] rationalized" beyond the scope of a simple command–obedience model, which is the sovereign power (Foucault, 1982, p. 793). Foucault elaborates on the latter point:

> [W]hat I mean by power relations is that we are in a strategic situation towards each other ... We are in this struggle, and the continuation of this situation can influence the behavior or nonbehavior of the other. So we are not trapped. We are always in this kind of situation. It means that we always have

possibilities of changing the situation. We cannot jump outside the situation, and there is no point where you are free from all power relations. But you can always change it. So what I've said does not mean that we are always trapped, but that we are always free. Well anyway, that there is always the possibility of changing.

(Foucault, 1996a, p. 386)

In making this claim about power relations, however, Foucault does not abandon altogether the supposition that power can work to prohibit or severely restrict the behaviour of those subject to it. Indeed, for Foucault, and as the chapters to follow show, "power [can and does] function[] repressively" (Allen, 1999, p. 34), and precisely because "although ... pervasive, it is not equally distributed" (McLaren, 2002, p. 39; Foucault, 1979, 1982).

Yet he is also at pains to qualify his view that power relations have been elaborated and rationalized beyond the scope of a simple command–obedience model: "I do not mean to say that power, from my point of view, is a foundational, unconquerable, absolute entity that one has to kneel before" (Foucault, cited in Afary & Anderson, 2005, p. 189). To the contrary, he asserts, and his explanation bears acknowledging once more, "the purpose of all my analyses is that, in light of them, we find out where are the weak points of power, from which we can attack it" (Foucault, cited in Afary & Anderson, 2005, p. 189).

Foucault and modalities of power

At one corner of Foucault's power triangulation stands state sovereign power foregrounded by authority figures—judges, teachers, fathers—the designated holders of power to whom allegiance is owed. Theirs is a power after the command-embodied-in-law model. It is a kind of power that at the highest political levels comes to be "exercised through [the] juridical and executive arms of the state" (Gordon, 2008, p. 13). For Foucault, the sovereign power, what he calls the "juridico-institutional power" (1978, p. 136), is the power over life and death or the "right to take life or let live" (Foucault, 2003, p. 240). It is exercised through what he calls deduction, "a subtraction mechanism, a right to appropriate a portion of wealth, a tax [on] products, goods and services, labour and blood, levied on the subjects" (Foucault, 1978, p. 136). Foucault (1978) cites the death penalty as a common mode of punishment meted out by the sovereign on all "those who attack [her/] his will [and/or] law," one that serves as an example of sovereign power at work (p. 136).

For Foucault, however, merely focusing on the repressive model is of limited utility, precisely because "what makes power hold good, what makes it accepted, is simply the fact that it does not only weigh on us a force that says no" (Foucault, 1980, p. 119). The latter observation in tandem with another, namely that in modern societies disparate forms of sovereign power have grown to be less efficient—in large measure due to the prohibitive cost of "visibly constraining subjects" through brute force (Baker, 1994, p. 204)—compels him to talk and speak of other power modalities. Consequently, sovereign power has come to be "both replace[d] [by] and [to] work in tandem" (O'Farrell, 2005, p. 102) with other modes of power that can achieve more at less cost and operate more subtly by permeating the "whole social body" (Foucault, 1977a, p. 209) far more efficiently than their naked, sovereign counterpart.

Foucault defines disciplinary power as an assemblage of specific techniques that "operates on the minute parts of daily interactions" (Gordon, 2008, p. 12) and has "individuals as objects and instruments of its exercise" (Foucault, 1977a, p.170), in the process producing and disseminating an array of norms and social practices. This particular modality, whose forms are synaptic and localized, strives to "keep [the individual] under surveillance ... to control his conduct, his behavior, [and] his aptitudes," deploying simple techniques such as hierarchical observation, normalizing judgement, and the examination in institutions as diverse as schools, universities, factories and prisons (Foucault, 1977a, p. 304).

The above techniques, moreover, are solidified by an inspecting and normalizing gaze, whose function is to shape the soul of individuals so that they "conform to the [prescribed] rules, codes, and [norms]" (Gordon, 2002, p. 129). In doing so, it generates a field wherein the behaviour of the individual can be compared to that of others according to a hierarchical, value-laden scale that establishes an average and sets parameters. Further, through normalizing judgement each individual exercises "surveillance over ... and against himself [, and others]" (Foucault, cited in O'Farrell, 2005, p. 104), ever aware that disobeying or deviating from the rules and codes would incur punishment.

The objective here is to produce docile bodies that "may be subjected, used, transformed, and improved" (Foucault, 1977a, p. 136) with a view to "carry[ing] out tasks ... perform[ing] ceremonies and ... emit[ting] signs" (Foucault, 1977a, p. 25), thus making it possible for state authorities as well as the individual to detect differences among members of a society as well as identify anomalous behaviours. This disciplinary gaze works to place the individual within a machinery of surveillance, the purpose being to prevent him/her "from doing wrong and ... tak[e] away [his/her] will to do wrong" (O'Farrell, 2005, p. 104). In other words, the gaze produces predictable individuals such that the "supervisors [become] perpetually supervised" (Foucault, cited in McLaren, 2002, p. 107). Moreover, it penetrates the individual so that he/she obeys, internalizes norms, follows laws and codes voluntarily and wholeheartedly, and applies them to others. It works in such a way that "the soul ... becomes the prison of the body" (Gordon, 2002, p. 129). Ultimately, such techniques and procedures "bear on society as a whole through the organization of a police apparatus concerned with the intricacies of individual behavior" (Taylor, 2011, p. 33).

If discipline has as its primary target the individual, biopower, defined as a power that imposes itself on human life by "foster[ing it] or disallow[ing] it to the point of death" (Foucault, 1978, p. 138), complements it by focusing on the population as a whole. As a mode of power embedded in state policy and its administrative techniques, biopower uses statistical devices and scientific methods as well as mechanisms of surveillance to regulate those within its purview. Its statistical devices include birth rates, unemployment rates, and rules and regulations governing the allocation of labour by age and gender. Its objective is "an explosion of numerous and diverse techniques for achieving the subjugation of bodies and the control of populations" (Foucault, 1995, p. 140).

Such regulation is invariably conducted at the level of the economy, health, sexuality and control of reproduction—categories concerned with the "life, death, and health of entire populations" (O'Farrell, 2005, p. 106). Thus, biopower concerns itself with public health practices, the regulation of heredity, and risk regulation, among many other regulatory mechanisms often linked less directly with the physical health of a population. Therefore, unlike the logic underlying sovereign power, the logic here is that of production, or to use Foucault's terminology "to make live and to let die" (Foucault, 2003a, p. 241), by means of controlling reproduction and optimizing life and health "through detailed forms of knowledge being put in place to gather knowledge and manage populations" (O'Farrell, 2005, p. 106). On the subject of biopower, Foucault writes:

> I wouldn't say exactly that sovereignty's old right to take life or let live was replaced, but it came to be complemented by a new right which does not erase the old right but which penetrates [and] permeate[s] it. This is the right, or rather precisely the opposite right. It is the power to "make" live and "let" die. The right of sovereignty was the right to take life or let live. And then this new right is established: the right to make live and to let die.
> (Foucault, 2003a, p. 241)

"We are, then," Foucault contends, "in a power that has taken control of both the body and life or that has, if you like, taken control of life in general—with the body as one pole and the population as the other" (2003a, p. 241). As such, power, health, birth, death, fertility, sexuality and body intermesh through a combination of biological and disciplinary knowledges and categories. Ultimately, these knowledges are connected, technologized and rationalized through the production and dissemination of norms. All three modes of power ultimately work in tandem, each constituting a "part of the parcel of the modern form of governing" (Gordon, 2008, p. 14).

Foucault, power and resistance

For Foucault (1980a), however, being an object of power "does not mean that one is trapped" (pp. 141–142), for the very existence of power relations has as its corollary the possibility of resistance. As Foucault (1978, p. 95) famously postulated, "where there is power, there is resistance;" without it, there can be, in fact, no relations of power, only a state of domination where the subject has no room whatsoever to manoeuvre. Hence, resistance is an integral aspect of power that embodies the possibility of defiance, disruption and subversion, a theme taken up in, among other works, his *History of Sexuality* wherein it is demonstrated that "bodies and pleasures" can serve as "a base of operations" for a "counterattack against the deployment of sexuality," in the process giving rise to and making possible a counterdiscourse that disrupts the power relations sustaining the dominant discourse on sexuality (1978, p. 157).

It is apparent that, for Foucault, power, rather than being resisted by a force external to it, is opposed "precisely at the point of its application" (May, 1993, p. 114). This means that it operates on the individual in two ways: first, he/she is subject to the constraints of social relations of power; second, and simultaneously, he/she can and may take up the position of a subject in and through those very constraints. This is what Foucault calls subjugation or subjection, a term that denotes the co-constitutive nature of power and resistance: while one can conceive power as a heteronomous, multiple and expansive phenomenon, one can also speak of "a multiplicity of points of resistance" made possible through the disparate mechanisms of power (Foucault 1978, p. 95).

The question this co-constitutive relationship raises has to do specifically with how Foucault's formulation of governmentality vis-à-vis the power–resistance nexus translates into a theoretical framework for elucidating social movements, the forms they assume and the conditions governing their emergence, and the process of solidarity building among the actors?

Foucault, governmentality and movements of counterconduct

In his elucidation of the power–resistance nexus Foucault identifies those moments of historical singularity when a people subjected to the techniques and mechanisms, the discipline, and the normalizing gaze feel compelled to initiate various forms of collective resistance. These moments, as Foucault understands them, manifest "the strategic codification of [various] points of resistance" (1978, p. 96), leading to "great radical ruptures [and] massive binary divisions" between the two poles dividing the conductors, i.e., those who govern through specific modalities of power, and the conducted, or the governed. Such moments of radical rupture embody, for Foucault, materialized ways to resist power, which are expressed in the form of full-fledged demonstrations and protestations, and whose possibilities are enabled through what he calls movements of counterconduct.

A "movement of counterconduct" may be broadly defined as a "[collective] struggle against the processes implemented for conducting others" (Foucault, 2007, p. 201). Such movements represent a collective rejection of the status quo by a people that, in Foucault's words, are preoccupied with the question of "how not to be governed like that, by that, in the name of those principles, in view of such objectives and by the means of such methods, not like that, not for that, not by them" (1996a, p. 384).

Foucault, moreover, understands the term "counterconduct" as "part of a localized struggle against a specific modality of government [or] a specific way of being conducted" (McCall, 2014, p. 7). It follows, then, and this is the critical point to grasp, that counterconduct is ultimately a "[collective] struggle against the processes implemented for conducting others" (Foucault, 2007, p. 201), one that can assume various forms of "resistance to processes of governmentality" (Death, 2010, p. 239). It constitutes, in other words, "a mode of action upon actions of [conductors]" (Foucault, 1982, p. 789), which means that it can encompass and/or manifest "a range of activities from civil disobedience to revolution" (McCall, 2013, p. 44).

As will be shown here, the principles, attributes and features Foucault assigns to movements/episodes[3] of counterconduct can be used to construct a theoretical framework for examining social movements, as both have the same aim: to contest power. Indeed, just as the both episodes/movements of counterconduct and social movements seek to circumvent or replace specific ways of conduct for the purpose of contesting power techniques in the service of governmental regimes, so, too, do social movements, however conceived and constituted, challenge governmental regimes, and by implication their power, at the level of both principles and practices of governance. Both social movements and movements/episodes of counterconduct do so by engaging in various forms of collective action aimed at advancing specific social or political agendas or resisting or reversing government policies, in the process mobilizing "people with [a] common purpose[] and solidarity" with a view to contesting, subverting and negating governmental rules formulated by political elites and implemented by their functionaries (Tarrow, 1998, p. 4).

Analyzing social movements through a counterconduct lens, however, constitutes "a particular style of analysis" (Walters, 2012, p. 38) in that while it does not abandon key concepts—the state, society, agency, and the mobilization of actors/agents, pivotal to social movement studies—it eschews their application in a rigid and universalistic manner to all scenarios, cases and contexts. Rather, all are to be treated as "'transactional realit[ies],'" as entities that have "not always existed" but are "nonetheless real" and "born precisely from the interplay of relations of power and everything which constantly eludes them" (Foucault, 2008, p. 297).

Thus, the chief merit of the analytical framework to be employed here lies in its sensitivity to contingency, to concepts and ideas in relation to historical processes specific to particular localities. This, in turn, opens up theoretical and empirical spaces to elucidate specific formations of social movements, understand the conditions governing their emergence, examine particular arts and techniques protestors engage, and interrogate the mentalities that drive them to embrace collective forms of action.

Movements/episodes of counterconduct emerge at those historical junctures when certain configurations of power, and by implication knowledge, leave mobilization, demonstrations, protestations and civil disobedience the only remaining avenues for expressing discontent. This is why for Foucault they possess the attribute of singularity; they appear upon the scene at those historical junctures when "life can no longer be bought" (Foucault, cited in Simons, 2013, p. 85) and/or when "no power can continue to rule over a people who refuse to be intimidated by death" (Simons, 2013, p. 310). Such singular moments, however, do not possess the attribute of universality, nor do they encompass a laundry-list of attributes to be applied to every contentious situation, hence Foucault's dictum that there is "no pure law of the revolutionary" (Foucault, 1978, p. 96).

Nonetheless, in their extreme forms, they may arise when a people give "preference to the risk of death over the certainty of having to obey," which occurs at "that moment when life will no longer barter itself" (Foucault, cited in Simons, 2013, p. 85); when a people "say, 'I will no longer obey'" (Foucault, cited in Afary & Anderson, 2005, p. 129). Under such circumstances, they will refuse to be governed by such principles, laws and regulations and will begin to speak and act against a governmental regime and/or its conduct of conduct, and do so "with a single [collective] voice" (McCall, 2004, p. 12), even if this means "risk[ing] their lives in the face of power that they believe to be unjust" (Foucault, , cited in Ghamari-Tabrizi, 2016, p. 180). It is at this intangible and contingent level that we can attribute specific causes to the emergence of a movement of counterconduct, such as certain exclusionary and/or repressive policies, certain arts, knowledges, and techniques of governing, or a crisis of legitimacy.

A movement and/or episode of counterconduct challenges power at the level of its objectives and procedures and mentalities, technologies and rationalities, practices and mechanisms of governance (Death, 2010). The state, according to this view, emerges as a historical construct that projects and sustains power by appropriating and adapting certain arts and techniques, thus, making, for Foucault, "the history of the governmental ratio" inseparable from "the history of the counter-conducts opposed to it" (2007, p. 357). In making this claim, Foucault conceives such movements as the by-product of the reciprocal interaction of state and society or as movements/episodes that emerge contingent upon particular technologies of power or as "a form of schematization appropriate to a particular technology of government" (1989, p. 113).

Perhaps nowhere does Foucault highlight the role of this reciprocal interaction in producing movements of counterconduct to greater effect than in his analysis of the 1979 Iranian revolution where he introduces the concept of "political spirituality" to describe the principal "mode of resistance to the Shah" (McCall, 2013, p. 39):

> For the people who inhabit this land, what is the point of [contestation and demonstration], even at the cost of their own lives, for this thing whose possibility [can only be realized by] a political spirituality[?]
> (Foucault, 2005, p. 209)

It would appear that, for Foucault, this political spirituality encompasses an understanding on the part of the people that to change society, they must first change themselves by way of "renew[ing] their entire existence" and by undergoing a spiritual experience, or, more precisely, "a spiritual experience that they thought they could find within Shi'ite Islam" (Foucault, 2005a, p. 255). Far from constituting some kind of irrational resurgence of a peculiar and/or regressive type, which Foucault is at great pains to clarify, is a function and at the same time a by-product of Iran's history and, by implication, that of the Pahlavi governmentalizing regime: "[W]hen I say that they were looking to Islam for a change in their subjectivity" (Foucault, 2005a, p. 255), I mean it in the sense that "there was something other than the desire to obey the law more faithfully" (Foucault, 2005a, p. 255), and that something was, it bears repeating, "the desire to renew their entire existence" (Foucault, 2005a, p. 255), in the teeth of "a modernization that [was] an archaism" (Foucault, 2005c, p. 195)—a most compelling oxymoron for the "Shah's [greatest] crime" (Foucault, 2005c, p. 195).

This so-called archaic modernization was part "Kemalist program ... of modernization" (Foucault, 2005c, p. 196), part yearning for a return to the grandeur and glory that was ancient Persia—a fantasy the Iranian monarch would "cling to ... as if it were his sole *raison d'être*" (Foucault, 2005c, p. 197). This grand social and political project was to be realized by "a corrupt and despotic system" (Foucault, 2005c, p. 195), in the form of "a sovereign regime with disciplinary features," and enforced by the SAVAK, Mohammad Reza Shah's dreaded secret police (McCall, 2013, p. 37). In 1979, Foucault (2005c, p. 196) concludes, it was "[t]his archaic] modernization [that was] utterly rejected" by the great mass of a people caught up in an irresistible revolutionary wave.

This last point suggests that what "was at stake in Iran was a revolt of subjectivity, [one] that cannot be explained solely in economic terms" à la European models of revolutionary ideology (McCall, 2013, p. 29). Indeed, "the very fact of [its] singularity" (Osborne, 1999, p. 52) makes Foucault's work on the revolution a project that defies the "temporal map of a universal history;" thus, it is to be viewed "as something radically new [that emerged and developed] outside the tried conception of linear revolutionary politics" (Ghamari-Tabrizi, 2016, p. 7). Foucault validates this point in opining that the 1979 "revolt [needs to be considered] the most modern and the most insane" case of collective action (Foucault, 2005d, p. 222), in part because it "lack[ed] ... political organization [and was] disengage[d] from ... [the kind of] internal politics" often associated with oppositional movements in the West (Foucault, 2005d, p. 222); in part because the revolutionary cadres used modern technology, e.g., cassette tapes, to mobilize the masses (Foucault, 2005b); in part due to the fact that the 1979 uprising was "the first great insurrection against global systems," the Western-backed political-economic project that had reinstated and sustained the Pahlavi dynasty (Foucault, 2005d, p. 222). All this suggests that, ultimately, his analysis can be seen as a seminal work upon which to build a "theory of multiple modernities or multiple projects of modernity" (McCall, 2013, p. 28). Put differently, in the Iranian case, "[a] political spiritualty had been born that owed nothing to Western models of [collective action]" (Osborne, 1999, p. 52).

This explains why Foucault's perspective on the 1979 revolution as a case of counterconduct—in particular his concept of political spirituality and focus on multiple modernities—is so germane to understanding MENA oppositional movements. It is so precisely because it transcends "Western models of revolutionary ideology and sociopolitical progress," and by implication the exclusivist and linear understanding of social and political development and the modernist assumptions and West-centric orientations embedded in them (Osborne, 1999, p. 52). Indeed, Foucault's work debunks the all-too-familiar universalizing and/or exclusivist project of modernity and political development and social progress that collective oppositional action is supposed to inspire and enable. In this way, in his analysis of the 1979 revolution, with its emphasis on political spirituality, Foucault aims to illustrate that modernity constitutes a set of multiple practices and that it is also tied to, and must be understood in relation to, trajectories of people outside Europe.

Relatedly, and on another level, part of Foucault's fascination with the 1979 revolution lies with the mode of resistance to the Pahlavi monarchy, which is the "political spirituality" that generated a kind of "political spontaneity on the part of the populace" (McCall, 2013, p. 40). For Foucault, the latter manifested itself in the form of a "political will" (Foucault, 2005d, p. 222) on the part of Iranians to "open up a spiritual dimension in politics" (Foucault, 2005, p. 208). In 1979, it was this general will that "transverse[d] the entire people" (Foucault, 2005a, p. 256) in that it transcended their "self-interested political calculations" (McCall, 2013, p. 48), something essential if a more just social and political order was to be established—became the "manifestation of counter-conduct against the Shah's regime" (McCall, 2013, p. 44), "the response" to (McCall, 2013, p. 38), and above all a mode of resistance in opposition to the Shah's archaic modernization (Osborne, 1999).

It was this political will, moreover, that galvanized the people to resist and reject the monarchy and prove to be a most effective surrogate for "the organized political resistance that serve[s] as the impetus for [various] forms of [collective action in the West]" (McCall, 2013, p. 41). As such, the Foucauldian view of counterconduct provides "an alternative account of collective [action]" (McCall, 2013, p. 41), and by implication collective agency. What emerges is a contextually conditioned political phenomenon to be understood vis-à-vis historically and socially and politically grounded forms of governmental power within the purview of which the subject is born, raised and disciplined. It is the various disciplinary modes that work to inform the actor's consciousness, and hence sense of agency, thus making collective action possible. The latter, then, is contingent upon the "multiple [historical] process[es] that constitute [it]" (Foucault, 1991, p. 76).

Demonstrations and protestations constitute for Foucault, then, a historical and practical means by which one can change oneself, and by implication one's society, or, as Thomas Osborne (1999) asserts, a form of stylization of oneself—whether as an individual or as part of a collectivity—"in relation to that by which we are governed and those who govern us" (p. 54). This is precisely why Foucault is at such pains to make the point that "the very word demonstration must be taken literally [because it references] a people [who are] tireless[ly] demonstrating [their] will" (Foucault, 2005a, p. 254). It both symbolizes and evokes, again quite literally, the transition to "a new order arising from the old" (McCall, 2013, p. 49).

In this schema, the notion of an acting subject engaging in collective action raises the possibility of being a certain kind of person, one "formed within the limits of a historically specific set of formative practices and moral injunctions" (Mahmood, 2005, p. 28) and, above all, of certain discourses competing for domination and/or constitution of the world (Baker, 1994).

Foucault (1972) clarifies the latter point in his analysis of the French Revolution, demonstrating that in the lead-up to 1789, the three modes of political power he references "produced increasingly radical contradictions in French political life" (Baker, 1994, pp. 198–199), which, as Keith Baker opines, "exhibited themselves in an increasingly intense conflict among competing discourses of power" (1994, p. 199). In this way, Foucault (1972, p. 176) contends, "the French Revolution ... does not play the role of an event exterior to discourse[s]," but rather, it must be understood as "the effect of ... political hierarchization of competing discourses" in their constitution of the world (Baker, 1994, p. 190).

Here lies an example of how a discourse, or rather a dominant discourse, can "provid[e] points of resistance for counter-strategies to develop" (Howarth, 2000,

p. 49). This means that in the context of a contentious politics, discourses not only sustain power; they also provide an impetus for the development of resistance. Investigating the relation between competing discourses and the formation of subjects can shed light on the very conditions for the possibility of contestation, protestation, and mobilization.

It is apparent from the above discussion that in the Foucauldian conceptualization of counterconduct, one can clearly discern a theoretical framework for analyzing social movements, wherein their "condition[s] of possibility" (Foucault, 1978, p. 121) are contingent upon a series of historical processes, competing discourses, discursive practices and heterogeneous events arising from specific forms of governmental conduct. In such a formulation, mobilization, protestation and contestation "rely upon, and are even implicated within the strategies, techniques and power relationships they oppose" (Death, 2010, p. 240), in turn opening up a space to analyse social movements based on the diverse "mentalities, practices, [techniques] and subjectivities" that constitute them (Death, 2011, p. 426).

According to this reading, social movements are more than heterogeneous parcels of defiance that seek to shape human conduct against governmental power techniques. By way of contestation, protestation and/or demonstrations, the actors showcase their collective political will to change and/or contest the status quo. They do so by employing a "technology of politicization" (Baker, 1994, p. 191), the purpose of which is to "redeploy the space of appearance" and to "contest and negate the existing forms of political legitimacy" (Butler, 2011, para. 13).

When such episodes/movements of collective contestation and refusal emerge, "everything," as Foucault (2007, p. 390) asserts, "can be politicized, [and] everything may become political" in that unexpected alliances can be formed, unlikely citizenship claims made, multiple identities/subjectivities enabled and repertoires of collective action practiced, remade and reinvented. This is because revolts of counterconduct are no less than "work[s] of ethical self-transformation on the part of those who say 'no' to power" (Osborne, 1999, p. 52).

Germaine to this process of self-transformation is the role of public spaces in mediating how social and political conflicts originate and develop. Indeed, for the Foucauldian active subject, such spaces are crucial as loci for conducting "all forms of communal life" (Foucault, cited in Crampton & Elden, 2007, p. 45). A Foucauldian analysis of collective action facilitates understanding an important kind of politics, namely the "politics of everyday life" (Fraser, 1989, p. 18), whereby public spaces mediate exposure to modalities of power, in the process creating actors capable of resistance.

The use of public spaces as domains of counterpower is likely to merge with the politics of everyday life where open political channels simply do not exist; where political parties are non-existent and/or their function(s) is rudimentary; and/or where oppositional groups are denied political rights, chief among them the right to lobby and petition governments and the right to freedom of expression, particularly where challenging government policy is concerned. It is under these circumstances that such subjects may appropriate public spaces in order to voice their demands, thus creating loci of resistance and defiance. This is so because public spaces can serve as alternative venues for everyday political expression and debate, to parliaments, legislative assemblies, etc. that, by virtue of being monopolized by conservative elements, are severely handicapped in this regard. As Jeffrey Nealon asserts, as "power becomes increasingly ... more invested" (2008, p. 107) in our everyday lives, while "increasingly saturat[ing] ... public [space]," our modes of [everyday] resistance ... [become] increasingly intense" (2008, p. 108), as everyday life becomes a domain from which new relations, alliances and subjectivities emerge and are enabled.

Once this occurs, politics may be attenuated or suspended altogether within those domains that are its natural milieu—again, parliaments, legislative assemblies, etc.—only to emerge in all manner of unexpected public spaces—urban streets and alleyways, rooftops, buses and taxis, private homes pressed into service as temporary refuges for political activists on the run. At this juncture "an immense new field of possibility for resistance is opened [up]" (Nealon, 2008, pp. 107–108) as everyday life becomes the domain wherein new relations, alliances and subjectivities are enabled. At such times, the subject can intentionally turn everyday life into social and political loci of defiance. It is then that various forms of collective action or counterconduct, even its most drastic mode, i.e., revolution, arise spontaneously out of innumerable altercations played out in the context of everyday life (Alvarez, 1992). Collective action, in this schema, becomes nothing less than a "feature of situated [, and hence everyday,] political events and conduct" (Osborne 1999, p. 51).

Iran's Islamist governmentality: The Green Movement as a localized case of counterconduct

It is my contention that the widespread demonstrations and protestations that convulsed some Iranian cities in June 2009 and continued well into April of the following year manifest that moment of historical singularity and grand refusal Foucault associates with movements of counterconduct. In this way, Iran's Green Movement represents a manifestation of a people's political will, a case of localized collective defiance on the part of diverse societal strata for the purpose of resisting specific modalities of governmental conduct.

The Iranian constitution is closely patterned on that of France's Fifth Republic (1958–present), replete with the latter's "multilayered and institutionally diffused" mechanisms (Moslem 2002, p. 35). Its institutional arrangements and the distribution of power are predicated upon a clear division of powers among the executive, judicial and legislative branches—a feature that establishes the Iranian state system as "a modern phenomenon" (Mahdavi, 2008, p. 145), one strikingly similar to the kind of governmental structures typical of "contemporary modern Western states" (Mahdavi, 2008, p. 146).

Not surprisingly, the Islamic Republic has availed itself of all three Foucauldian modes of power—sovereign, biopower and disciplinary—to foreground its programme of conduct of conduct, which includes monitoring, supervising, controlling and disciplining individuals as well as whole populations, for the purpose of both governing them and for conditioning them to govern themselves and that of their counterparts. Moreover, in more than four decades of its existence, the state's technologies of power has employed disciplinary measures to, for example, control individuals in institutions as diverse as schools, universities, prisons and factories, themselves sites of power relations, norm productions and disseminations, and domains for competing discourses, as part of a programme aimed at creating a disciplinary society. It has also introduced biopolitical techniques, such as scientific and statistical methods, to manage the lives of Iranians in such diverse arenas as health care, sexuality and family matters.

It is the justice system that is charged with institutionalizing and systematizing Tehran's disciplinary and biopolitical techniques and ensuring that its conduct of conducts, such as the rationalities, arts, techniques and tactics of governance, work in tandem with sovereign power to render the populace governable by, among other things, segregating schools along gender lines, adopting school curricula that promote the dominant ideology, compelling women to wear the *hijab* (veil) in public at all times, and imposing a plethora of rules, codes and regulations pertaining to family matters and sexuality, among them laws relating to abortion, divorce, inheritance and polygamy.

All these macro-micro practices, techniques, tactics and rationalities of governance gave rise in the post-revolutionary period to a mode/form of what I call an Islamist governmentality, by which I mean exclusively a form of conduct of conduct wherein Islam is, and continues to be, instrumentalized and politicized, and by extension governmentalized, to advance a particular religio-governmentalized form of governance. The latter modality of governance, one that entails a combination of formal and informal rules and norms and macro and micro techniques and tactics, can best be described as a complex and multilayered set of religio-governmentalized practices and rationalities so as to make the individuals and the whole of the population conform to certain rules, codes, norms and regulations, and to discipline them to engage in forms of self-regulation and self-governance, of both his/herself and the broader population.

Specifically, as will be discussed in the next chapter, these complex modes of ruling and/or techniques of governance or conduct of conduct are rationalized by a set of seemingly religious imperatives: that the Islamic Republic constitutes a "divine entity ... [ordained] by God," with the Supreme Leader as his earthly representative as well as a manifestation of his divinity (Khomeini, cited in Abrahamian, 2008, p. 165); given that Western ways of life, and the culture that informs them, foster widespread corruption and deceit, they must undergo a process of state-sponsored Islamic "purification," a process in which both the "public and private sectors" are to cooperate (Amir-Ebrahimi, 2006, p. 3). These examples, broadly speaking, are complemented by a further conviction on the part of the conductors, namely that religion can prescribe all the rules and regulations necessary for managing the conduct of conduct of Iranians. By way of these rationales, then, the individuals and the whole of the population are expected to engage in self-governance and to disseminate the prescribed rules, codes, and norms.[4]

It is in light of this religio-governmentalized mode of governance—and, most importantly, the discursive arts and forms of knowledge that sustain them, the artificial rules and norms that breathe life into them, and their effects and contradictions—that one can come to understand the complex conditions responsible for the emergence of Iran's Green Movement. Put another way, the 2009 uprising manifested diverse and strategic points of resistance instigated by historically specific relations, practices, rationalities, and technologies of power. It represents that Foucauldian moment of great radical rupture and historical singularity, when a people fed up with the status quo—the disciplining and monitoring, the rationalities and techniques that legitimize them, the submissions and coercions that underwrite them, the threats and intimidations that sustain the operation of power—pour onto the streets to challenge power at the level of the objectives and procedures, practices and techniques, rationalities and mentalities that underscore the Islamist governmentality.

This refusal "to be governed like that" (1996, p. 384), to use Foucault's cogent phrase, renders the Green Movement as a historical and localized struggle against a specific modality of governance, waged mostly by students, women, youth, *bazaaris* and workers (Abrahamian, cited in Hashemi & Postel, 2010), who in 2009 "[took] up and occup[ied]" the position of acting/mobilizing subjects within the "socio-historical context available to [them]" (Taylor, 2011, p. 7). Thus, to understand the Green Movement, one must first examine the history and trajectories of these groups, which requires examining earlier cases of political contestation and social mobilization, as well as interrogating the localized, and hence varied, tactics, techniques and technologies of defiance and/or contestation of the status quo, along with historical processes of solidarity-building at work in post-revolutionary Iran.

Investigating that history can also shed light on the ways in which Iranians, through collective action, brought the "space of politics into being" (Butler, 2011, para. 15), or how they used for political purposes the public spaces of urban centres— in the Middle East and North Africa the traditional locus of opposition to state rule—to metamorphose from subjects to "modalities of power" in their own right, determined to be counted and heard as demand-making and rights-bearing citizens (Butler, 2011, para. 12). This "politics of empowerment," to borrow Patricia Collins's (2000) phrase, involves, and is to be understood in terms of, certain mentalities, techniques, arts and practices—factors that constitute, as Foucault would put it, a form of stylization of oneself (Osborne, 1999) in relation to that by which one is governed—that Iranian demonstrators developed and directed at disrupting, reversing and re-balancing asymmetrical power relations between the state and its opponents.

Analysing the Green Movement through the lens of a movement of counterconduct lends this book the theoretical rigour and solid foundation required to conceptualize it as a movement of movements, as a phenomenon as heterogeneous as it is dynamic. Both frameworks—albeit the former at the level of theory, the latter at the level of concept formation—showcase the multiplicity of sites of resistance and contestation with a view to illuminating the radical historicity and contingency, and by implication specificity, of social movements, in the process aiding us in understanding them on their own terms: with respect to the context in which they develop and conduct operations.

Triangular research methodology

Understanding the Green Movement as a case of multiple resistances or a resistance of resistances and addressing the research questions posed here requires examining its history, composition and development, its sudden emergence and eventual retreat underground, and its influence on sociopolitical trends of the post-2009 era. Given that the Green Movement was comprised in the main of youth, student and women's groups, this project focuses primarily on documenting and analysing their cadres' experiences during the years leading up to 2009, with particular emphasis on President Mahmoud Ahmadinejad's first term (2005–2009). This time frame covers the critical period when conditions were ripe for the emergence of the Green Movement.

A combination of historical and analytical approach is used here to trace the trajectories of these three groups and to place the Green Movement in the context of earlier cases of contention politics, most notably the 1999 Student Movement and the 2006 Women's One Million Signature Campaign. Elucidating these cases, something that requires contextual analysis, will enable an understanding of the genesis and character of the Green Movement as a movement of movements years in the making.

The research will be operationalized by applying a triangular methodology, anchored at one corner by discourse analysis, a method that elucidates "the mutual constitution of conceptions and practices" (Tripp 2012, p. 90). Discourse analysis offers a way to identify "a group of ideas or patterned way of thinking which can be [located] in textual or verbal communications, and ... also ... in wider social structures," and which entails analyzing both "serious [policy texts and] speech acts" (Dreyfus and Rainbow 1982, p. 48) as well as the kinds of sociopolitical practices that the latter enable with a view to "[shaping] human lives" (Baker 1994, p. 192). Discourse analysis will be applied to Iran's constitution, in addition to relevant government policy documents and publications and official speeches and rhetoric covering the post-revolutionary era, with one purpose in mind: to elucidate how state policies and practices worked to discipline, subordinate and marginalize the three aforementioned groups. This will allow for a multidimensional and fluid approach to delineating the rationales, techniques and mentalities underlying diverse forms of governmental conduct as well as provide insight into the strategies and tactics aimed at resisting that conduct.

Archival resources comprising primary and secondary sources will also be examined. The former includes the diaries and speeches of prominent activists; YouTube clips of cell-phone footage shot during the demonstrations; manuscripts and letters published by Green Movement leaders and activists prior to, during and following the 2009 uprising; and news stories and journal and magazine articles documenting their personal experiences in the lead-up to the 2009 elections and immediate aftermath (L'Eplattenier, 2009; Thomassen, 2001). These texts will be subjected to historical and interpretive analysis to identify the conditions that triggered the Green Movement; delineate how a united front was formed; and examine the ways in which collective action was organized.

The secondary sources include both published and unpublished material—textbooks, editorial commentary, book reviews, biographies, video documentaries—describing, summarizing and analysing the history of social mobilization and contestation in post-revolutionary Iran, as it pertains to the student, youth and women's groups. These sources provide the requisite background information for examining multiple characters of the Green Movement in relation to earlier contention episodes, such as the 1999 Student Movement and the 2006 Women's One Million Signature Campaign; investigating how these events shaped its agenda and strategies; and elucidating the genesis of its democratic ideals and demands for political accountability, gender equality and human rights. Thus, the aim of the archival work to be undertaken here lies in analyzing the broad historical context within which the Green Movement took shape, articulated its demands and conducted its operations.[5]

Lastly, over a two-year period, extending from February 2015 to March 2017, semi-structured personal interviews were conducted with various authorities on Foucault's work, chief among them William Walters and Corey McCall; leading social movement activists, including political prisoners, such as Rouzbeh Safshekan; participants in the 2009 demonstrations, among them Zeynab Peyghambarzadeh as well as leaders like Ali Abdi, who were among those arrested and brought to trial; activists in the 2005 Women's One Million Signature Campaign, such as Sabra Rezaei; and leaders of the 1999 Student Movement, most notably Ali Afshari. Former student activist and political prisoner, and currently a doctoral candidate at the University of Alberta, Rouzbeh Safshekan possess a wealth of knowledge regarding the post-revolutionary Iranian scene and student politics in particular. Zeynab Peyghambarzadeh, Sabra Rezaei and Ali Abdi, who played prominent roles in both the One Million Signature Campaign and the Green Movement, number among the best known and widely respected of the former activists and political prisoners of the post-revolutionary period. In 1999 Ali Afshari was a prominent leader of the *daftar-e tahkim-e vahdat*, or Office for Consolidating Unity (OCU), the largest and among the most important subversive student organizations in post-revolutionary Iran. It was he who led several street demonstrations, often appearing at the head of crowds estimated at between fifty and sixty thousand strong.

Recruiting interviewees proved challenging to say the least. The majority of the 1999 Student Movement leaders had been summarily exiled and/or marginalized politically. Most were unwilling to participate for political reasons. Thus, for a personal account of this seminal movement, I had to rely solely on Ali Afshari and the diaries kept by activists. I endeavoured to address this shortcoming by interviewing Afshari for more than seven hours over the course of a two-year period (February 2015–January 2017).

The great majority of the One Million Signature Campaign leaders and activists still residing in Iran or living in exile also refused to be interviewed, and for much the same reasons. That said, while those interviewed were few in number, their reflections on the great events in which they participated contributed to this project in invaluable ways, in particular, by shedding light on the disparate modes and forms of resistance employed every day.

The respondents were selected on the basis of their ability to shed light on the Green Movement's relationship to earlier episodes of contention politics; identify and analyse the obstacles it encountered and the opportunities it created; interrogate its impact on sociopolitical trends of the post-Ahmadinejad era; and assess its contribution to bringing about a paradigm shift in the social and political landscape. The interviews were semi-structured and open-ended so as to allow respondents to answer in detail, qualify and clarify their responses, and discuss alternative viewpoints.

By far the greatest constraint facing this project would prove to be my status in Iran as a *persona non grata,* which precluded my conducting fieldwork in the country. This problem has been addressed in part by using to best effect the triangular methods described above, which is contingent upon selecting both the most relevant archival sources and interviewing the most knowledgeable and best informed respondents.

Conclusion

This chapter has delineated a Foucauldian model of social movements, which I suggest is superior to leading social movement theories in respect to analysing social movements in general and the Green Movement in particular, and in three respects. First, in transcending many of the difficulties posed by the universalistic and grand-casual narratives, it provides a contextual approach, focusing on the social and political relations that underlie oppositional movements; second, in emphasizing the particular localities in which social movements arise, evolve and operate, it facilitates an examination of oppositional movements based on the reciprocal relationship between state and society; lastly, by elucidating the trajectories and experiences of such movements, along with the motives that impel their actors to undertake collective forms of action, it offers a more historicized account of oppositional movements, thus revealing in detail relations to the specific states whose power they seek to contest. Herein lies a theoretical approach predicated upon the recognition that episodes of mobilization and collective action are never wholly reproducible; rather, they are contingent upon the settings and contexts within which they emerge; in other words, each is embedded in a unique historical and social web of relations whose specificities must be delineated if the dynamics at play. Thus a Foucauldian model, with its emphasis on historical contingency and sensitivity to particular localities, holds out the promise of providing a theoretical underpinning sufficiently rigorous to analyse social movements in a way that reveals their contextual character and dynamics.

Notes

1 Notable exceptions include Sveinung Sandberg (2006) "Fighting neo-liberalism with neo-liberal discourse;" Colin Death (2010) "Counter-conducts: A Foucauldian analytics of protest" and "Counter-conducts in South Africa: Power, government and dissent at the world summit" (2011); Catherine Wilson (2009) "Beyond state politics: Subjectivities and techniques of government in contemporary neoliberal social movements." Note, however, that these works focus mainly on oppositional movements within Western polities, in particular the so-called 'anti-globalization movements.'
2 For a detailed examination of why a Foucauldian model of social movements has been underutilized in the field of Social Movement Studies, see Colin Death (2010) "Counter-conducts: A Foucauldian analytics."
3 A case of counterconduct need not be a movement such as a social movement and/ or revolution per se; as will be seen in the subsequent pages, it may and can involve

other, for example milder, manifestations of discontent, such as civil disobedience and work sabotage, among other things.
4 As will be seen in chapter 3, the above rationales and practices are not necessarily shared with all political/religious elites and/or political factions at the helm of Iran's Islamic mode of governmentality. Nonetheless, by virtue of their stranglehold on key governmental domains—the judiciary, media, security apparatus—the hardliners have parlayed this representation of the conduct of conduct into a dominant leitmotif informing official discourses.
5 Note that most of the archival materials— textbooks, editorial commentary, book reviews, biographies, film and video documentaries—can be accessed through the University of Alberta. Some, particularly those pertaining to the student and women's movements, can be accessed through, most notably, Vista News Hub. Others, such as historical films and documents and cell-phone footage, are available on YouTube; and manuscripts and letters published by Green Movement leaders prior to, during and following the 2009 uprisings are accessible online. For example, since June 2009, Mousavi has issued a total of eighteen news releases that are available at the khordaad88 website.

3 The coming of a disciplinary society to post-revolutionary Iran

Ordinary Iranians and everyday resistance

Introduction

As suggested by Foucault's famous dictum "where there is power, there is resistance" (1978, p. 95), power and resistance exist in a state of interaction, sometimes violent, and flux. If this is the case, then, as Lila Abu-Lughod (1990, p. 42) asserts, "where there is resistance, there is power," given that that the former is "an essential fact of everyone's everyday struggle[] with power" (Nealon, 2008, p. 111). Thus, far from emerging "in opposition to an institution or a group," resistance arises "in opposition to the effects of … particular technolog[ies] of power," almost all of which "operat[e] [on] our immediate everyday life" practices (Canavez & Miranda, 2011, p. 156). As Foucault argues in the "Lives of Infamous Men":

> There was never a thought that there might be, in the everyday run of things, something like a secret to raise, that the inessential might be, in a certain way, important, until the blank gaze of power came to rest on these minuscule commotions.
>
> (2003a, p. 289)

Thus, for Foucault, everyday life embodies not only a site wherein the "body," that chief "object and target of power" (1995, p. 136), is mobile in its most visible and ubiquitous form, it also acts as "a figure for the proliferation, saturation, and intensification of power (which is to say, resistance) relations" (Nealon, 2008, pp. 107–108).

Using a Foucauldian approach, this chapter analyzes the phenomenon of everyday resistance on the part of ordinary people in the context of semi-authoritarian settings, in this case post-revolutionary Iran. My purpose here lies in demonstrating how, in relation to various arts, rationales and technologies of power employed by the Islamic Republic, everyday resistance worked to challenge the status quo, underwritten by an Islamist governmentality. I begin by showcasing how, during the post-revolutionary period, public spaces and various modes of ruling, enabled by governing arts and rationalities and techniques and tactics of governance, have over time become domains of resistance to the

Islamic Republic's conduct of conduct, challenging, disrupting and often compelling the authorities to reformulate, or at least relax, their semi-authoritarian rule.

An enquiry of this kind is warranted in that it serves to demonstrate that, far from constituting mundane practices, everyday forms of resistance represent, both in themselves and in the debates they spawn, political acts carried out at the very point at which power is applied. As such, they work to communicate to the authorities profound disaffection with the status quo. It is inevitable that, in the absence of anything resembling open political debate, these resistances should become politicized. "What is politics ... in the end," Foucault ponders, "if not both the interplay of [the] different arts [and technologies] of government with their different reference points and the debate to which these different arts of government give rise? It seems to me it is here that politics is born" and thus where resistance is concurrently politicized (2008, p. 313).

For Foucault (1984), "[n]o immensity is greater than a detail" (p. 184). It follows, then, that to understand power and resistance, we must investigate "the tiny residues, the minute particles of the power relations circulating at the heart of everyday life" (Canavez & Miranda, 2011, p. 155). Only then will we be in a position to grasp how social mobilization and political contestation—in Foucauldian terms, those episodes of counterconduct, when bodies pour onto the streets to challenge the technologies of power—might erupt and gain momentum in a particular locality. After all, as Julia Alvarez reminds us, revolution—for Foucault "the most drastic form of [counterconduct]" (McCall, 2004, p. 13)—or any form of collective action/resistance, requires nothing more than interrogating the "constant skirmishes on an everyday [and] mundane level" (Alvarez, 1992, p. 111).

"If we want to do an analysis of power," asserts Foucault, "we must speak of powers and try to localize them in their historical and geographical specificity" (2012, para. 12). Thus, far from taking the state, society and acting subjects as given categories, this chapter will subject them to a contingent, historicized enquiry, with a view to shedding light on those dynamics and processes that create the conditions of possibility for their emergence, thereby delineating how the Islamic Republic "has become what it is through its adaptation and appropriation" of various technologies of power (Walters, 2012, p. 39). The latter constitute, for Foucault, asserts William Walters (2012), "a politics of combination," meaning that they embody "quite different arts of government" that in unison can make the state a formidable entity (p. 41).

I begin by explicating what a Foucauldian analysis of power and resistance entails in light of his notion of governmentality and the arts, techniques and tactics of governance. I then interrogate the various processes of what I call Islamist governmentality at work in post-revolutionary Iran, along with the rationales that underwrite them and make possible their existence, in the process demonstrating how, over time, such processes have enabled the various biopolitical and disciplinary norms, rules, and codes that inform the conduct of the individual and ultimately the citizenry. This historical investigation of the processes of governmentality involves interrogating "[macro-]micro practices of government," in addition to the major as well as "the humble and mundane mechanisms by which the authorities seek to instantiate government" (Rose & Miller, 1992, p. 183), something that will serve to demonstrate that governance, or to use the Foucauldian term conduct, "is an extremely pervasive and heterogeneous activity" (Dean & Hindess, 1998, p. 2).

Next, I focus on how the Islamic Republic's everyday regulatory norms, rules and codes that have paradoxically, and over time, become both enabling (in opening up a space/rationality for action) and productive (in producing the very individuals it seeks to control), particularly in reference to empowering and politicizing women, students and youth who presently constitute the bulk of the Iranian population as well as the most volatile groups demanding social and political change.

Governmentality: A Foucauldian account of power and resistance

A vantage point for analyzing contention politics is discernible in Foucault's writings on governmentality and power, or more precisely governmental power, understood as "the way[s] in which the conduct of individuals or groups might be directed" (1982, p. 790). In essence, this phenomenon represents a complex of modes, arts and techniques predicated upon specific knowledges, mentalities and methods. For Foucault (1982), the exercise of power, whether disciplinary, biopolitical or sovereign, involves bringing these elements to bear in the right combination.

These modalities of power in no way guarantee, however, domination on the part of the state, for, according to Foucault (1978), they also create, as a corollary, the potential for resistance. But what, one might ask, does the term resistance mean, and what does it entail in the context of the Middle East and North Africa? Drawing on Foucault, I take it to be a contextually conditioned phenomenon closely intermeshed with geographically specific governmental power relations to which the subject is exposed, socialized and disciplined. This means that resistance counteracts the effects of particular technologies of power working to subordinate, marginalize, discipline and control the individual in his/her everyday life, and to condition him/her to engage in self-governance and in governing others. But far from constituting any and/or all acts or random acts of defiance, resistance entails specific ways of saying "no," or at least challenging and/or undermining, multiple processes of governmentality, such as those macro- and micro-actions and techniques and rationalities that are peculiar to technologies of power. As a result, resistance, especially the everyday variety, entails the everyday art of "not being governed like that," comprised of a varied and persistent opposition to diverse technologies of power (Foucault, 1996, p. 384).

In this sense, resistance does not counterpoise the exercise of power at every moment and at every point in every domain of social life. Rather, it comes into its own only when subjugated bodies are willing and prepared to confront the exercise of power, for which disciplinary and governing techniques, norms and regulations constitute a vehicle, that is, when it aims specifically to contest governance (Foucault, 1982). Thus, while resistance manifests and showcases the seemingly paradoxical effect of specific technologies, norms, codes and spaces of power, make no mistake, it is ultimately an intentional act directed at "making fresh [and persistent] demands" on the authorities (Bayat, 2013, p. 44), and precisely because it unfolds at that moment when we, as Foucault would say, begin to stylize ourselves in relation to certain modalities of power (Osborne, 1999; Pourmokhtari, 2017), or when we recreate ourselves in a fashion that is no less than "a work of art" and for the express purpose of resisting and/or contesting specific modalities of power (Foucault, cited in McLaren, 2002, p. 70). In this way, forms and acts of resistance are contextually bound to certain forms of political conduct given that they "implicate[] the strategies, techniques and power relationships they oppose" (Death, 2010, p. 240). After all, as Foucault (2007) puts it, the story of counterpower is "inseparable [from] the history of ... governmental [conduct]" (p. 357).

An Islamist governmentality: The Islamic republic and the governmentalization of religion

Soon after its birth, the Islamic Republic of Iran set in motion a project of Islamist governmentality, enabled by Republican and Islamic principles (or more precisely a particular reading of the latter) living in uneasy combination; while the former inform the mechanisms of governance, they are often times subordinated to the latter. But, how, one might ask, did so strange an alliance come into being following the collapse of the Pahlavi monarchy in February 1979?

Addressing this question requires delving into the activities of Ayatollah Rouhollah Khomeini, the future Supreme Leader of Iran, in the 1970s, during which time he was living in Najaf, Iraq, having been exiled there on the order of the monarchy. It was there that Khomeini (1979) authored *Islamic Government: Governance of the Jurist*, outlining "the major doctrines of [what he envisioned to be an] Islamic government" (Dabashi, 2011, p. 274). Though simple and straightforward, the book's thesis would have momentous consequences for Iran. Drawing on a "series of Qur'anic passages and prophetic traditions" (Dabashi, 2011, p. 274), Khomeini proposed that in the absence of the Twelfth Imam of Shia's, who is believed to be in occultation, the task of governing Muslim nations fell to a *valiy-e faqih*, a Supreme Islamic Jurist, who would, as a religio-political leader, regulate the "daily affairs of Muslims [so as] to assure their other worldly [salvation]" (Dabashi, 2011, p. 274). The *vilayat-e faqih*, or Rule/Guardianship of the Jurist, would be assigned to a Supreme Jurist who would undertake this grand task of conduct of conduct.

With the revolution drawing to a victorious conclusion in the winter of 1979, one of the first tasks confronting its leadership, among whom the Ayatollah Khomeini was the most prominent and iconic figure, lay in drafting a new constitution. Whether or not Khomeini "appear[ed] at first to ... attach[] much significance to drawing up a constitution" (Amir Arjomand, 1992, para. 4), there can be no question that, as Ervand Abrahamian (2008) points out, seizing this opportunity would have presented the Ayatollah and his supporters with a golden opportunity to governmentalize, and in so doing, "institutionalize their concept of *vilayat-e faqih*" (p. 162).

One obstacle, however, stood in the way: the revolution. The latter had, after all, "been carried out not only under the banner of Islam, but also in response to demands for liberty, equality and social justice" (Abrahamian, 2008, p. 167). Indeed, Mohammad Reza Shah had been toppled by a multilayered movement made up of nationalists, liberals and leftists of all stripes that included sub-variants such as Islamist and Muslim liberals and nationalists, nearly all of whom were males, in addition to women, students and *bazaaris*, who now expected a payback.

While the new constitution was being drafted, Khomeini came under intense pressure from rival factions that had mobilized the masses against the Shah, and particularly the nationalists, one of whose leaders, the liberal Muslim Mehdi Bazargan, was now Prime Minister of the transitional government appointed by Khomeini himself. It was widely known that Bazargan wanted a constitution patterned on that of Charles de Gaulle's Fifth Republic, one that was "Islamic in name but democratic in content" (Abrahamian, 2008, p. 162).

At this juncture, it is important to note, Khomeini in no way represented the sole Muslim or even Islamic voice within the dominant order. Indeed, his notion of Islamist governance was hotly contested by certain high-ranking Shiite clerics, chief among them the Grand Ayatollahs Seyyed Kazem Shariatmadari and Abol Qasem Khoi, based in Iran and Iraq respectively, who emerged as fierce critics of the Khomeinian concept of the Rule/Guardianship of the Jurist (Cooper, 2016; Pahlavi, 2004). It was this multilayered opposition, among other factors, that compelled Khomeini to recognize that conceding "a 'partial' role to the people ... was at least politically necessary'" in crafting a new constitution (Moslem, 2002, p. 20). Thus, the end product was an Islamist mode of governmentality that was, in the words of Ervand Abrahamian (2008, pp. 163–164), torn "between divine right and the rights of men; between theocracy and democracy; between *vox dei* and *vox populi*; and between clerical authority and popular sovereignty."

One end of the continuum representing Tehran's mode of Islamist governmentality is anchored by Islamic principles as expounded by the Supreme Jurist. The latter, according to the constitution, is charged with determining "the interest[s] of [the] state" as well as "the interest[s] of Islam," in addition to "set[ting] general guidelines for the Islamic Republic" and mediating between the executive, legislative and judicial branches (Abrahamian, 2008, p. 164). He is, moreover, the commander-in-chief of the armed forces, with the authority to declare war and make peace and appoint military commanders. He is also charged with appointing the heads of all governmental bodies, including, to take but two examples, that of the Islamic Republic of Iran Broadcasting (IRIB) system and of the so-called Revolutionary Foundations or *nihadha-ye inghelabi*, charged with ensuring political and religious conformity and "realiz[ing] the egalitarian and redistributive rhetoric of the revolution" (Moslem, 2002, p. 22). The Supreme Leader's authority does not end here, however; he can also dictate what is referred to as practicable law. Thus, for example, he can "enact any laws ... or suspend any existing laws, or make any changes in the judicial, legislative or executive laws" deemed necessary to ensure the survival of the Islamic Republic (Rafizadeh, 2011, p. 29).

Furthermore, the *valiy-e faqih* "[has] many institutional 'extended arms'," ranging from the "powerful Revolutionary Foundations" to their supervisory bodies, often referred to as parallel institutions (Mahdavi, 2008, p. 146). The latter are informed by Ayatollah Khomeini's reading of Islamic principles and accountable solely to the *valiy-e faqih*. The most powerful of these is, arguably, the Guardian Council, a body consisting of six clerics and six lawyers, all either directly or indirectly appointed/approved by the Supreme Leader and entrusted with "review[ing] all laws passed by the *Majlis* ... check[ing the] Islamic credentials [of the members,] ... [exercising the right of veto [over] interpreting the Constitution, and supervising the elections of ... the president[] and the *Majlis*" (Moslem, 2002, p. 30). These supervisory bodies, as exemplified by the Guardian Council, ultimately, have an "overriding authority that supersedes all other decisions made within the political system, and over and above the three branches of the government" (Moslem, 2002, p. 33).

The republican end of the constitutional continuum is anchored by the executive, legislative and judicial branches of government, signifying the Iranian state system as "a modern phenomenon" (Mahdavi, 2008, p, 145), strikingly similar to its counterparts among "contemporary modern Western states" (Mahdavi, 2008, p. 146). That said, republican principles of governance are invariably trumped by divine rule. The Iranian parliament, the *Majlis*, for example, has the authority to pass laws, investigate complaints brought against the executive and judiciary, question the president and cabinet ministers, and appoint six members to the twelve- member Guardian Council, with the remaining six selected by the Supreme Leader (Moslem, 2002). This arrangement allows the latter to wield great influence within a Guardian Council charged with, among other things, selecting candidates to run for parliamentary office. This is but one example of how republican principles of governance are effectively subverted.

The judiciary, whose chief justice and lower court judges are appointed by the Supreme Leader, has jurisdiction over the criminal and civil courts, in addition to the Islamic revolutionary courts, the mandate of which is to try suspects "on ... charges of [committing] un-Islamic [acts]" and common crimes such as the breaching of "national security laws," both of which are lacking in precision and open to broad interpretation (Ghaemi, 2010, para. 1). The fact that in neither case the law is precise leaves it open to broad interpretation, invariably in the interests of the state. It is important to note here that the revolution in no way spelled the end of the Pahlavi judiciary; rather, it merely substituted seminary-educated jurists for secular ones and "codified more features of the *Shari'a*" (Abrahamian, 2008, p. 177).

Lastly, the general electorate selects through secret and direct balloting the president, members of Parliament, and provincial and local councils, among other political bodies. Elected every four years and limited to two terms, the president is, according to the constitution, "the highest official authority after the supreme leader," responsible for residing "over the cabinet and appointing[] its ministers as well as all ambassadors, governors, mayors, and directors of the national bank, the National Iranian Oil Company [, and] the police" (Abrahamian, 2008. p. 166).

Although ostensibly modern, these political institutions are constitutionally informed by divinely ordained values—the very values embodied in the Rule/Guardianship of the Jurist responsible for overseeing the conduct of conduct. Thus, "[a]ll laws and regulations must conform to the principles of Islam," which are, in part, vested in *Shari'a* Law (Abrahamian, 2008, p. 167). As it is the Guardian Council that determines such principles, the *Majlis* is devoid of sovereignty unless supervised by this body.

Thus, while ostensibly it is the uneasy admixture of secular-republican and religio-clerical principles that provides the Islamic Republic with a veneer of legitimacy, its *de facto* legality rests mainly on the latter, for it is these principles that inform the concept of the Rule/Guardianship of the Jurist, and hence its mode of Islamist governmentality. How that legitimacy came to exist, however, is a matter of contention between the country's two main political factions: reformists and conservatives. As will be discussed in Chapter 4, the majority of reformers hold the legitimacy of the Supreme Leader to be predicated, in one way or another and to varying degrees, on public consent. To the contrary, the conservative establishment sees in the divine will of God a rationale for legitimizing the elevation of one figure among the senior clergy to the position of His representative on earth, in effect "signifying [its] commitment to traditional Islamic principles and ... unwillingness to change" (Safshekan & Sabet, 2010, p. 546). As such, the conservatives have often pledged "their ... loyalty and obedience [to the] Guardianship of the ... Jurist [, which translates into absolute] obedience to the *faqih*" (Safshekan & Sabet, 2010, p. 546). Moreover, by virtue of their stranglehold over the media, judiciary and security apparatuses, they have succeeded in authenticating an exclusive Islamist governmentality.

But, and here is the crucial question, just how truly Islamic are the religio-clerical principles informing the concept of the Rule/Guardianship of the Jurist, and, by implication, Islamist governmentality? Addressing this question requires examining what became the official view of *Shari'a* law, which constitutes "the basis for the country's legal system" (Moslem, 2002, p. 30). As *Shari'a* is not codified, it is open to broad interpretation and is flexible in its application. In the case of the Islamic Republic, however, both interpretation and application were to become contingent upon political exigency. In 1989 the Ayatollah Khomeini went even further, indeed much further, in decreeing that the *mamlekat-e valiy-e faqih* (the land ruled by the Supreme Jurist) could, if necessary, "stop the implementation of the *Shari'a* and dismiss the founding pillars of Islam in order to protect the general interests of the state" and in particular to ensure its survival (Mahdavi, 2008, p. 145).

Moreover, all the secondary rulings of *Shari'a*, such as those pertaining to prayer, fasting, and the *haj*, or pilgrimage to Mecca, could be suspended for the purpose, again, of preserving Islam and/or the governance of the Islamic Jurist (Abrahamian, 2008; Moslem, 2002). In so doing, Ayatollah Khomeini politicized *Shari'a,* thus providing a religio-legal basis for the abuse of power on the part of various authorities, including the judiciary and supervisory bodies such as the Guardian Council, intent on gaining political office or membership to key government committees, defeating rivals, and/or purging opponents. Political imperatives have thus come to trump religious values and principles in the context of this conduct of conduct.

And, indeed, political considerations have often prevailed over constitutional legalities intended to entrench religious authority within the sphere of governance. For example, with no apparent successor in line, Khomeini, shortly before his death in 1988, appointed a Constitutional Reform Council to amend the constitution and appoint the next Supreme Leader. According to the first version of the constitution, the latter had to be a *marja'e taqlid*, a source of emulation, of the highest religio-clerical ranking. The new version dispensed with this stipulation altogether; henceforth, while still required to be a *mujtahid* (religious scholar), the Supreme Jurist was excused from being a *marj'ae*, so long as he possessed, among other attributes, "'honesty,' 'piety' and 'administrative abilities' and was well "versed in the political issues of the age" (Abrahamian, 2008, p. 182). Thus, in post-revolutionary Iran, it was not the religious clergy per se that exercised real power, one can argue, but rather "a politicized section of it" (Chehabi, 2001, p. 52).

From the preceding discussion, two conclusions may be drawn regarding Tehran's Islamist governmentality. First, the Iranian polity constitutes a complex of bodies, cooperating or competing with one another as the situation demands—all having legal or semi-legal, and often conflicting, mandates, and all seemingly directed at preserving the status quo, something that requires rationalizing and normalizing the conduct of conduct. Second, as we have seen, even the notion of an Islamic Jurist, "the [principal] symbol of the religiosity" of the Islamic Republic (Moslem, 2002, p. 100), had effectively become politicized. Thus, it is safe to assume that in the Iranian case, religion, or to be more precise Islam, had at one and the same time been governmentalized, instrumentalized and, as will be shown, disciplinized and biopoliticized, so that *asl-e nezam*, or the foundation of the Islamic Republic, of which the *vilayat-e faqih* remains the cornerstone, could be preserved at all costs, and to the exclusion of alternatives.

The emergence of a disciplinary and biopolitical society in post-revolutionary Iran

The governmentalization of Iranian society during the post-revolutionary period involved implementing a complex of diverse practices, techniques and rationales aimed at creating a governable, hence Islamic, society. Islam was to be instrumentalized with a view to producing a disciplinary and biopolitical society, wherein the individual could be governed, naturally and rationally, on the basis of rules, codes, norms and regulations aimed at authenticating and perpetuating Islamist governmentality. As will be shown, this process of instrumentalization, hereafter referred to as state-sponsored Islamization, was systematically and rigorously implemented by conservatives and their backers in the administration, civil service and security forces.

A primary objective here was to "mould a post-revolution generation of … Iranians … into the backbone of … a [future] Islamic [polity]" (Yaghmaian, 2002, p. 48). In effect, Iranian society had to be detoxified to eliminate every sign of Westoxification (Sreberny & Torfeh, 2013). All this was underpinned by the unshakeable conviction that the West was, and is, on a diabolical mission "to incite a coloured revolution on Iranian soil" (Pourmokhtari, 2014, p. 153). Countering the latter would require exporting the revolution beyond Iran's borders, by conducting a campaign aimed at disseminating the state-sponsored Shi'a ideology throughout the Mid-East region and ultimately throughout the globe (Ansari, 2006).

In addition, according to the senior clerics who dominated the revolution, Islam had the authority and capability to prescribe all the rules and regulations necessary for managing the everyday conduct of Iranians (Moslem, 2002; Abrahamian, 1993, 2008). This largely religio-political view provided a rationale for imposing disciplinary and biopolitical measures on the whole of Iranian society. This new order found its ultimate justification, in particular among the conservative right, in the conviction that the Islamic Republic was a "divine entity given by God," and for this reason its "laws," regulations and, one might say, codes of conduct, had the full force of "his commands" (Khomeini, cited in Abrahamian, 2008, p. 165). Thus, "'non-Islamic' social behaviour" were soon to be purified "through a process of social engineering" (Yaghmaian, 2002, p. 48), entailing "the ... transformation of society [through] the creation of hegemonic Islamic social ... norms" that would create the conditions necessary for introducing specific arts and techniques of governance (Fadaee, 2012, p. 138).

The Islamic republic and the governmentalization of public spaces

Immediately following the revolution, the Islamic Republic, under a clerical oligarchy, took in hand the work of Islamizing various social domains, especially public spaces. The chief instrument for achieving this end was the Islamic code of public appearance, which, among other things, required women to wear the *hijab*, or veil, in all public places or risk fines or even imprisonment. It was just this accoutrement that Janet Afary (2009) would cite as the principal symbol of the ideological and political hegemony of the Islamic Republic. In the case of men, Western-style dress, and in particular ties and short-sleeved shirts, along with long hair, were proscribed; later, such restrictions were relaxed, as will be shown, after flaunting them became a general practice and hence source of embarrassment for the authorities. And though not compelled to do so, men were encouraged through the media as well as official rhetorical pronouncements to grow beards and wear plain cloth shirts, buttoned up to the neck and descending well past the waistline (Talabegi Blog, 2014).

The dress code's political objective lay in managing bodies, chiefly by implementing a disciplinary mode of control, something that required distinguishing between *khodis* (us) and *gheir-e khodis* (them) (Fadaee, 2012). The former were expected to adhere strictly to the Islamic code of conduct, hence the official designation *arzeshi* or *inghelabi*, the moral/revolutionary ones, a status to which only the most dedicated of revolutionaries might aspire. And while much was expected of this elite group, much was given in the form of prestigious jobs, pensions, educational opportunities, healthcare benefits, and social welfare, among other things (Aftab News, 2017; Golkar, 2015; Radio Farda, 2017). In contrast, the *gheir-e khodis* were deemed to lack revolutionary zeal, hence the designation *gheir-e arzeshi*, the immoral ones. It was their unhappy lot to incur the wrath of a vengeful state determined at all costs to conduct the conduct of all citizens, Muslim or otherwise. Thus, some among the *gheir-e khodis* were denied educational, employment and/or political opportunities (Fars News, 2017; Tavaana, 2016), others something called *dieh*, or compensation for bodily injury or death (Asoo, 2017); still others had their passports confiscated, effectively precluding them from leaving the country (Tavaana, 2016), or had their property expropriated (Bahai News, 2006; Iran Press Watch, 2010); many were intimidated or imprisoned, and in extreme cases some were tortured or even executed (Rejali, 1994; The Atlantic, 2012; Human Rights & Democracy for Iran, 2017; Radio Zamaneh, 2017).

Beyond the latter classification, in post-revolutionary Iran, moreover, the "segregation of the populace [was to be become] a permanent rule of social life," primarily manifest in diverse domains of public life (Amir-Ebrahimi, 2006, p. 3). It soon became commonplace, for example, to witness female passengers occupying the rear of buses, male passengers the front. Moreover, disciplinary measures aimed at segregating the sexes were soon impinged upon all religio-cultural and state-sponsored events, including weddings, Friday prayers and other religious ceremonies, political rallies, and anniversaries of the revolution, the purpose being to limit opportunities for subversive, in this case anti-establishment, acts and behaviours.

The holy rituals of *muharram*, arguably the most significant of Shi'a holidays, provides but one example of how the Islamic Republic uses public spaces to reproduce its official narrative/discourse. *Muharram* commemorates the heroic death of the third Shi'a Imam, Hussein, martyred during the course of a battle in which his greatly outnumbered forces were overwhelmed by an army under Bani Umayyah Caliph, Yazīd ibn Mu'āwiya. By recalling in song the story of Imam Hussein's death, professional cantors (*rowzeh-khans*)—some aligned closely with the Islamic Republic—reproduce and naturalize Tehran's revolutionary ideals and values, along with its political ideology. So important are the political ends served by this particular ritual that the authorities allocate spatial domains, e.g., streets, squares, parks, even alleyways—sites the Islamic Republic is keen to governmentalize—to religious organizations (*hey'ats*) so that they might mourn the death of Imam Hussein in "a series of spectacular street processions (*dasteh*) and passion plays (*ta'ziyeh*)" (Azam, 2007, p. 140). In recent years, and with the development of information technology and its capability to bring people together, *muharram* rituals have attracted even greater numbers of participants and spectators.

Though Iran has had the Internet since the mid-1990s, its use was limited until the early years of the new millennium (Ansari, 2006): indeed, it was only in the 2010s that the number of Internet users began to grow at a rapid pace, rising from 250,000 in 2000 to nearly 47 million by 2015 (57% of a population numbering some 82 million) (Internet World Stats, 2015). Today, it is commonplace for people from all walks of life to have Internet access. Many, if not most, of the leading clerics of the Islamic Republic have personal websites that feature lively debates and discussions covering a broad range of religious and secular, even political, topics, in both Farsi and English (Khamenei, 2015; Makarem.ir, 2017). The Islamic Republic views the Internet, along with other information technology, as an important means of disseminating its rhetoric and promoting its policy of exporting the revolution (Ansari, 2006). In this regard, Ayatollah Khomeini made it clear that not just the Internet, but modern information technology in general, had a major part to play in his governmentalizing system:

The claim that Islam is against (technical) innovations is the same claim by the deposed Mohammad Raza Pahlavi that these people (Islamic revolutionaries) want to travel with four-legged animals, and this is nothing but an idiotic accusation. For, if by manifestations of civilization it is meant technical innovations, new products, new inventions, and advanced industrial techniques ... then never has Islam ... opposed their adoption.

(cited in Ansari, 2006, p. 66)

Since the introduction of the Internet, the Islamic Republic has developed the requisite means to control virtual spaces, principally by creating a legal and regulatory framework for controlling Internet service providers (ISPs) and monitoring email, chat rooms and VoIP conversations, and by establishing a state-owned monopoly over the provision of Internet services, the sole exception being the smaller ISPs. Thus, for example, DCI, the country's largest ISP, is owned and operated by Iran's Revolutionary Guard (Anderson, 2013; Rhoads & Fassihi, 2011).

As the Green Movement gathered steam and news reports and images of street protests began appearing on social media, the state moved quickly to clamp down even more tightly on the Internet. In the vanguard of this effort stood FATA, a cyber police force created in January 2011 to fight "cyber crime[]" (Cyber.police. ir, 2017). According to its official website, FATA's mandate included

... secur[ing] cyber space[,] protect[ing] national and religious identity, community values, ...liberty, [and] national critical infrastructure against electronic attack ... [and more generally] preserv[ing the country's] interests and national authority in cyberspace ... in order to preserve national power and sovereignty.

(Cyber.police.ir, 2017)

Thus, FATA possesses the legal authority to close any website or halt any online activity and/or use of cyber space perceived as a threat to national security. In effect, it "uses the same [computer] technology ... to beat and destroy enemies and criminals and tries to fight them and sends them to the hands of justice to guarantee the security of cyberspace" (Cyber.police.ir, 2017).

Appointed by the Supreme Leader, the head of FATA is responsible for regulating Internet Service Providers operating in each of the country's thirty-one provinces (ISNA News, 2013). Perhaps its most controversial operation to date involved the October 30, 2012 arrest of Sattar Beheshti, an Iranian dissident and blogger. Accused of undertaking "actions against national security on social networks and Facebook," Beheshti was detained at an unknown location for several days, whereupon he died after being tortured (The Atlantic, 2012).

Thus, though fully sanctioned by the state, information technologies, and the Internet in particular, are rigorously regulated and controlled under the guise of defending the state against a foreign soft war or velvet revolution. The aim of the authorities, as will be shown later, lies in ensuring these technologies will never be used for subversive purposes, especially by dissident groups operating within the country.

The Islamic republic and the governmentalization of Iranian strata

Since its birth, the Islamic Republic has used its disciplinary apparatus to good effect in shaping and controlling the lives of men and women of every social stratum. Of particular interest, however, are three groups: youth, students, and women. As will be shown, each has, by virtue of its demographic significance and unique position in Iranian society, been a primary target for finely calculated disciplinary measures.

Shortly after the beginning of the Iran–Iraq War (1980–1988), the authorities implemented a series of biopolitical policies aimed at remaking Iranian society. Included among these was a Family Planning policy, predicated on Ayatollah Khomeini's writings and his reading of *Shari'a* Law, that lowered the age of puberty for girls to nine and the marriage age to thirteen, in addition to laying the ground work for a series of measures aimed at promoting "polygamy ... large family [sizes] and temporary marriages" (Rafizadeh, 2011, p. 56). All this was intended to Islamize sexuality, by which I mean instrumentalizing Islamic precepts to promote a programme of sexually-inspired Islamist governmentalization, and to do so in a way that could increase the rate of population growth—an important consideration given that the war with neighbouring Iraq was exacting a heavy toll on the country's manpower reserves. More births would in time translate into more soldiers, thereby fulfilling Ayatollah Khomeini's dream of an *artesh-e 20 millioni*, an army of 20 million, which could effectively safeguard the Islamic Republic (Pourmokhtari, 2017). Thus, rapid population growth, spurred by incentives aimed at encouraging families to have additional children, became part of the national agenda. Moreover, since food and consumer goods were distributed on a per capita basis through a state-controlled rationing system, it was relatively simple and easy to reward fecundity (Tejarat News, 2000; Afary, 2009). Note that the population policy remained in force until the end of the Iran–Iraq conflict in 1988, at which point the authorities realized that continual rapid growth in population would exceed the country's carrying capacity.

The consequences of the latter policy took a decade to play out as the population grew from 38.9 million in 1980 to 58.2 million only twelve years later (Worldometers, 2016). The long-term ramifications proved even more dramatic: by 2013, of a population numbering 77 million, 60 percent were under the age of 30 (The World Bank, 2016). With more youth came more university students: by 2014 the number stood at 4.5 million—one out of every 20 Iranians—of whom, and for reasons to be explained later, 60% were women (World Education News & Review, 2013). Thus, the three social strata targeted by the Islamic Republic share the "triple identities of being young, schooled and increasingly female" (Bayat, 2007, p. 66); of equal importance, they constituted a dynamic and volatile social force whose concerns, needs, aspirations, even fates, were largely interconnected and interdependent. This, combined with their enormous numbers, proved to be the greatest concern for the state, which duly made them the chief target for everyday disciplinary measures.

Since its earliest days the Islamic Republic has worked assiduously to subordinate women, the purpose being to contain what it views as an insidious threat to patriarchy. This has translated into marginalizing an enormous—and, as will be shown, politically charged and volatile—segment of the population. In the immediate post-revolutionary period women required the consent of husbands prior to engaging in all manner of civil matters, ranging from filing for divorce—"unless the right was stipulated in marriage contracts" (Esfandiari, 2010, para. 4)—to travelling abroad. The state went even farther to entrench patriarchy. The Civil Code of Iran (1928), as amended between 1982 and 1983, stipulated that the "[h]usband inherits all the property of the deceased wife, but the wife of a deceased husband inherits only movable property of any kind and buildings and trees" (The Library of Congress, 2009, para. 1).[1]

Nor were women permitted to serve as judges or enter other restricted occupations such as construction and mining (Halper, 2005), and many "were purged from government positions" (Esfandiari, 2010, para. 3); they were also banned from participating in certain sports such as wrestling at the professional level (Shilandari, 2010; Tahmasebi, 2012)—all of which was intended, as Haleh Esfandiari asserts, to "put women at the mercy of men in the family [and in the public domain as well]" (2010, para. 1).

These measures were justified, according to Farah Shilandari, on the grounds that—and this is crucial to understanding the techniques and modes of contention typical of counter-governmentalizing efforts of an everyday kind to be discussed in subsequent chapters—only "[invisible and] obedient [daughters], wives and mothers" could be regarded as decent and righteous (2010, para. 7). It is these gender norms that the hardliners sought to normalize, and nowhere more so than in their official rhetoric. This explains why the state invested so heavily in ensuring that every woman was "properly veiled, invisible in public by her attitude, manners, and behavior, submissive and obedient" (Amir-Ebrahimi, 2008, p. 99). In particular, obedience represented "the most [desirable] quality for Muslim women" (Shilandari, 2010, para. 7) in that it served the key political objectives of containing their voices and integrating them as invisible and silent subjects into the very fabric of the revolutionary state.

These kinds of policies left their mark on both students and university life in general. In the immediate post-revolutionary period, the universities were closed and would remain so for a period of three years (1980–1983). For Ayatollah Khomeini, it was vital that higher education undergo a revolution of its own, one aimed at Islamizing the universities, thereby ridding them of Western and secular influences. As the Supreme Leader warned, "[w]hat we are afraid of is Western universities and the training of our youth in the interests of West or East" (Khomeini, cited in Bakhash, 1984, pp. 69–70). This explains the emergence of a cultural revolution centered in Iranian universities, which, though Islamic in name and principles, was in reality a political manoeuvre intended to segregate students along gender lines. This, it was believed, could greatly facilitate the dual project of normalizing Islamic women according to patriarchal imperatives, and combatting counter-revolutionary thought and behavior. Again, seemingly Islamic measures served an important political end: to contain dissent within a traditional hotbed of social radicalism.

With gender segregation came a policy of banning books and classes deemed pro-Western or secular, in the process preparing the way for state-friendly curricula (Mashayekhi, 2011; Razavi, 2009). These steps were accompanied by a systematic purge of numerous so-called liberal and secular faculty members and students, including "thousands of women," whose continued presence posed, or so it was perceived, a political challenge to the state's hegemony within the universities as well the broader society (Amir-Ebrahimi, 2006, p. 3).

The policy of Islamizing the universities continued well into the new millennium. Indeed, the debate over further Islamizing higher education ramped up in the post-2009 era, ushering in what might be called a second cultural revolution. The latter was presided over by conservative heavyweights Ayatollah Mohammad-Taghi Mesbah Yazdi and the Supreme Leader himself, Ali Khamenei. It was Mesbah Yazdi who attributed the 2009 uprising, in part, to the "social sciences on offer" at the universities, which indoctrinated students with "Westernizing values such as individualism, liberalism and secularism" (Tasnim News, 2015). In lockstep with Mesbah, Khamenei called for further "nativization" of higher learning, a move designed to counter Western-inspired curricula based on "materialism and disbelief in Godly and Islamic teachings" (Aviny, 2009, para. 5). Since then, a number of universities have followed Khamenei's prescription. In 2011, for example, Aallameh Tabtabai University eliminated no less than 13 social science departments, among them Sociology and Psychology, whose courses ranked perennially among the most popular (Radio Farda, 2011).

Women and students were not alone in feeling the sting of these disciplinary measures. Immediately following the revolution, the Islamic Republic had made it clear that disciplining politically charged youth was to be a chief priority. In this way, all that the authorities condemned as Westernized joy, a magnet for the young, came under heavy scrutiny. Included under this rubric were a host of so-called immoral behaviours, including, but by no means limited to, the consumption of alcohol, playing music at high volume, the wearing of make-up, and gambling, for which the remedy was detoxification (Rafizadeh, 2011). Ironically, the state effectively exploited some of these behaviours for its own ends. During the Iran–Iraq war, both the army and the Revolutionary Guard used loud and highly emotive music, based on religious or revolutionary themes, to help recruit civilians as well as motivate troops prior to engaging in combat (Afshari, 2015).

More recently, the conservative establishment, with the backing of the Supreme Leader Ayatollah Khamenei, has sought to extend its control over other areas of youth culture by governmentalizing joy. To take but one example, the simple and seemingly innocent act of clapping, has become, at least in theory, the subject of codes, rules and regulations stipulating the occasions and settings deemed appropriate for this kind of behaviour—usually religious or national holidays (Hawzah Net, 2004; Kheybar Online, 2014; Gooya News, 2016; Khamenei.ir, 2016a).

Moreover, as decreed by Khamenei (2015, p. 49), the wearing of fashionable clothing—indeed, any kind of speech or behaviour that might reflect a fashion-conscious attitude—is forbidden lest it "propagate the empty culture of the foreigners" (see also Talabegi Blog, 2014). According to Ayatollah Khamenei (2015, p. 47), it is not permissible "to wear clothing which in color, style, or cut imitates or propagates the cultural assault of the enemies of Islam and the Muslims." In the same vein, men and women are forbidden to wear clothing, the "designs and colours [of] which stand out or attract attention" (Khamenei.ir, 2016b). For the latter, this means no article of clothing or accoutrements or cosmetics that might showcase, in any public space, their "bod[ies] and the[ir] curves and forms" (Khamenei, 2015, p. 43; Khamenei.ir, 2016b). As will be seen, however, these measures would have a paradoxical effect, in particular by way of whetting the appetite of diverse social groups for fundamental social and political reform.

The crucial point to be grasped, however, is that the so-called governmentalization of joy remains largely *pro forma*. Though seldom operationalized, it still numbers among the disciplinary strategies in place for conducting the lives of the masses, and hence a target for operations of counterconduct. It is at this contingent and intangible level that the focal point of the analysis of governmentalizing joy emerges, lending us a vantage point, as Foucault contends, to identify and expose "the weak points of power, from which we can attack it" (Foucault, cited in Afary & Anderson, 2005, p. 189).

The management and control of sexuality constituted the principal focus of the governmentalization of joy, as evinced by the host of rules prohibiting everything from homosexuality to extramarital affairs to the comingling in public spaces of unmarried couples. That bodies, sexuality and the pleasures of the flesh represent the chief targets of disciplinary power speaks to a prurience on the part of the conservative establishment that would appear unseemly. The effect on the broader society, moreover, has been far from wholesome. As Behzad Yaghmaian asserts, in a "society of repressed worldly desires" (2002, p. 48), wherein, the "... political process [is]," according to Ziba Mir-Hosseini, "gendered" (1999, p. 73), sexuality has become taboo and pleasure an unforgiveable crime, particularly where youth are concerned.

The Islamic republic: The everyday mechanics and techniques of control

The governmentalization of Iranian society, as with everywhere else, involved the "overlayering of many techniques ... complex articulations, majorings and minorings, [and] combinations of quite different arts of [governance]" (Walters, 2012, p. 40). Such mechanics and techniques of disciplinary power, as will be shown here, have been applied to the general populace, and in particular women, students, and youth, who, as discussed above, have come to dominate contemporary Iranian society owing to their dynamism/volatility and numbers. Note, however, that the techniques and mechanisms of control to be examined here are but a few of the many comprising the state repertory; they have been selected with a view to familiarizing the reader with the specificity of the power relations at work in the Islamic Republic with respect to students, women, and youth.

Following the revolution, the Islamic Republic lost no time in creating what soon came to be known as the "morality police," with a mandate "to impose order and discipline and to enforce Islamic codes of behaviour," particularly within the context of everyday life (Golkar, 2015, p. 75). In the immediate post-revolutionary era, the morality police came to represent the chief manifestation of a disciplinary power aimed at asserting the conduct of conduct within public spaces.

In the major cities their special units remained very much in evidence throughout the early years of the revolution. Their green-striped vehicles prowled the boulevards, streets and alleyways at all hours. Generally, though not always, any breach of the innumerable disciplinary laws and codes resulted in the arrest of the code-disobeyer (Asr Iran, 2013; Meidaan, 2015). The efficacy of the special units depended primarily upon their unpredictability; potential violators could never be certain when or where they might suddenly appear, their ever-watchful gaze directed at detecting violations of the dress code, something particularly common during the summer months when, seeking relief from the heat, the unwary or reckless might be tempted to expose more than the law was prepared to allow. For this reason, in more recent years the morality policy have concentrated their efforts during those particular months (Aftab News, 2016; Mashregh News, 2013).

For the most part, all that is required of the morality police is to target the individual with a vigilant, normalizing gaze, a reminder of his/her place in the disciplinary domain and hence of the need to observe its rules and codes. The disciplinary principle at work here applies every minute of every hour of every day, as no one ever knows if or when the special units will make an appearance.

If and when apprehended, those in breach of the rules, norms and codes are subject to disciplinary measures. The usual punishment for violating the dress code varies with the violator's gender. Females are usually detained at a police station, required to sign an agreement pledging not to repeat the offence, and then released, albeit not before donning a black *chador*, a long veil provided by family members at the request of the authorities (Jerusalem Post, 2015; Meidaan, 2015). After signing an agreement pledging not to reoffend, males are released, often after having their heads shaven as a sign of wrongdoing for all to see. Depending on the severity of the crime, the guilty may be fined or receive the requisite number of lashes, something that can usually be avoided by paying a fine (Afary, 2009; Rafizadeh, 2011).

It is important to note, however, that with the ascendancy of the reform-minded Hassan Rouhani (2013–present) to the presidency, the morality police have been reined in. For example, in April 2016, Tehran's chief of police, Hossein Sajediniya, announced a new initiative aimed at further "safeguarding the moral security" of society (Fars News, 2016). This involved deploying no less than 7,000 undercover agents at strategic checkpoints located on busy thoroughfares, the purpose being to report drivers and passengers who "fail to observe the *hijab*" rule (Fars News, 2016). Violators would have their license plate numbers recorded and texted to a local police station where the miscreants were required to present themselves. This initiative was repealed after only one month, however, owing largely to the intervention of President Rouhani who ruled it to be an affront to "the dignity of the population" (Asr Iran, 2016). Nonetheless, owing to factional infighting within government circles,[2] the morality police continues to serve an important disciplinary function, even under the aegis of a reform-minded administration (YouTube, 2017a, 2017b, 2017c).

The disciplinary technique employed in this particular case involved subjecting the populace to observation during the course of everyday life with a view to instilling the desired disciplinary norms that over time become routinized and habitual. Should this approach fail to deter potential resistors, the authorities may resort to punishment. By undergoing punishment, witnessing it firsthand or learning of its trials and humiliations from either the victims or those who have witnessed it or heard of it second-hand, the individual will be schooled, so it is assumed, to shun wrongdoing. It is the watchful gaze of the morality police that reminds all and sundry of their position in the disciplinary domain of conduct, thus relieving the authorities of any need to enforce the standing norms and codes themselves.

Yet, paradoxically, it is under the normalizing gaze that the observed may metamorphose into a subject bent on subverting state-sanctioned norms, thereby opening up another avenue of resistance. As will be seen in the following pages, despite what appears at first glance a formidable redoubt turns out to be a point of weakness to be discovered and exploited by oppositional movements, which brings us back to Foucault's famous admission, one worth repeating here: "the purpose of all my analyses is that, in light of them, we find out where are the weak points of power, from which we can attack it" (cited in Afary & Anderson, 2005, p. 189).

Thus, it is not the scale or frequency of operations conducted by the morality police or even the severity of the punishments meted out that is important here, but rather the capability on the part of the government to instil among the entire populace an acute awareness of its seemingly all-pervasive watchful gaze—a capability that speaks to a prodigious and unrelenting effort to governmentalize bodies in the domain of everyday life.

Religious teachings were also appropriated by the authorities with a view to conditioning the populace to tow the official line. The morality police and the state-controlled media had long advocated enforcing the aforementioned Qur'anic injunction *amr-e be maruf and nahy az monkar*, "command[] the right and forbid[] the wrong" (Golkar, 2015, p. 76). Ironically, this commandment was originally intended to empower all Muslims to monitor state officials with a view to ensuring just and accountable governance. Time and time again, the Islamic Republic has shown itself not to be averse to instrumentalizing Qur'anic injunctions for the purpose of promoting its disciplinary project.

By conducting so-called *amr-e be maruf* campaigns, the authorities sought to normalize and internalize officially sanctioned definitions of what constitutes a decent Islamic man, woman, girl, boy, youth and student. To take but one example, during one such campaign in the winter of 2015, female vigilantes affiliated with the paramilitary *Sāzmān-e Basij-e Mostaz'afin*, better known as the *basij*, backed by the morality police, were set the task of rewarding any woman identified as decent and obedient—as evinced by their modesty, humility, and self-effacing behavior—with a single rose as a token of official approval (Khabar Online, 2013; Bahejab, 2015; Faradeed News, 2015). Photographs and videos of code and law abiders were often featured on national media to provide the public with exemplars of ideal womanhood. Audiences, including the violators among them, were expected to internalize state-approved gender norms, the aim being to produce docile and obedient bodies sufficiently motivated to discipline themselves and others, thus helping to reproduce the status quo.

The creation of docile bodies requires the production, dissemination and internalization of specific knowledges relating to various disciplinary domains. Carrying out the first two steps is the responsibility of conservative clerics and intellectuals with close ties to the authorities. Every opportunity, in particular state-sanctioned ceremonies and events, including Friday prayers, anniversaries of the revolution or of the birth or death of an Imam, is exploited for this purpose.

During an April 16, 2010 Friday prayer gathering, Ayatollah Kazem Sadighi, among the best known of Tehran's clerics, took the opportunity to catalogue the dire consequences occasioned by women wearing revealing clothing and behaving promiscuously: "[m]any women who do not dress modestly ... lead young men astray, corrupt their chastity and spread adultery in society, which increases the frequency and severity of earthquakes" (Fars News, 2010). And on June 10, 2016, Isfahan's Friday prayer leader, Yousef Tabatabaeinezhad, attributed the exceptionally low water level of the Zayandehrood, a major river cutting through the heart of the city, to the appearance of photographs of *hijabless* women on social media as well as several websites (Zistboom News, 2016).

Disciplinary knowledges are disseminated in other domains as well. As part of the campaign to Islamize the universities, and in particular the social sciences, the authorities have sponsored major international seminars and conferences that draw sympathetic academics with impressive credentials (Mizan Online, 2015). These convocations serve to make the so-called Islamization of the universities, and through them the whole of society, appear simultaneously normal, religious and scientific, hence grounded in morality and reason.

Such knowledges, along with the various rationales intended to legitimize them, are routinely disseminated through mainstream and social media, government agencies, religious institutions and academe, among other channels. For example, it is commonplace for women of a conservative stripe working within government agencies to disseminate and normalize the new knowledges. Thus, there appeared in the December 25, 2017 edition of *Kayhan*, a conservative daily, an op-ed piece by Zahra Ayatollahi, head of the Women and Family Socio-Cultural Council (WFSCC),[3] condemning a bill recently tabled in the *Majlis* aimed at combatting violence against women. "If [the Bill of Prohibition of Violence Against Women] ... is approved, young men wound not dare get married," asserted Ayatollahi, who then added, "experience has shown that the best form of protecting women is to leave them at the mercy of their men; that is, [their] father[s], spouse[s], brother[s], and father[s]-in-law [, in sum,] those who can support and defend women" (Shabtab News, 2017). "A woman who has a father, brother, and a spouse," she concluded, "would not need the law" (Shabtab News, 2017).

The conservative establishment, which effectively controls the Islamic Republic of Iran Broadcasting (IRIB) network, moreover, funds regular television and Internet programming aimed at persuading audiences, and in particular youth, students and women, that abiding by Islamic principles, codes and rules offers the surest guarantee of both earthly and heavenly salvation.

Zolal-e ahkam,⁴ which is broadcast live on the IRIB network and which is also available online, epitomizes this kind of programming. Audience members with questions and concerns of a religious nature, or to do with everyday needs Tehran deems to be of social and political relevance, are invited to call in and imbibe the advice of a cleric (Ahkam TV, 2016). Topics can vary from the *hijab* to the role of men and women in the family, from the aspirations of youth to Islamizing fashion, from student life on university campuses to social and political affairs. It is not uncommon for callers to confess their wrongdoings or sins. Having heard out the caller, the presiding cleric proffers advice in the form of religious rulings (Ahkam TV, 2016; Telewebion, 2016). The aim of this exercise lies in producing trained bodies capable of self-examination and, by implication, self-governance. The objective, in other words, is to produce docile bodies that adhere to *Shari'a* norms, thereby reproducing the governmentalizing system.

The IRIB is, moreover, notorious for broadcasting serial programming and films that valorize and normalize codes and rules of conduct. It is usually the case that unsavoury male characters are clean shaven and attired in Western dress; where their female counterparts appear heavily made up and attired in ways both revealing and, equally repugnant, colourful—the very antithesis of all that is prescribed by Islamic Republic rules and codes of conduct. It is not uncommon, moreover, for characters of this ilk (especially in politically-inspired productions) to be foreign agents bent on toppling the Islamic Republic, which they proceed to do by engaging in destructive acts such as damaging public and private property, torching buses and taxis, assaulting innocent bystanders and generally causing mayhem.

To take yet another example, in February of 2012, the Islamic Republic produced and distributed *Ghalladehaye Tala*, The Golden Collars, a feature-length film that reduces the Green Movement to the status of a cabal aiming to bring about a velvet revolution (Fars News, 2012). Thus are Green Movement activists shown to be, at best, naïve individuals manipulated by foreign powers intent on regime change, or, worse, agents of Tel-Aviv and the West determined to topple the Islamic Republic by orchestrating unlawful demonstrations, destroying public property, and attacking ordinary Iranians on the streets.

These specific micro-measures and techniques to which the individual is exposed virtually every day, however insignificant and unobtrusive they may seem, nonetheless, have the accumulative effect of demonizing those whom Tehran views to be non-conformist, in the process rationalizing and justifying its disciplinary knowledges and the apparatus used to inculcate or internalize them.

Beyond the domain of broadcast media, one is routinely confronted in public spaces with placards, banners and billboards featuring slogans, often accompanied by images, which serve a distinctly disciplinary end. Some liken a woman properly attired to "a pearl in a shell" (Welayatnet, 2013); others declare that "the *hijab* is immunity, not a limitation" for women confronted by lascivious men (Hejab Bartar, 2012). Some banners are inscribed with quotations from great Shi'a Islam figures of the past, sometimes edited or taken out of context to better serve the Islamic Republic's disciplinary project. Moreover, one often encounters street banners and placards quoting the charismatic third Shi'a Imam, Hussein, that declare: "I want to follow the commandment of *amr-e be maruf*, continuing the same path that my father [Imam Ali] and my grandfather [the prophet Muhammad] followed" (Afkar News, 2017).

These examples indicate just how far the Islamic Republic, and the conservative establishment in particular, is prepared to go in order to produce trained and docile bodies. Their efficacy lies in invoking religious sentiment, the purpose of which is to exhort the individual to conform to state-prescribed rules, norms and codes so that the governmentalized project go unchallenged. In the case of those billboards and placards promoting the *hijab*, a clear-cut socio-moral message is being communicated to both men and women: "[to] be safe in Islamic public spaces, one should wear the *hijab*, which functions like a protective enclosure and can provide security for women against strange[] men" (Amir-Ebrahimi, 2006, p. 5).

In the case of the *amr-e be maruf* billboards, one can clearly discern how the authorities rationalize and normalize disciplinary practices, in this case combining micro practices of governance with the aforementioned macro practices of the morality police, such that the individual is socialized to accept, as part of the natural and normal order of things, the routine exercise of this kind of authority. In addition, that the latter is endorsed by one of the most holy and charismatic figures of Shi'a Islam, confers upon it a religious and moral imprimatur. These micro-measures and techniques, however insignificant and unobtrusive they may appear, were designed to producing obedient and conformist bodies incapable of challenging the status quo.

The Islamic Republic and the art of repression

As the previous discussion reveals, the Islamic Republic employs a mix of different arts, techniques and measures to control individual conduct and, by implication, that of the masses. The majority of these have as their objective the production and reproduction of docile bodies that can be trained, instrumentalized and put to various uses in the service of power. Among its manifold methods of governance, the Islamic Republic has perfected the art of repression, which entails the use of brute force that can be summoned at the shortest notice to contain othering voices, including those of dissent. It is referred to as an art because its techniques have been masterfully intermeshed with the psychology of fear, such that the body and the soul come to internalize the full consequences of wrongdoing. The objective here lies less in devising creative and innovative measures aimed at compelling the individual to submit to state-prescribed norms, codes and regulations; rather, the chief purpose is to inculcate fear so that dissident voices might be silenced without the need to resort to force.

The chief rationale underlying the art of repression is predicated on the notion that the Islamic Republic constitutes a "divine entity … [ordained] by God," with the Supreme Leader as his earthly representative as well as a manifestation of his divinity (Khomeini, cited in Abrahamian, 2008, p. 165). Herein lies the essence of the conservative establishment's religio-governmentalized view of the republic as "a holy phenomenon where sovereignty and leadership belong ultimately to God, who relegates … power[] to the [Supreme] *faqih*" (Mahdavi Kani, cited in Moslem, 2002, p. 100). By virtue of their stranglehold on key governmental domains—the judiciary, media, security apparatus—conservatives have parlayed this representation of the state into a dominant leitmotif informing official discourses. In invoking the principle of divine right to rule, it serves to legitimize the Islamic Republic, and in particular the rule of the Supreme Leader; thus, any challenge to the state amounts to undermining divine rule. In this schema, preserving the system, or *nizam* as it is popularly known, and along with it ""Islamic rule" (*vilayat*) ... takes precedence over all other obligations" (Bayat, 2013, p. 293). According to this logic, as the Supreme Leader is both holy and a sovereign, any challenge, be it to him or to the state, may be seen as undermining divine rule, entitling him "to [make] die [and] let live," should the situation demand (Foucault, 2003, p. 240).

In this way, any act perceived as a threat to the status quo may be viewed as un-Islamic, hence a challenge to the authority of the Supreme Leader and, by implication, the very existence of the Islamic Republic, warranting unlimited retaliation on the part of the authorities. It is little wonder then—as the many verbal accounts and diary entries of Iranian prisoners so vividly attest—that torture is seen by its practitioners as a sacred practice to be put in the service of the government of God and his earthly representative (Rejali, 1994; Qhaneei Fard, 2013). According to this line of thinking, acts of defiance against the authorities may be seen as un-Islamic and those charged with punishing the perpetrators as servants of God. And that such a view happens to coincide with preserving at all costs the social and political status quo must appear in keeping with the natural order of things.

Perhaps one of the most commonplace tactics used to inculcate fear among dissidents is the spectacle of police and military manoeuvres and parades held frequently throughout the country. This show of strength is complemented by broadcasts over the national media describing in considerable detail the most advanced technologies available to the security apparatus for dealing with internal unrest (Fararu Daily, 2013; 110nopo, 2013). In addition, special police units parade through the streets, stopping occasionally to demonstrate equipment and tactics designed to crush any threat to the status quo. The chief exemplar of such spectacles is mounted annually by the *nirooy-e vije-ye poshtiban-e vilayat*, Guardian of the Supreme Faqih's Special Force, whose chief responsibility lies in "crush[ing] internal riots or unrest" (Fararu Daily, 2013, para. 7). The marchers, clad in black uniforms and black vehicles, are often accompanied by armoured busses capable of holding large numbers of rioters (Shabestar News. 2014; 110nopo, 2013).

Fear tactics are often complemented by media campaigns aimed at dispensing misinformation and framing events in ways calculated to discredit or intimidate oppositional groups. To take but one example, in the immediate aftermath of the 2009 street protests, the media mounted a vigorous campaign to depict the Green Movement as a cabal that was funded by foreign enemies. The IRIB began featuring documentaries and other types of programming, wherein "experts" were invited to analyze the events of 2009 with a view to comparing them to the so-called colored revolutions, funded, instigated and orchestrated by Western governments bent on undermining the Islamic Republic (Fars News, 2015).

Staging show trials, replete with *eterafat-e ejbari*, forced confessions, constitutes yet another means of inculcating fear in dissidents. One such parody of justice, conducted in the aftermath of the 2009 street protests, was broadcast live via the state television network as well as online. Of all those appearing on trial, Mohammad Ali Abtahi, former Vice President of Iran under Mohammad Khatami, stood out for "confessing" that the Green Movement was intended to be the vanguard of an *inghelab'e makhmali*, a velvet revolution, orchestrated by foreigners (Jahan News, 2013a).

But what if these tactics should fail to deter opposition to the ruling clerical oligarchy? What makes the Islamic Republic's art of repression so singularly effective is that beyond the police, and even the special forces assigned to deal with dissidents, there exists two paramilitary groups, both affiliated with the Office of the Supreme Leader, whose chief responsibility lies in suppressing oppositional voices by any and all means, including brute force, even to the point of taking lives or exercising the sovereign right/power of making die and letting live.

Officially designated the fifth branch of the Islamic Revolutionary Guard Corps, the *basij* constitutes a paramilitary force whose head is appointed by the Supreme Leader. Its mandate is to serve "as the eyes and ears" of the Islamic Republic (Golkar, 2015, p. 87). Among its manifold responsibilities, none is more important than maintaining security and suppressing demonstrations and other forms of public unrest with which the regular police are unable to cope. Operating independently of the regular police forces, the *basij* makes its presence felt throughout the country's urban areas by establishing temporary checkpoints at major street intersections, the purpose of which is to discourage dissent. In recent years its jurisdiction has been greatly expanded to include schools, universities and public and private institutions; factories and even tribal groups fall within its purview. So ubiquitous is its presence that the *basij* represents, according to Saeid Golkar, "the equivalent of a parallel society" (2015, p. 37).

The *basij* is not alone in enforcing governmental rule; indeed, its zeal in this regard is matched by the *ansar-e hizbollah*, Followers of the Party of God. Known variously as *lebas shakhsiha*, those who wear plain and/or civilian clothes, and *gorouh-e feshar*, pressure group, its members are fanatically dedicated to upholding the *vilayat-e faqih* principle (Pars News, 2015). The *ansars* are part of no law enforcement agency; they function solely on extralegal grounds (Radio Farda, 2016). That said, one can speculate, based on statements by former leaders as well as rank-and-file members, that they have covert ties to the office of the Supreme Leader, from whence they receive the green light to conduct operations (Boghrati, 2006; Afshari, 2015; Safshekan, 2015).

The *ansars* are best described as a vigilante group that would not hesitate to use brute force and intimidation to contain dissent at whatever the cost (Jonoub News, 2014; Peyk Iran, 2014; Yalsarat News, 2015). They are, for example, quick to respond violently to all forms of dissent and to anything that strikes them as pro-Western or subversive: they vandalize cinemas, disrupt lectures delivered by intellectuals whose political tendencies are best described as othering, set ablaze publishing firms deemed to be of an anti-establishment character, and much else besides (Ansari, 2006; Iran Briefing, 2012; Noghrehkar, 2009).

The *ansars* are especially active during demonstrations and uprisings, putting their machinery of repression into motion with the greatest zeal. They were, to take but one example, instrumental in crushing opposition during the 1999 student movements and the 2009 Green Movement (Afshari, 2015; Safshekan, 2015). In both cases, as accounts of eyewitness testify, they took to beating students, hurling them from balconies, and setting their rooms afire, in the process killing one and five students, respectively (Akhbar Rooz, 2009; Daneshjoo News, 2015). During the 2009 disturbances, photographs of these vigilantes brutally assaulting activists were distributed widely via social media.

The machinery of repression and intimidation highlighted here cannot be explained simply in terms of disciplinary vs. repressive modalities of power; the picture is far more complex, as is revealed by interrogating the vigilante activities of the morality police, a law enforcement agency whose role was discussed above in reference to the Islamic Republic's subtle disciplinary programme. For a mandate, the morality police, in common with other police/security forces operating within the country, relies on the aforementioned religious injunction of *amr-e be maruf*, or "commanding the right and forbidding the wrong" (Golkar, 2015, p. 76). However, while their respective mandates may have been identical, in the case of the former the means employed and consequences to follow differed substantially.

According to "official sources," in October 2014, in the city of Isfahan, the second most populous metropolitan area after Tehran, a group of vigilantes took it upon themselves to "fling[] acid [on]to the faces of women [, estimated to number between seven and ten,] with whom they had no history of personal grudges" (cited in Centre for Human Rights in Iran, 2015, para. 6). According to the Centre for Human Rights in Iran (CHRI), those involved in this gruesome incident were "male acid throwers [who were presumably scandalized by the victims'] loose clothing" (CHRI, 2015, para. 7). The same source reported that the perpetrators were "morality vigilantes with close ties to ... *basij* militias" (CHRI, 2015, para. 12). Moreover, "eyewitnesses [to the incident] reported that the assailants declared they were defending *hijab* during the assaults" (CHRI, 2015a, para. 4). In this way, concluded CHRI, "the link between the acid attacks and the *hijab* issue is strong" (CHRI, 2015, para. 8).

And indeed, that the acid attacks coincided with the June 2013 election of the moderate, reform-minded Hassan Rouhani to the presidency would appear to lend credence to the CHRI report. Rouhani's ascendancy coupled with the defeat of the ultraconservative incumbent, Mahmood Ahmadinejad, "triggered a backlash by hardline state officials and conservative clerics anxious to assert their dominance in the domestic sphere" (CHRI, 2015a, para. 1). According to CHRI, "[w]omen's issues, always [central] to the [conduct of conduct], assumed particular importance in this power struggle; moreover, the use of the 'bully pulpit' to promote a more restrictive view of women's place in society increased palpably after Rouhani's election" (CHRI, 2015a, para. 1).

In this move to reassert the political power of patriarchy, moreover, the "[h]ardliners ..., including Parliamentarians and [senior] clerics, focused [increasingly] on imposing [an] ultraconservative [interpretation] of *hijab* on all Iranian women, seeing the issue as a litmus test of allegiance to the Islamic Republic" (CHRI, 2015, para. 8). In April 2014, for example, a bill, entitled Plan to Promote Virtue and Prevent Vice, was tabled before the *Majlis* and passed into law some two months later (CHRI, 2015). The law "explicitly"

> [m]andated the *Basij*, under the auspices of Iran's Revolutionary Guards, to enforce proper *hijab* on all Iranian women. [In thus mobilizing the] *Basij* … it entrust[ed] law enforcement to untrained (and unaccountable) individual citizens—in other words, it effectively create[d] a system of vigilante justice.
> (CHRI, 2015, para. 10)

The new law was promoted by "the state-run media, [the clerical establishment at] Friday prayers, and official speeches throughout the country" (CHRI, 2015a, para. 2). More specifically, the Plan to Promote Virtue and Prevent Vice

> presented ultraconservative views on women and gender policies as mandated by their interpretation of Islam (as well as a national security imperative to guard against infiltration by the West), and, through their explicit references to the necessity of public enforcement of these views and policies, lay the groundwork for vigilante groups to take matters into their own hands.
> (CHRI, 2015a, para. 2)

Thus, on July 9, 2013, the Grand Ayatollah Makarem Shirazi, a conservative heavyweight, declared:

> The issue of improper *hijab* has … become a political issue. The enemies of the state believe that they can harm us through spreading bad *hijab* practices. On the other hand, we believe if we deal with (and end) improper *hijab* we will strengthen the state … If we don't protect *hijab* in society, we will harm the state. Anti-revolutionaries would use every opportunity to get rid of the *hijab* and harm us. Unlike what Westerners claim, the *hijab* should not be a choice. Protecting *hijab* is our moral and religious duty.
> (CHRI, 2015a, para. 3; see also Ghatreh, 2013)

And on October 19, 2014, only days[5] before the acid attack, Isfahan's Friday Prayer leader, the cleric Mohammad Taghi Rahbar, "[delivered] a sermon suggesting women with bad *hijab* should be confronted by more than just words" (CHRI, 2015, para. 11). For the conservative establishment, enforcing *hijab* was tantamount to defending Islam itself because the *hijab* represented a cornerstone of the conduct of conduct. Speaking before a group of Revolutionary Guard Commanders at Qom on September 22, 2013, the Grand Ayatollah Lotfollah Safi Golpayegani warned:

> Getting rid of the *hijab* is the most significant way of diverting society (from the righteous path). You Guards are the protectors of our beloved Islam, and

as such you must be in the forefront of promoting virtue and preventing vice [,i.e., *amr-e be maruf*]

(CHRI, 2015a, para. 5; see also Ghatreh, 2013a)

Responsibility for the Isfahan acid attacks would be laid at the feet of one Abdolreza Aghakhani, a self-proclaimed "soldier of the *vilayat*" (Quds Online, 2017, para. 1) and the city's Chief of Police as well as director and supervisor of the morality police for Isfahan province. Six years following the acid attacks, "the police and security forces ha[d] not apprehended a single individual" (CHRI, 2015, para. 1). As it turned out, the incident appears to have advanced Aghakhani's career, for on May 10, 2016 he was officially recognized as pre-eminent among the country's Chiefs of Police for his "committed endeavours to fulfill the great objectives of the *nizam* [the system]" and for his unrelenting efforts to ensure the "moral security of the public" (Quds Online, 2016, para. 3). Thus, the machinery of repression and intimidation at work here disrupts the simple dichotomy of disciplinary vs. repressive modalities of power relations, meaning that under Islamist governmentalization a disciplinary force such as the morality police can be pressed into service to enforce laws and codes, if necessary by the use of force.

Post-revolutionary Iran: Iranians, the everyday life and everyday resistance

Post-revolutionary Iran, in common with other countries in the Middle East and North Africa, has witnessed a multiplicity of resistances, driven by the paradoxically empowering effect of regulatory norms, codes and laws (Butler, 1993; Foucault, 1978). Understanding how acts and modes of resistance actually materialize requires examining their historical context. The founding of the Islamic Republic set the stage for the coming of age of socially charged and politically volatile social strata for whom the state's governmentalizing rules, regulations and norms, proved anathema. The 1979 revolution itself had galvanized and politicized disparate social strata like "no other event in the country's recent history" (Vahdat, 2010, para. 7), thus preparing the ground for the emergence of a highly politically conscious post-revolutionary society. A number of other historical factors and developments further politicized Iranian society.

First, and notwithstanding its many non-democratic features, the Islamic Republic has held elections regularly at the district, municipal and national levels, making it "the only country in the Muslim Middle East [to have] enjoyed regular elections" over the course of the past four decades (Mahdavi, 2008, p. 142). This is highly significant with respect to politicizing the citizenry in that elections, along with the political campaigning that accompanies them, provide a large numbers of citizens opportunities for at least some "degree of civil society participation" (Mahdavi, 2008, p. 142).

Certain state policies have also contributed to mass politicization. Most notably, those responsible for setting in motion the cultural revolution, which was, among other things, intended to Islamize universities by purging faculty members and administrators, had the unforeseen consequence of radicalizing hundreds of thousands of students. This governmentalization of the universities turned many students into staunch proponents of social rights, including the right to access information and study non-Islamic curricula. The universities thus became hotbeds of political radicalism, as evinced by the 1999 student protests that rocked the Islamic Republic to its foundations.

Women were also politicized by discriminatory laws, rules and codes intended to regulate every facet of their behaviour. Under a post-revolutionary constitution designed to Islamize society, they had been granted voting rights as well as the right to stand for political office, at once politicizing them and at the same time transforming them into active citizens seeking fundamental rights. This represented a giant step toward participating fully in the political, social, and economic life of the country.

Ultimately, the campaign to Islamize society would have a paradoxical effect, especially where women adhering to the traditional ways were concerned. The law making it compulsory to wear the *hijab* in public represents a case in point. Intended to make women invisible, it instead, as Masserat Amir-Ebrahimi asserts, "facilitated their access to new public spaces and to modernity" (2006, pp. 4–5). For the first time, women could enter the professions, in addition to other occupational areas traditionally reserved for men, such as the civil service, wholesaling, retailing, and the trades. All this led Mehrangiz Kar (2006) to conclude that the Islamic Republic's "biggest gift to women" was the right to venture "out of … [their homes] [so that] the sky replaced the roof and politics … prayers" (p. 284). More broadly, the Tehran's policy of permitting women to engage in political and religious activities, among them the Islamic Republic's orchestrated demonstrations and religious rituals had the contrary effect of radicalizing them, thus making for a much more volatile society.

The Iran–Iraq War (1980–1988) also played a role in politicizing the masses. During this long, bloody conflict, women, youth and students were recruited to serve as workers, soldiers, and volunteers, something that required "participat[ing] in the political, social, military, and … economic affairs of their country" as never before (Vahdat, 2012, para. 3). This proved transformative, giving rise to bold, confident, demand-making citizens, conscious of their newly acquired status as active agents.

Everyday resistance and post-revolutionary movements of counterconduct

The combination of these government policies and historical developments, along with their paradoxical effects, would play a key role in the birth and consolidation of a politically charged post-revolutionary society, of which large sections—women, students, youth, workers, the urban poor, among others—were acutely aware of their social and political rights and steadfast in demanding them. It was these elements that in the post-revolutionary period filled the ranks of various movements of counter-conduct that in 2009 coalesced into the Green Movement.

What qualified each of these groups as a movement of counterconduct, moreover, was a commitment to subvert, negate and resist a religio-governmentalized order or Islamist conduct of conduct. Toward this end, each engaged in the same politics of negation and subversion, the hallmark of which was a politics of everyday life. In this sense, "counterconduct" is to be understood as "part of a localized struggle against a specific modality of government [or] a specific way of being conducted" (McCall, 2014, p. 7). For example, owing to the semi-authoritarian setting within which they operated, the post-revolutionary movements of counterconduct lacked anything resembling a formal organizational structure or recognizable leadership. Moreover, as they were denied the political rights, freedoms and opportunities available to oppositional groups operating in Western democratic polities—the right of assembly, the right to lobby and petition government, the right of freedom of expression—their activism was restricted to the "shared practices of large numbers of ordinary people" bent on challenging the status quo through everyday life practices (Bayat, 2013, p. 15). Consequently, their oppositional activities were, for the most part, carried out in the passing minutes of everyday life. Thus, it can be argued that this form of resistance represents, not just a politics of protest per se, but also a social campaign aimed at bringing about change through "direct and disparate actions" of an everyday kind (Bayat, 2013, p. 20).[6]

Moreover, as will be shown, their experience of the Islamic Republic's security apparatus dictated two strategic imperatives: first, to counter the government's rules, norms and regulations through the repetitive public display of their numbers, commitment, unity and worthiness; second, to promote slow-paced, incremental change, both of which would play out, again, in the arena of ordinary life practices (Amir-Ebrahimi, 2006; Bayat, 2013). It is there that an "immense new field of possibility for resistance ... opened," a site where subjugated bodies paradoxically, albeit in an intentional fashion, exploited the mechanisms, techniques and technologies of control in order to counter, reverse and/or rebalance power relations (Nealon, 2008, pp. 107–108).

In the post-revolutionary period, it was by no accident that women, students and youth made up the rank and file of these movements of counterconduct. Apart from being marginalized and subordinated, all three, henceforth referred to as movements, shared much in common: enormous numbers, youth, education and, in the case of students and youth, an ever-growing female contingent. Their sheer numbers and, more importantly, shared objectives and interests "ha[d] the effect of normalizing and legitimizing those acts that [would] otherwise [be] deemed illegitimate" (Bayat, 2013, p. 21). Moreover, "their practices of big numbers [made it possible to] capture and appropriate spaces of power in society [where they could] semireproduce their counterpower" (Bayat, 2013, p. 21). Hence, the chief dynamic driving their everyday resistance was their subordination and marginalization. In response, the authorities, as has been shown, implemented manifold governmentalizing measures and techniques aimed at macro and micro-managing every facet of social life—sex, education, the family, dress, and much else besides. The net effect was to both alienate and antagonize these groups, thereby pushing them to the breaking point.

In the post-revolutionary period, women, youth and university graduates ranked consistently among the most economically marginalized groups in Iranian society. According to the state-sponsored Statistical Centre of Iran (SCI), while the overall rate of unemployment in 2014 was 10.9%, that for those under 30 was 27.8%, or 2.5 times greater than the overall rate (Mehr News, 2015). No less astonishing was the unemployment rate for women that between 2003 and 2013 doubled, leaving 830,000 jobless (Ilna News, 2015). At its peak in 2014 mass unemployment stood at a staggering 28% (Mehr News, 2015; Ilna News, 2015; Farda News, 2016). In 2017 the SCI reported an estimated 17.8 million "educated women to be inactive economically" (Melliun, 2017, para. 1). Moreover, according to an SCI report published in 2013, the unemployment rate for women under 30 stood at a staggering 85.9%, with nearly 48% holding a post-secondary degree—and this despite government policy initiatives aimed at opening up the professions and other occupational areas to women (Farda News, 2016). In 2014 an estimated 42% of university graduates, the majority of whom held a Bachelor's degree, were without work. The same report indicates that of the nearly 1.5 million graduates with a Master's degree or a degree in medicine, 40% were unemployed (Farda News, 2016). As grim as these figures are, the reality was even worse, for according to the SCI to be classified as employed required that one need work only one hour per week (Ramezanzadeh, 2015).

For an explanation of the very high unemployment levels, especially among marginalized groups, including women, students and youth, one need look no farther than the government policies discussed above. While aimed at enhancing the nation's military and political strength, these had the effect, it bears repeating, of fuelling a baby boom that in the new millennium outstripped the economy's ability to provide employment for the young. To the latter explanation must be added escalating economic sanctions imposed on Iran by the West, beginning in January 2012, targeting the key energy and financial sectors, most importantly the oil industry. Their express purpose was to rein in Tehran's uranium enrichment programme believed to be close to developing a nuclear capability. The sanctions had a crippling effect on the whole economy. It is estimated that oil exports, the country's chief source of income, declined from an average 8.2 million barrels per day in July 2011 to under 1 million by July 2012 (Bultan News, 2014), forcing Tehran, according to Hassan Hakimian, "a) [to] find new customers, b) offer discounts to maintain customers, and c) enter into barter arrangements or conduct transactions in ... [foreign] currencies, like [the] rupee [,] which reduce[d] the range of imports" (2012, para. 10). These efforts, however, did little to stem the tide of mounting unemployment, especially among youth, women and university graduates, or lower the rate of inflation (Ramezanzadeh, 2015). And though the sanctions were finally lifted in January 2016, the Iranian economy would require years to recover.

Denied the right to lobby or petition government, conduct anti-government demonstrations, or exercise freedom of expression, the women's, student and youth movements adopted everyday life practices as a way to resist the rules and codes of conduct. Through micro-level actions, they succeeded, as will be shown, in "enforce[ing] [their] collective sensibilities on the state" (Bayat, 2007, p. 203), making their presence felt, in an incremental fashion, on the social and political scene, with each micro victory over the regulatory apparatus inciting further demands for change.

In response to official indifference to mass unemployment, these marginalized and disaffected movements adopted strategies grounded in everyday life practices with a view to bettering the economic lot of their members. To take but one example, as early as 2001, Jamileh Sadeghi and Marzieh Khatoon Shari'ati, a former taxicab company owner and a former driving instructor, respectively, began pressuring the authorities to permit women to enter an occupation formerly the exclusive preserve of men: that of taxicab drivers (The Guardian, 2007; Shafaf News, 2014; Tavaana, 2016). As this sector was largely unregulated—for example, neither government licences nor visual means of identifying cabs was required—women seeking entry had only to press their private cars into service as taxis. Driven by the spectre of unemployment without end, coupled with their exclusion from certain occupations, many women flouted the state ban on female taxicab drivers—so many that the authorities had no choice but to acquiesce, albeit on one condition: that female cabbies cater only to women. And even though gender discrimination within this industry was not entirely eliminated, the patriarchal order was delivered a stinging rebuke.

Women were quick to exploit this new employment opportunity. In Tehran alone approximately 700 were working as taxicab drivers by 2008, serving 60,000 to 70,000 female passengers annually (The Guardian, 2007; Asr Iran, 2008). And though subject to some new regulations—the requirement for standardized identification for their vehicles being the most important—female cabbies were for the most part free to choose their workdays and schedule working hours (The Guardian, 2007; Asr Iran, 2008; Ebtekar News, 2008). They would soon be joined, moreover, by youth, students and even college/university graduates, lured by the prospect of earning annual incomes that could "[exceed] $12, 000 [US] a year, almost twice Iran's average annual household income" (Time Magazine, 2008, para. 4). Thus did some women succeed in "turn[ing] gender segregation on its head," in the process carving out, as Roksana Bahramitash points out, "an independent lifestyle" that transgressed gender norms through everyday life practices (cited in Time Magazine, 2008, para. 5).

Everyday life practices were also a means of undermining, and in some cases even appropriating, various disciplinary domains. For example, in spite of the officially-mandated gender segregation in public spaces, the purpose of which was to discourage the sexes from fraternizing, the disaffected and marginalized of all ages and backgrounds persisted in attending daily exercises held in the public parks of urban centres (My Stealthy Freedom, 2017). Much to the vexation of the authorities, the so-called exercises invariably degenerated into singing, dancing, and playing various sports, all to the accompaniment of music. Ironically, videos of the crowds obviously enjoying themselves began flooding the social media in February of 2017, the anniversary month of the 1979 revolution (My Stealthy Freedom, 2017).

The appropriation of disciplinary spaces by movements of counterconduct did not stop here, however. For example, for the first few years following the revolution, religious services, so numerous and pervasive as to be almost part and parcel of everyday life, were used to disseminate official rhetoric. These gradually lost their efficacy as propaganda outlets, however, owing primarily to the activities of the counterconduct movements in attendance. To explain why the latter were so keen to attend these convocations, one must look, not to any efforts on the part of the Islamic Republic to attract them, but rather to the paucity of opportunities afforded by the authorities to gather and socialize. It was only a matter of time before certain subcultures within these movements appropriated these disciplinary domains with a view to reaffirming and strengthening their bonds.

One occasion for this kind of appropriation was provided by the rituals of *muharram*, commonly referred to as Hussein Parties (Bayat, 2013; Yaghmaian, 2002). Though they always retained an important religious function, these rituals had to share centre stage with something best described as part fashion show, part dating site, replete with boys attired in tight jeans and sporting slicked-back hair and heavily made-up girls wearing revealing *mantos*, which were a kind of long overcoat. The now-common protocol is for the two groups to eye one another, then mingle; soon telephone numbers are exchanged and dates arranged, in effect appropriating *muharram* for a purpose very different than the original.

In more recent years, these movement of counterconduct began appropriating non-Islamic events that did not appear in the Islamic Republic's official calendar, among them International Women's Day, World Student Day, and Valentine's Day (Amir-Ebrahimi, 2006; Yaghmaian, 2002; Mehrkhane, 2014), the purpose being to express their solidarity and commitment to bringing about fundamental social and political change. Commemorating non-Islamic holidays has become, in effect, a manifestation of worldly aspirations and, by implication, a demonstration of discontent—a way to challenge officially sanctioned religious holidays and the moral and political authority of which they are an expression.

It was often the case that activities and rituals that were integral to affirming solidarity within movements of counterconduct unfolded spontaneously within university dormitories, city streets and alleyways, private homes, indeed, wherever the opportunity afforded—often the very spatial sites the authorities were so eager to governmentalize. News of upcoming events is disseminated by word of mouth or flyers (Safshekan, 2015). Again, their diffusion, combined with their enormous popularity and impromptu character, leave the authorities with little choice but to tolerate their existence.

Violating the official dress code presents another example of how everyday forms of resistance on the part of movements of counterconduct worked to bring about change. During the first decade of the revolution, public space was a site of uniformity and conformity, wherein the dress code was strictly observed: women often wore the black *chador* and little to no makeup, men, for the most part, long-sleeve, plain-cloth shirts and loose-fitting trousers. Both sexes scrupulously avoided clothing that could be construed as non-conformist (Amir-Ebrahimi, 2006; Rafizadeh, 2011). While its real purpose lay, as mentioned above, in facilitating the detection of abnormalities and subversive acts, the dress code was justified on the grounds of preserving Islamic virtues, such as righteousness, obedience, and modesty.

In the aftermath of the Iraq–Iran war this situation changed, however. Partly as a result of gaining access to proscribed television programming—the requisite equipment for receiving satellite signals had become available owing to the efforts of smugglers—a large portion of Iranian households now had an alternative to state media. According to official figures, 38% of the population could, by 2014, access satellite television programing, 70% by 2016 (ISNA News, 2016). Members of movements of counterconduct figured large in these audience segments: 46% of satellite users were youth between 18 and 29 and 47% held college or university degrees (Eghtesad Iran Online, 2014); there was, too, a marked preference among these two movements for foreign programming, focusing on youth, students and women vis-à-vis the fare offered up by the IRIB, which was heavily weighted with religio-political propaganda (Asr Khabar, 2015).

Moreover, despite the illegality of satellite receivers and concerted efforts by the authorities to collect them, their number soared, transforming smuggling operations and black-market activities into thriving, albeit underground, businesses (Matin, 2014). Viewing proscribed television programming would for many Iranians become woven into the fabric of everyday life, compelling the authorities to all but abandon efforts to control and/or regulate it (Alef News, 2012). Consequently, in July 2016 Ali Jannati, Iran's Minister of Culture and Islamic Guidance, declared that "the law that prohibits the use of satellite television must change," given that "while its use is currently illegal, the majority of the population elect to use it" (ISNA News, 2016, para. 5).

Exposure to uncensored satellite television programming contributed to instilling in women, students and youth a new fashion consciousness, one that inspired a movement aimed at Iranianizing fashion, something that required paying lip service to the dress code while at the same time adopting the bold colors and innovative designs, influenced to some degree by Western tastes. This entailed challenging the official dress code on an everyday basis. Increasingly, within some social strata the traditional *chador* gave way to the far more revealing *mantous* and the *hijab* shrank to reveal an abundance of hair; the loose-fitting trousers and shirts, once *de rigueur* for men, was in some city quarters eclipsed by tight, form-fitting shirts, t-shirts and jeans—much to the dismay of the authorities. And a virtual flood of innovative designs and bold colours overthrew the hegemony of traditional loose-fitting and monochromatic, clothing so enamoured of conservative elements. Thus, in "adopting new styles of dress [and] coiffure [as a mode of] self-representation in public space" (Amir-Ebrahimi, 2008, p. 98), the fashion-conscious succeeded brilliantly in trying the patience of the authorities.

In the 1990s and early 2000s, the security forces, backed by the conservative establishment, responded to what can only be described as mass civil disobedience by directing the *basij,* the morality police, and the even more notorious *ansars*, to harass and/or arrest dress code violators in large numbers (Dolate Bahar, 2014; Satrs News, 2014; Akhbar Rooz, 2015; Golkar, 2015). This crackdown on the fashion-conscious proved difficult to sustain, however, due to the sheer number of dissidents—the majority being women, students and youth who by then constituted the bulk of the population.

For the authorities, the worst-case scenario unfolded when those arrested refused to board the vehicles that were to transport them to detention centres, thereby attracting large crowds that only added to the mayhem in the very public spaces that Tehran was so determined to control (BBC News, 2008; Shafaf News, 2015). The unenviable choice before the Islamic Republic lay in arresting large numbers of dress-code violators daily, ignoring the violations altogether or relaxing the code's more stringent provisions. The first would disrupt "the normal flow of life" (Bayat, 2013, p. 13), the second and third undermine Tehran's authority and lead to demands for further reform.

Mohammad Khatami's 1997 landslide election victory, made possible in large part by the support of women, students and youth, signalled the coming of social and political reforms aimed at, among other things, abrogating or moderating a host of reactionary policies. However, and as will be seen in the next chapter, while these reforms were indeed significant, they served only to create an appetite for further change. Thus, the dress code continued to be assailed (Iran Eslami News, 2015) and public spaces transformed, as the drab, uniformly clothed crowds gradually gave way to fashionistas (Amir-Ebrahimi, 2006).

In challenging what the conservative establishment held to be religiously sanctioned norms and standards for governing behaviour in the public domain, movements of counterconduct succeeded in "contest[ing] many fundamental aspects of ... state prerogatives, including the ... control of public space" (Bayat, 2013, p. 80). This meant that for youth, women, and students, all that had formerly signified modesty and obedience in the context of the public sphere—the *hijab*, abstinence from make-up, the plain cloth shirt, closely cropped hair—was now turned on its head; moreover, this was especially the case in the modern quarters of cities and on university campuses. Here, in particular, the forbidden now appeared in plain sight: men with hair slicked down with jell, wearing skin-tight jeans and designer t-shirts; women attired in skimpy *mantous*, headscarves exposing a rich abundance of hair, eyes highlighted, brows artfully uplifted and lips painted (Webshad, 2013). For many, all this and more was now *de rigueur*.[7] What mattered here was not so much the absolute numbers involved in defying the dress code but what this signified, namely the rejection of the state-sanctioned conduct of conduct.

These disparate acts of micro-resistance, played out in the streets, on university campuses, on playing fields, wherever people gather, would take on a momentum of their own, leading to further acts of defiance. This was especially true of resistance centred upon the *hijab*, which constitutes for the Islamic Republic, so Janet Afary (2009) asserts, the chief symbol of patriarchal hegemony. Ziba Mir-Hosseini goes even further, declaring it to be nothing less than a "cornerstone" of governmental rule (2002, p. 42), and for this reason, as Haideh Moghisi argues, a focal point for "... women's defiance and resistance" (2004, p. 225).

That this kind of resistance would for women become an imperative has little, if anything, to do with any lack of religiosity; rather, the whole point lay in resisting and defying governmental rule. The two ought not to be confused. Indeed, many within these movements of counterconduct, including those with international reputations, among them Jamileh Sadeghi and Fakhr Al Saadaat Mohtashamipour, were devout Muslims. What they opposed was its legalistic, i.e., mandatory, status. Here lies the answer to a question posed by Haideh Moghisi (2011, p. 8): "Why is it ... that after [decades] of imposing mandatory veiling on Iranian women, ceaseless resistance against the Islamic veil has continued?" Clearly, for many female members of movements of counterconduct, the *hijab* had become a signifier, not of anti-religiosity, but of resistance to hegemonic rule.

In solidarity with the women's movement, Masih Alinejad, a dissident residing in the United States, launched, in 2014, My Stealthy Freedom, an online campaign intended to publicize the plight of Iranian women who had made a life-long commitment to defying the *hijab* rule. With a Facebook following that surpassed the one million mark in July 2016, it would prove one of the most popular online campaigns in the history of the Internet in Iran (Iran Wire, 2016). Its huge audience ratings testify to the willingness of ordinary Iranians to embrace the Internet and its oppositional programming despite the tight regulatory controls in place. This would require the use of software, such as Hotspot, Freegate, and Puffin, to counteract efforts on the part of the authorities to filter social media—in and of itself an act of empowerment (Rezaei, 2015).

The My Stealthy Freedom website features thousands of photographs of *hijabless* women, some adherents of the traditional black *chador*, intent on expressing solidarity with their non-conformist sisters. In encouraging women to submit video clips of some everyday oppositional activity in which they took part, such as appearing *hijabless* in public in the presence of men who were non-family members, it sought to challenge the normalizing notion that only through the *hijab* could women feel safe in public spaces and that the *hijabless* woman represents a moral threat to men, for which retaliation would be a rational response.

Since launching the campaign, Alinejad has broadened its scope with a view to encouraging oppositional youth and students to engage in subversive acts, in the process bringing pressure to bear on the authorities to relax some of the rules and regulations that subordinate women. In 2015, for example, when the captain of Iran's Futsal team, Niloofar Ardalan, was denied her husband's permission to travel to the World Cup competition in Guatemala, My Stealthy Freedom solicited Iranian men to submit photographs of themselves, each of which was to include a written statement denouncing the discriminatory law requiring a woman to obtain her husband's consent to travel abroad (BBC News, 2015; Iran Wire, 2015b).

Interestingly, just as this campaign was gathering momentum in Iran, President Hassan Rouhani, then on a diplomatic trip to Paris, was questioned by journalist David Pujadas of France 2, a French public television channel, about the Stealthy Freedom Facebook page and the restrictions placed on Iranian women (Independent News, 2015). To underscore the latter, Pujadas produced a photograph of a *hijabless* woman downloaded from the page. Shortly after concluding his trip, President Rouhani directly intervened to grant Ardalan permission to join her teammates in Guatemala, without the consent of her husband (Gibbs, 2015).

Micro-victories of this kind encouraged more women to engage in everyday subversive acts, including gender cross-dressing (Iran Wire, 2016b). In January 2016, following the appearance of a series of photographs of *hijabless* women posted on social media and several online applications and websites, including Instagram and My Stealthy Freedom, *Fars News*, the Islamic Republic's semi-official news agency, reported what it viewed to be a new and disturbing trend, namely that "[women in ever growing numbers] were employing a new tactic to circumvent the *hijab* regulation" (Fars News, 2016, para. 1). These malefactors had discovered that shaving their heads and dressing in male attire would allow them to move about

94 *Ordinary Iranians and everyday resistance*

freely in public spaces, despite the presence of morality police units, often on the alert for *hijabless* women.

The cross-dressing, head-shaving dissidents were of two minds as to the purpose of these practices. For some, it was a matter of freedom of choice: "the authorities wish to impose on us," declared one "malefactor," "the mandatory *hijab*, but I and many others wish to show them that this practice must be a matter of [individual] choice" (Iran Wire, 2016b, para. 13). For others, the aim was to sow subversion, "[to] challenge and undermine a rule imposed on [them]" (Iran Wire, 2016b, para. 5). Whatever the intent, the authorities could only view such acts as a threat to the status quo, especially as their frequency grew. Again, they were confronted with an all-too-familiar dilemma: accept the occupation of public spaces by *hijabless* women and have their authority compromised or crackdown on the dissenters and disrupt the flow of urban life across the entire country.

That the authorities were reluctant to risk the latter only incentivised women to engage in even bolder acts of everyday subversion. As early as June 2017, those that had elected to flout the *hijab* rule took it upon themselves to resist both the *basij* vigilantes and the morality police, in addition to those ordinary Iranians bent on enforcing the Qur'anic commandment of *amr-e be maroof and nahy-e az monkar,* or "commanding the right and forbidding the wrong" (Golkar, 2015, p. 76), which provided a rationale for enforcing the compulsory *hijab* rule in public spaces. This religious injunction, which the state appropriated to normalize its disciplinary project, has since been turned on its head, judging by the sheer number of videos featuring *hijabless* women that appear daily on the My Stealthy Freedom page.

One video-clip, for example, depicts a woman defying a female vigilante who demands she adjust her *hijab*. She responds by declaring, "[m]y camera is [my] weapon," then informs her that a "peaceful movement against the compulsory *hijab*" has emerged, and consequently "I have no fear of you" (My Stealthy Freedom, 2017a). Another shows a man demanding of a rule-violator that she "[p]ut [her] veil on, otherwise [he would] slap [her]," to which she replies, "I will not; this is none of your business," all the while video-recording the event until the would-be assailant leaves the scene (My Stealthy Freedom, 2017b). Yet another video-clip chronicles a father and *hijabless* daughter being confronted by a man who orders her to "put [on her] veil" (My Stealthy Freedom, 2017c). When the father protests and asks that he leave, the norm/rule-disseminator complies. The webmaster tagged this video-clip upload with the following comment: "[t]his is how we should stop the morality police or individuals interfering in our personal choices" (My Stealthy Freedom, 2017c). Still another captures a clerical vigilante ordering a rule-violator to "put on your scarf, you lascivious and perverse woman," to which she replies, "repeat your earlier remarks, if you have guts," all the while recording the proceedings on a cell phone. Her assailant abruptly departs the scene (Stealthy Freedom, 2017d). Another video-clip features yet another woman being harassed for not observing the *hijab* rule: "if you were my daughter," her assailant threatens, "I would … kill[] you for not wearing the *hijab*," to which the rule-violator replies, "What is this vocabulary? Why d[o] you … look at me [as] if my *hijabless* appearance … makes you uncomfortable? If you have a problem with my appearance, simply walk away" (Stealthy Freedom, 2017e). When a curious crowd gathers, the man complies. So ubiquitous were such everyday acts of resistance and negation on the part of women that, on December 27, 2017, Tehran's chief of police, Hussein Rahimi, announced that those who refuse to observe the full *hijab* rule would no longer be "arrested and/or criminalized" but rather conveyed to special disciplinary centers where they would undergo "re-education" (Mehr News, 2017; Tejaratemrooz.ir, 2017).

This new development represents a categorical defeat for the hardliners, who, despite decades of implementing disciplinary and normalizing measures directed against women, have failed to enforce the *hijab* rule. Through everyday life practices, ordinary people involved in movements of counterconduct have brought to bear a counterpower sufficient to compel the authorities to back down. This example drawn from the everyday life experiences of women bent on resisting power, along with the many others documented here, make a mockery of the Tehran's disciplinary rules and normalizing practices aimed at perpetuating its hallmark conduct of conduct.

What the above examples reveal is that movements of counterconduct, however disparate, use similar practices, in conjunction with everyday micro-techniques, to challenge the rules, codes and regulations underwriting governmentalizing systems, and in so doing sometimes succeed in reconfiguring power relationships between themselves and the state, in the process undermining the latter's moral and political authority. These various forms of resistance are, as Stellan Vinthagen & Anna Johansson (2013) remind us, "conditioned by the [modes and technologies] of power that [in turn] determine ... what to resist" (p. 27). In other words, what renders them politically transformative is the context within which they unfolded, in this case a semi-authoritarian setting that had, among other things, governmentalized, and by implication politicized, joy, the presentation of the body in public, and university life, among much else besides, with a view to perpetuating the status quo. Put differently, it is abundantly evident that the "... state [had] made activities taken for granted in [other] polities both political and risky" (Meyer, 2001, p. 168).

It is by means of the very ordinary and everyday practices catalogued above, moreover, that these movements of counterconduct have over the years asserted themselves on the social scene, resisting and subverting the Islamic Republic's rule. By tirelessly renewing their commitment to solidarity on behalf of a common cause, in addition to exploiting their enormous numbers, they have succeeded in presenting an existential alternative to the status quo, in the process normalizing and legitimizing acts otherwise deemed unnatural, taboo or illegitimate.

It is these ordinary practices that have had the "consequential effect on norms and rules ... of many people simultaneously doing similar, though contentious, things" (Bayat, 2013, p. 21), in combination with a set of everyday techniques—altering the character of public spaces, transforming personal appearance and re-ordering state-sanctioned rituals through repetitive and prolonged practices rooted in everyday life—that have worked to challenge and negate the Republic's mode of Islamist governmentality. Here is an everyday form of resistance that aims to effect "a subtle ... transgression" of the rules, codes and regulations that underwrite the status quo (Amir-Ebrahimi, 2008, p. 94); one that entails a slow, creative, meticulous, and above all persistent "encroachment of the ordinar[ies]" (Bayat, 2013, p. 15), which in its various micro-forms has succeeded in challenging and disrupting technologies of power.

These everyday resistances, directed at challenging and disrupting power relations, are enabled by what may be called an everyday solidarity conditioned and made possible by the Islamic Republic's rule of conduct and made manifest by a people's engagement with the politics of everyday life. Grounded in the minute practices of everyday life, this everyday solidarity binds a people together by virtue of their being ruled within the same governmental domain, and by implication by the rules, codes and norms that define that space. It is very much an expression of sympathy existing within and among the disparate post-revolutionary movements of counterconduct, one that enables mutual support and generates counterpower through ordinary life practices. It is also a condition of possibility in that it provides a basis for challenging norms, rules and regulations in diverse domains of public space. In either case, everyday solidarity may and can open up possibility for resistance of all kinds. As will be shown in the following chapters, it can even provide among disparate marginalized, subordinated and dispossessed movements of counterconduct the requisite social cohesion and political convergence to coalesce into a united front.

In the Iranian context, everyday solidarity plays out in domains as diverse as streets, transit stations, parks, social media, and even households, to name but a few. It achieves concrete expression in everyday life when scores of ordinary Iranians rush to rescue those about to be arrested by the morality police for violating some governmentalizing regulation or other; when taxi/bus drivers and/or their passengers air personal grievances against the authorities; when those awaiting the services of a doctor, barber, or government clerk seek clarification on some point or other concerning the latest government rulings; when crowds gather in public squares in the evening hours to debate and/or criticize Islamic Republic policies; or when, as occurred on the Stealthy Freedom Campaign website, thousands of men call upon the authorities to rescind discriminatory laws against women.

Conclusion

This chapter demonstrated how, through everyday and seemingly mundane life practices, ordinary Iranians would succeed in challenging the status quo in a setting that is less than auspicious. The technologies, rationalities and modes of power employed by the state can doubtless create docile bodies, in the process marginalizing, subordinating and controlling disparate social groups. But at the same time and paradoxically, they can produce resisting bodies willing and prepared to contest power.

As has been shown, the techniques and tactics of conduct and control used by the Islamic Republic were, for the most part, geographically specific, and thus were the tactics of resistance used to counter them. Creative, meticulous and repetitive, these resistances, moreover, were a mere reflection of technologies of power, a condition of possibility in relation to those modes of power, which in turn galvanized the resistant bodies in the ways of how and what to resist.

As has also been shown, Iranian society was simultaneously governmentalized, politicized and, by implication, biopoliticized and disciplined, by a radical politicized faction of the clergy and their adherents, who claimed to rule by divine right. However, upon questioning the latter claim, and denaturalizing it through investigating its mode of governance, which amounts to no more than an artificial assemblage of disparate techniques, arts, and rationalities, developed during the course of the pre/post-revolutionary period, we can discern that, far from constituting the vanguard of some divine plan, Islamist governmentality was, and remains, in every sense an artificial construct and thus very much of this world, a conduct of conduct that, in large measure, sought to monopolize power in the service of an agenda that was, for the most part, profane.

The state's programme of rationalization and governmentalization of every facet of Iranian life worked to politicize mundane and everyday life practices—music, sport, fashion, education, to name but a few. This is precisely why everyday forms of resistance to the codes and regulations aimed at bringing about the new order became inherently political acts with political implications and outcomes, leading over time to significant social change. Apprehending the equivalence of such forms of resistance and political acts is crucial for understanding the processes by which resistance unfolds and plays out in a given society; it also provides the general background and perspective required to understand the particular localities, social and political specificities, and geographical particularities that shape movements of counterconduct as they develop and emerge.

Notes

1 Note, however, that this same law "provide[d] that if the other survivors of the husband refuse to pay the wife the price of the real property, then the wife can acquire the real property itself" (The Library of Congress, 2009, para. 1).
2 This point requires clarification. Responsibility for supervising the morality policy lies with the head of Iran's police force, officially the Law Enforcement Force of the Islamic Republic of Iran (NAJA), who is appointed by the Supreme Leader. NAJA itself, however, is supervised and directed by the Ministry of the Interior whose head is appointed by the President. This dual chain of command is the cause of an ongoing conflict in which the Ministry of the Interior, and the President himself for that matter, are at a marked disadvantage.
3 The WFSCC is a government body tasked with, according to its official website, "develop(ing) and propos(ing) policies ... [aimed at] generat[ing] a favourable environment [in which] to promote the growth of the personality of women and to expedite the recovery of human values and nobility, [and] to provide women[] [with] multilateral rights" (WFSCC, 2017).
4 *Zolal-e ahkam*, which translates literally to limpid rulings, refers to the sacred nature of *Shari'a* rulings.
5 There appears to be no official statement on the part of the authorities regarding the precise date (beyond the month of October) of the initial acid attack.
6 This does not necessarily disqualify these movements from participating in full-fledged demonstrations or other forms of radical collective action. They might do so, for example, when the latter "enjoy a reasonable [degree of] legitimacy" (Bayat, 2013, p. 40). What is important to note here, and this point will be reiterated in the chapters to follow, is that there exists no universal criteria for determining under what conditions these smaller movements of counterconduct might elect to engage in full-fledged forms of protestation.
7 Despite tight controls on importing cosmetics, in 2013 Iran ranked seventh globally in the consumption of these products, most of which were smuggled into the country via Western and Southern borders of Iran (Samimi, 2013). That same year, *Jahan News*, a news agency affiliated with the conservative faction in Iran, reported that while a Middle East woman spent on average $36 (US) on make-up annually, the dollar figure for her Iranian counterpart was almost three times higher, i.e., $150 (Jahan News, 2013b). This is yet another example of how Iranians chose to repudiate a governmental agenda aimed at reordering post-revolutionary society.

4 Social mobilization and political contestation in Iran at the turn of the millennium

The 1999 student movement and the 2006 women's one million signature campaign

Introduction

Using a Foucauldian perspective grounded in the twin concepts of governmentality and counterconduct, this chapter examines the two outstanding cases of social mobilization and political contestation in Iran at the turn of the millennium: the 1999 student movement and the 2006 Women's One Million Signature Campaign. An enquiry of this kind is warranted on three interrelated grounds. First, it serves to elucidate how in a semi-authoritarian setting such as Iran social mobilization and political contestation driven by grassroots protest movements develop and are sustained and how new subjectivities are constructed. Second, it shows how, on the one hand, in these kinds of contexts, certain practices, techniques and tactics of resistance are developed, and, on the other, how solidarities are forged among oppositional elements in a semi-authoritarian setting. Lastly, it sheds light on the precise ways in which policies implemented by semi-authoritarian states, along with the overweening use of power in enforcing them, can create the conditions of possibility for political contestation and/or social mobilization—what Foucault refers to as episodes/movements of counterconduct—directed at promoting radical political and social reform.

Drawing on Foucault's work, in particular his analysis of governmentality, understood as the rationalities and mentalities, knowledges and techniques, and programme and tactics, that sustain certain technologies and modes of power, I show that social mobilization and political contestation are not only manifest forms of resistance to governmental regimes and "to processes of governmentality" (Death, 2010, p. 239); they are also historical and localized struggles against a specific way of being governed, which ultimately means that power and resistance, "government and dissent [,] are mutually constitutive" (Death, 2010, p. 240).

According to this Foucauldian formula, the acting subject engaged in collective oppositional action has a constitutive nature as well, one "ineluctably bound up with the historically and [politically] specific [governmental] disciplines through which … [it] is formed" (Mahmood, 2005, p. 29). In other words, the existence of an acting subject raises the possibility of the emergence of a certain kind of person, one "formed within the limits of a historically specific set of formative practices and moral injunctions" and certain discourses, i.e., dominant and oppositional, competing to construct the world (Mahmood, 2005, p. 28).

For the Foucauldian active subject, moreover, public spaces are crucial as loci for conducting "all forms of communal life" (Foucault, cited in Crampton & Elden, 2007, p. 45), and this is especially the case where social and political reform is likely to be blocked, or at least impeded, by factions possessing a monopoly over power; where open political channels simply do not exist; and/or where oppositional groups are denied political rights, chief among them the right to lobby and petition government and the right of freedom of expression, particularly where challenging government policy is concerned. It is under circumstances like these that such subjects may appropriate alternative spaces, most often of a public kind, to voice their demands, thus transforming them into spaces of resistance and defiance. In this way public spaces are an essential element of all relations and exercises of power.

To understand how public spaces become domains of resistance and defiance for acting subjects, moreover, one need look no farther than the historical context in which the subjects themselves are constituted. Of particular importance for Foucault (1978) in this respect are the respective roles played by dominant discourses and counterdiscourses in constituting them, hence his interest in historical context or what he refers to as the conditions of possibility informing its development. While certain rationalities, mentalities and knowledges of governing are articulated within a dominant discourse(s) where they work to inform disciplinary institutions and construct the subject in a particular way, they can also be countered by an opposing or counterdiscourse(s) that calls into question their legitimacy as well as the way they constitute the world, leading in some cases, as Foucault (1978) reminds us, to massive social ruptures and deep-seated political divisions between the conductors and the conducted. To this end, as Britta Baumgarten and Peter Ullrich assert, "[g]overnmentality studies are especially helpful in investigating the relation between discourse/societal practices and the formation of subjects and thus the very conditions for the possibility of protest" (2012, p. 17).

Following Foucault's lead, then, I focus, first of all, on the dominant discourse that emerged in the aftermath of Ayatollah Khomeini's death in 1989. By way of being promoted by the state, in particular that part of the state apparatus with a monopoly over certain technologies of power, the new dominant discourse informed Tehran's Islamist governmentality, in addition to giving rise to certain policies and disciplinary techniques, in the process profoundly impacting the lives and the day-to-day conduct of Iranians, in this case students, youth and women. Next, I delineate how the emergence of this dominant discourse provided the conditions of possibility for the creation of a counterdiscourse that questioned, and by questioning undermined, not only its legitimacy but also its particular way of constituting the world.

In examining these kinds of political operations, I address three key questions: At what point, under what conditions and in response to what kinds of social and political issues did these discourses come into existence? How did they enable the specific policies and practices adopted by Tehran's Islamist mode of governmentality? And, finally, how did the latter contribute to creating the conditions of possibility for massive resistance of a radical bent. The first step in addressing these questions requires investigating the relationship among various processes of governmentality—the operation of specific technologies of power, the production of discourses, and the formation of subjects—with a view to providing a road map with which to examine the very conditions for the possibility of protest, including particular modes of resistance, such as political contestation, social activism/mobilization and solidarity building.

Governmentality, discourse, and the politics of contestation

As noted earlier, Foucault defines the term "governmentality" as the "encounter between the technologies of domination of others and those of the self" (1997, p. 225) or "the way[s] in which the conduct of individuals or groups might be directed" (1982, p. 790). This conduct of conducts embodies various articulations and exercises of technologies of power that are in turn underwritten by certain mentalities and rationalities that when combined constitute governance (Foucault, 1982; Walters, 2015; McCall, 2015), defined as a set of "techniques and knowledges that underpin attempts to govern the conduct of [people] in diverse settings" (Walters, 2012, p. 38).

Given the intimate relation between power and resistance that Foucault takes such pains to foreground in his famous maxim "where there is power, there is resistance" (1978, p. 95), it follows that, for him, technologies of power, and by implication their application to the processes of governance, paradoxically incite resistance on the part of those who elect to "refuse forms of governmentality" (McCall, 2004, p. 8). Such refusals have the potential to morph into various forms of collective action, or, in Foucauldian terms, episodes/movements of counterconduct. This is most likely when certain configurations of power, and by implication the knowledges and rationalities that sustain them and the governmental policies and social practices they implement, become so intolerable as to leave political contestation and/or social mobilization of various kinds the only remaining avenues for expressing discontent (Walters, 2015; McCall, 2015). Moreover, as Foucault reminds us, under circumstances of such historical singularity a people may undergo a process of (collective) self-transformation, and by implication societal transformation, by recreating themselves as defying/resisting subjects, for better or for worse. In such circumstances, unexpected alliances may be formed, citizenship claims made, and subjectivities enabled.

Germane to these transformative processes are the ways in which, according to Carl Death (2015), such cases of collective action emulate the interrelationship between power, marginalization and subordination, on one hand, and counter-power, resistance and defiance on the other. This means that episodes/movements of counterconduct that emerge in a semi-authoritarian setting are a consequence of, or are conditioned by, the transformation of public spaces by acting subjects engaged in the politics of everyday life. By engaging in such politics, acting subjects work to transform public spaces into domains of subversion, negation and defiance of the conduct of conduct. In this way, protest, contestation and various forms/arts of resistance are nothing short of "concrete practices, techniques, and technologies" (Death, 2010, p. 241) that work to undermine efforts by state authorities to harmonize subjects or bodies within a particular domain of conduct. This is because for Foucault (2003), power and discipline are "used to ensure the spatial distribution of individual bodies (their separation, alignment, serialization and surveillance) and the organization, around those individuals, [in order to produce, rationalize, and naturalize] a whole field of visibility" (p. 241).

Movements/episodes of counterconduct, however, represent something more than the contestation of public spaces or collective action on the part of those "wanting to be conducted differently" (Death, 2010, p. 240). They are also discursive practices given they are engaged at the level of discourse where worldviews compete for legitimacy. Conceived as such, Christian Bröer and Willem Duyvendak (2009, p. 339) argue, such movements manifest "the struggle for dominance implicit in the rendering of certain ideas, expressions ... and aspirations" as invariably true, normal, scientific, and legitimate.

It is in this context that an understanding of the role discourse plays as an element of power can shed light on the emergence and development of radical forms of resistance, in this case movements of counterconduct. As a "collection of statements" and/or texts and signs, discourses are constructed "by the designation of a common object of analysis" and "by particular ways of articulating knowledge about that object of analysis" (Foucault, cited in Bartilet, 2016, para. 5). However, beyond this, Foucault notes,

> [o]f course, discourses are composed of signs [texts, languages, and/or statements]; but what they do is more than use these signs to designate things. It is this more that renders them irreducible to language (langue) and to speech. It is this 'more' that we must reveal and describe.
>
> (1972, p. 49)

Even the most cursory survey of Foucault's work reveals that discourse aims at either promoting or contesting some forms of power/knowledge. He makes this point clear elsewhere, opining that "the longer I continue, the more it seems to me that the formation of discourses ... need[s] to be analyzed ... in terms of tactics and strategies of power" (Foucault, 1980, p. 77). Conceived as such, discourses, according to Margaret McLaren, can be seen to exist at "the conjunction of power and knowledge" (2002, p. 90).

Discourses, moreover, entail particular ways of speaking and writing, such as buzzwords, that can be extended beyond language games to the milieu of wider social practices and can also demarcate "the boundaries of what can be thought of and communicated at a given time in a given society" (Baumgarten & Ullrich, 2012, p. 2). They also "determine[] ... certain type[s] of political life and practice[s]" while "actualiz[ing] certain possibilities and omit[ing] others" by, among other things, informing consciousness and/or serving to advance a political agenda (Bashiriyeh, 2001, p. 1). The point to be grasped here is that discourses are "the means of transmitting [certain] ideas and sets of beliefs" within the context of a given society (Holliday, 2011, p. 12).

For Foucault, moreover, a discourse can become dominant by, for example, being promoted by the state or part of the state apparatus commanding a monopoly over certain technologies of power, in the process working to sustain, legitimize and/or produce certain knowledges regarding, practices and power relations that serve to reproduce the social and political status quo (Walters, 2015).

For the French luminary, any dominant discourse can or may be opposed by a competing discourse(s), known as a counter, reverse, or resisting discourse(s), contesting its supremacy and legitimacy, in addition to questioning its particular way of constituting the world. In this way, one may speculate that, for Foucault, both discourses and counterdiscourses constitute the will to power:

> [D]iscourse can be both an instrument and an effect of power, but also a hindrance... a point of resistance and a starting point for an opposing strategy. Discourse transmits and produces power; it reinforces it, but also undermines it and exposes it, renders it fragile and makes it possible to thwart it.
> (1978, pp. 100–101)

It is clear that for Foucault, a counterdiscourse(s), which is in and of itself a product of opposition, arises out of material and historically specific conditions and emerges, not in isolation, but in relation to a historically specific dominant discourse. While discourses can limit the possibilities with respect to what can be said, written or thought, they can also be enabling in the sense of inspiring and precipitating counter strategies/resistances, both in the realm of ideas and the social policies and political practices they inform. In other words, discourses are the "means for different forces to advance their interests and projects, while also providing points of resistance for counter-strategies to develop" (Howarth, 2000, p. 49).

The question that arises at this point has to do with how discourses are germane to investigating oppositional social movements and the contentious politics to which they give rise. The answer may be found in Foucault's analysis of the French revolution, in which he "seeks to derive [an understanding of the phenomenon] ... from the operation of ... specific technolog[ies] of power" (Baker, 1994, p. 191) by focusing on how discourses shape disciplinary institutions and create the subject who then engages in collective, revolutionary action (Foucault, 1978, 2000, 2005). The revolution can be placed "in the context of a heterogeneity of discourses overlapping and/or competing in their constitution of [the] world" (Baker, 1994, p. 193).

For Foucault, analysing competing discourses provides a lens through which to peer "into the functioning of bodies and knowledge in their specific situated context" (Powers, 2007, p. 18). Only then, he believes, is it possible to explicate how power constructs and/or renders the individual body in a productive way—as a resisting body and/or acting subject engaged in concerted oppositional action. After all, it is more often than not the case that "political life and [social] practices are articulated within dominant political discourses" (Bashiriyeh, 2001, para. 1)—and precisely because the latter have the ability to "contribute to sustaining existing power relations" (Fairclough, 2001, p. 64). Put another way, it is the dominant discourse(s) that, sustained by certain rationalities and particular knowledges promotes, inspires and/or evokes a certain type of political life and types of societal practices.

In this schema, collective action of an oppositional kind would most likely erupt when certain policies and practices, typically those of some government faction(s) commanding a monopoly over power, work to the detriment of a people. Herein lies, for Foucault, that sublime oppositional moment when for the subjugated masses, life can no longer sustain itself, that moment of singularity when a people engage in collective political contestation and social negation, leading in some instances to social mobilization and/or political contestation against the status quo. The point to be made here is that every case of counter-conduct "designates the myriad forms of resistance to state power," and thereby a localized case of resistance against particular technologies of power and conduct (McCall, 2014, p. 7). Such a struggle can manifest itself in forms of oppositional action as mild as civil disobedience or as tumultuous as a revolution (McCall, 2013; McCall, 2017).

In the following section, I map out the history of, and conditions of possibility for, the emergence and development of both a dominant and counterdiscourse in the aftermath of the Ayatollah Khomeini's death in 1988, examining, in particular, how the two discourses shaped a battle of ideas that drew in all manner of disparate social groups and parties determined to have a say in how the lives of Iranians would be conducted. In particular, it will be shown how the dominant discourse informed government policies formulated by the conservative establishment—policies that dominated the political process, in addition to directing the all-important state security/disciplinary apparatus whose efficacy in subordinating, marginalizing and silencing oppositional groups will be examined later. It was the policies of this governmentalized faction that would provoke a grassroots backlash, culminating in the 1999 Student Movement and the 2006 Women's One Million Signature Campaign.

The death of the Ayatollah Khomeini: The emergence of two antithetical discourses, one absolutist the other reformist

According to William Walters, "[t]he analysis of governmentality builds outwards from localities ... it starts with events, encounters, and government in particular places, under particular circumstances" (2012, p. 6). In the context of post-revolutionary Iran, the death of the Ayatollah Khomeini, founder of the Islamic Republic, Supreme Jurist, and the country's most charismatic figure, represents just such an event. Always remaining above factional politics and political rivalries, Khomeini "provided the new Islamic Republic with a semblance of unity in both direction and ideology" throughout much of the 1980s (Povey, 2016, p. 73). His immense power and stature were underwritten by three forms of legitimacy: a charismatic legitimacy forged while leading the revolution; a tradition-based legitimacy as the *marj'a-e taqlid*, the source of emulation, for Shi'ites the highest position to which a cleric can rise; and a legal legitimacy invested in him by the constitution (Abdi, 2001). Notwithstanding the importance of these three forms of legitimacy, it was the principle of *vilayat-e faqih*, the Rule/Guardianship of the Supreme Jurist, that conferred upon him a stature in Iranian politics that was unparalleled. Indeed, in the aftermath of his passing, it was this very principle that would play a dominant role in shaping the emerging political landscape of the country.

Three months earlier, in March 1989, Khomeini had dismissed his designated successor, the Ayatollah Hussein-Ali Montazeri (also a *marj'a*), on account of his opposition to the mass execution of political prisoners in the late 1980s. With no heir apparent waiting in the wings, the Supreme Leader appointed a Constitutional Reform Council numbering twenty-five members, with a mandate to amend the post-revolutionary constitution with a view to broadening the pool of available candidates (Abrahamian, 1993).

The Council dispensed with the original requirement that the head of Islamic Republic had to be a prominent *faqih* who was also officially recognized as source of emulation. And so it came to pass that before the year had ended, the Council would draw up and push through the *Majlis* constitutional amendment decreeing that the Supreme Leader could be a seminary-trained cleric, provided he possessed the appropriate qualifications, such as ""honesty," "piety," "courage," and "administrative abilities," and was sufficiently well "versed in the political issues of the age" (Abrahamian, 2008, p. 182). What had transpired was nothing short of a politically- motivated manoeuvre that propelled Ali Khamenei, a mere middle-ranking cleric, to the Islamic Republic's highest office, that of the Supreme *faqih*.

The coming of an absolutist discourse in the post-Khomeini era

As the new Supreme *faqih*, Khamenei confronted a number of obstacles. For one thing, he possessed none of the charisma of his predecessor, which, along with clerical credentials that while solid enough could hardly be said to be impressive, made him a far less prepossessing leader than his predecessor. Beyond this, as Ali Banuazizi (1999, p. 3) notes, the status afforded the Supreme *faqih* amounted to little more than "a *de jure* recognition of the unusual stature of the Ayatollah Khomeini," which like charisma was not easily transferable to the new leader. Thus handicapped, Khamenei became "dependent on his conservative peers," some of whom by this time were, or would soon be, occupying powerful government positions (Mahdavi, 2011, p. 96). This set the stage for the emergence of a politicized section of the clergy that would, in the immediate aftermath of Khomeini's death, dominate the political scene through "a system of collective rule by clerical assemblies or councils" (Amir Arjomand, 2005, p. 506). This faction of clerics and their supporters would soon constitute the far right of the political spectrum, occupying key positions, especially in the judicial and legislative branches of government as well as the Islamic Republic's supervisory bodies, all with the backing of the new Supreme Leader. In this way Ervand Abrahamian (2008, p. 182) christened the Islamic Republic of the post-1990s as "the regime of ayatollahs."

Of crucial importance, these developments gave rise to an absolutist discourse that would legitimize and sustain the authority of the new Supreme *faqih* and his clerical supporters. Under the cloak of that authority, a profound political transformation took place: a "clerical oligarchy [that] replaced the revolutionary charismatic legitimacy with an absolutist version of the *vilayat-e faqih* ... suggesting a complete and full obedience to the *faqih*, or 'melting into the *vilayat*' (*zob-e dar vilayat*)" (Mahdavi, 2011, p. 96).

At the heart of this absolutist discourse lay a seemingly religio-political view of the Islamic Republic as "a holy phenomenon where sovereignty and leadership belong ultimately to God, who relegates [the] ... powers [associated with each] to the *faqih*" (Mahdavi Kani, cited in Moslem, 2002, p. 100). Evoking the principle of the divine right to rule had the dual effect of authenticating this discourse while legitimizing the position of the Supreme *faqih* as the central pillar of the Islamist governmentality.

While clerics within the conservative establishment and their adherents may have differed as to the precise nature of the relationship between the Supreme Jurist and society, none doubted that absolute obedience was owed this most august of figures, and by virtue of the principle of the divine right to rule—in effect, the country's head of state governed on the basis of the authority invested in him by God. It follows that the "leadership had no [secular] responsibility to the people, being accountable only to God—a God, moreover, whose meaning in practical terms was defined by the state" (Abdi, 2001, para. 3). The state, however, have a religious duty, which was "to lead and guide the people towards heaven, preventing them from becoming God's lost children" (Abdi, 2001, para. 3). Divinely ordained, the Supreme Leader was both in theory and practice above the law; indeed, it was his duty and that of the state to create new laws or interpret existing ones in accordance with whatever was deemed to be the will of God.

It follows that in this divine right scheme of governance the wishes of the leader amount to nothing less than commands that all true believers are duty-bound to obey. It further follows that no individual or group has a right to "engage[] in politicking (*siasat bazi*) [; rather] all are [required to] perform[] their religious duties," or *taklifs*, a celebrated buzzword that features prominently in the absolutist discourse of the time (Badamchian, cited in Moslem, 2002, p. 103). Moreover, the "utility, role, and function of the will of the people [as delineated] in the constitution and [manifested in] the *Majles* appear superfluous" (Moslem, 2002, p. 103). Accordingly, Ali Akbar Parvaresh opines, while in many governmental systems "people seek to ensure the sovereignty of the nation ... in an Islamic [polity] they seek ... [to] implement[] [the] sovereignty of divine laws, because ... they believe that the nation's sovereignty can only be achieved under the beacon of [the] sovereignty of Islam" (cited in Moslem, 2002, p. 104).

In this absolute governmentalizing framework, moreover, the Supreme *faqih* steers the ship of state, assisted by "a 'second stratum' of lay civil servants in control of the administration" (Amir Arjomand, 2009. p. 120). However, and again according to this absolutist framework, it is the Supreme Leader, along with the governmentalized clerics he appoints, that actually govern, exercising power in the service of a single all-encompassing cause: the reproduction of a "[religio]-moral system that [has] answers to all human problems" (Bayat, 2007, p. 54). "The clergy," asserts the Ayatollah Mahdavi Kani, "must not only guide the nation but be directly involved in ruling, because ... it is entrusted with the task of ensuring that the [system] is at all times Islamic" (cited on Moslem, 2002, p. 101).

For its part, the citizenry is required to relegate "all of its rights to the *faqih* [as] the embodiment of the state" (Moslem, 2002, p. 103). This leaves little, if any scope for self-determination; indeed, as Badamchian notes, "in the government of God, sisters and brothers do not fight, and in the case of disagreements they will submit to the will of the *faqih,* hence God" (cited in Moslem, 2002, p. 103).

In this schema, religion functions as a totalizing project, a mono-politicized calculus for governing life and a framework for regulating the general as well as the day-to-day conduct of individuals. The success of this project is contingent upon *dini kardan-e jameeh*, or "making society religious" (Holliday, 2011, p. 117). For Ayatollah Khamenei (1994, para. 7), "religious society" or what he termed *jame-eye armani-e islami* (literally an Idealistic Islamic Society) are interchangeable, each having precisely the same governing principles drawn from "a reading of Islam ... as a complete social, political, economic, and moral system" (Bayat, 2007, p. 54)—in other words, a utopia (Khamenei, 2015). Moreover, it is only by means of what Ayatollah Javadi Amoli and other clerical sympathizers call *hokumat-e islami*, or "Islamist government"—yet another buzzword celebrated in the absolutist discourse—that such a society can be brought into existence (Hawzah News, 2010). It bears repeating that the latter embodies a kind of divine societal utopianism formulated by a clerical establishment on the basis of an exclusivist reading of Islamist law (Khamenei, 2000).

As will be shown in the following section, in the aftermath of the Iran–Iraq War (1980–1988), the absolutist discourse would inform the conservative position, in addition to promoting a strategic alliance among conservatives, the newly-elected President Hashemi Rafsanjani, and the various disciplinary power regimes and institutional mechanisms of the Islamic Republic, thus profoundly shaping the day-to-day lives of Iranians during the first half of the 1990s.

Reformism as counterdiscourse: Roots, ideas, and genesis

In the late 1980s, just as the conservative right was consolidating its political power base with the blessing of the new Supreme Leader, a new politico-religious movement was emerging. With the conclusion of the Iran–Iraq War in 1988 and the death of the Ayatollah Khomeini the following year, a circle of religious intellectuals, or *roshanfekran-e dini*, initiated a series of discussions and debates regarding the character and future of Islamist governmentality as a mode of governance (Dabashi, 2006; Nabavi, 2012).

This movement was driven by two interrelated factors. First, the eight-year-long conflict had taken a very heavy toll on the country's resources, infrastructure and manpower, virtually crippling the state. During the war the Islamic Republic had sought "to avoid any polarization or fragmentation within the polity, and [toward this end had] exercised a high degree of control over the society" (Fadaee, 2012, p. 76). However, in the aftermath of the war, this policy no longer proved effective, in large measure owing to the growing dissatisfaction on the part of ordinary Iranians who during the course of the conflict had been politically marginalized and dispossessed of much of their wealth, and who now were yearning for change (Afshari, 2015). Second, the death of the Ayatollah Khomeini and the ensuing succession crisis, combined with a constitutional amendment bestowing upon the new leader the title and authority of an absolute ruler or the *faqih,* had alarmed many, especially those within religious-intellectual circles, who saw these developments as a threat to the ideals of the revolution. In their view the revolution had ultimately triumphed due to the collective will of a people to replace an autocracy with a rule-bound and more inclusive polity (Ansari, 2006).

It is in this context that there emerged a debate within religio-political circles focusing on the aims and ideals of the 1979 revolution—liberty, freedom and the promise of a better life—and the failure to realize them in the post-Khomeini era. At the same time, the conservative establishment's totalizing reading of Islam as an instrument for legitimizing and exercising power was cause for alarm within these circles as well as a spur to advocating on behalf of "new approaches" to politics and religion (Fadaee, 2012, p. 76). Out of this intellectual ferment a new discourse emerged that advanced an alternative to the conservative establishment's reading of Islam and its absolutist Islamist governmentality as a mono-governmentalized project capable of addressing all of society's needs and ills.

Among the numerous critiques informing the new discourse, perhaps the best known and most incisive were penned by Abdol Karim Soroush, a former member of the Commission for Cultural Revolution, established by Khomeini in 1983, and Mohammad Mojtahed Shabestari, a cleric and member of the first *Majlis* and contemporaneously a professor of philosophy and theology at Tehran University.

Labelled by some a "pioneer of ... Islamic modernism" (Fadaee, 2012, p. 80) and chief source of inspiration for the future President Mohamad "Khatami's [reformist] ideas [centering on] democracy and rule of law" (Holliday, 2011, p. 101), Souroush (1994) argued that Islam as a religion should be differentiated from those charged with interpreting it and that much of what had been handed down through the generations and come to be regarded as core religious beliefs was in fact little more than human interpretation and hence subject to human error. This was as much an application of critical hermeneutic philosophy to Shi'ite theology as it was a critique from within Muslim intellectual circles. It aimed at reforming the political status quo and in particular undermining the whole notion of a state authoritarianism rooted in a religio-governmentalizing and monolithic dogma (Ansari, 2006).

Soroush had been published in various journals, including the prestigious monthly *Kiyan*, which in October 1991 featured his critique of government and religious institutions that took aim at the conservative interpretation of Islamic theology and the state interpretation of the Rule/Guardianship of the Jurist as a divine/absolute figure (Povey, 2016). It is noteworthy that for him and other Islamic-intellectual reformers, the primary task of re-affirming the pluralistic and inclusive legacy of Islamic philosophy and law was coupled with the need to "establish[] political reforms which would allow ... [that legacy] to be realised in Iranian society" (Povey, 2016, p. 79).

To this end, Souroush (1994) argued for a democratic reading of religion that rested on three pillars: rationality, pluralism and human rights. While acknowledging "there are perennial unchanging religious truths," he also held that "our understanding of them depended on our knowledge in the fields of science and philosophy" (Fadaee,

2012, p. 80). The implication here is clear: religion assumed to be divinely revealed cannot be equated with exegeses regardless of how valid in terms of sociological and historical knowledge (Souroush, 1994; Ghamari-Tabrizi, 2004).

In the same vein, Mohammad Mojtahed Shabestari argued that a totalizing view of religion and rigid enforcement of religious dogma is at best insufficient for "organizing a modern society" (Fadaee, 2012, p. 80), adding that a state based on a "traditional reading" of religion is undemocratic and "violates [basic] ... human rights" (Yaghmaian, 2002, p. 221). In *Hermeneutics: The Book and Tradition,* published in 1996, he formulated a critical theory aimed at rethinking Islam's place in the contemporary world. In his view modern Islam must eschew all claims to being monolithic, all-encompassing and omniscient. In "the society of the faithful," he declares, "there are no red lines to demarcate the limits of critique" (cited in Povey, 2016, p. 81), nor does "Islam ... recognize[] []or recommend[] any single form of polity" (cited in Vahdat, 2004, p. 217). Herein lies a rebuttal of the absolutist discourse and its view of Islam and the Supreme *faqih*.

The religious intellectuals were soon joined by another group of Muslim thinkers and activists who subscribed to the so-called neo-Shariati line of thinking.[1] The latter, including Ehsan Shariati, Hassan Yousefi-Eshkevari, Reza Alijani, Narges Mohammadi, and Ahmad Zeidabadi, advanced a view of governance that "reject[ed] the concept of an Islamic state and advocate[d] [instead] a secular, or *urfi*, democracy" (Mahdavi, p. 105). This position rested on the assumption that the state ought to be "a neutral secular entity ... neutral to all religions and ideologies" (Mahdavi, 2011, p. 105). In this schema, the legitimacy of the state, rather than resting on divinely ordained values, would be predicated on reason and the collective will of the people.

Equally important was a significant role played by an array of so-called non-religious intellectuals, many of whom, such as Mohammad Jaa'far Pouyandeh, Mohammad Mokhtari, Dariush Forouhar, Shirin Ebadi, Mehrangiz Kar, were writers and activists. The latter provided a liberal critique of the religio-political order amounting to a clarion call for freedom of the press, freedom of information, and separation of church and state (Kar, 2006; Ebadi, 2006). Clearly, the aim here was to offer an alternative to the state's religio-governmentalizing agenda, one that would allow political reform to move forward.

This diverse group of dissidents were soon joined by those who in the 1980s had been branded Islamic leftists, so-called because of their Third Worldist and anti-imperialist views, advocacy of big government, and emphasis on developing the economy, and particularly domestic industries. During this period they had held key government positions and "had ... been strong supporters of [the] *vilayat-e faqih* during the lifetime of Ayatollah Khomeini" (Povey, 2016, p. 80). And though sharing a common critique of the absolutist rule, the leftists, whose ranks included Abbas Abdi, Mostafa Tajzadeh, Mohsen Mirdamadi, Saeid Hajjarian, Mohammad Mousavi Khoeiniha, Mohammad Khatami, Mehdi Karoubi, Masoumeh Ebtekar, to name but a few, came from diverse backgrounds and were by no means undivided in their views. Some like Abdi, numbered among the student leaders at the time of the revolution, others such as Mousavi Khoeiniha, Khatami and Karoubi were clerics, yet others, for example, Hajjarian, a former deputy minister of intelligence, had held key government positions during the decade following the revolution. However, by the early 1990s, and with the accession of Khamenei to the position of Supreme Leader, this faction had been largely relegated to the margins of political life.

More precisely, they were purged by Khamenei and his supporters within the conservative establishment, joined in what Ghoncheh Tazmini (2009, p. 41) describes as a "tactical alliance" with the newly elected President Akbar Hashemi Rafsanjani (1958–2017). As the first president of the post-Khomeini era, the latter was determined to "create a strong executive that would allow him to reshape Iran" (Povey, 2016, p. 74). Most were dismissed from their positions and/or disqualified by the powerful Guardian Council from seeking political office, given they were perceived by Khamenei and Rafsanjani to pose a threat to the political establishment (Moslem, 2002; Povey, 2016).

Pushed to the margins of political life, and at the same time appalled by the social ills of the post-war era, many leftists, "despite their commitment to Islam and the 1979 revolution" (Abdi, 2001, para. 6), began to rethink their political views. As Abbas Abdi (2001) argues, they embarked on "a scientific analysis of all that had happened since the revolution" (para. 28). Some chose to pursue or complete university educations, most often in the social sciences; others went to work in the print media, using whatever opportunities available to criticize the political status quo. Chief among all that united this disparate band of dissenters was their opposition to the "use of the language of Islam to bypass popular sovereignty," particularly with respect to designating and legitimizing an extra-legal role for the Supreme *faqih* (Povey, 2016, p. 80). In proposing an alternative, they made the case for reforms to all three branches of government based on "democratic principles and the rule of law" (Mir-Hosseini, 2002, p. 100). As a result, the Islamic leftists re-invented themselves and re-emerge on the political scene as reformists, armed with a reformist discourse.

At the heart of the reformist discourse lied an admixture of "republican ideas and religious ethics, with religious democracy as its political mission" (Bayat, 2007, p. 49). Its underlying assumption was that religious democracy could accommodate religious ethics not only in theory, but also in practice. This required rejecting the view of Islam as a totalizing project, in favour of making it democratic as a governmentalizing system (Bayat, 2007). This could be achieved by both rationalizing and democratizing key religio-political institutions, thus making them accountable to a democratically elected *Majlis,* and by creating a democratically-inspired governmentalized version of Islam, or a religio-democratized Islam, an inclusive Islam wherein citizens could be self-determining agents whose needs and aspirations were formally recognized and addressed as a chief priority for the state's project of conduct of conduct.

The reformist discourse was, moreover, predicated on the view that "[n]o single person [and/or institution, including the Supreme Leader and his office] can be the ultimate arbiter of right and wrong, justice and cruelty" (Abdi, 2001, para. 7). It follows that "the duty of the state is not to guide people but to implement their demands" (Abdi, 2001, para. 7), which in turn allows for their "maximum participation [in the political life of the country] ... [while incurring the] minimum cost in terms of social conflict and repression" (Abdi, 2001, para. 8).

Clearly, what lent this discourse legitimacy was not the principle of divine right to rule espoused by the absolutist clerics, but rather the people's will.

With a view to advancing a democratic agenda, and influenced by all those disparate religious and non-religious intellectuals who earlier had critiqued the political status quo, the reformists began articulating, in the early 1990s, the concept of *tawse'ehye siyasi* (literally political development), developed by Saeid Hajjarian, a figure viewed by many to be the theoretician of the 1997 reform movement (Nabavi, 2012). Political development was seen as a precondition for what they called *islahat*, meaning reforms—a buzzword within the reformist discourse—aimed at building and securing *mardumsalari islami*,[2] or Islamic democracy. At the heart of this homegrown democracy, in most respects antithetical to the conservative establishment's exclusivist vision of Islamist government, or *hokoumat-e islami*, laid the principles of "freedom, equality, and … [individual] rights" (Abtahi, cited in Holliday, 2011, p. 115). Of these, the last was of singular importance, for only by guaranteeing them, it was believed, could the people "[exercise] civil and political [agency]" (Abtahi, cited in Holliday, 2011, p. 115). It was for this reason that the term *haqq*, meaning right, became so prominent a reformist discourse buzzword, one often pitted against the absolutist notion of religious duty. Moreover, the defence and institutionalization of individual rights, along with the principles of freedom and equality, or so it was envisioned, was to be one of the "central duties of the state" (Armin, cited in Nabavi, 2012, p. 46). Only then could *mardumsalari* triumph.

The term civil society, perhaps the most celebrated of all reformist discourse buzzwords, was used as a "kind of euphemism for a democratic system of governance" (Mir-Hosseini, 2002, p. 99) and means of sorts for bringing about a "more balanced relationship between the rulers and the ruled" (Kamrava, 2008, p. 141). In this capacity it served as a counterweight to the establishment's concept of a "religious society," or what the Ayatollah Khamenei (1994) termed an "idealistic Islamic society," a utopia informed by an exclusivist understanding of Islamic precepts, and by implication Islamist governmentality, and hence a reductionist view of the people as duty-bound subjects.

In sum, reformism as a discourse and reform as a religio-democratized governmental project, constituted a reaction to a flawed vision of society, one that featured the instrumentalization of religion, the downgrading of republication institutions, vast social inequality, corruption, violence and the enforcement of unjust laws. Reformism was rooted, moreover, in the belief that "political change was necessary, but that there were no quick fixes" (Nabavi, 2012, p. 44). Whether its component strands emphasized, respectively, pluralism, civil society, human rights, respect for the rule of law, gradualism, or non-violence, there was never any question that "any attempt to bring about change must come from within" the existing framework/system of governance, that is, Islamist governmentality (Abdi, 2001, para. 8).

Islamist governmentality negated: Reformism as a religio-democratized governmental project

It was the afternoon of May 23, 1997, and my hometown of Shiraz lay under a thick blanket of clouds I was winding my way through familiar streets and alleyways, returning home from a nearby bakery where each day I bought bread. On this day, however, I sensed something was different; the crowds were unusually dense and the atmosphere electrified, as when the national soccer team won a crucial match, sending thousands, sometimes hundreds of thousands, of celebrants, pouring into the streets. Euphoria gripped the crowds: drivers sounded horns, young people danced on the sidewalks, motorcyclists cruised the back alleys, their passengers waving Iranian flags. Mohammad Khatami had just been elected the fifth president of the Islamic Republic.

Christened the epic of May 23, that day will forever live as a watershed event of the post-revolutionary period. What lent it special significance was that a full 70% of the thirty-million-strong Iranian electorate voted for Khatami and the reformist agenda (Abrahamian, 2008). Elucidating the factors responsible for so massive a renunciation of the political status quo requires investigating certain macro and micro social trends unfolding prior to 1997.

Iranian society prior to presidential election of 1997

By the mid-1990s Iran was undergoing a major demographic shift, accompanied by a growing sense of disillusionment with the social, economic and political direction the country was headed, attributable in large measure to policies introduced during the Iran–Iraq war (1980–1988). These included, to take but one example, the biopolitical Family Plan, introduced in 1980, the consequences of which came to fruition at this time. Intended to, among other things, boost the manpower reserves of the country and create a post-revolutionary generation committed to defending the revolution, this policy, though terminated immediately following the war in 1988, was to have unintended results. On the one hand, by 1996, 60% of the country's population of some 60 million was under the age of 24 as planned; on the other, this demographic was comprised mainly of women, youth, students and the unemployed or underemployed who found themselves relegated to the margins of social life—hence the sense of disillusionment among so many (Tazmini, 2009).

A second factor fuelling discontent among this demographic and the populace in general had to do with a set of policies aimed at reconstructing the country following the disastrous war with Iraq. Post-war reconstruction began with the election of the late Akbar Hashemi Rafsanjani to the presidency in 1989, raising hopes that social development and economic prosperity would follow. A strong advocate of privatization and trade liberalization, Rafsanjani vowed to halt public sector growth, which had spiralled out of control during the war (Karbassian, 2000). To this end, the new "administration drew up a five-year economic development plan" (1989–1993), which included a programme of structural adjustment aimed at promoting privatization and removing or reducing subsidies, tariffs and price controls (Niakooee & Ejazee, 2014, p. 193). Under its auspices, fiscal discipline was tightened, the economy deregulated, consumer subsidies cut, private foreign investment encouraged, budgetary control exerted over parastatal public foundations, and unprofitable state-owned enterprises privatized (Karbassian, 2000).

The five-year economic development plan was financed by tapping state revenues derived from oil exports and by borrowing heavily abroad as well as from the Central Bank and domestic banking sector. The result was "[m]assive state budgetary deficits ... financed by large-scale Central Bank loans and commercial bank credit" (Karbassian, 2000, p. 636). This in turn "caused inflation to ... increase" to 24% per year on average well through the mid-1990s, soaring to 50% in 1996 (Karbassian, 2000, p. 636). Hardest hit were women, students and young workers, for whom the cost of living outpaced incomes by a considerable margin, causing real hardship and fomenting further discontent and disillusionment.

An additional factor further alienated this demographic: rapid urbanization. By the mid-1990s, the baby boomers, conceived during the heyday of the biopolitical Family Plan introduced in 1980, were leaving the countryside and pouring into the cities seeking employment and educational opportunities, in the process swelling urban populations. According to Safar Ghaedrahmati and Mohammad Reza Rezaei (2012), whereas in 1976 the county could boast only one city with a population exceeding one million, by 1996 the number had risen to five. During the same twenty-year period, the number of cities grew from 373 to 614 and the percentage of the urban population from 47% to 61.3%, the majority of which consisted of the young and educated of both sexes (Mashayekhi, 2011). Tehran simply had no social or economic policies in place with which to address this crisis. Many rural migrants were left to fend for themselves in increasingly overcrowded cities lacking employment opportunities and essential services.

By the mid-1990s, the combination of economic stagnation and population growth had sent unemployment rates soaring as high as 30%, with students, women and young urban workers, many of them rural migrants, hit the hardest (Bayatrizi, 2007). Many eked out a living in the informal economy, the majority by resorting to street vending. The thoroughfares of the major urban centres resounded with the cries of hawkers selling everything from balloons, plastic sandals, socks and hand-made bath sponges to chewing gum, Cheetos, grilled corn, samosa, and the fava beans and turnips so beloved by Iranians. For young rural migrants, conditions were particularly harsh given that they lacked social support networks as well as familiarity with urban environments. As a consequence, many crowded into urban slums that flourished on the outskirts of major cities (Afshari, 2015; Bayat, 1997). These masses of the poor and marginalized soon swelled the ranks of various movements of counterconduct.

It was in the gloomy economic climate of the post-war period that women emerged as a social collectivity, albeit one with little in the way of organizational structure or leadership. The wartime experience of providing frontline troops with logistical and other forms of support, and increasing state-sponsored participation in social and religious activities, heretofore the almost exclusive preserve of men, inculcated in women a new sense of purpose and social agency as well as discontent with their traditional roles of homemaking and childrearing (Afshari, 2015; Peyghambarzadeh, 2015).

This new consciousness expressed itself most dramatically in the enormous numbers of women entering universities and colleges. By 1996 women represented an estimated 70% of university freshmen, despite little prospect of employment upon graduation given the dismal state of the economy (Bayat,

2007). The resulting huge and ever-expanding pool of unemployed or underemployed women, many educated, represented a daunting challenge for any political party or presidential candidate seeking election in 1997.

The same social, political and economic pressures transforming the consciousness of women were also being felt on university and college campuses. Though lacking the kind of formal organizational structure and coherent ideology of the student revolutionaries of 1979, those of the post-war period were just as eager to reassert themselves on the social and political scene after a long period of political dormancy following Cultural Revolution of the 1980s. What they lacked in revolutionary zeal, they more than made up for in numbers—an estimated 1.2 million in all institutions of higher education in 1996 (Mashayekhi, 2011). Clearly, here was a force to be reckoned with. Moreover, the high inflation rate and the prospect of future unemployment added a note of desperation to a cause upon which they were willing to stake all.

In the post-war period the country's youth joined the women and students in challenging the social and political status quo, in the process, "creat[ing] one of the most remarkable youth movements in the Muslim world" (Bayat, 2007, p. 190). Having lost friends and family members during the war and now having to bear the social and economic consequences, many youth elected to "move away from the culture of self-sacrifice that had informed the first decade and a half of the Islamic Republic in favour of a worldly attitude to material life" (Bayatrizi, 2007, p. 27). Moreover, with wartime restrictions lifted, foreign-made products, ranging from Japanese and Korean electronics to European clothing, were once again available, as was foreign television programming that could be received by means of the satellite dishes that were becoming a common sight in residential neighbourhoods. All this combined to create among youth a keen appetite for fashion scorn for "official religious dogma," which "symbolized and crystallized everything that they thought was wrong with their circumstances" (Bayatrizi, 2007, p. 27).

A stagnant economy and high unemployment, combined with official prohibitions on public dating and drinking, strict enforcement of the dress code and patriarchal legal codes, and the ban on distributing Western pop music "contributed to a deep scepticism" regarding the establishment's religio-governmentalized agenda (Bayatrizi, 2007, p. 27). However, notwithstanding these strictures, and despite the "[h]ardliners repeated calls] for vigilantes to take to the streets to fight ... anti-Islamic sentiments," the country's youth succeeded in establishing a culture of worldly joy by employing disparate and fragmented, at times clandestine, means, along with everyday life practices, in the process creating a counter-culture of everyday defiance (Bayat, 2007, p. 62).

The two cultures soon merged. It was not, for example, uncommon to see young men taunting the authorities by appearing in public spaces wearing tight leather jeans and jackets and trendy T-shirts and listening to music, particularly foreign pop music. At wedding receptions or private parties, break dancing was all the rage, and Michael Jackson's moon dancing had no shortage of devotees.[3] And exchanging or selling illegal cassette or video tapes or playing cards—the made-in-America Kem brand was especially popular—often as a desperate measure to earn income, was as widespread among youth as it was irksome to the conservatives, who saw it as corrupting influence.

For girls during the period, joy combined with defiance in everyday life practices such as the wearing of fashionable, brightly coloured clothing—in particular, the multicoloured *mantous* that replaced the full-length black *chadors*—and the use of cosmetics (Amir-Ebrahimi, 2006)—all officially proscribed on pain of "clerical indoctrination and resocialization"—measures that most violators succeeded in resisting (Mahdavi, 2011, p. 96).

In dramatic fashion these practices unshackled from the yoke of patriarchy heretofore "exclusionary, masculine, harsh, segregating" and uniformly monochrome (Bayat, 2007, p. 55). What emerged at this time was a female subculture, whose members were young and in headlong pursuit of worldly pleasure, of which the chief signifiers were fashionable clothing and heavily made-up countenances. In sum, regardless of how onerous the restrictions on so many life practices and pleasures may have been in theory, in practice the country's youth, male and female, simply ignored, and sometimes even defied, them—and this was true even of those misdemeanours the government was most anxious to prosecute, among them, drinking alcohol, gambling and dating. Put another way, the brand of Islam to which they subscribed in no way prevented them from pursuing worldly joy at the expense of heavenly salvation.

The presidential campaign and subsequent victory of Mohammad Khatami

It was under the socio-economic and political conditions delineated above that the presidential campaign of 1997 was waged. Politically repressed, socially marginalized and economically deprived students, women and youth belonging to various movements of counterconduct were primed to challenge the dominant status quo, chiefly by resisting "the clerical cultural code and insisting on their social, if not political, rights" (Mahdavi, 2011, p. 96). In their view, the dominant order "had failed to create the men and women or the society" envisioned during the revolution (Mahdavi, 2011, p. 96). Now it was time to assert their interests, which they believed could be addressed by establishing a polity based on an "inclusive religion and democratic ideals" (Bayat, 2007, 59). Thus, all three groups threw in their lot with the reformists and their presidential candidate Mohammad Khatami, to which they were most closely aligned politically.

As the presidential campaign got underway, few among the establishment viewed the reformist camp and their candidate as a serious threat; indeed, Khatami was dismissed as an underdog, a "political lightweight" according to Ali Ansari (2006, p. 94). There were two reasons that so few "took seriously his prospects as a contender for the presidency" (Ansari, 2006, p. 94). First, in the outgoing administration Khatami had served as Minister of Cultural Guidance, a relatively junior office that placed him far down the pecking order vis-à-vis his principal rival, Ali Akbar Nateq-e Nouri, then speaker of the *Majlis,* one of the most powerful offices in the legislative branch. Ironically, as some have argued (Ansari, 2006), Khatami's apparent weakness proved advantageous in that it qualified him to run as a presidential candidate. This point requires elucidation. As mentioned earlier, according to the Iranian constitution, all presidential candidates had to be approved by the Guardian Council, a body consisting of six clerics and six lawyers, all either directly or indirectly selected/appointed by the Supreme Leader for the purpose of determining the eligibility of presidential candidates. In the lead-up to the 1997 presidential campaign, it had found 234 of the 230 contenders to be ineligible to run for office (Mashayekhi, 2011).

Presumed to have little chance of winning, Khatami was an ideal choice for a presidential candidate; he would also help bring out the electorate, lending the election a veneer of legitimacy, while splitting the reformist vote. With all the cards seemingly stacked in his favour, the establishment candidate Nateq-e Nouri appeared certain to triumph in the upcoming presidential election.

As the Nateq-e Nouri campaign progressed, however, it soon became apparent that within establishment circles "the inner despair" of the young, students and women had gone largely unnoticed and therefore unheeded (Bayat, 2007, p. 59). Ignoring the plight of these groups, the Nateq-e Nouri campaign focused, in large part, on defending the Islamist principles upon which the Islamic Republic, and hence Islamist governmentality, had been founded, which required, among other things, a vigorous defense of the *vilayat-e faqih*. "The main purpose of the Islamic Republic," declared Nateq-e Nouri, "is the implementation of the words of God," and by implication that of the Supreme *Faqih* (cited in Moslem, 2002, p. 100). Beyond this narrow focus, there was yet another problem. For the most part, the establishment, the late Mehdi Moslem (2002, p. 241) asserts, "sounded so righteous and so sure about ... the Nateq-e Nouri" candidature and his subsequent victory, that little effort was invested in the campaign, which consequently fell far short of what was needed in terms of both organization and ideas if it was to woo an electorate made up of diverse social strata. In sum, the very convictions that galvanized the Nateq-e Nouri camp led to complacency, and complacency failure to mount a strong campaign.

In contrast, acutely aware of the myriad social, political and economic ills plaguing Iranian society, and the degree to which they were alienating large segments of the populace, Khatami wisely tailored his agenda to mirror a reformist discourse promoting the rule of law and religious democracy, precepts that informed a religio-democratized conduct of conduct. Of crucial importance to the campaign and the future of his administration, Khatami held that economic development "must be accompanied by political development" (cited in Moslem, 2002, p. 246). Herein lay the inspiration for one of Khatami's most celebrated political projects, namely constitutionalism and, more specifically, the "protection of civil liberties guaranteed by the ... Constitution" (Ashraf & Banuazizi, 2001, p. 250), through which the rule of law, or *hokoumat-e qanun*, was to be achieved.

Rule of law, a principle pressed into service as one of Khatami's campaign slogans, informed the entire reformist agenda; it also shaped his plans to promote civil society, or, as he preferred to call it, Islamic civil society, within the future religio-democratized order. The latter, according to Khatami, differed from the status quo, or Islamist governmentality, in three respects: first, citizens had the right to control their "destiny [to manage] their affairs and [to] question [the policies of] their rule[rs]" (Khatami, cited in Ansari, 2006, p. 146); second, "rights and responsibilities [was to be] transparent, and no-one [could be] beyond the law or [be] denied his/her legal rights" (Khatami, cited in Mehran, 2010, p. 317); lastly, there existed the requisite institutional framework "for [ensuring] popular participation, especially among ... women and youth, and [guaranteeing] the right[] of the people to intervene in fundamental decisions that affect their lives" (Khatami, cited in Mehran, 2010, p. 314). In an "Islamic civil society," Khatami declared, "there should be no sign of individual [or] group despotism or even [a] dictatorship of [the] majority [or] efforts to destroy the minority" (cited in Ansari, 2006, p. 146). In this way, the republican principles enshrined in the constitution of the Islamic Republic could be reasserted.

In promoting civil society, Khatami was, in effect, proposing a programme of political reform, or a religio-democratized governmentality aimed at guaranteeing equality, individual rights and freedoms and constitutionalism, establishing the rule of law, and making government accountable to the electorate.[4] The essence of this programme was captured in two campaign slogans, "freedom in the realm of thought; rationality in the realm of dialogue; and law in the realm of action" (Khatami, cited in Mehran, 2003, p. 317) and "Iran for all Iranians" (Khatami, cited in Mehran, 2003, p. 318) that ran counter to the conservative establishment's "totalitarian mode of governance" (Mir-Hosseini, 2002, p. 99).

In voicing opposition, however, Khatami had to tread carefully. On the one hand, he often professed loyalty to the Supreme Jurist, on one occasion declaring the Rule/Guardianship of the Jurist to be "the pillar of the Islamic Republic;" on the other, he asserted repeatedly that "one of the [Islamic Republic's] missions is the institutionalization of the Islamic system based on the constitution as the foundation of our political system," indirectly criticizing those who "think they hold a monopoly on the correct reading of the [rule of the Jurist]" (cited in Moslem, 2002, p. 247). In foregrounding such a critique, Khatami was, in effect, proposing to "rationalize the office of the *vilayat-e faqih*" (Mahdavi, 2008, p. 151), thereby institutionalizing it and, by implication, making it accountable to the *Majlis*. This was an initiative intended to move "Iran one step forward in transition[ing to a] democratic [polity]" within a future religio-democratized order (Mahdavi, 2008, p. 151).

Unsurprisingly, then, Khatami appealed to a broad spectrum of students, women and youth. For one thing, acutely aware that these groups had become disaffected owing to policy failures on the part of the outgoing government, Khatami proposed that "rather than estranging them, [any future government] must involve the young in politics, economics and the affairs of the country" (cited in Moslem, 2002, p. 246). He also warned that the marginalized and oppressed might one day be driven to become dissidents, adding that "a society that resorts to force will face instability" (Khatami, cited in Moslem, 2002, p. 246). Buoyed by such pronouncements, a vast host of students, women and youth declared loyalty for Khatami in the upcoming presidential election.

A former minister of Culture and Islamic Guidance (1982–1992), Khatami was also an intellectual and writer, which, along with his social and political views, made him popular with students, who were to rank among his most loyal, enthusiastic and active supporters/campaign workers. Over the course of a hundred-day campaign that criss-crossed the country, Khatami delivered the majority of his speeches on college and university campuses, the first of which was organized by what was then the largest student group in Iran, the Office for Consolidating Unity (OCU), or *daftar-e tahkim-e vahdat*, based at Sharif University (Mashayekhi, 2011). Speaking before several thousand students, mostly youth, Khatami outlined his views on the crucial importance of both the rule of law and the institutionalization of individual rights. For students who had long been agitating for greater intellectual and political freedom, his decision "to address them first [was] a good sign, [and] his comments and philosophy seemed at one with their own" (Ansari, 2006, p. 97). In the following days leading up to the May election, thousands of students served as Khatami campaign workers. One source estimated the number working at the campaign headquarters alone at 5000 (Raad, cited in Mashayekhi, 2011).

While students were the most enthusiastic and active Khatami supporters, none were more so than the women among them, and especially the younger ones. Many worked tirelessly throughout the campaign, canvassing voters, including family members, debating with opponents, explaining the candidate's agenda to the uninformed, distributing pamphlets, and attending to the host of details that crop up in every election campaign (Afshari, 2015; Motlagh, 2012).

Perhaps the greatest contribution made by the women lay in publicizing the enormous gap between Khatami and the conservative establishment in terms of their positions on women and gender relations. On March 2, roughly midway through the campaign, *Zanan,* the leading women's progressive magazine of the day, invited Khatami and his chief conservative rival, Nateq-e Nuri, to address a series of questions on issues and concerns of interest to women. Some carried great social weight, "What do you believe to be the most significant problem facing women in our society?" Others were of a personal nature, and though often seemingly humorous, served to highlight a growing feminist consciousness, "Do you help your wife with the housework?" Khatami responded to every question in a forthright and candid fashion, often referencing the term civil society when outlining how women might attain social and legal parity in Iran (Motlagh, 2012). His responses delighted the magazine's readership who declared him to be the "only candidate who respected women" (Kian-Thiébaut, 2002, p. 56). In sharp contrast his rival, Nateq-e Nouri, declined to answer any of the interview questions, prompting the magazine's editor, Shahla Sherkat, to run an article entitled "*Zanan's* Unanswered Questions Posed Presidential Candidate Nateq-e Nouri" (Motlagh, 2012).

And so it was that on May 23, 1997, with the backing of students, women and youth, Khatami won a landslide victory. It was these marginalized social strata that were, in large part, responsible for creating what Ali Banuazizi (1999, p. 1) refers to as the "Khatami phenomenon," and for ensuring a sweeping victory, with 70% of the voters declaring for the reformist candidate. In reality, however, what happened on that May day was as much a manifestation of the will of a people longing for change as it was a "social phenomenon with profound political consequences" (Ansari, 2006, p. 109). Most importantly, a new political paradigm had emerged, one predicated on religio-political reform from within the "confines of the existing framework of the Islamic Republic" (Maloney, 2013, para. 1). This represented a reformist religio-democratized project, a bottom-up movement drawing its strength from the grassroots mobilization of a post-revolutionary generation of the marginalized and subordinated.

The real significance of Khatami's landslide victory lay in marking a seismic shift towards a more inclusive and democratic polity, one that opened up "a new sphere of public life" and paved the "way for [the] emergence of new kinds of civic activities" (Fadaee, 2012, p. 74). In particular, his intention to establish a rule-bound polity—whose corollary was a legalistic polity, with a rationalized and constitutionally-bound role for the *valiy-e faqih*—was ultimately realized due to grassroots activism on the part of a people longing for change. The aim of this political project was clear: to challenge and "undermine the institutions of power" that functioned to legitimize and enable political domination by a conservative establishment and by implication the institutionalization of Islamist governmentality (Moslem, 2002, p. 246).

Political contestation in post-1997 Iran: Reformists vs. absolutists

In the immediate aftermath of the 1997 presidential election, Iranians of all political persuasions waited with bated breath to learn whether, in light of the formidable opposition expected from conservative quarters, Mohammad Khatami would be able to deliver on his campaign promises, and if so how. Few doubted that a titanic clash pitting reformists against absolutists could be avoided. For the new administration, the primary objective lay in building a governmentalizing order, a religio-democratized order responsive to the needs and aspirations of ordinary people. It was believed by the reformists that the most effective way of pushing for social and political change, however modest and/or fundamental, lay in constitutionalism, a central theme of Khatami's campaign and presidency as well as a "key component of [his] vision of [developing and strengthening] civil society" (Nabavi, 2012, p. 46). This meant, in Khatami's own words, "institutionalising the rule of law ... promoting and consolidating the principle of accountability ... [and] empowering the people in order to achieve and ensure an ever-increasing level of their discerning participation [in all facets of government]" (cited in Tazmini, 2009, p. 64)—all prerequisites for an Islamic civil society.

Vital to the success of the administration's governmentalizing project was a free and independent press. At once the harbinger for the development of a civil society, and at the same time a signifier of the new governmentalizing order, the press could now propose alternatives and champion views unpalatable to vested interests. Most importantly, in the absence of a multi-party political system,[5] it rested with a fledgling media, and particularly the press, to disseminate the views of nongovernment actors, ranging from intellectuals to ordinary citizens.

In this regard, May 23rd ushered in a policy change that had far-reaching political consequences. Acting on the instructions of the new president, Iran's Minister of Culture and Islamic Guidance, Ata'ollah Mohajerani, removed many of the restrictions that had long handicapped the media and issued licenses to a select group of newly created newspapers, including *Jame'eh, Khordad, Rah-naw,* and *Neshat,* soon to be joined by *Toos* (Amir Arjomand, 2000; Mashayekhi, 2011). These became channels for a reformist political discourse while at the same time articulating demands on the part of the citizenry for "'pluralism,' 'law-orientedness' (*qanun-gara'i*) and 'law-abidingness' (*qanun-mandi*)" and the rights of dissidents (Amir Arjomand, 2000, p. 287).

The reformist press, joined by other media, ventured far beyond political cliché by articulating the needs and concerns of students, women and youth and by criticizing the political establishment. So unprecedented was the effort to create a free and independent press that Geneive Abdo regarded it as "the most ambitious attempt [of its kind] in the Islamic world" (2003, p. 878).

To cite but one example, *Jame'eh*, or Society, the self-described "first newspaper of the Iranian civil society" (Fadaee, 2012, p. 82), began life as a forum for open and often-heated debate among disparate social groups emboldened by the new press freedom. Responding to the public demand for change, *Jame'eh* was the first daily to lend a voice to public opinion, thus making its presence felt on the political stage for the first time. The inaugural edition featured a headline entitled "Greetings to Society," the second "[w]e hope, God willing, we will perform our duties in order to create a civil society in Iran" (Abdo, 2003, p. 880). Both remained alive in the memory of every reform-minded citizen.

Jame'eh routinely violated political taboos. Rather than featuring the supreme leader's every utterance on the front page, as was customary with the state-sponsored and conservative press, it relegated his pronouncements to the inside or even back pages (Abdo, 2003). Moreover, the front pages carried photographs of women or scenes from real life, such as restless youth congregating in city parks or male and female university students conversing with one another. In this way, *Jame'eh* opened up a new world "to a reading public thirsting for something more than official pronouncements, clerical sermons, and scripted rallies in support of the establishment's domestic and foreign policies" (Abdo, 2003, p. 881).

As a result, mid-way through the paper's initial three-month run, in early April 1998, its readership had surged to an estimated 300,000 (Jalalipour, 2003). *Jame'eh*'s brief, and as will be seen below, not uneventful, existence illustrates how at this time the press functioned as an organ for those with new ideas and chief advocate for a civil society in a land where traditionally all media and other channels of information were tightly censored or monopolized by conservative ruling elites.

During the first four months following the May 1997 election, the Ministry of Culture granted 90 licenses to print-media start-ups, twice the number issued over the course of the previous six months (Mashayekhi, 2011). Moreover, in a 12-month period, spanning part of 1998 and 1999, licenses were issued for 168 new publications—seven daily newspapers, 27 weeklies, 59 monthlies, 53 quarterlies and two annual periodicals (Fadaee, 2012). By 2000, the country boasted no less than 1,485 newspapers and periodicals (Mashayekhi, 2011). Moreover, the press could for the first time, and with a relative degree of openness, articulate the views of intellectuals, indeed those of any individual or group wishing to make their voices heard.

The easing of press censorship, along with the growing number of newspapers sprouting up, was accompanied, moreover, by a massive surge in the number of NGOs operating in disparate social, political and cultural domains—a phenomenon aided and abetted by the new government. With the blessing of Mohajerani and his deputy Ahmad Borgani, the first Assembly Guild for Writers and Journalists of the Press was established in December 1997 with a view to institutionalizing and rationalizing and protecting these most vulnerable of professions from arbitrary harassment and/or illegal encroachment on the part of the authorities (Tazmini, 2009). With government encouragement and support, the number of NGOs exploded, from no more than a dozen in 1996 to 400 by the turn of the century (Bayat, 2007).

The expansion of the press and proliferation of NGOs had the effect of suffusing Iranian society, as never before, with new and radical ideas and strange and disparate voices that found expression in myriad debates often "focus[ing] on citizenship rights" (Fadaee, 2012, p. 83). This development was the outgrowth of Khatami's policy of tolerance towards alternative/othering voices, which in his view "no longer [constituted] an act against the security of the country" (cited in Fadaee, 2012, p. 82). For reformists in general and Khatami in particular, individual rights were no mere abstractions, for what the latter envisioned was a society wherein "every human being has rights [within] a framework of law and order," which meant that their defence numbered among the "central duties of the state" (Armin, cited in Nabavi, 2012, p. 46).

In this new climate of tolerance, religious intellectuals could more freely articulate their views, and most especially their critiques of the state of governance in an Islamic society. Some were quick to make explicit the political implications of their reformist-religious hermeneutics. For example, in "Straight Paths," an essay published in 1998, Soroush made it clear that institutionalizing religious and cultural pluralism necessitated the formal acceptance of social pluralism (Amir Arjomand, 2002). Others, including Mohsen Kadivar, a junior yet prominent reformist cleric, used the press as a platform from which to disseminate a "most thoroughly detailed critique of every aspect of" Ayatollah Khomeini's concept of the Rule/Guardianship of the Islamic Jurist (Amir Arjomand, 2002, p. 728). For Kadivar, the latter was, at best, "one among many recognized Shi'i views of the state" in the tradition of Shi'i jurisprudence (Amir Arjomand, 2002, p. 728); at worst, the embodiment of an "absolutist authority reminiscent of the Monarchic rule" (Kadivar, 2011, para. 11), the very political system loathed by the revolutionaries, for whom it represented the very antithesis of the major principles of the revolution.

This new freedom of expression meant that ordinary Iranians were exposed to a different concept of governance, one dramatically at odds with the status quo that had long been promoted by state-owned and operated media, such as the Islamic Republic's television and radio station, and conservative newspapers such as *Kayhan* and *Etela'at*. Thus encouraged, some began blogging or submitting articles or letters to newspapers, magazines or journals, articulating views often highly critical of government policy (Abdo, 2003; Amir-Ebrahimi, 2008).

Moreover, several of those observing the scene recognized the role of a free press in promoting an embryonic civil society. One witness to the events unfolding described the press as, variously, "a platform for the publication of new ideas and the frontier of civil society" (Fadaee, 2012, p. 82) and as "the most active section of the newly emerged civil society" (Fadaee, 2012, p. 81), another as "the voice of a civil society in the making" (Yaghmaian, 2002, p. 4). For the reformists, the chief objective here lay in articulating the disparate voices of dissent, which, they believed, could foster a new political openness among the masses that would percolate to the uppermost echelons of Iranian society, leading eventually to a religio-democratized system of governance. Saeid Hajjarian described this master strategy for reform as one of "build[ing] up pressure at the bottom [to drive] negotiat[ions] at the top" (cited in Mahdi, 2000, para. 43).

With the press no longer muzzled, the way was open for the Khatami administration to initiate the second in a series of sweeping reforms aimed at "institutionalizing the rule of law ... [through] promoting and consolidating the principle of accountability ... [and] empowering the people in order to achieve and ensure an ever-increasing level of their discerning participation [in the political life of the country]" (Khatami, cited in Amir Arjomand, 2000, p. 286). The best way to bring this to fruition, Khatami believed, was through electing village, municipal and provincial councils, which, along with the *Majlis,* formed, as intended by the constitution, the decision-making and administrative organs of the state, entrusted with appointing mayors, supervising the activities of municipalities, and determining the social, cultural, educational, health, economic and welfare needs of constituents. Note that although these bodies were specified in article 7 of the Iranian Constitution, both in the original and amended versions, it was only in 1999 that they were elected and began to function as originally intended.

In February 1999 the President called for the election of village, city and provincial councils. In that spring, "over half a million candidates competed for seats in 35,000 village and over 900 municipal councils" (Amir Arjomand, 2005, p. 508). Some four-fifths of the popular vote, based on a 65% turnout, went to reformers and other Khatami supporters, who won a large majority in all three jurisdictions (Amir Arjomand, 2005). In terms of promoting a progressive politics, the newly elected councils signified a milestone in the process of decentralizing governmental power. Ghoncheh Tazmini (2009, p. 72) hailed this democratization of local government as one of Khatami's "most unambiguous successes," signifying "both an exercise in the development of civil society and an implementation of the rule of law" (Tazmini, 2009, p. 72)—the very foundation of the reform movement. Here was the pinnacle of reformist project in practice.

Though momentarily stunned by these developments, the establishment soon struck back, mobilizing support among conservatives and bringing into play the technologies of power wielded by the institutions—the office of Supreme Leader, the Council of Guardians, and the judiciary—that it still very much dominated. The stage was set for a mighty clash between the two governmental camps.

Perhaps nowhere was the establishment more deeply entrenched than in the judicial sphere. With the backing of the courts, it had at its disposal the means to impede, in various ways, the operations of a free press. In what Saeid Amir Arjomand (2000, p. 290) describes as "clerical judiciary activism against the press," scores of newspapers, magazines and journals were shut down. *Jame'eh* ceased operations in June 1998, only three months following its launch, after leaking a threat made by then the Commander of the Revolutionary Guard, General Rahim Safavi, to "cut the throats and tongues" of those journalists acting against the interest of the *nizam* (the system) (Navabi, 2006, para. 1). Three months later, following an ultimatum to halt press attacks directed against Islam, issued by the Supreme Leader, Ayatollah Khamenei, clerical judges revoked the licence of the reformist newspaper *Toos* and that of the weekly *Rah-e Naw* for publishing articles refuting the legitimacy and legality of the Mandate of the Jurist, first propounded by the late Grand Ayatollah Kho'i, in addition to an interview with the reformist Abdollah Nouri, whose views on this matter were equally critical (Amir Arjomand, 2000). And in October 1999, the reformist newspaper, *Neshat*, was closed down and its editor arrested for printing disrespectful material relating to "[Qu]r'anic sacred beliefs and certainties" (Amir Arjomand, 2000, p. 290).

In April 1999, "judicia[l] intervention in the politics of contestation" reached new heights with the arrest and subsequent trial of a group of reformist clerics, among them Mohsen Kadivar, who was at the time engaged in critiquing the principle of the Rule/Guardianship of the Supreme Jurist (Amir Arjomand, 2000, p. 290). He was eventually sentenced to eighteen months in prison on the order of the Special Court for Clerics (Povey, 2016). In sum, while one can argue that the period 1997–1999 witnessed the birth of a free and independent Iranian press, the degree of conservative establishment censorship, along with the persecution of reformists, including many intellectuals, suggests that these two years might be viewed, paradoxically, as a time of press carnage.

Contention between the establishment and reformists was in no way confined to intellectual and elite political circles. Acutely aware of the reformists' grassroots support, the latter called upon the *basij*, the elite paramilitary organization under the direct supervision of the Supreme Leader, to infiltrate society at all levels, the purpose being to disseminate propaganda and engage in mass ideological indoctrination (Golkar, 2015).

The objective of this strategy lay in countering efforts to build a civil society and promote grassroots participation in the political process; the means were to be an all-encompassing social project, the aim of which was to manufacture a counterfeit/replica society that reproduced the political status quo from below. Crucial to this operation was ensuring the cooperation of the *basiji* operatives whose task was to indoctrinate ordinary Iranians so as to ensure "conformity with social and political norms, and thereby maintain social order" (Golkar, 2015, p. 7). To this end, the newly created Department of Propaganda and Basij Culture played a key role, chiefly by incentivizing field operatives to recruit ordinary citizens for the establishment's programme of social and ideological indoctrination by, among other things, allocating them housing as well as providing access to welfare, job training and higher education, in addition to cultural amenities (Afshari, 2015; Golkar, 2015).

The conservatives did not stop here, however. Flouting constitutionalism and the rule of law, they seized upon extra-legal means to rule and govern with a view to "demobili[zing] the reform movement," including the use of *ansar-e hizbullah*, vigilante groups to harass and even physically assault intellectuals, along with other reformers and their supporters among ordinary Iranians (Povey, 2016, p. 83). In the years leading up to the new millennium, *ansar* operatives frequently interrupted speeches by intellectuals, most notably Soroush, prior to dispersing the crowds by whatever means necessary, including intimidation and beatings (Ansari, 2006).

The autumn of 1998 marked a new and more intensive phase of the conservative establishment's campaign to halt the reform process through extra-legal means. Whereas heretofore, it had stopped short of liquidating citizens, now anything was permissible even chain murders, the name given a series of related homicides and kidnappings, whose victims included more than eighty writers, translators, poets, political activists and even ordinary citizens. Among the most prominent were Dariush Forouhar, a leading member of the oppositional liberal-nationalist *hezb-e mellat* (Nation Party) and his wife Parvaneh Eskandari, who were brutally assassinated in their Tehran home on November 23 (Mahdi, 2000). A month later, on December 3, Mohammad Mokhtari, a writer and political activist, was found strangled to death. On December 12, the body of Mokhtari's colleague, Mohammad Ja'afar Pouyandeh, was discovered on the outskirts of Tehran. He too had been strangled.

Responsibility for the kidnappings and assassinations was traced to the Ministry of Information,[6] whose leadership and operational management were known to be under the direction of none other than the Supreme Leader. Thus, it appeared that the extra-legal actions presumably ordered by the conservative establishment were intended to counter the Khatami administration's policy of social and political openness at whatever the cost.

Reformist and absolutist discourses and students and the battle of ideas

In the aftermath of the Khatami presidency, the general plight of the students became a major bone of contention between the conservative establishment and the reformists. As discussed earlier, reformism, in the form of a counter-discourse and counter-governmentalizing project, had been eagerly embraced by large numbers of students, who had been instrumental in securing Khatami's electoral victory in 1997.

To elucidate the opposing positions regarding the students, particularly with respect to their future political roles and individual rights, one need only reference the absolutist and reformist discourses on this demographic. According to the former, and in keeping with the theocratic character of the Islamic Republic as a holy entity whose sovereignty and leadership were ultimately the prerogatives of God, such roles and rights were to be "defined by the state" (Abdi, 2001, para. 4). Based on this premise, student life, in all its multiplicity of forms, can have but one ultimate purpose: to "solidify the Islamic [Republic's] legitimacy" (Bayat, 2007, p. 68). It follows then that in the absolutist discourse student activism was signified as "an obligation [owed the Islamic Republic], not a right" (Bayat, 2007, p. 68).

This is necessarily the case given that at the heart of the absolutist discourse lay the notion of the Islamization of society, which was at one and the same time an injunction, a panacea and a totalizing project, aimed at addressing all of society's ills. According to this line of thought, students were required to strive to "Islamize the universities," in Ayatollah Khamenei's view "a priority and a goal" that had to be met if the grander project of Islamizing Iranian society was to be realized (Khamenei, 2015, para. 5). To this end, according to the absolutist discourse, students had nothing less than a religious duty to facilitate the process of Islamization. In particular, the *taklif madar*, or "duty-oriented" youth, among them must be prepared to defend the religious values of the Islamic Republic, against subversion whether encountered on campuses or in the wider society (Khamenei, 2013, para. 38).

Radicalized student organizations, along with those students inclined to scepticism, were viewed with the utmost alarm, and with good reason, for taken together they posed a serious obstacle to the grand project of an exclusive and all-encompassing Islamizing of Iranian society. Where these students were concerned, however, there were to be no concessions, and hence no negotiations (Holliday, 2011). This in turn, legitimized the presence on university campuses of vigilante groups, mainly the paramilitary *basij*, something the Ayatollah Khamenei viewed to be essential if Islamist governmentality was to succeed in eliminating non-Islamist and non-revolutionary elements working to turn students against the grand Islamic project (Khamenei, 1998).

The reformist discourse, on the other hand, rejected the notion of a totalized religious polity that casted the people, including students, in the role of subjects with religious duties to the state. This is reflected in Khatami's declaration that "[w]e are not people's guardians or owners of society; we just serve the people ... and must be able to cater to their needs and answer their questions" (cited in Mehran, 2003, p. 319). Thus, in sharp contrast to the conservative establishment's position, "voicing criticism" was in Khatami's view "no longer considered ... an act against the security of the country," but rather a means of democratizing it (Khatami, cited in Fadaee, 2012, p. 82).

The reformist discourse promoted the view that student activism was a prerequisite for building a democratic polity. This position was itself predicated upon the conviction that "any society that suppresses the voices of critical dissident groups, in particular students" is doomed to failure (Khatami, 2008, para. 15). The government and students, according to this line of thinking, must engage in a constructive, interactive dialogue so that the latter's voices might be heard and their demands acknowledged. This was essential if the reformist project was to succeed in fostering a democratic political development, an imperative for establishing and sustaining a religio-democratic system of governance, that is, an Islamic democracy (Khatami, 2008). "Students must be able to voice criticism," Khatami declared, "without fearing the consequences" (2015, para. 1). He later affirmed the centrality of university life for political development, adding that both "universities and university students are [in essence] dead if they cease to voice criticism [of the status quo]" (Khatami, 2015, para. 1). This required, first and foremost, that universities be independent, self-governing, and free from meddling, whether on the part of the state or special interests (Khatami, 2013).

In the following section, I show how the aforementioned ideas regarding students embedded in both the conservative establishment and reformist discourses translated into specific governmental policies and practices. Indeed, with the reformists at the helm of the executive branch and the conservative establishment controlling the legislative and judicial branches as well as the supervisory bodies, there commenced a battle of ideas that would inform policies and practices and that out of which "different conflicts and movements ... would emerge[]" (Fadaee, 2012, p. 74).

Student activism in post-revolutionary Iran: A brief history

Unlike their predecessors at the beginning of the revolution and throughout the 1980s, the post-1997 generation of Iranian university students were for the most part non-ideological, pragmatic in their demands for social and political reform, and, above all, deeply alienated by the establishment's monopolization of political power and social policy making. As stated earlier, the profound shift in the social and political orientation of this new generation can be traced, in part, to two factors: criticism of the status quo in the late 1980s and 1990s on the part of intellectuals of a mainly religious or reformist bent, many of whom held teaching or administrative posts were otherwise affiliated with the universities at the time; and their having borne witness to the appropriation of power by a politicized faction of the high clergy during the post-Khomeini era. These two factors, which are elaborated upon below, led many students to embrace the cause of reformism, viewing it to be a political project aimed at delivering a democratic polity.

This shift in political and discursive outlook was most apparent in the organizational structure and activities of the principal student association of the time: the Office for Consolidating Unity (OCU). Founded in September 1979 on the order of the Ayatollah Khomeini, the OCU was, during much of the 1980s, "closely affiliated with ... radical clerics" (Mahdi, 2000, para. 20) as well as exploited by the Ayatollah "as a tool to Islamize universities and combat ... campus Marxists and liberals" (Rivetti & Cavatorta, 2013, p. 650). The OCU advocated a brand of politics informed by "[a]nti-imperialism, a radical critique of materialism and a strong faith in Khomeini's religious and political leadership" (Rivetti & Cavatorta, 2013, p. 650). More than anything else, it represented "all strands of Islamism," albeit with the Islamic left dominating (Rivetti & Cavatorta, 2013, p. 650). However, with Khomeini's death and subsequent efforts on the part of the Khamenei and Rafsanjani to "challenge the ideological hegemony of the Islamic left" (Rivetti & Cavatorta, 2013, p. 650), of which the epicentre was the universities, the organizational structure and leadership of the OCU underwent radical transformation; at the same time, the latter found itself increasingly marginalized.

These developments brought about a profound change in outlook among many within the leadership as well as the rank-and-file, who began to "view the law [to be] above the *faqih*" and/or longed for "the limitation of power, greater accountability, [and the rule of law]" (Bayat, 2007, p. 69). The OCU's falling out with the Rafsanjani government and the conservative establishment was attributable, in part, to growing criticism from an oppositional media dominated largely by intellectuals. In addition, a long and costly war with Iraq ending in stalemate, along with the government's failure to achieve some of its social and economic goals, had pushed many among the rank-and-file to adopt a pragmatic, non-ideological approach to achieving an alternative political status quo (Afshari, 2015).

Reformism in practice: Khatami and students

By 1997, the OCU had by and large abandoned state-sanctioned Islamization and Third Worldism in favour of a democratic/republican and manifestly secular agenda. In their new emerging subjectivity "they had become ordinary;" they wanted to live their lives, study, and secure stable employment, all within the context of a religio-democratic order that could guarantee their individual rights and freedoms (Bayat, 2007, p. 69). In this way and in the aftermath of the Khatami presidency, their commitment to politics and political activism took a democratic turn. Reflecting this development, and in response to the government crackdown on student radicals, the OCU adopted a diffuse and semi-structured organizational format (Mahayekhi, 2001).

Owing in large measure to the Khatami administration's relaxation of restrictions limiting political participation, moreover, both the OCU and a large number of student groups, among them the United Student Front, the Society for Defense of Political Prisoners, and the Society of Intellectual Students, that had sprung up in the new climate of toleration, including many ordinary students, could now engage in press activism, to a degree unparalleled since the revolution (Afshari, 2015; Mahdi, 2000). A single event, the Student Press Festival held in October 1998, will suffice to illustrate the unprecedented growth in student print media at this time. No less than 260 student journals participated in what was a remarkable show of numbers and solidarity (Mashayekhi, 2011). According to the late Mehrdad Mashayekhi (2011), the student press came to exert a decisive influence over students as well as the general public, particularly youth, representing a crucial factor in informing public opinion during the lead-up to the 1999 urban and rural Council elections that swept reformists into power.

A free student press was complemented by relaxing restrictions on political activism, both on and off campus. In the first two years of the Khatami administration, students in large numbers began participating in rallies and demonstrations marking historical occasions such as Student Day and the May 23rd convocation commemorating Khatami's accession to the executive office. Later, in 1998 and 1999, they took part in a series of demonstrations protesting the closure of several newspapers, harassment and imprisonment of activists and intellectuals, use of torture in prisons, serial murders of intellectuals and political activists, and much else besides (Afshari, 2015; Mashayekhi, 2011). According to a 1999 report released by the Revolutionary Guard, between May 24, 1997 and January 11, 1999, there were "104 cases of associations, demonstrations and confrontations" in the Tehran University housing complex alone, reflecting not only the executive branch's commitment to open political activism, but also a growing student radicalization of an everyday kind stemming from profound dissatisfaction with the status quo (cited in Mashayekhi, 2011, p. 298).

Absolutism in practice: The conservative establishment and students

Rather than calming the political atmosphere on university campuses, however, these developments heightened tensions, thereby alarming the conservative establishment, who were quick to push through legislation aimed at unleashing the state security apparatus to deal with any perceived threat to the status quo. The establishment-dominated *Majlis* of the day introduced a series of measures aimed at bringing the universities, and particularly the student activists, to heel. October 1998 witnessed the passing into law of a bill establishing on every university campus a *basij* unit recruited from the student body and charged with "defend[ing] the achievements of the Islamic Revolution and advance[ing] *basiji* thinking" (Mahdi, 2000, para. 37). This micro-governmentalizing measure was intended to regulate student life, control the OCU as well as other radical student groups. Responsibility for deploying and supervising these units, moreover, fell to the High Council for Coordination and Support of the Student Basij, established the same year. In addition to encouraging student participation in "educational plan[ning]" having to do mainly with the religious actions, these units were to engage in "disciplinary activities," both of an educational and coercive kind, aimed at suppressing student organizations by, among other things, disrupting seminars and conferences, using intimidation and brute force as required (Mahdi, 2000, para. 36).

By the beginning of 1999, student life, and student activism in particular, was being disciplinized as well as, in the words of Nayereh Tohidi, "sabotaged ... by totalitarian Islamists" within the legislative and judicial branches (1999, para. 6). But rather than cowing the students, this crackdown produced the paradoxical effect of further radicalizing them as did additional repressive measures taken by conservative forces within the security forces. As Ali Afshari (2015) reports, at this time the OCU stepped up its support for the reformist project by, among other things, staging political rallies, in addition to "numerous [small scale] protests opposing conservative attacks on [Khatami's] policies" (Mahdi, 2000, para. 39). In this way, a kind of everyday solidarity, one enabled and conditioned by the politics of everyday life, was made possible and fostered within the student movement. It was this sense of solidarity that represented the requisite condition of possibility for engaging in acts of contestation.

The 1999 student uprising

Unrest on the campuses boiled over in 1999 when students staged a mass demonstration protesting the government closure of *Salam,* a popular reformist daily. On the evening of July 8, some 200 Tehran University students, the majority affiliated with the OCU, staged a peaceful demonstration in front of their dormitories that spilled over onto the adjacent streets (Afshari, 2015). This prompted the local security forces to intervene and order the demonstrators to return to their dormitories, which they agreed to do. The short-lived demonstration was at an end. Around 00:45 a.m. the following morning, however, the Acting Chief of the Tehran Police Department, accompanied by a large security force, arrived at the student dormitory complex and began engaging the students in a discussion (Mahdi, 2000). The director of the dormitory complex soon arrived on the scene and sought to persuade the Acting Chief to remove his forces, which, reinforced by anti-riot police, had now surrounded the complex.

Having learned of a police action intended to "finish the matter once and for all" and quash a pocket of student resistance, several officials, including the Interior Minister, Abdolvahed Mousavi Lari, and his Deputy, Mostafa Tajzadeh, rushed to the scene hoping to defuse the situation (Mahdi, 2000, para. 48). Mousavi Lari "ordered the security forces to leave, but they refused" (Mahdi, 2000, para. 48). Meanwhile, Tajzadeh had assured the students that they would not be attacked and that they should return at once to their dormitories. Confident that the crisis had passed, Mousavi Lari and Tajzadeh left, assuming the security forces and anti-riot police would soon withdraw. This assumption proved to be unfounded.

At 3:30 a.m., as the Acting Chief and his forces looked on, mayhem broke loose: some 400 members of the vigilante group *ansar-e hizbollah,* armed with batons and carrying shortwave radios and wearing their trademark plain white shirts, broke into the compound and proceeded to indiscriminately attack students, some shouting that even the president could do nothing to save them (Afshari, 2015). Doors were smashed to pieces, rooms set on fire, and students hurled from balconies onto the pavement below, resulting in the paralysis of at least one and the death of another; 300 others were injured, some seriously, and unknown scores detained (Afshari, 2015; Mahdi, 2000).

So brazen was this unprovoked attack that students inspecting the scene later the same morning were momentarily at a loss as to how to proceed. At this crucial juncture, however, many among them began chanting slogans directed against the conservative establishment who, they believed, had given the *ansars* the green light to attack (Afshari, 2015). As news of the violence spread, the students were joined by angry crowds in the cities, whose ranks included, apart from other students, women, youth and intellectuals, each, as will be seen below, with their own objectives, interests and grievances, albeit united in a common cause: to avenge what had transpired earlier that morning.

Demonstrations, for the most part spontaneous, erupted in Tehran and later in Shiraz, Isfahan, Tabriz and Mashhad—indeed, virtually every major city in the country (Afshari, 2015). Angry masses poured into public spaces, parks, squares, streets, university campuses, even alleyways, intent on waging a collective struggle against a conservative establishment whose Islamist governmentality could no longer be tolerated. As Ali Afshari (2015), one of the student leaders, recalled, the demonstrators, of which the majority were students, also included intellectuals as well as women and youth with very different agendas: some demanded the arrest and trial of the establishment figures responsible for the attack on the student compound; others, particularly liberal-nationalists, a radical liberalization of the political and social system; certain women's groups an end to patriarchy, particularly the mandatory *hijab* regulations; the relatives of political prisoners the release of family members; still others an end to the Islamic Republic itself.

In Tehran, site of the largest demonstrations, a crowd numbering between fifty and sixty thousand, comprised mostly of students and youth staged a peaceful demonstration (Afshari, 2015), albeit their slogans left the authorities in no doubt that those responsible had to be brought to justice and the legal system reformed to accord with the rule of law and the principle of accountability. Every so often, however, a different note sounded as when the crowds demanded the release of political prisoners or called into question the policies of the conservative establishment (Afshari, 2015). A movement inspired by student activists and borne along by the masses of ordinary people had suddenly emerged upon the scene, posing a daunting challenge to the status quo.

Though alarmed by the unexpected turn of events, the conservative establishment showed no sign of abandoning or even relaxing its hardline stance. Indeed, as early as July 10, the Office of the Supreme Leader "had warned the OCU leadership that further acts of subversion" was to be viewed as an "attempt to topple the Islamic Republic," warranting an iron-fisted response on the part of the state security forces (Afshari, 2015). This dire warning succeeded in halting further mass demonstrations. Nevertheless, scattered, small-scale disturbances continued for the next three days, providing the authorities with a pretext to unleash its machinery of repression with a view to stamping out the last vestiges of a massive grassroots rebellion.

To this end, on July 12 the elite Revolutionary Guard were deployed in all the major urban areas. In what quickly degenerated into a campaign of fear and intimidation, mobile Guard units seized control of those cities where the demonstrations had taken place. According to Ali Afshari (2015), the stage set for the arrest of "dozens of student activists," the majority OCU members, many on trumped-up charges of conspiring to topple the Islamic Republic on the order of undisclosed foreign powers. A formidable opposition movement had been crushed in its infancy.

What united these disparate groups in common cause was a shared conviction that the political status quo was fundamentally unjust, undemocratic and unaccountable. This merging of a heretofore fragmented people was enabled by their sharing in common interests and objectives. It was the latter that provided the conditions of possibility for uniting in opposition to the Islamist conduct of conduct, and thus defying the entire system of Islamist governmentality. It was this condition of possibility that produced a singular moment of social rupture. In this way, the events of July 1999 were marked by the coming together of a people bent on collective action and united by virtue of their being ruled by way of exclusionary and repressive rules governing the conduct of conduct.

What July 9 witnessed, moreover, was a rejection of the status quo by a people who had "imagine[d] themselves empowered to effect change even under the most inauspicious circumstances" (Pourmokhtari, 2014, p. 146). This act of collective defiance made manifest a people's "political will" (Foucault, 2005, p. 222) that generated a kind of political spontaneity, which in turn translated into a movement of counterconduct directed against the conservative establishment's governmentalizing rule. The political will manifest in these acts gave rise to full-fledged episodes of radical resistance, negation and defiance directed at "not being governed" in a certain manner, form, and way and, equally, "of not being governed ... so much" (Foucault, 1996, p. 384).

Nowhere were these radical acts of resistance, defiance and negation showcased to greater effect than in the public spaces of major urban centres—parks, streets, boulevards, and alleyways, university campuses, the very spatial domains demonstrators had occupied in July 1999. In this way, the protestors transformed what had hitherto been within the purview of the state's disciplinary/security apparatus into nodes of defiance. The latter became operational centres for conducting a movement of grassroots opposition understood here as a strategy of defiance aimed at turning governmentalized zones into strongpoints where marginalized, subordinated and subjugated bodies might defy power.

In intentionally disrupting the natural stream of everyday life by way of demonstrations and protestations, those subjugated bodies de-normalized the "very public character of [public[space[s]," which is normally orderly, fluid, disciplinized and, above all, governmentalized, the purpose being to manifest their resistance, defiance and negation to the Islamist rule of conduct of conduct (Butler, 2011, para. 1). In July 1999, the one factor that lent this intentional act its political significance, moreover, was the demonstrators' awareness of the conservative establishment's stranglehold over the country's political institutions and of how the latter were being misused, with a view to blocking reform and containing dissent. It was this awareness that impelled them to commandeer urban spaces as alternative avenues for expressing discontent and voicing demands in ways the authorities could not ignore—an awareness born of their shared interests, objectives and values.

For Iranians, engaging in this political act of disrupting the normal sequence of everyday life was motivated in part by their understanding that, given the conservative establishment's political dominance, the status quo could be contested most effectively only by transposing politics from its normal and natural domain, that is, from mainstream political arenas such as the *Majlis,* to the public domain of urban spaces. Thus, the demonstrators elected to bring politics into the heart of urban centres, the very public spaces that the Islamic Republic, like all governmental regimes, was obsessed with routinizing—in the process un-routinizing them and turning them into political loci of defiance wherein the rules and rationalities of Islamist governmental conduct might be challenged.

And despite what at first glance appeared to be a decisive victory for the establishment, the events of early July would signal a sea change in relations between state and citizenry. In unprecedented numbers, student activists as well as ordinary people with little in the way of organizational structure or formal leadership succeeded in challenging, however briefly, the Islamist governmentality, and on a scale never witnessed before, in the process undermining Tehran's moral and political authority.

And though incapable of bringing about significant social and political change, the 1999 uprising, or more precisely the lived experience of it, would become, in the years to follow, imprinted on the political conscious and imaginary of

Iranians. The experience of defying power gave rise to new collective values predicated on common interests, such as promoting political accountability, the rule of law and democratic process—all to be achieved, for the most part, through collective non-violent action carried out in public spaces. The latter came to serve as a template for the various forms of defiance adopted by the 2006 Women's One Million Signature Campaign and the 2009 Green Movement. In a highly visceral way this multilayered mode of collective action constituted a "corporeal challenge to the norms of political conduct" (Meade, 2014, p. 9) as well as a form of stylization, manifest in a willful desire to reject normalizing rules of conduct formulated by the most reactionary elements within the Islamic Republic.

Above all else, the events of July signified a "[great] conflict between human ... and divine subjectivity," a titanic struggle born of the battle of ideas raging between two discourses, one oppositional/reformist, the other dominant/absolutist (Mahdavi, 2006, p. 22). The former sought to challenge the legitimacy of divine right principles as well as provide an alternative to the status quo in the form of a "revitalized and redefined Islam" that could provide the basis for "the social and cultural cohesion [essential to] the operation of [an Islamic] democracy" capable of "transform[ing] [Iranians] from subjects to citizens ... with rights" (Ansari, 2006, p. 115). The latter, which in large measure informed the existing political order, was predicated upon a dogmatic religiosity in search of the kind of utopia prescribed by divine rule, one populated by duty-bound subjects. The events of July, therefore, were grounded in a "widely held dissent against a religious polity that had denied [so] many ... individual liberty, gender equality, and meaningful participation in public life" (Bayat, 2007, p. 49); they also served to map out ways and means to resist what Foucault calls "absolute[] absolut[ism]" (cited in Ghamari-Tabrizi, 2016, p. 201).[7]

Women and politics of social contestation

Early on in the post-revolutionary period, women's issues, in particular those pertaining to the nature and scope of their social and political rights, became a dominant feature of Iranian politics. The new Islamic Republic moved swiftly to replace the Family Protection Laws of 1967, which had afforded women a modest degree of security and protection, with a legal code "based on an extremely conservative interpretation of *Shari'a* law [that] ... discriminat[ed] against women" (Tahmasebi, 2012, para. 2). According to the biopolitical code, women lost, among other things, the right to be judges, to initiate a divorce, to win custody of children, and to travel abroad without first obtaining the permission of husbands. In addition, testimony given by a woman in a court of law now counted for half that of a man, and her share of an inheritance would be half that of a brother (Bayat, 2007; Rafizadeh, 2011). Moreover, the state, at different times, promoted polygamy, large families and temporary marriages, depending on the political exigencies of the moment or whatever interpretation of *Shari'a* law was in vogue (Rafizadeh, 2011; Tahmasebi, 2012).

A revolution Triumph: Women's activism in the early and mid-1980

Perhaps one of the greatest impositions borne by women was the legal requirement to wear the *hijab* in all public spaces. Article 102 of the state Islamist Punishments (*ta'zirat*) stipulates that failure to wear this article of clothing in public constitutes "an offence against public morality, punishable by ... up to seventy-four lashes" (Mir-Hosseini, 2002b, p. 42). The *hijab* law "was defended and enforced with such vigour in those years [that it] gradually became one of the cornerstones of the Islamic Republic" (Mir-Hosseini, 2002b, p. 42). In their Friday sermons, lectures and writings, conservative clerics went so far as to attribute the success of the Islamic Republic to its *hijab* policy (Mir-Hosseini, 2002b).

This clampdown on the rights of women did not go unchallenged, however. In the early years of the revolution, many so-called secular women participated in street demonstrations and other forms of protest directed against state-sponsored patriarchy (Bayat, 2007). By the start of the Iran–Iraq War (1983–1988), however, opposition of this kind had been crushed by the authorities; moreover, the exigencies of total war had the effect of pushing the debate over the *hijab*, along with women's issues in general, to the margins of both social and political life.

Along with their male compatriots, women rallied to the flag. And while the conservative establishment sought initially to confine them to their traditional roles of homemaking and childrearing, if only to produce sufficient manpower to wage future wars for the "glory of Islam ... and the nation" (Bayat, 2007, p. 73), mounting casualties, combined with the pressing need to recruit workers for auxiliary roles behind the front lines, meant that patriarchal ideology and tradition had to be subordinated to the needs of the war effort. As a result, many women served in an administrative or logistical capacity or as health workers—doctors, nurses, first-aid practitioners—many stationed at hospitals close to the front; others took up teaching positions at schools and universities and army bases (Afshari, 2015).

With hostilities drawing to a close in the late summer of 1988, the authorities anticipated with some confidence that the war experience had effectively marginalized and silenced women both socially and politically; this, however, proved to be nothing more than wishful thinking, a miscalculation that was to have profound implications. Indeed, in the aftermath of Ayatollah Khomeini's death and the accession to power of a politicized faction of conservative clerics, women's issues again came to the fore. Moreover, what more than anything else politicized this very large demographic was the hardline views of the conservative clerics and, in particular, their exclusivist interpretation of *Shari'a* law that underpinned so many facets of social life. Paradoxically, their uncompromising stance on women's issues would have precisely the opposite effect to the one intended, namely that of "speeding up the ... [development] of [a] feminist consciousness" among Iranian women (Tohidi, 2006, p. 627).

The absolutist discourse and women

The absolutist discourse was "premised on the notion of duty," or more precisely religious duty, which in the case of women meant strict adherence to the role of dutiful wife, sister and mother (Mir-Hosseini, 2002b, p. 50). "Understanding fully this [religious] duty," Ayatollah Khamenei (2014, para. 3) declared, is essential to "defin[ing] women's greatness and glory." It would be a mistake, however, to assume that all conservative clerics spoke with one voice. One faction, often referred to as traditionalists, was committed to "preserv[ing] ... a patriarchal ... regime" (Tohidi, 2006, p. 625), viewed to be ordained by divine law, and thus part of "the natural order of things" (Mir-Hosseini, 2003, p. 3). For them, "wifehood and motherhood [were] to be the sole roles and obligations of women" (Tohidi, 2006, p. 625).

A second faction, known variously as radical Islamists or neo-traditionalists, sought to advance an all-encompassing Islamist political project "as an alternative or solution for all of the social ills and gender-related moral decadence ... [endemic to] traditional and modern [social] systems" (Tohidi, 2006, p. 625). Their stance on gender issues was essentially reactive, meaning that it was directed against the "gender regimes and sexual mores promoted by secular Westernized modernists, liberals, socialists, and feminists" (Tohidi, 2006, p. 625). Specifically, they "reject[ed] gender equality [in favour of the] complementarity of gender rights and duties" (Mir-Hosseini, 2003, p. 17). In contrast to their traditionalist rivals, however, they advocated "mobilizing women and engaging them in social and political activism," albeit only in so far as this underwrote "their bid for political power" (Tohidi, 2006, p. 625).

What traditionalists as well as the majority of neo-traditionalists agreed to be non-negotiable regarding the social status of women was the "Islamic dress code[8]... sex-segregation, control of women's sexuality, and *Shari'a*-based family law," which meant that both camps were committed to reproducing a neo-patriarchal system (Tohidi, 2006, p. 626). In the late 1980s both supported efforts on the part of the conservative establishment to promote gender subordination; in addition, many of their respective members joined the ranks of the governmentalized clerics where they were strategically positioned to inform state policy in this respect.

The coming of post-Islamist feminists to the political scene

The traditionalist/neo-traditionalist agenda did not go unopposed, however; by the late 1980s, there appeared the first signs of what Ziba Mir-Hosseini (2006) calls "a new [feminist] consciousness" (p. 640). Inspired in large part by the aforementioned hermeneutic project aimed at subjecting religious/sacred texts to an exegesis informed by modern-day realities, women mounted "a politically and ideologically heterogeneous challenge to conservative and patriarchal interpretations of Islam" (Povey, 2016, p. 75). Their principal strategy lay in eliminating ideological barriers to a democratic polity through a programme of "Islamic reformation," directed at *Shari'a* law and *fiqh*, or Islamic ruling (Tohidi, 2006, p. 628). Only then, it was believed, could equal rights for women be achieved and state-sponsored patriarchy rolled back.

Those advocating this approach came to be known as post-Islamist feminists.[9] In post-revolutionary Iran, it was this group, more than any other, which dominated the feminist camp. Post-Islamist feminism was informed by "a blend of piety and choice, religiosity and rights" (Bayat, 2007, p. 76); and while "Islamic in its language," it remained "feminist in its aspirations and demands" (Mir-Hosseini, 2006, p. 640). For them, "Islam ... as a system ... could accommodate women's rights only if it was seen through [a] feminist lens" (Bayat, 2007, p. 76). As a result, they placed a premium on women's autonomy and choice, along with "gender equality in all domains" (Bayat, 2007, p. 76).

The post-Islamist feminist project, moreover, was decidedly ecumenical, embracing all strands of feminism aimed at "[ending] women's subordination in general" (Bayat, 2007, p. 76). This could only be achieved by removing the patriarchal constraints on women entrenched in the legal system and rigorously enforced, something that, given the nature of the Iranian polity, required problematizing, critiquing and de-monopolizing the interpretation of Islamic law, thereby usurping the role of the conservative clergy. The strategy to be employed was one of "utiliz[ing] ... Islamic [language] to push for gender equality within the constraints of the Islamic Republic" (Bayat, 2007, p. 76).

Lastly, it was the inclusive approach adopted to women's politics that lent it legitimacy in the eyes of many ordinary women. This sense of inclusivity was best captured in a remark by Shirin Ebadi, a prominent feminist lawyer and Nobel Laureate for Peace in 2003: "[so long as] Islamic feminism means that a Muslim woman can also be a feminist and feminism and Islam or Muslimhood do not have to be incompatible, I would agree with it" (cited in Tohidi, 2006, p. 632).

Post-Islamist feminists in the late 1980s and 1990s were joined by other feminist factions, most notably secular feminists, in contesting state-sponsored patriarchy. Theirs was largely a horizontal, and by implication diffused and multipronged, strategy for change that included prominent feminist lawyers such as Ebadi and Mehrangiz Kar discussing legal issues in the oppositional media; religious and intellectual reformers holding public forums in large urban centres and on university campuses; media-based educational programmes targeted at ordinary women; and articles and op-ed pieces published in the print media, most notably *Zanan*, a monthly magazine that became the voice of the women's movement during this period (Peyghambarzadeh, 2015; Povey, 2016; Tohidi, 2006). All this was intended to compel the clerics among the conservative establishment "to rethink notions of the sacred and the mundane" as stipulated in Islamic texts and rulings, including *Shari'a* law, thereby challenging some of their fundamental assumptions (Mir-Hosseini, 2006, p. 637).

All this intellectual ferment could not hope to bring about a repeal of the discriminatory laws and social control mechanisms that had been a staple feature of the Islamic Republic since its birth. What it did do, however, was to provide an impetus for introducing legal reforms, which, albeit modest, represented a major concession on the part of the authorities. These included removing restrictions on the academic subjects women were permitted to study (1986); access to family planning and contraception (1988); amendments to divorce laws curtailing the right of men to divorce spouses and requiring them to provide greater compensation in the form of alimony (1992); the appointment of women as advisory judges (1992) (Mir-Hosseini, 2002b; Rezaei, 2015).

Reformist discourse and women

As noted earlier, the reformist discourse was informed by the principles of equality, freedom of expression, and individual rights, existing within the framework of constitutionalism and the rule of law—all essential to establishing an Islamic democracy and civil society in which women could play a key role as equal partners with men. "Iran for all Iranians," the reformist rallying cry, was no mere utopian slogan but rather an expression of a coherent vision of an Islamic democratic polity wherein, according to Khatami, "all men and women who live [i]n this land" must according to it be treated equally (cited in Mehran, 2010, pp. 317–318). Realizing this vision required creating equal opportunities for women, which could only be achieved by "eliminating prejudice ... valuing knowledge and intellect, and respecting [individual] rights" (Mehran, 2010, p. 315). It is precisely the government, declared Khatami, that must "prepare the ground for women [by] recogniz[ing] their rights and capabilities and acknowledg[ing] their merits" (Khatami, cited in Mehran, 2010, p. 318). "We are not the guardians of women," asserted Khatami in a bid to distinguish his administration from the conservative clerics and their patriarchal agenda, but rather the means of empowering them (cited in Mehran, 2010, p. 318). The latter, as Golnar Mehran (2010) notes, could only be realized by "increasing female knowledge, awareness, and education [to the point where they might] recognise and demand their rights" (p. 318). As will be seen, with Khatami's ascendency to the presidency, women would have an unprecedented opportunity to pursue their social and political rights.

The reformist government and the new activism on the part of women

With Mohammad Khatami's victory in the 1997 presidential election and the birth of a reformist movement, committed to promoting a more "egalitarian reading of Islamic law" (Mir-Hosseini, 2002b, p. 51), the great mass of women, including secular and post-Islamist feminists, ramped up their activism to an unprecedented level. As shown earlier, these women had played a major role in underwriting Khatami's bid for the presidency; they also constituted a core element of the reform movement itself. In common with the students, they were quick to use the media, most notably print media, to develop a critique of Islamist governmentality and its rationalities and rules of conduct. Scores of dailies, monthlies and magazines, many newly created in response to demand, took up the women's cause, the majority taking their cue from the post-Islamist feminists.

Among the print media, two in particular stood out owing to the degree of influence they wielded. The post-Islamist feminist-orientated *Zanan* (women), a magazine established in 1992, emerged in the aftermath of Khatami's victory as a leading voice of the women's movement (Tohidi, 2006). It was soon joined by *Zan* (woman), launched in 1998, which became "the first-ever women's [daily] newspaper" (Mir-Hosseini, 1999, p. 275). Together, they brought women's issues, both great and small, to the forefront of mainstream analysis and debate, in the process articulating a wide range of subjects considered taboo—ways to improve one's sex life, plastic surgery, domestic abuse, housework tips for men, the *hijab* and gender equality, feminism and patriarchy (Rezaei, 2015; Mir-Hosseini, 1999). Contributors included Muslim scholars of the likes of Mohsen Saeidzadeh and Abdolkarim Soroush, in addition to feminist lawyers such as Shirin Ebadi and Mehrangiz Kar, the latter herself a member of the *Zanan* editorial board. Work by early feminist authors such as Virginia Woolf, Charlotte Perkins Gilman and Simone de Beauvoir, among many others, also found a home at *Zan* (Bayat, 2007).

In the new climate of political openness, *Zanan* soon asserted itself as the leading exponent of the women's agenda. Shahla Sherkat, one of its editors, best captured a sense of the magazine's mission during this period:

> At *Zanan* we tried to discuss the concept of feminism and open up the discussion around the different meanings [attached to] feminism and different forms of feminisms. We also tried to [correct] the ... conservative[] [mis]perception ... [of] this concept. Feminism was ... taboo for many women or a bad word, so we tried to change this. Against this trend, we argued that anyone can be a feminist whether secular or Muslim or ... [of] any other ideological affiliation.
>
> (cited in Povey, 2016, p. 77)

Perhaps, *Zanan*'s most singular initiative laid in deconstructing patriarchal religious texts and proposing an alternative gender-sensitive account that would allow women to stand as the equal of men in both the public and private sphere. Thus, in a move that was in part strategic, in part pragmatic, *Zanan*'s editorial board "shifted the basis of hierarchy from sex to piety" by highlighting gender inequality embedded in orthodox readings of Islamic religious texts and the rulings predicated upon them (Bayat, 2007, p. 77). And so it was demonstrated that gender inequality, far from being "a manifestation of divine justice ... [was, in fact,] a construction by male jurists which [was] contrary to the very essence of [the] divine will as revealed in the sacred texts of Islam" (Mir-Hosseini, 2003, p. 20).

In a bid to further legitimize a feminist agenda, the magazine enlisted sympathetic clerics, among them Mohsen Saeidzadeh, who were arguing for a feminist concept of justice within the context of a religio-ethical order. Hitherto little known, these religious scholars were now thrust before a national audience. For Saeidzadeh, equality represented Islam's supreme principle as revealed in the Qur'an. In a series of commentaries on theological and jurisprudential issues, seemingly inspired by no less an authority than Soroush, he argued in *Zanan* that "in understanding ... doctrine and [in] inferring *Shari'a* rulings" (Saeidzadeh, cited in Mir-Hosseini, 1999, p. 249), theologians and jurists, alike, "have sacrificed the principle of [gender] equality to endorse a set of theories [which rest] on assumptions" that continue to be "part of *fiqh* [Islamic rulings]" but are "no longer valid" (cited in Mir-Hosseini, 1999, p. 250). This was nothing short of a call for a renewed commitment by clerical jurists to adopt a gender-sensitive interpretation of Islamic texts and rulings that reflected the "politics and social customs of the age and milieu in which they operate" (Saeidzadeh, cited in Mir-Hosseini, 1999, p. 250).

The feminist press campaign was met with a favourable response on the part of the Khatami administration, one that translated into first time political and social gains for women that were unprecedented. In 1997 Masoumeh Ebtekar was appointed Vice-president of Iran, a first for any woman in the post-revolutionary period. In 1999, Zahra Rahnavard was selected to be president of Al-Zahra University, making her the "first woman ever to hold such a position" (Beck & Nashat, 2004, p. 159). Women also succeeded in securing one-third of all the seats in the country's first city council elections held in 1998. In all, 114 women in 109 cities would serve in this capacity. Lastly, the first ever post-revolutionary performance of an all-woman orchestra was broadcast on Iranian television (Osanloo, 2009). All in all, these were impressive gains for women.

Women and the conservative establishment

Confronted by the spectre of unprecedented numbers of women engaged in the social and political life of the country, the conservative establishment, with the blessing of traditionalist and neo-traditionalist clerics, struck back, bringing to bear, as in the case of the student activists, the full weight of the *Majlis*, judiciary and state disciplinary apparatus. The conservative-dominated fifth *Majlis* (1996–2000) was the first to act, passing two bills "infamous for their anti-women slant" (Mir-Hosseini, 2002b, p. 39). The Adaptation of Medical Services to Religious Law brought medicine under the purview of *Shari'a* law for the first time, effectively segregating physicians and their patients along gender lines. This was soon followed by the Banning the Exploitation of Women's Images and the Creation of Conflicts between Men and Women by Propagating Women's Rights Outside the Legal and Islamic Framework bill, aimed at "prohibit[ing] the lively press debates [over] women's rights as well as press coverage of the dynamic film industry" (Mir-Hosseini, 2002b, p. 40). Both bills became law in July 1998 and played a major "part [in] a concerted conservative effort to frustrate" the reform movement in general and women's rights in particular (Mir-Hosseini, 2002b, p. 40).

The stage was now set for a renewed onslaught against the media or, more precisely, the feminist print media. *Zanan* was taken to court in 1998 and eventually banned for "inciting women against men and "spreading homosexuality"" (Bayat, 2007, p. 96). Saeidzadeh, a cleric and regular contributor, was unfrocked and imprisoned the same year and his writings banned (Mir-Hosseini, 2002b). The following year, *Zan* was shut down by judicial order for insulting Islam, apparently by featuring a cartoon depicting a man pleading with a mugger to victimize his wife on the grounds that "... according to *Shari'a* her "blood money" would be only half that of his" (Abrahamian, 2008, p. 192).

All this was complemented by a systematic effort on the part of the *basij* to conduct through its dispatchers a propaganda campaign directed against women. The latter, in conjunction with the conservative print media, strove to disseminate the view that feminists and their supporters, including NGOs, were stooges of Western governments bent on promoting immorality (Sadr, 2012).

The reformist victory in the 2000 parliamentary election, however unprecedented, failed to pave the way for legislation aimed at advancing a feminist agenda. This was due chiefly, as will be shown, to the power wielded by the conservative-dominated supervisory bodies and, most importantly, the Guardian Council, which had the final say in approving or rejecting legislation passed by the *Majlis*.

Ultimately, more than anything else, the reformist parliamentary victory fuelled "a broader conflict over two [diametrically opposite] notions of Islam:" one was "absolutist and legalistic," inspired by a religio-governmentalized clergy inherently opposed to conceding individual rights or "making concession[s]," especially to women; the other a "pluralistic and tolerant" religio-democratized order committed to "promot[ing] democratic values and human rights—including women's rights"—and supported by the mass of the people (Mir-Hosseini, 2002b, p. 37).

Perhaps nowhere were conservative and reformist differences over the status of women and the character of Islam more sharply highlighted than in the debate over ratifying the Convention on the Elimination of All Forms of Discrimination against Women (CEDAW), a United Nations initiative hailed by feminists as an international bill of rights for women. If adopted by Iran, CEDAW would have directly challenged a host of laws, customs and practices that worked to marginalize and subordinate women.

Following a press campaign, mounted by post-Islamist and secular feminists, demanding the government deliver on its promise to "reconcile Islam with democracy and human rights" by joining CEDAW, the Khatami administration, in December 2001, drafted the requisite legislation and submitted it to the *Majlis* for ratification (Mir-Hosseini, 2002b, p. 38). However, immediately prior the final vote, the enabling bill was placed on hold by the head of the *Majlis*, Mehdi Karoubi, owing to concerns on the part of the conservative clerics regarding its compatibility with *Shari'a* law (Tohidi, 2006). Reformist deputies, over the course of the next two years, demanded a transparent answer to every enquiry made about the bill, but to no avail. Finally, in August 2003, the Guardian Council announced that the CEDAW bill would not be ratified (Pourmokhtari, 2017).

Presence-as-resistance: Women, public spaces, and the politics of social contestation

The *Majlis*' rejection of CEDAW emboldened the conservative clerics and their sympathizers to mount a campaign aimed at discrediting reformists, post-Islamist and secular women guilty of crossing what they referred to as red lines. Thus, for example, in the city of Rasht the Friday prayer leader, Zein-al Abedin Ghorbani, condemned all who "questioned religious authorities on ... *Shari'a*;" he went on to warn "not to cross the red line, not to dismiss the Qur'an and Islam" (cited in Bayat, 2007, p. 79). At the same time, women among the conservatives, most notably Monireh Noubakhat and Marzieh Dastjerdi, motioned to have feminist debates in the press censored for "creat[ing] conflict between women and men" as well as undermining *Shari'a* and the fundamental principles of Islam (Bayat, 2007, p. 79).

The dispute over the ratification of CEDAW brought to the fore fundamental differences between conservative and reformists over the rights and status of women; it also exemplified efforts on the part of the former to "block and frustrate every move of [a] reformist government" (Mir-Hosseini, 2002b, p. 39) committed to "formulat[ing] a more egalitarian reading of Islamic law" (Mir-Hosseini, 2002b, p. 51). With the crackdown on the press and other print media aligned with the feminists and their post-Islamist and secular allies, along with the failure to close legal loopholes allowing for gender discrimination, women were once again pushed to the margins of social and political life. However, rather than serving as a deterrent, this backlash only politicized women further, thus empowering them to pursue certain everyday strategies directed at asserting their collective will to counterpower.

No longer able to advance a reformist agenda through official channels, masses of disaffected women turned to an everyday form of defiance that entailed less risk. It is examined here under the rubric of what I call *presence-as-resistance*, by which I mean an everyday mode of resistance, visible and therefore public, on the part of the subordinated and marginalized, which involved making their presence felt by performing in public spaces the everyday life practices normally, and hence governmentally, reserved for the private sphere of the home. It was this strategy that eroded the efficacy of government power, which was very much contingent on marshalling human bodies in public spaces. By way of operationalizing it, and in the absence of anything resembling a formal leadership or organizational structure, these movements of women transformed spatial domains—streets, squares, parks, alleyways, university campuses, classrooms, whatever was at hand—into venues where grievances might be aired and discursive interests and objectives communicated, demands made, subjectivities enabled, everyday solidarity fostered, and the social and political status quo contested, negated and subverted.

For their part, the authorities, though backed by a battery of laws and regulations for controlling public spaces, were loath to intervene to restore order, for to do so meant turning public spaces into virtual militarized zones, effectively curtailing the normal, everyday sequence of life (Bayat, 2013). That this brand of activism was infused with ordinary life practices further complicated, and made more unpalatable, state intervention.

Presence-as-resistance, and the everyday life practices that were its life-blood, assumed disparate forms. Thus, for example, women in unprecedented numbers entered the universities where they acquired specialized knowledge in a broad range of academic fields, in the process building solidarity with their peers, both male and female. This great influx into the halls of academe prompted the *Majlis* in 2007 to publish a report, which drew a comparison between the proportion of female students admitted to universities in the 1980s with that in the 2000s. The report concluded that this figure had risen from 32% in 1983 to 65% by 2007 (Amir-Ebrahimi, 2008). The dramatic increase in the presence of women on campuses had the effect of nurturing campus subcultures of educated women and youth whose members saw themselves as active agents working to undermine the political and social status quo. All this was, of course, an anathema for a conservative establishment that had set its sights on raising a generation of obedient and docile housewives, mothers, sisters and daughters.

Other like-minded women took up the arts or music, much to the consternation of a conservative establishment for whom such pursuits were tantamount to crossing yet another red line (Khabar Online, 2013; Khamenei.ir, 2016). Conservatives were dismayed to discover so many women attending vocal/singing classes, while others studied traditional Persian musical instruments, such as the *tombak*, *taar*, *ney* and *santoor*, in addition to piano, guitar and other Western instruments, often taking advantage of public classes open to all.

Still others took up sports, in particular rowing and cycling, which necessarily took them out of the private sphere and into public spaces monopolized for the most part by men, in one stroke eliminating a formidable barrier to gender inequality (Rezaei, 2015; Peyghambarzadeh, 2016). Others simply appeared in the streets, making their presence felt by revealing heavily made-up faces and/or wearing brightly coloured *mantous* or diminutive *hijabs* from which spilled scandalous amounts of hair (Amir-Ebrahimi, 2006)—all an affront to the establishment's brand of Islam. Consequently, by transgressing dominant norms, codes and rules, hundreds of thousands of women from diverse social strata transformed public spaces into domains of subversion, resistance and defiance.

The express purpose of these public displays—in and of themselves acts of empowerment, assertions of a collective will and expressions of everyday solidarity—lay in resisting, and by implication de-authenticating and de-moralizing, the state-sanctioned Islamist governmentalization of women's lives. The strategy employed to this end was one of exploiting ordinary life practices, thereby challenging the authorities in ways that could only be met by violently disrupting the tenor of daily life—something they were not prepared to do. As so often happens, the best-laid plans—in this case aimed at producing a generation of model women that reproduced the status quo—did indeed go awry, and in spectacular fashion.

The 2006 Women's One Million Signature Campaign: The everyday politics of social contestation

As discussed above, it was the everyday public acts of resistance and solidarity, grounded in ordinary life practices, that in the waning years of the Khatami administration inspired and empowered women to launch what came to be popularly known as the Women's One Million Signature Campaign. One of the most seminal events of the post-revolutionary period, the later was initiated in August 2006, only a year following the ascendancy of Mahmood Ahmadinejad to the presidency. Its single objective laid in repealing family, civil and criminal laws discriminating against women through petitioning the *Majlis* (Rezaei, 2015; Tahmasebi, 2012). The changes proposed would result in equal marital rights for women, including the right to divorce spouses; abolition of polygamy and temporary marriages; the right of women to pass on their nationality to their children; gender equality with respect to *dieh*, or compensation for bodily injury or death; equal inheritance rights; the reformation of laws relating to honour killings, the objective being to increase their deterrent value; and equal weight given testimony provided by women in courts of law (Peyghambarzadeh, 2015; Rezaei, 2015).

The Women's One Million Signature Campaign was initially conceived by a group of 54 activists, including several distinguished journalists and secular and post-Islamist feminists, among them Shirin Ebadi, Noushin Ahmadi Khorasani, Narges Mohammadi, Parvin Ardalan and Zhila Bani Yaqoub (Tavaana, 2016). "[The founders] chose to avoid a traditional hierarchical leadership model," fearing it precluded opportunities for ordinary women, especially the young and those with low incomes, "to become involved in trying to [abolish] unjust laws" (Tavaana, 2016, para. 13). As Ali Abdi (2015) explains, this key decision drew ordinary Iranians from all social strata and walks of life—in particular, youth but also feminists, secularists and intellectuals of every persuasion—to participate in the campaign, which was set in motion in the public spaces of urban centers.

To facilitate recruitment the campaign sponsored workshops, initially in Tehran and later in most major Iranian cities, which quickly metamorphosed into loosely-coordinated cells, where canvassers and other workers could be trained as well as educated regarding women's rights and the legal issues pertaining to them (Peyghambarzadeh, 2015; Rezaei, 2015). Many future activists, however, were recruited in public spaces while engaging with campaign workers or through friendship networks, comprised mainly of urban youth (Abdi, 2015).

What created among these disparate elements a sense of solidarity and willingness to engage in collective action directed against the status quo was their everyday experience of misrule and misconduct. It was this lived experience and the sense of solidarity it instilled that impelled many men to join the campaign.[10] As former campaign member Ali Abdi (2015) asserted during an interview with the writer,

> [t]his campaign was all about a struggle on the part of activists, both male and female, for full citizenship rights. We understood intuitively that, as men, if we d[id] not fight on behalf of women, our own struggle for social and political rights would come to nothing. In this way, many male activists elected to join the campaign, because they, too, wished to end the state-sponsored patriarchy that had worked to subordinate and marginalize women.

According to Abdi, what united both men and women was the conviction "that the status quo [was] unjust with regard to women" and that "collecting signatures constituted a pragmatic way of addressing the discriminatory laws against [them]." It was this deep-rooted conviction that fostered a sense of everyday solidarity among the campaigners and fired them with a determination to engage in collective forms of activism of an everyday kind.

A tactic much favoured by the campaigners involved gathering in crowded public spaces, usually streets, parks, alleyways and metros, in groups numbering anywhere from three or four to a dozen and then engaging ordinary citizens in discussions aimed at raising public awareness of patriarchal laws and their consequences, not only for women but for the whole of Iranian society (Peyghambarzadeh, 2015; Rezaei, 2015). They then encouraged their interlocutors to sign the petition. All this played out in the context of performing ordinary life practices, such as shopping, socializing, engaging in sports, picnicking with families or simply strolling along alleyways, streets and boulevards (Peyghambarzadeh, 2015).

And indeed, such urban spaces became sites of contestation, wherein the campaigners, with women in the vanguard, performed everyday subversive acts. Thus, for example, in one especially popular skit, two activists, supposedly married to the same man, engaged in a heated argument, sometimes accompanied by mock fisticuffs, during which each revealed how a polygamous relationship had worked to undermine her rights, dignity and authenticity as a woman (Peyghambarzadeh, 2016; Rezaei, 2015). Performed in public domains, this became the campaign's signature sketch (Abdi, 2015). So realistically staged were these performances that they drew large crowds, at which point other activists appeared on the scene and proceeded to engage the audience on the subject of legally sanctioned gender discrimination and the need for reform (Abdi, 2015). Theirs proved to be an easy sell as the performances so precisely mirrored the reality of everyday life for so many women making up the audiences.

In order to broaden their appeal, especially to religious groups, the campaigners, many of whom were themselves devout Muslims, took pains to ensure that "the legal reform[s] [they were advocating were] based on a dynamic interpretation of *Shari'a* law" (Tavaana, 2016, para. 21). They succeeded in this respect chiefly by referencing the views of prominent clerics sympathetic to the reformist position, among them the late Ayatollahs Yousef Sanei and Hussein-Ali Montzaeri. The campaign "cast its demands within the framework of Iran's existing laws without [appearing to] ... [undermine] ... the state's political foundations," a necessary stratagem if the wrath of the state security apparatus was to be avoided (Tavaana, 2016, para. 23). This initiative on the part of the Women's One Million Signature Campaign exemplifies the mechanisms Foucault associates with "resisting the processes implemented for conducting others" (2007, p. 201). It is a form of everyday negation of the status quo that finds expression in subtle and artful forms of "[collective] resistance to processes of governmentality" (Death, 2010, p. 239) while reflecting a geographically specific and context-dependent collective struggle against specific technologies of power, in this case, the Islamist conduct of conduct.

Notwithstanding that the campaign was scrupulous in framing its demands in compliance with existing laws, as its popularity among the public waxed and the cause gained momentum, the authorities grew increasingly alarmed. Things reached a head in early 2008 when the state security forces began a systematic crackdown, banning meetings and workshops, arresting members and shutting down the campaign website (Peyghambarzadeh, 2015). By the end of 2008, "over 50 members ha[d] been arrested ... while hundreds more ... had [had] their passports revoked or ... been barred from the education system," thereby forcing the campaign underground and thus rendering it inoperable (Tavaana, 2016, para. 19).

Despite failing to garner the requisite number of signatures, the campaign may, according to Farhad Khosrokhavar, be viewed as "the most prominent feminist [initiative] in [post-revolutionary] Iran" (2012, p. 65), and precisely because it worked so "effectively [to] raise[] ordinary peoples' awareness of women's rights, promote[] the idea of societal equality, and publicize[] women's demands," such that the latter could no longer be ignored (Tavaana, 2016, para. 8). It did so specifically by "creat[ing] a [public] discourse on women's rights" to which the authorities had to respond (Tahmasebi, 2012, para. 10). That response came in the form of "the movement's [sole] practical achievement[]" (Tavaana, 2016, para. 8): pressuring the *Majlis* to repeal, over the course of 2008, two patriarchal laws and replace them with gender-neutral legislation. Specifically, women were granted the right to inherit a husband's property and to receive equal blood money in the event of an accident covered by an insurance company (Rezaei, 2015; Tavaana, 2016).

The One Million Signature Campaign succeeded in challenging gender discrimination embedded in a legal system, informed both by state-sanctioned patriarchy and a religio-governmentalized reading of Islamist governmentality. And though it was to produce little in the way of practical gains for women, it, nonetheless, galvanized them, as will be seen in the next chapter, into reinventing themselves by opening up a new dimension in their social lives, in the process empowering a generation of rights-bearing women committed to asserting themselves on the social and political scene as citizens determined to claim their fundamental civic rights. As will be seen, it was these women, in combination with students and youth, that would provide the 2009 Green Movement with the majority of its activists and footsoldiers.

Conclusion

This chapter has shown how the triangular relation among processes of governmentality, competing discourses, along with the social and political practices they inspire, and the formation of the subject can provide a roadmap for examining solidarity building, modes of radical resistance and, above all, the very conditions for the possibility of protest in a semi-authoritarian setting. To this end, I have examined the emergence in late-1980s Iran of both a dominant ideology and a counterdiscourse and demonstrated how the competing social and political practices they inspired came to create an unbridgeable rift between the conservative establishment and certain social strata, in particular students, women and youth.

It has also been shown that certain state policies, practices and religious knowledges that were the hallmark, mainstay and public face of the Islamic Republic's conduct of conduct—or to be more precise that of the conservative establishment that dominated the judiciary and supervisory bodies and monopolized technologies of power—had the effect of inducing strategic forms of everyday resistance. Put differently, the policies implemented by the conservative establishment, in particular those that worked to the detriment of oppositional groups, contributed in no small way to politicizing and radicalizing them to the extent that they were willing to engage in collective action. Indeed, upon finding the mainstream political institutions such as the *Majlis* closed to them, these groups, and in particular students and women, elected to transform the public spaces of urban centres into zones of political defiance, all with a view to asserting their political will and contesting the status quo.

In a semi-authoritarian setting collective action on a mass scale constitutes a corporeal challenge to dominant attitudes, values, norms, knowledges and rules of political conduct and, by implication, to the status quo itself. It is, moreover, the expression of a collective will to contest power at a thousand points on the part of a people shaped by specific relations of marginalization and subordination. In such settings, resistance to processes of governmentality assumes the form of disparate and ubiquitous arts, technologies and tactics of contestation, that mirror not just the enabling aspect of state power, by which I mean its propensity to induce resistance, but the power and potential of the subjugated masses. This was particularly true in the case of women's groups whose resistance to the status quo was bound up in ordinary life practices and unfolded in governmentalized public spaces.

Lastly, for the semi-authoritarian state to turn a blind eye to presence-as-resistance and other expressions of opposition and/or make significant concessions would have run the risk of losing its grip on power. This explains why the conservative establishment felt compelled to crush the 1999 student movement and drive the 2006 Women's One Million Signature Campaign underground. Despite these apparent reversals, however, the hegemonic frame did in fact shift, if only slightly, as evinced, for example, by amendments to the marital law providing for greater gender equality. More important for the future, the student movement and the Women's One Million Signature Campaign would each play a decisive role in developing a new social and political consciousness among Iranians, who increasingly came to see themselves as rights-bearing and politicized citizens determined to assert their collective political will.

Notes

1 Neo-Shariatism represents an updated version of Iranian intellectual Ali Shariati's ideas on governance that were formulated during the early 1970s. In his view, the real agents for bringing about sociopolitical change are not political or religious elites, but the people whose political authority is sacrosanct. He even went so far as to equate God with the people in social issues, declaring, "We can always substitute the people for God" (cited in Mahdavi, 2011, p. 104).
2 The term *mardumsari*, a Persian rendering of democracy, means literally that the people are at the top of the hierarchy.
3 Indeed, so popular were Michael Jackson's dance moves among Iranian youth during the 1990s, for those of my generation, watching video clips of his performances evokes a profound nostalgia.
4 Clarification is required here. As Saeid Amir Arjomand argues, in the context of the Islamic Republic, the very notion of 'civil society' "in the sense of an autonomous sphere of associations whose growth is facilitated by the legal system is an empty slogan" (2000, p. 296). This view has led Hossein Bashiriyeh (2001, para. 16) to argue that the practice of using the term as a 'buzzword' in the context of a reformist discourse may be seen to be "a reaction to a deep discursive crisis in Iranian politics." This last point has been articulated, in one way or another, in the literature examining the promotion of civil society during the Khatami era. For some, e.g., Masoud Kamali (1998), the interest around developing a civil society at this time may be attributed to Iran's encounter with modernity. For others, it marks "... [a] long standing attempt[] to come to terms with the West and Western modernity by way of comprehending and incorporating it in homegrown visions of what the Iranian society should look like" (Bayatrizi, 2007, p. 22). Still others see the political developments of the early years of the twentieth century, and particularly the 1906 constitutional revolution, as the first fledgling efforts at creating a civil

society (see Mir-Hosseini, 2002). Though differing in most respects, these views share one thing in common, and that is the conviction that civil society can function as a catalyst for a democratic polity, something deeply ingrained in the Iranian collective conscious.

5 Note that two-and-a-half years into the Khatami presidency, 64 new political parties and civil society groups had been granted operating permits. The fact remains, however, that despite this progress, the number of active and influential parties and groups barely exceeded a dozen of which *Jame-eh ye Rouhaniyat-e Mobarez, Jamiyat-e Motalefeh-ye Islami, Majma-e Rouhaniyun-e Mobarez, Jebheh-e Mosharekat-e Iran-e Islami, Kargozaran-e Sazandegi* and *Mojahedin-e Inqelabi-e Islami* were among the more significant. Their operations, moreover, were severely restricted owing to the conservative establishment's control of the judiciary and the *Majlis* at that time (Afshari, 2015; Tazmini, 2009).

6 More precisely, Ayatollah Khamenei and the hardline media at first assigned blame for the chain murders to "foreign enemies," whom they accused of creating "insecurity ... [with a view] to block[ing] the progress of Iran's Islamic system" (BBC, 1998, para. 6). However, in January 1999, the Ministry of Intelligence issued a statement accusing "rogue elements" within the ministry of having committed the crimes (Iran Press Service, 2000). Several of its operatives were arrested and the alleged mastermind, one Saeid Emami, reported to have committed suicide by drinking a bottle of hair remover while being held in prison.

7 Foucault borrowed this concept, which was originally spelled "absolutely absolute," from Amir Parviz Pouyan, leader of a leftist guerilla group called *Fadaaian-e Khalq* (the Devotees of People), established in Iran in 1970. For a further discussion of this point, see *Foucault in Iran: Islamic Revolution After the Enlightenment* (2016) by Behrooz Ghamari-Tabrizi.

8 Neo-traditionalists generally take a more liberal stance on the *hijab*.

9 They are more popularly known in the West as Islamic feminists (Mir-Hosseini, 2004; Tohidi, 2006; Povey, 2016).

10 As Farhad Khosrokhavar (2012) reports, in late 2008 men comprised 30% of all campaign members.

5 The Green Movement as a movement of movements and the rise of a home-grown rights-based society in post-revolutionary Iran

Introduction

This chapter uses a Foucauldian-inspired model of collective action to analyse the formation, emergence and subsequent development of the 2009 Iranian Green Movement. The purpose here lies in elucidating the multiple components, dimensions and processes, along with the aspirations of the actors, which either constituted or defined this unprecedented phenomenon. Special emphasis will be placed on interrogating the historical processes at work, culminating in a social and political movement that in June 2009 shook the Islamic Republic to its very foundations.

In particular, I examine the manifold historical conditions responsible for the emergence and development of what became, by the time Mahmood Ahmadinejad assumed office in 2005, the Islamic Republic's official/dominant discourse, one that promoted neo-Islamist governmentalization by raising the conduct of conduct to the level of a fine art. I also explicate how this process unfolded by identifying its principal discursive elements and delineating what they signified. How this dominant discourse gave rise to certain knowledges, practices, laws and rules for conducting the lives of Iranians in general, and students, women and youth in particular, between 2005 and 2009 is also examined. This enquiry examines the laws, policies, knowledges, mentalities of governing and practices operative during the period 2005–2009, in effect creating a vantage point from which to analyse the various factors leading to the emergence of the Green Movement; it also elucidates those knowledges and rationalities and social and political rules and practices the demonstrators were actively resisting. This historical investigation will enable me to delineate and explain how the 2009 uprising gave rise to and solidified a counterdiscourse that contested the legitimacy of the dominant discourse by challenging and negating its knowledges and politically-inspired practices and, ultimately, its very way of constituting the world.

A Foucauldian-inspired model of collective action, or in Foucauldian terms counterconduct, designates the various forms/modes of resistance to governmental power or governmentality. The latter refers to an amalgam of "quite different arts of government" or what Foucault would call variously techniques of governance, arts of governance or rationalities (Walters, 2012, p. 41). For Foucault, the term counterconduct, then, captures the processes and modalities that run, in various ways and forms, counter to such arts, techniques and rationalities of governance.

Suffice it to say that, on one level, a movement of counterconduct projects "the ubiquity of the refusal of power"—power that may and can "be resisted by the force of collective will" (Osborne, 1999, p. 52). Conceived as such, counterconduct embodies resistance on the part of a people engaged in the game of "des-ubjectification [or] what could [be] call[ed] ... the politics of truth" (Foucault, 1996, p. 386), which is what a governmentalized regime strives to promote as normal, rational and truthful with respect to official knowledges and the social and political practices they inform. At the level of discourse lies an approach to analysing the emergence and development of a movement of counterconduct. As Foucault explains in reference to his analysis of the French Revolution, to be discussed later, the latter assumed the character of a battle of discourses in the sense that the forces of revolution advanced an agenda, and a form of knowledge production that can best be described as a discourse on resistance, which worked to de-legitimize and disrupt hegemonic discourses. This means, for Foucault, that understanding the French Revolution entails "analy[zing] ... the conflict of discourses [that numbered among its singular features]" (Baker, 1994, p. 198). The same approach has been applied here to understanding the Green Movement.

Discourse, both as an instrument and as an effect of power, informs what can be discursively thought, communicated and/or demanded at a given historical juncture, thereby shaping policies and practices. Consistent with this understanding of discourse, a movement of counterconduct has as a first priority the de-legitimization of official knowledges, and by means of "turning [them] against [themselves] ... or mobilizing some forms of [knowledge] against others" (Medina, 2011, p 13).

In order to grasp how state-sponsored knowledges, and by implication counter-knowledges, emerge and develop, it is essential to analyse the day-to-day processes and events that culminate in their genesis and development. This can be facilitated by viewing everyday life, as informed by everyday life practices, wherein power collides and interacts with counterpower to create new ways of thinking, new forms of expression and, most importantly, new forms of knowledge, which may and can run counter to the dominant knowledge(s). In this way, one is able to discern how seemingly mundane and everyday life practices become politicized, and how they transpire strategic points of resistance to negate state power. The politics of everyday life is thus crucial to understanding how a movement of counterconduct emerges from the shadows, conducts operations and evolves.

The chief importance of analysing the politics of everyday life can be summed up both in the Foucauldian formulation that "everywhere that power exists, it is being exercised" and in the dictum that disciplinary power, that most ubiquitous modality of power, operates at the level of minute practices of everyday life (Foucault, 1977, p. 213). It follows, then, that resistance may be viewed as a galvanizing force within everyday struggles to resist, subvert and reject power relations. For Foucault, power "is a total structure of actions brought to bear upon possible actions" (1982, p. 789), meaning that while power is a "way of changing people's conduct" throughout the course of day-to-day life, it also offers the opportunity to resist and negate it (O'Farrell, 2005, p. 99). The everyday becomes the domain of ubiquitous power relations whereby governmental conduct is imposed and resisted.

In what follows, the above observations are put to the test with a view to analysing the emergence of the Green Movement as a case of counterconduct. In particular, I examine the context, or what Foucault (1972; May, 1993; O'Farrell, 2005; Gallagher, 2008) calls the conditions of possibility for thought or conditions for the emergence and existence of knowledge, that is, for the emergence and development of what became, by the time Mahmoud Ahmadinejad assumed office in 2005, the Islamic Republic's official/dominant discourse and rationality. With a view to explaining how this process unfolded, I interrogate dominant discursive elements and showcase what they signify. The ways in which the dominant discourse informed specific knowledges, practices, arts and rules for governing Iranians in general, and students, women and youth in particular, between 2005 and 2009 are also examined.

In interrogating the historical experiences and trajectories of the Green Movement, and taking account of the specific historical context within which it emerged, developed and conducted operations, I argue that the Green Movement may be best described as a movement of movements, a mega social movement of disparate movements or a coalition of smaller movements of counterconduct that in June 2009 merged to form a broad front in opposition to the neoconservative establishment's conduct of conduct. Moreover, it was this willingness to coalesce on the part of what heretofore had been smaller oppositional movements with diverse agendas that constituted a primary attribute of the Green Movement as a movement of movements—a willingness that signified a new historical phase in post-revolutionary Iran, one marked by growing demands for democratic civic rights among political activists and ordinary citizens alike. As will be seen, it was precisely a yearning for these rights that would in June 2009 drive hundreds of thousands to occupy the streets and other public spaces of Iranian cities.

Foucault, governmentality and counterconduct

According to the Foucauldian model of collective action, oppositional movements seek to challenge and negate governmental power at the level of certain techniques, knowledges and mentalities of ruling. These arts of governing constitute the zone between the poles of strategic relations and states of domination (Walters, 2012). Foucault refers to them under the rubric of "governmentality," an umbrella term that in the context of collective action "captures the close interrelationship between protes[tors] and the forms of government they oppose" (Death, 2010, p. 236). Pitted against this conduct of conduct was "the art of not being governed like that" and "the art of not being governed so ... much" (Foucault, 1996, p. 384). Foucault describes some of the diverse ways of de-authenticating, de-legitimizing and, above all, challenging and negating governmental regimes through collective action, or more precisely what he calls movements of counterconduct. All work to resist processes of governmentality predicated upon macro and micro, formal and informal, intense and subtle arts/modes of governing that together constitute not just the idea of modern governance, but the very notion of the modern state (Walters, 2015; McCall, 2015).

As highlighted in Foucault's analysis of the 1979 Iranian revolution, a movement of counterconduct showcases a people's collective political will to challenge and negate certain configurations of power, knowledge and techniques of governance (Foucault, 2005a, 2005b). For example, a moment of singularity or social rupture can and sometimes does emerge when the conduct of conduct becomes so intolerable as to leave mobilization and collective action the only remaining avenues for expressing discontent. In such circumstances, Foucault (2005a, 2005b) asserts, a people come to prefer death to obeying the rules, arts and techniques for controlling their conduct. Moreover, at precisely that stage when oppositional movements take shape or are about to emerge, certain concerns become paramount, specifically "how not to be governed like that, by that, in the name of those principles, in view of such objectives and by the means of such methods, not like that, not for that, not by them" (Foucault, 1996, p. 384).

This politics of rejection, of saying "no" to specific forms of governmentality, represents a response to what Foucault calls "power at its extremities" (1980, p. 96), enabled by various power techniques and knowledges that in combination have the potential to "make the state so dangerous" (Walters, 2012, p. 41). This "politics of combination" provides a lens through which one can discern how the "state ... become[s] what it is" and how in response a people become what they are, and by implication how movements of counterconduct take shape, emerge and operate (Walters, 2012, p. 39). Perhaps what is most essential to grasp here is that counterconduct is conceived at that moment when docile bodies declare collectively, "I will no longer obey" (Foucault, cited in Afary & Anderson, 2005, p. 129).

In this Foucauldian formulation, it is the web of relations between rulers and ruled, conductor and conducted, that provides a focal point for analysing a movement of counterconduct. While the state seeks to project power and consolidate authority throughout the whole social body, the resistance encountered, or, more accurately, "the strategic codification of ... points of resistance," may, at certain historical junctures and at certain moments of pure singularity, lead to ubiquitous social ruptures and fundamental divisions between those who govern and those being governmentalized (Foucault, 1978, p. 96).

Part of the reason Foucault takes such pains to emphasize the singularity of movements of counterconduct lies in the specific social modes and circulation of governmental power. For him, such movements must be understood in relation to "those [strategic] points where [power] becomes capillary, that is, in its more [social,] regional and local forms and institutions" (Foucault, 1980, p. 96). It is there, where power is confronted at its outer limits, that the reader is invited to analyse oppositional movements.

For Foucault, this minute exercise of governmental power is to be understood with reference to two phenomena that elucidate, each in its own way, the intimate relationship existing between power and resistance, and thus the emergence and operations of movements of counterconduct: the politics of the everyday (or everyday politics), and discourse as counterknowledge.

Everyday politics is political because the efficacy of governmental power is contingent upon orchestrating, harmonizing and, above all, governmentalizing bodies in public spaces. For example, disciplinary power, that most ubiquitous modality of power, "depends upon the creation of novel physical arrangements in which people can be monitored in the minute details of their activities" (Barnett, 1999, p. 378). In this way, Foucault (1978) opines, disciplinary power is predicated entirely upon, and feeds on, spatial enclosure, fixity and isolation, all of which are intended to promote uniformity and manufacture harmony. Above all, it is the "constitution of an empty, closed space [that enables] ... artificial multiplicities ... to be constructed and organized" (Foucault, 2007, p. 17). All this transpires, as Judith Butler reminds us, because the "state apparatus ... depends upon the public space [for its] theatrical self-constitution," and hence its survival (2011, para. 13).

Yet, even as all this unfolds, and especially during those periods when disciplinary monitoring and surveillance reach unprecedented heights, new possibilities for contestation may open up, as those who are the objects of power transform public spaces into domains of resistance wherein the social and political status quo can be contested and negated. As might be expected, where institutional channels for bringing about change are sclerotic, it is in these very public spaces that mass demonstrations and other forms of resistance against processes of governmentality erupt. Thus, in the politics of everyday life, power and resistance, "in all their material ... and everyday manifestations," are always inseparable and reciprocal (Ballvé, 2011, para. 3). In the case of movements of counterconduct, this means "a spatial perspective allows us to historicize power relations and to grasp them in their transformations" (Tazzioli et al., 2015, p. 6). For only in the space of power, it can be argued, can a domain of resistance, defiance and protestation emerge (West-Pavlov, 2009). In this way, scrutinizing what Nancy Fraser (1989, p. 18) calls the "politics of everyday life," anchored in those everyday power techniques, rules and norms that work to subordinate the individual, is essential to discerning how subjugated bodies can defy and/or resist these manifestations of power by means of counterstrategies involving everyday life practices, even those that may appear to be mundane and apolitical, for example weblogging, bicycling, singing. Ironically, the latter are hardly immune to the operations of power in the sense that they can in some instances be governmentalized and, by implication, routinized and regularized, monitored and surveilled, controlled and manipulated by applying disparate disciplinary techniques.

As to why the politics of everyday life is so germane to understanding movements of counterconduct, we need look no farther than Foucault's formulation of governmental power and how it circulates through a given society. Foucault (1982) has famously argued that beyond a single sovereign mode of power, the modern state employs a host of subtle rules, norms and regulations aimed at subjecting and disciplining the individual through various techniques, such as observation, normalization and the disciplinary gaze. This "disciplinary power," Foucault (1995, p. 170) argues, permeates the "whole social body" and does so far more subtly, and by implication effectively, than its sovereign counterpart, which, relying mainly on brute force, imposes far greater social and political costs. As a result, everyday life constitutes a domain of power relations, precisely because "power [is] an unavoidable element of social life" (Allen, 1999, p. 44), which means that to understand the dynamics of collective action, in particular of a radical kind, requires an understanding of the scuffles that erupt spontaneously at the level of the everyday.

Bodies are, according to Foucault (1995), the chief object, marker and objective of disciplinary power. Thus, not surprisingly, it is in the domain of everyday life that one can best bear witness to the Foucauldian phenomenon of subjection, which paradoxically constitutes a double-edged sword: on one hand, bodies are subjected to laws, rules and regulations aimed at securing their submission, by way of, among other things, internalizing certain norms and codes; on the other, these same bodies can take up the position of acting subjects, thereby becoming not just "counter ... modalities of power" but also "modalities of power" seeking to wrest, resist and contest the legitimacy and authenticity of a "governmental regime" (Butler, 2011, para. 12).

Subjection or subjugation, a phenomenon that induces everyday struggles with power, plays out at the level of the minute practices of everyday life, thereby providing a portal through which to discern how individuals become resistant bodies and, furthermore, how, at certain moments of historical singularity, they may transmute into agents seeking to transform themselves, and by implication their society and the governmentalizing system ruling it. Thus, asserts Patrick Ffrench, analysing the politics of everyday life is crucial for analysing "the potential emergence of 'new relations,' 'new virtualities,' ['new pleasures,' 'new alliances,' etc.]" (2004, p. 302). In this way, through the politics of everyday life a people can develop a "new consciousness about themselves and their individual ... rights" (Amir-Ebrahimi, 2006, p. 4), and precisely because such a politics undermines the very rationales, norms and mentalities at work to produce docile, disciplined, subordinated and marginalized bodies.

The second requirement for apprehending movements of counterconduct and the so-called politics of everyday life that are their most common form of expression is an understanding of power and resistance in relation to discourse. According to Williams and Davidson (1996), the latter refers to, as was noted in the previous chapter, "a collection of statements (frequently, though not exclusively, a body of texts) unified by the designation of a common object of analysis [and] by particular ways of articulating knowledge about that object" (pp. 88–89).

It is in the context of discourse where power and knowledge are conjoined, hence Margaret McLaren's (2002) observation that discourses embody the juxtaposition of power and knowledge. Clearly, for Foucault, a study of discourse "entail[s] a focus on discourse-as-knowledge" (Hook, 2007, p. 132). Knowledge, then, is an integral part of a Foucauldian-inspired notion of discourse; the latter not only refocuses it "as a matter of the social, historical and political conditions under which statements come to count as true or false" (Hook, 2007, p. 132), but also demarcates "the limits of acceptable speech" and, by implication, the limits of "possible truth," not just in the world of theoretical abstraction, but also in practice (Butler, 1997, p. 34). It is precisely the latter observation that constitutes the basis upon which Foucault (1978) acknowledges that at any given moment in any society, one can discern a dominant discourse at work—as demonstrated in *History of Sexuality* with respect to the dominant discourse on modern sexuality—underpinned by a set of historically and sociopolitically specific conditions of possibilities, developed by a complex of signs, texts and statements, and solidified and sustained by the state or by some political faction with a monopoly over specific levers of power and conduct. In this way, a dominant discourse is, for Foucault, in a very real practical sense, "an instrument" or producer of power (1978, p. 100). It demarcates the boundaries of the good, bad and ugly in the context of real life practices; backs up the knowledges and mentalities required to exercise power; provides a rationale for formulating certain laws, rules and regulations, and for their application. All this is enabled through a set of discursive functions that "break [down] the concept of the discourse ... into different aspects" (Baumgarten & Ullrich, 2012, p. 17).

Herein, and this is the crucial point to grasp, this power–knowledge–discourse triangulation can only be fully comprehended when analysed in reference to a complementary element: resistance. Foucault (1978) writes and speaks of a discourse of resistance in the sense that the dominant discourse simultaneously "transmits and produces power; it reinforces it, but also undermines it and exposes it, renders it fragile and makes it possible to thwart it" (pp. 100–101). In *History of Sexuality*, for instance, he cites a counterdiscourse capable of calling into question the legitimacy of the dominant discourse on sexuality. Discourse, or more precisely the dominant discourse, can and often does provide conditions of possibility for resistance, including the production and dissemination of counterdiscourses, replete with their own particular truth and knowledges (Howarth, 2000). The latter are a product of discursive practices that inform what can be produced and disseminated in a particular geographical/societal domain as the given truth and/or dominant mode of knowledge. Moreover, so omnipresent is the effect of the dominant discourse that the counterdiscourse will at times appropriate some of its signs and terminology to foreground its own way of constituting the world. This is because, according to Carl Death (2010), various forms of resistance replicate, project and manifest the arts, techniques and mentalities of power and the relationships that underpin them.

But what of counterconduct in this power–knowledge–discourse–resistance formulation nexus? Perhaps, this question is best addressed by first acknowledging that to understand movements of counterconduct requires "the recovery of discourses and discursive contexts," meaning that it is the discursive functions of the dominant discourse, that determine what can be said, demanded, and contested by the opposition at a given time in a given society (Vucetic, 2011, p, 1300).

For Foucault, understanding how the dominant discourse(s) shapes social and political practices must be understood in relation to "its arbitrariness in terms of knowledge, its violence in terms of power, in short, its energy" (1996, p. 395)—particularly in those historical situations where such practices have become intolerable for those over whom power is exercised—is key to grasping how movements of counterconduct emerge and develop, hence Foucault's insistence that the French revolution of 1798 "does not play the role of an event exterior to discourse" (1972, p. 176).

This means that, strictly speaking, at the level of discourse or discourse-as-knowledge, counterconduct is to be understood as a signifier for, and by-product of, conflicting discourses competing to inform how the world is to be imagined and perceived. This is necessarily so because, on one level, a movement of counterconduct signifies a conflict of discourses, and by implication worldviews and knowledges; indeed, as Corey McCall (2004, p. 9) posits, a movement of counterconduct emerges as "a necessary response" to those "existing relations of power and knowledge" embedded in the dominant discourse(s). In this sense, counterconduct signifies a clash of discourses.

The latter formulation for understanding a movement of counterconduct speaks to, above all else, a "critical battle against the monopolization of knowledge-producing practices" by the dominant discourse(s) (Medina, 2011, p. 13). It becomes, regardless of how it may emerge, an insurrection of subjugated knowledges (Foucault, 2003), and brings to the fore new visibilities, knowledges, techniques and above all new ways of envisioning the world (Death, 2010). This is because such movements are ultimately about the hermeneutics of the subject, that is, of those who have a deep and abiding desire/urge to transform and/or renew themselves (Foucault, 2005b) and their society through a "[collective] struggle [that aims to] present a different way of thinking" about social life and political processes at work (Foucault, cited in Ghamari-Tabrizi, 2016, p. 62). Hence, Foucault is to be taken both literally and figuratively when he asserts that "one must recognize the transformative character of a moment when [a] people say, 'I will refuse to obey'" (Foucault, cited in Afary & Anderson, 2005, p. 263).

In the next section, I examine the context, or in Foucauldian terms the conditions of possibility, for the production and development during the late 1990s of what became, by the time Ahmadinejad assumed office in 2005, the state's official/dominant discourse and narrative. I also explicate how this process unfolded by identifying their principal discursive elements and delineating what the latter signify. How this dominant discourse gave rise to certain knowledges, practices, laws and rules for conducting the lives of Iranians in general, and students, women and youth in particular between 2005 and 2009 is also examined. This will require investigating the policies, laws, practices, knowledges and mentalities of governing operative during the period 2005–2009, in effect creating a vantage point from which to analyze the various factors leading to the emergence of the Green Movement as well as elucidating the knowledges and social and political practices and rules and norms the demonstrators were actively resisting. This historical investigation will enable me to delineate and explain how the 2009 uprising gave rise to and solidified a counterdiscourse that contested the legitimacy of the dominant discourse by challenging and negating its knowledges and sociopolitically-inspired practices and ultimately its very way of constituting the world.

Ahmadinejad's rise to power: The emergence of a neo-absolutist discourse

On June 24, 2005, Mahmood Ahmadinejad became the sixth president of the Islamic Republic, having garnered no less than 64% of the popular vote (Takeyh,

2009). So decisive a victory was due less to Ahmadinejad's personal popularity than to domestic and geopolitical factors. First and foremost of these was economic mismanagement on the part of the outgoing, reform-minded Khatami administration. Note that while the consequences of the aforementioned neo-liberal policy initiatives introduced by the Rafsanjani administration (1990–1997) were responsible in part for the gross economic mismanagement that plagued the Khatami administration, the latter's free trade policy and heavy borrowing abroad did little to improve the lot of ordinary Iranians or address the ever-growing gap between rich and poor. The fallout from these policies, notes Mojtaba Mahdavi (2008), proved devastating:

> By March 2002, Iran's foreign debt stood at $20 billion [US]. By [the] year 2000, 20–23 percent of ... urban and rural households lived under the absolute poverty line and the vast majority needed two [income earners to survive]. By [the] year 2001 ... inflation ranged from 20 to 50 percent, and more than 4 million Iranians remained unemployed. Each year more than 750,000 individuals entered [the] labour market while the economy [produced] only 300,000 new jobs annually. (p. 8)

In addition, the reformists failed to meet fully the expectations of their primary constituencies—women, students and youth—that in 1997 had been instrumental in rallying the bulk of the electorate to the reformist cause—and this despite the fact that after 2001 reformists made up the majority in the *Majlis*. Youth in particular fared poorly in an economy tottering on the brink of disaster. In 2005, "[w]ith almost two-thirds of ... [a population numbering] seventy million ... under ... thirty years [of] age," apart from the urban and rural poor, it was youth who were "most vulnerable to unemployment, inflation, and economic instability" (Mahdavi, 2008. p. 9).

A great many students, moreover, were disenchanted with the Khatami administration, believing it had shirked its responsibility "during periods of crisis such as the attacks on ... student protest[ors in] 1999" (Povey, 2016, p. 86)—which was indicative of what Tara Povey refers to as "Khatami's inability to put the movement before the state" (2016, p. 86). Rather than protecting those students who had unconditionally thrown their support behind him, Khatami elected instead to "call[] for calm and national stability, [all the while] emphasizing his loyalty to the supreme leader" (Povey, 2016, p. 68).

Saeid Amir Arjomand (2009) and Tara Povey (2016) assert that Khatami was adopting a conciliatory approach towards the conservative establishment as evinced by his refusal to support student demands for political accountability and transparency. In retaliation, the Office for Consolidation of Unity (*daftar-e tahkim-e vahdat*) (OCU), the country's largest student organization—some of its members had been in the vanguard of the 1999 student movement—"[began to keep its] distance ... believing it had been badly let down by the President and the reformists" (Amir Arjomand, 2009, p. 108). In alienating the students, and in particular the activists comprising the backbone of student organizations, the Khatami administration lost the support of an important constituency.

Nor was the government able to make good on its promises to women's groups. Reformists in the *Majlis,* Ervand Abrahamian reports, "passed more than a hundred reform bills," with the majority being blocked or disqualified by supervisory bodies, most notably the conservative-dominated Guardian Council (2008, p. 190). What raised the ire of women in particular was the failure on the part of the reformist-dominated *Majlis* to ratify the Convention on the Elimination of All Forms of Discrimination against Women (CEDAW), a United Nations initiative hailed by feminists as an international bill of rights for women. In December 2001, the Khatami administration drafted the requisite legislation and submitted it for ratification to the *Majlis*. However, and as was discussed in Chapter 4, immediately prior the final vote, the enabling bill was placed on hold owing to concerns on the part of conservative clerics that it was incompatible with *Shari'a* law. In August 2003, the Guardian Council would finally reject the bill, shattering all hope of reform (Feminist News, 2013). This single incident is indicative of the Khatami administration's inability to advance a reform agenda, in the process alienating women, one of its primary constituencies: and especially the young among them.

More broadly, the CEDAW debacle illustrates what Saied Amir Arjomand (2009) describes as the "paradox of Khatami's rule of law," whereby "he and his supporters [for example, the nation's law makers] were seen to be powerless to either mak[e] laws or enforc[e] them" (p. 94). This political impotence speaks to Khatami's ambiguous position within Iran's power structure: he "was neither a mere extension of the will of the political establishment nor an [opponent within] the establishment" (Mahdavi, 2008, p. 14). Viewed in the most charitable light, Khatami was unable rather than unwilling to push for the kind of political reform required to meet the expectations of his constituencies.

The foregoing examples speak to Khatami's limited success in maintaining the support of the broad coalition that had worked to bring about his electoral victory. This is reflected in the makeup of his administration, which was dominated by a closed circle of political elites described by Fred Halliday as a "post-revolutionary ruling group of around 5,000 men, cleric and lay alike" (2005, para. 4). Popularly perceived as "a kind of Islamic *nomenklatura*" (Halliday, 2005, para. 4), that "relied on negotiations from above" and by-passing the grassroots (Mahdavi, 2006, p. 3), these insiders concentrated in the executive branch of government would later be accused of exploiting the economy and political process for personal gain. Thus, one can argue, the reform movement and "the reformist leadership suffered from too much elitism" (Mahdavi, 2006, p. 15), a shortcoming that took the wind out of the sails of the reformers and in so doing contributed to a conservative victory in the 2005 presidential election.

In addition to the Khatami administration's economic mismanagement and its mediocre performance in delivering on social and political reforms, geopolitical factors played a major role in Ahmadinejad's ascendancy. Under Khatami, foreign policy had two interrelated objectives: integrating the country into the global community and promoting what was officially referred to as a dialogue of civilizations, both deemed to be prescriptions for reducing global conflict (Abrahamian, 2008; Takeyh, 2011). These initiatives received a fatal blow, however, when in a 2002 State of the Union address, President Bush denounced Iran, North Korea and Iraq as an axis of evil.

"Domestic audience[s]," Tara Povey argues, could not help but view "such statements ... as the continuation of a hypocritical policy on the part of the US, which criticized Iran while supporting ... [authoritarian] Arab regimes and the Israeli occupation of Palestine" (2016, p. 87). Conservatives in Iran were quick to exploit Bush's axis-of-evil speech, by dismissing reformist foreign policy as naïve, short-sighted and devoid of any real grasp of global politics. The subsequent invasion and occupation of Iran's neighbours, Iraq and Afghanistan, by a Western coalition further undermined the administration's foreign policy position and raised doubts as to the competence of the political elites running the country. In the 2005 presidential election, conservatives would capitalize on these foreign policy blunders, much to the discomfort of reformists.

While Khatami's reformist project "was not a total failure" (Mahdavi, 2011, p. 97), its elitism and neglect of social and economic rights, along with limited success in improving the lot of students, women, youth, its chief constituencies, as well as the urban poor, in combination with geopolitical developments, ensured a conservative victory in the 2005 general election and the subsequent political marginalization of reformists.

At the same time that the Khatami administration was floundering, there emerged a new conservative right, one capable of capitalizing on reformist blunders and creating an agenda that would appeal to a broad constituency. It was this formidable coalition of reactionary elements that in 2005 propelled Ahmadinejad into the executive office. But whom precisely did Ahmadinejad represent, what was his political agenda, and how did the right come to capture the executive office in Iran's complex, multilayered and factional system of governance?

The new right, the neo-absolutist discourse and the rise of a neo-Islamist governmentality

The year 2005 witnessed a wholesale reconstitution of Iran's ruling elite, marked by the rise of the new right, the so-called neoconservatives, also known as Iranian neocons or *Osoulgarayan*, translated literally as Principalists. "Commit[ted] to traditional Islamic principles and unwilling[] to change," the latter viewed with the utmost alarm the reformist's project of change/reform from within the system (Safshekan & Sabet, 2010, p. 546). At the same time, the neoconservatives differed from the traditional right in several respects. Many of their leading lights, including Mahmood Ahmadinejad, Rouhollah Hosseinian, Sadegh Mahsouli and Mohammad Hossein Saffaar Harandi, were younger than their counterparts on the traditional right, such as Nateq Nouri, Javadi Amoli and Mahdavi Kani, and consequently had played no significant role in the revolution.

Many, including Ahmadinejad himself, however, had served during the Iran–Iraq War (1980–1988) as "young, middle-ranking ... members" of the Iranian Revolutionary Guard Corps (IRGC), some in one of its security or intelligence branches (Safshekan & Sabet, 2010, p. 546). The neoconservatives, moreover, were critical of what they saw as the traditional right's overly abstract view of social and political affairs, which precluded political pragmatism. At the same time, they condemned the practice of *servat andoozi,* or self-enrichment, to which many clergymen among both the traditional and moderate right, and most notably Hashemi Rafsanjani (1958–2017), subscribed, equating it with corruption (Hunter, 2014).

Fortified by a neo-absolutist discourse, the neoconservatives soon came to dominate the executive branch. As with its absolutist predecessor, at the heart of this discourse lay a religio-governmentalized view of the Islamic Republic as a holy phenomenon whose right to rule was based on "the blessing" of a divine/ God (Ahmadinejad, cited in Amanat, 2009, p. 240). Moreover, as with the earlier project of conduct of conduct, theirs was structured around the concept of *hokoomate dini* or "Islamist Government" (Khamenei, 2000, para. 9), which meant that "all rules and regulations [were to be] derived from religious rulings" (Mesbah Yazdi, 2017). Thus, "all those who occup[ied] major ... [positions] in the system [were] in fact appointed by God" (Mesbah Yazdi, 2017).

While the neo-absolutist discourse, like its absolutist predecessor did not necessarily rule out elections per se, ultimately, it "rejected the principle of popular sovereignty ... convinced that sovereignty only belong[s] to God" and his representative on earth, namely the Supreme *faqih* (Schwerin, 2015, p. 210). In this schema, the people were relegated to the status of duty-bound subjects. And while permitted to participate in elections, they had "no role in bestowing legitimacy on the system and its *faqih*" (Mesbah Yazdi, cited in Andisheh Siasi, 2017, para. 2). Rather, by virtue of divine sanction, this virtually divine being possessed "all the rights necessary to govern" (Javadi Amoli, cited in Alvadossadegh, 2011).

Where the neo-absolutist discourse and its project of governmentality departed from its absolutist predecessor was in emphasizing that, in addition to God and the Rule/Guardianship of the Supreme *faqih,* there existed yet a third source of political legitimacy, namely the Imam Mahdi, the twelfth Imam of the Shiites, believed to be in occultation. It was imperative that this august figure be the focal point of the new administration's project of conduct of conduct, the centrepiece for neo-Islamist governmentality.

Underpinning the project of neo-Islamist governmentalization was a messianic narrative, according to which the 12th Imam had voluntarily "relinquished his authority to the Supreme *faqih*," thereby providing the neocons, as will be seen shortly, with a rationale for their social, political and economic policies. Within this new messianic political order, "[a] new class of clerics" (Rahimi, 2012, p. 67) led by Ayatollah Mohammad Taqi Mesbah Yazdi, the neocon theorist *par excellence,* called for the social and economic justice and equality deemed to be a prerequisite for the Mahdi's return, which they believed was imminent. Their programme would soon be appropriated by the new right eager to assume the mantle of reform—a purely opportunistic move on their part aimed at filling the political vacuum created by the policies of the departing Khatami administration. The stage set for a "resurgence of ... Mahdism" at the state level (Rahimi, 2012, p. 66), fuelled by an unshakable conviction on the part of its proponents that "it was the [role] of politics to prepare for [the Imam's] return" (Schwerin, 2015, pp. 210–211).

The neo-Islamist governmentalizing project was to be promoted by a populist rhetoric, one that was manufactured and opportunistic, as evinced by artificial values and suffused with buzzwords, religious, messianic and otherwise. Bereft of anything resembling authenticity, it represented a political/strategic initiative aimed at winning the support of the masses, in particular those socially and economically dispossessed. Moreover, its opportunism lay in its intent to capitalize on the shortcomings of reformist economic and social policies. In this way, slogans peppered with buzzwords and catchphrases such as economic and social equality, social and economic justice, anti-corruption, justice and human dignity, fight against aristocratic and luxury-loving tendencies, came to dominate the political scene (Hunter, 2014; Schwerin, 2015; Takeyh, 2009).

This kind of nomenclature speaks to a form of nativism that entailed in part a return to revolutionary values, chiefly justice and equality, something that held forth the prospect of fulfilling the "unfulfilled promises of the Islamic revolution," especially where the "disadvantaged and underprivileged segments of society and the less developed and deprived regions of the country" were concerned (Hunter, 2014, p. 195). Indeed, as Shirin Hunter notes, "eliminating deprivation (*mahrumiyat zodaei*)" (2014, pp. 195–196) became one of Ahmadinejad's chief campaign slogans, signifying the "pursui[t of] a kind of distributive economic justice" (2014, p. 196). All this was to transpire, moreover, under the "management" or *mudiriyat* of the Imam of the age (Ahmadinejad, cited in Amanat, 2009, p. 241), who would conjure up "a new Islamic vision of politics [inspired by a] Shi'i revolutionary model of [governance]" (Rahimi, 2012, p. 66), one that would "lead … to justice" (Ahmadinejad, cited in Amanat, 2009, p. 241). It was this narrative that underwrote the post-Khatami (2005–2013) rational for the state's project of conduct of conduct.

The new political rhetoric, with its mix of messianic fervour and populist principles, led the Supreme Leader, Ayatollah Khamenei, to back the new right in the lead-up to the 2005 election.[1] For their part, the neoconservatives and their ideological godfather, Mesbah Yazdi (2017), were more than willing to embrace the Supreme Leader as "the true and authentic representative of the twelfth Imam during his occultation." The same was true of most rank and file neocons, many of whom were appointed to government posts. It is noteworthy that the majority of these functionaries had formerly served in the IRGC at one time or another during Khamenei's tenure as Supreme Leader (1989–present) and thus had pledged absolute loyalty and obedience to the *valiy-e faqih* or Supreme Jurist (Fadaee, 2012; Safshekan & Sabet, 2010).

The neo-Islamist conduct of conduct idealized by neoconservative apparatchiks was driven by an imperative to consolidate power with a view to neutralizing a reformist project of governmentalization intent on decentralizing power by promoting political pluralism and advocating for a more rule-bound polity. Notes Mesbah Yazdi:

> [T]he prophets of God did not believe in pluralism. They believed that only one idea was right … [and that] what is being termed reform today is in fact corruption. What is being promoted in the name of reform and the path of [the] prophets is in fact in total conflict with the objectives of the prophets.
>
> (cited in Takeyh, 2009, p. 36)

And so there emerged a strategic alliance between the new right and the Supreme Leader, aimed at further entrenching the political role of the *faqih*. Soon after the neoconservatives seized control of the executive office, Mesbah Yazdi, with the blessing of the Supreme Leader, began delineating the broad contours of an "Islamist society," wherein the individual would be "duty-bound to follow the divine rule, [as laid down by] the prophets and [interpreted by] the Imams" (Mesbah Yazdi, cited in Andisheh Siasi, 2017, p. 3). Anyone who dared oppose this neo-Islamist governmentalized project, meaning those "electing to do otherwise," were in essence "committing a sin and, by implication were sinful" (Mesbah Yazdi, cited in Andisheh Siasi, 2017, p. 3). Such individuals, in Mesbah Yazdi's view, were to be treated as "second-class [citizens]," at least "as far as their rights were concerned" (cited in Hawzah News, 2010, para. 6).

Within this exclusive neo-Islamist governmentalizing framework, moreover, the citizenries were, yet again, divided into *khodis* (us), those "who believe in the [worldview]" subscribed to by the establishment, and *gheir-e khodis* (them), those "who have a critical mindset towards th[at worldview]" or who refuse to conform to its rules and the mentalities and rationales underpinning it (Fadaee, 2012, p. 83). For Simin Fadaee, this dichotomy of believers and non-believers constitutes "one of the most undemocratic" strands making up the neo-absolutist discourse, in that it serves to cultivate a climate of extreme intolerance (2012, p. 83).

Women played a strategic role in sustaining the new societal order by raising a generation of revolutionaries committed body and soul to perfecting the new governmentalizing order. "Islam," declared Ayatollah Khamenei (2009), "measures the true value of a woman based on how well she can turn around the life of her husband and children at home and help elevate their state of spiritual being" (cited in Hawzah News, 2009). It follows then that "to encourage women [to take up] ... executive and administrative [positions would be] to fall [into the] trap [of] the West's ill-intended [social, political, and cultural] invasion" (Khamenei, cited in BBC News, 2013). Thus "anyone who value[d] the participative role of women outside ... their households," was, in fact, "holding [the] wrong view, not only of religion, but also of what constitutes the natural social order" wherein "housekeeping is the most important role for women, followed ... by childbearing" (Khamenei, 2014).[2]

For Khamenei, "gender equality" represented "one of the most fundamental mistakes [made by] the West[ern world]" (Khamenei, 2014a, para. 13), the reason being "men and women possess different capabilities, and by implication qualities" (Khamenei, cited in VOA News, 2016). This implies that women's education ought to be limited only to those areas compatible with "[their] emotions and sentimentalities," such as the arts, literature, and religious studies (Khamenei, 2014a; Khamenei, 2014b).

The project of actualizing a truly neo-Islamist society was the central focus of the new discourse, given that it was perceived as the prerequisite "for the glorious reappearance of [the] Imam Mahdi" (Ahmadinejad, cited in Amanat, 2009, p. 242). For this reason, any and all means of advancing it, including violence, were justifiable according to Mesbah Yazdi (2017; Takeyh, 2011). Such reactionary views, which lay at the heart of the neo-absolutist discourse, sat well with many neoconservatives, particularly those with a military or security background, who were obsessed with the specter of internal enemies "always lurking about and plotting to subvert the ... state" (Takeyh, 2011, p. 238). The two groups most likely to pose such a threat were none other than students and youth, those "nefarious enemies ... [intent on] erod[ing the Islamic Republic's] foundations through secularism and material greed" (Takyeh, 2011, p. 225), along with modernism and liberalism—all of which they viewed to be at odds with their particular amalgam of "[Islamism], populism and nativism" (Schwerin, 2015, p. 212).

In this way, the new discourse inspired "a new style of politics" (Takeyh, 2011, p. 225), which was an amalgam of "top-down Islamization [and militancy]" (Nazifkar, 2011, p. 8), whose presence was felt not just within the corridors of power but in the lives of ordinary Iranians. That this meant "diminish[ing] the republican ... [character] of the Islamic Republic" (Rahimi, 2012, p. 67) was of little, if any, concern to the architects of the neo-Islamist governmentalizing order. The die was cast: forming a neo-Islamist government would now be the chief priority, even if this meant eliminating every vestige of republicanism.

In sum, beset by what they saw as an implacable enemy, the neoconservatives set about building a new religio-governmentalized conduct of conduct, informed by the rationales, justifications and knowledges that figured so prominently in the neo-absolutist discourse, soon to become manifest in the various new social and political practices, rules and regulations devised to govern the lives of Iranians.

Neo-Islamist governmentalization in practice: The micro-macro practices of governing life

Once in office, Ahmadinejad, with the support of his neoconservative faction, began implementing the neo-Islamist governmentalized order so long envisioned. This section examines how that order would impact Iranian society, and in particular the everyday lives of women, students and youth. An immediate priority for the neoconservatives lay in bringing to heel the media, in particular those organs of a reformist or subversive inclination. Doubtless, the neocon worldview, informed by a messianic mission, predisposed its adherents to regard alternative media with the deepest suspicion. According to a 2010 study by Reporters Without Borders, an NGO promoting freedom of information, "suppression of the press and the detention of reporters and editors had become a natural and normal, even everyday, act on the part of the Ahmadinejad government" (Khodnevis, 2010, para. 6). By the end of Ahmadinejad's second term in 2013, 46 of the country's dailies, weeklies and monthlies, chief among them *Ayandeh Noe, Shahrvand Emrooz, Shargh, Kargozaaraan, Etemad-e Melli*, had either been closed or had their operations curtailed on the grounds of "breaching national security," publishing photographs that violated "public chastity," or disseminating information that "deprived people of their psychological security," to cite only a few (Peyk Iran, 2009; Goftegoo News, 2014).

With the press muzzled, the neoconservatives, who by 2005 controlled both the executive branch and the *Majlis*, set about formulating policies aimed at controlling the conduct of students, women and youth. The government's first initiative in this regard was to rename the Centre for Affairs of Women's Participation, established by the Khatami administration with a view to "safeguarding, developing and solidifying women's participation in social and political affairs" (Hamshahri Online, 2010). The new Center for Women and Family Affairs (CWFA) was given a mandate to "safeguard women's dignity" and foster a sense of the importance of household duties, of which none was more important than "raising a generation of religious [revolutionaries]" (Hamshahri Online, 2010).

CWFA became the "ideological [vehicle] and [institutional] back[bone]" of the new governmentalizing order's project to govern the lives of women (Sadeghi, 2012, p. 127). Its new head, Zohreh Tabibzadeh Nouri, appointed by the president himself, announced on May 31, 2007 that Iran was no longer committed to "Western[-affiliated women's] treaties," as their purpose lay in "corrupting Iranian women and destroying Islamic values" (cited in Sadeghi, 2009, para. 13). Next on her "to do" list was denouncing the Convention on the Elimination of All Forms of Discrimination against Women (CEDAW), which, in the post-revolutionary period, had come to symbolize the struggle on the part of women for gender equality. "So long as I am alive," Tabibzadeh Nouri declared, "I will not allow Iran to join CEDAW or any other international treaty for women" (Sadeghi, 2009, para. 14).[3]

The CWFA became the country's leading women's think-tank, developing and promoting initiatives intended to restrict the personal freedom and mobility of women. One such initiative aimed at confining women to the domestic sphere where they would be subject to the authority of fathers and husbands. *This required a steady stream of propaganda directed at educating and socializing the public on the virtues of female domestication* (Golkar, 2015). Those logging onto the centre's website or tuning into state-owned/-controlled television and radio stations could expect to be assailed by all manner of preposterous claims, for example, that "the absence of working women from home had led sexually frustrated men to infidelity ... [compelling] the state to remove the temptation of vice by means of reinstating polygamy and *sigheh* [or temporary marriage]" (Sadeghi, 2009, para. 19).

The public opinion was prepared for the next CWFA initiative: a formal proposal for a biopolitical Family-friendly Plan. The Ahmadinejad administration seized eagerly on this initiative and in 2006 implemented the *Tarh-e Rahmat,* or Compassion Plan, the express purpose of which lay in "indoctrinating housewives to be more obedient to their husbands" (Sadeghi, 2012, p. 127). More CWFA-inspired biopolitical legislation was to come in the form of a Family Bill ratified by the *Majlis* in the summer of 2007. This legislation effectively removed many of the legal barriers to practicing polygamy, thus "making it easier and more straightforward for men to take a second wife," while also "impos[ing] taxes on ... alimony," thereby discouraging women from seeking a divorce (Sadeghi, 2012, p. 127). These legal instruments were followed by a set of complementary measures, the most important of which was a mandatory reduction in working hours for women from 44 to 36 per week, the object being to "allow women to have more time for family chores" (Sadeghi, 2012, p. 127).

In addition to legislation, the new administration employed various tactics aimed at combatting the feminist cause. For example, the state-owned/controlled media were set the twofold task of "[revealing] non-governmental organizations and feminist groups [to be] stooges of Western governments ... [duped into] promot[ing] immorality and ... [of] call[ing] for [a] ban [on] their activities" (Sadr, 2012, p. 202). At the same time, loosely-organized cells of paramilitary *basij* operatives, the Sister's Basij Organization and Women's Society Basij, were assigned to educate and guide families by conducting door-to-door visits and street workshops (Golkar, 2015; Sadeghi, 2009). The aim here laid in normalizing homemaking and childrearing as the principal societal and religious roles for women. For their part, feminists were to be singled out, more often than not, as agents of Western governments (Sadr, 2012). The administration's objective, in other words, was to "penetrate the social spheres" with a view to marginalizing, discrediting, even demonizing, feminist groups and their sympathizers (Golkar, 2015, p. 37).

The neocon project aimed at domesticating women had serious implications for female university students, who up until 2008 accounted for 63% of university and college enrolments (Hosseini, 2012). Taking its cue from the CWFA, the government mounted a systematic media campaign, the object of which lay in cataloguing the social costs of higher education for women. According to Fatemeh Sadeghi, the state-run media "blamed [co-eds] for the deterioration of the quality of university education and the demoralization of male students who are unable to marry" (2009, para. 19). They were also held partly responsible for "snatch[ing] up ... job[s] [resulting in a] high rate of male unemployment" (Sadeghi, 2009, para. 19).

As might be expected, conservative clerics were especially zealous in denouncing co-eds as a destabilizing element. On November 29, 2008, during Friday prayers, Ayatollah Ahmad Jannati, head of the Guardian Council, asserted:

> Our problem with women going to universities is that when a man wants to marry them, the first question that is brought up has to do with "how many years of education does that woman have?" This is astonishing ... How would a woman's education benefit the health of a family, its peace, and its [well-being]? What plays a role in a family's success is her piety, her morals, and her [modesty.]
>
> (cited in Mobarezeh News, 2013)

Jannati concluded by warning that the entry of women into universities "has become a problem," requiring government intervention (cited in Fararu, 2008). The *Majlis* picked up where Jannati left off with a report published by its Research Centre expressing concern over the increasing number of women in higher education, something it viewed to be "a waste of the country's resources" and "severely damag[ing to] the ... institution [of the] family," and hence a source of social instability (cited in Akbari, 2009, pp. 11–12). These calculated efforts on the part of the establishment prepared the ground for the introduction in 2008 of a bill establishing a gender quota system for universities and colleges, designed to limit the number of co-ed enrolments. Passed by the neocon-dominated *Majlis* the same year, this legislation restricted co-ed enrolment for the 2009 academic year and thereafter to 30 percent of the total (Zanaane Emrooz, 2014).

Female students were not alone in bearing the brunt of the neoconservative backlash. Viewed as bastions of liberalism and secularism, the universities had to be cleansed of all that was non-Islamist, including liberal, secular and Marxist tendencies, thus completing the unfinished work of the revolution (Aviny, 2009; Mesbah Yazdi, cited in Tasnim News, 2015). Indeed, only in this way would it be possible "to realize [its] original principles" (Schwerin, 2015, p. 212). The neoconservatives were not found wanting in either zeal or determination in this regard; in the summer of 2006 "about 200 professors perceived as ideologically unreliable [were] forced into retirement" (Schwerin, 2015, p. 21).

Neither would the OCU, the largest student organization in the country, be spared. The administration's opportunity came in the summer of 2007, in the aftermath of what came to be known as the Gaza War pitting Israel against Palestine. Following its conclusion, the OCU published a statement that, while condemning Israeli aggression, criticized what it viewed to be Tehran's policy of encouraging militancy among Palestinians (Afshari, 2016). The state propaganda machine, with *Kayhan* and *Fars* in the vanguard, began systematically attacking the OCU. On January 4, 2009 the Ministry of Science declared it illegal and ordered its offices closed (Khabar Online, 2009).

As part of the process of cleansing the universities, the government adopted a tactic aimed at curbing rogue elements operating within their respective student bodies. *Daneshjooyan-e setarehdar*, meaning literally asterisked students, required that an asterisk be affixed to the name of each student deemed a threat to the Islamic Republic (Pourmokhtari, 2014). In the summer of 2006 this approach was refined with the introduction of a three-tier classification scheme (Fassihi, 2009). Students assigned one asterisk were permitted to return to school on condition they sign a document stipulating they would no longer engage in any form of political activism. Two asterisks meant suspension from classes and interrogation; three a life-long ban from all institutions of higher learning. To identify the culprits, the government turned to its national security apparatus, a network of security forces and informants under the aegis of the Ministry of Intelligence, whose mandate included the monitoring of email and telephone conversations of suspected dissidents and activists of every stripe. According to Ali Nikounesbati, a former OCU activist, between 2005 and 2007 an estimated 1,700 students were asterisked and 41 student organizations banned (cited in Radio Farda, 2007).

The practice of asterisking students was part of a comprehensive policy, aimed at securitizing the universities, to be operationalized by *basiji* militia members who from 2005 were enrolling in undergraduate programmes in unprecedented numbers under a government-approved quota system. According to Saeid Golkar (2010), by 2004 420,000 *basiji* students were attending Iranian institutions of higher learning; by 2007 the number had climbed to 600,000. These campus watchdogs were set the task of enforcing rules and regulations aimed at silencing dissenting voices and curtailing nonconformist behaviour. These two objectives were realized in two ways: screening those university and college applicants suspected of being subversive with a view to eliminating dissidents (Pourmokhtari, 2014); and the disciplinary gaze, directed at instilling, through fear and anxiety, a broad conformity, especially to Islamist principles, rules and norms, particularly those regulating both physical appearance and behaviour (Golkar, 2010; 2015). Clothing and hair styles, along with relations between male and female students, were especially targeted.

These measures were intended to complement a project aimed at normalizing the ever-increasing Islamization, and by implication securitization, of the universities. One of the most important strategies for achieving this end involved using the media, in combination with educational workshops, to normalize and justify the rules, norms, regulations and codes for the new forms of personal conduct aimed at transforming campuses (Golkar, 2015).

An article appearing in *Mashregh News,* a news agency affiliated with the neo-conservatives, illustrates how the official media conspired to carry out this programme. The reader is first apprised of the existence within Western universities of a dominant cultural relativism whereby the rules and codes governing student conduct are perceived to vary with "[the] particular culture and customs [of the country in question]" (Mashregh News, 2014). According to the article, these institutions, all operating in "the context of non-religious and secular countries," have even "tougher and more aggressive policies in place" than those of their opposite numbers in non-secular countries, and precisely because

> [i]n the absence of religious ideals [and] values ... those who devise the rules and regulations in non-religious societies are forced to come up with tougher rules and regulations in order to prevent their societies, and by implication universities, from ... disintegrating.
>
> (Mashregh News, 2014)

All this is intended to convince the reader that Iranian universities are, if anything, more tolerant than even elite Western universities such as Oxford and Harvard, their "codes of conduct" governing everything from clothing to dating less rigid (Mashregh News, 2014). The message is clear: discipline in the service of controlling bodies is part of the natural order of things, albeit it varies across space and time. Nonetheless, whatever the context, those over whom power is exercised are obliged to conform to official rules, regulations and norms and to internalize and disseminate them in the broader society, for to do otherwise could potentially undermine the natural order of things.

With women, students and youth subjugated by means of the aforementioned laws, regulations, techniques and norms, the stage was now set for the re-Islamization of public spaces. The objective here was to construct a solid platform upon which to build a just Islamist society. This required, first and foremost, eradicating all "'non-Islamic' [forms of] behavior [and appearance in public spaces, and in particular] among youth" (Khatam, 2009, para. 15). This initiative, like the others discussed above, was set in motion by a media campaign aimed at contrasting unfavourably the status quo in Iran and that in other countries. "Why do secular states expend such great effort to protect their youth from moral decadence," protested the conservative daily *Kayhan* in its August 15, 2005 issue, "while our Islamic [counterpart] is painfully indifferent ... toward the degradation of ethics among our youth?" (cited in Khatam, 2009, para. 20).

That same month, *Kayhan*'s outrage was appropriated by the Tehran city council, which formally approved an initiative called Strategies to Extend Piety, whereby various bureaucracies, including a coordinating committee drawn from various ministries and executive bodies, were required to cooperate with police in punishing those found guilty of transgressing Islamist moral codes, particularly in public spaces (Khatam, 2009). This initiative set a precedent for various Social Security Plans, targeting youth, of which the most infamous was the *Tarh-e Amnyate-e Ejtema'i,* or Public Safety Plan (Pourmokhtari, 2014). Introduced in 2006, the latter provided the moral police and the *basij* the requisite legal means to target improperly-veiled women or code- disobeying men in public places (Sadeghi, 2012). The objective was threefold: to "impose order and discipline[,] enforce Islamic codes of behaviour [and dress]" (Golkar, 2015, p. 75) and "exert moral control over society" (Golkar, 2015, p. 76). This, according to Ahmad Reza Raadaan, chief of the Tehran police at the time, would "[restore] the ... mental security" of a society that in his view had been undermined by the appearance in public of code-disobeyers (BBC News, 2007). Only then, according to Raadaan, could the "harmony of the society" be restored (BBC News, 2007). The new Public Safety Plan would target all code-disobeyers but none more so than those wearing brightly coloured trousers or skin-tight *mantous* or T-shirts and jeans or sporting improper hairstyles (BBC News, 2007). Once again, it was the body in public space that was the primary target of disciplinary power.

These initiatives were enforced in part by the disciplinary gaze of the watchful morality police and *basij*, in particular those plain-clothes operatives among them, who were more often than not, impossible to distinguish from ordinary citizens. Patrolling the streets day and night, ever on the lookout for infringements of the dress code or unlawful fraternization between the sexes, these enforcers of public order and propriety represented the government's first line of defence against the forces of chaos (Rezaei, 2015; Peyghambarzadeh, 2016). It was these two formations, moreover, that were responsible for manning checkpoints where vehicles could be stopped and searched (Rezaei, 2015). The young were most often targeted, and young couples often required to present a marriage certificate and/or other proof that theirs was no illegal relationship. In this way, within Ahmadinejad's new governmentalizing order, the public presentation of the body and sexuality were so tightly intermeshed that one can speak of both the politicization of sexuality and the "sexualization of public spaces" (Sadeghi, 2010, p. 1).

Lastly, these governmentalizing disciplinary measures were complemented by subtle micro-measures. With a view to "increas[ing its] presence in cyberspace," the government launched, in 2005, no less than 10,000 blogs managed by *basiji* operatives who were also responsible for producing the content (Golkar, 2015, p. 73). The aim here was in part to "enlighten" the masses, in particular youth, regarding the moral depravity of the West, as evinced by the devaluation of its peoples to the status of marketing objects devoid of human dignity; in part to counter "[its] supposed cultural war against the [Islamic Republic]" (Golkar, 2015, p. 43). This initiative was followed up by a government programme introduced in 2007 to recruit additional *basiji* dispatchers and operatives and provide them with greater access to information technology. Key to its success was the active involvement of the *basij*, which was assigned the task of establishing and managing a chain of Internet cafés to "provide ... *basiji* operatives and ... famil[y members] ... Internet access" and serve as a gathering place for Internet users, where they could be indoctrinated online with values, attitudes, assumptions and norms deemed appropriate by the government (Golkar, 2015, p. 73).

Presence-as-resistance: The everyday politics of negation and rejection

Neoconservatives' policies directed at governmentalizing the lives of Iranians did not go unchallenged by those disaffected, in particular women, youth and students. As was shown in the previous chapter, during the Khatami administration (1997–2005), and in particular the period 2001–2005, women's groups had daily resisted the conservative establishment's policies. The strategy of choice was one of making their presence felt by performing in public spaces those everyday life practices normally confined to the home or some other private sphere. Examined under the rubric of what I have called presence-as-resistance, these practices included such contentious public acts as singing, dancing and performing music—contentious because governmentally, and by implication normally, reserved for men. Presence-as-resistance, then, represented a localized mode and strategy of everyday resistance whereby women could challenge, negate and subvert the prevailing gender codes, norms and taboos underwriting the status quo.

Presence-as-resistance, and the everyday life practices that were its lifeblood, contributed in no small measure to instilling among women a sense of everyday solidarity by binding them together through shared and discursive interests and objectives, thus laying the foundation for a counter-politics and fostering a new consciousness that impelled them to fight for gender equality, as evinced by the 2006 Women's One Million Signature Campaign and other initiatives aimed at advancing a feminist agenda.

During Ahmadinejad's first term in office (2005–2009), presence-as-resistance emerged as the dominant counter-governmentalizing strategy. Over the course of this period, it was adopted by movements other than those comprising women, in particular youth and students. It was also applied in new public domains, such as cyberspace and the peripheries of urban centers—new frontiers of resistance, defiance and subversion, and hence everyday solidarity building. It was in these public arenas that it functioned as an everyday art of "not being governed like that" (Foucault, 1996, p. 384), operating at the heart of the politics of everyday life as a manifestation of mass discontent on the part of the disaffected seeking to reclaim fundamental rights.

As a strategy of defiance, presence-as-resistance worked to de-subordinate the subordinated, by transforming them into agents committed to contesting the established order by making their presence felt in public spaces, principally by conducting within the latter those everyday life practices normally reserved for the private sphere of the home. What amounted to a public discourse on the negation and subversion of official norms and codes was intended to undermine the efficacy of state power predicated on the government's ability to marshal governmentalized bodies in public spaces, which for the Ahmadinejad administration, as with any government, represented a top priority, and precisely because nothing is more crucial to the survival of the state than the ability to control the streets and other public domains.

At the same time, presence-as-resistance may and can embody a mode of visibility that communicates to the authorities in no uncertain terms that we are here, we are active, we are alive. This phenomenon is to be understood as a form of the bodily presentation of collective actors bent on using public spaces to engage in acts normally reserved for the private sphere of the home, and for the express purpose of resisting and negating norms, codes and rules of conduct dictated by officialdom. In this way, presence-as-resistance is, for the disaffected, no mere mode of visibility; rather, it has the "consequential effect [of] mirror[ing], invert[ing], subvert[ing], [and] reproduce[ing] spaces of power and domination"—something possible only when enormous numbers of people engage in doing "similar, though contentious, things" (Bayat, 2013, p. 21). And as will be shown shortly, presence-as-resistance can create and/or make visible "an immense new field of possibility for resistance" (Nealon, 2008, pp. 107–108) by fostering among resisting, subjugated bodies a new awareness of their civic rights.

In response to the neoconservative imperative that public life "reflect religion" (Farhi, 2015, para. 6), many students, women and youth, acutely aware of government efforts to regulate interactions between the sexes in public spaces by regulating sexuality and heterosexual relations, began socializing on the peripheries of urban centres where public spaces were subject to less scrutiny by the security apparatus and thus less governmentalized (Peyghambarzadeh, 2015; Rezaei, 2015). There soon sprang up in major cities like Tehran, Shiraz, Tabriz and Isfahan so-called hang out places—teahouses, cafés, restaurants—where "young men and ... women [could] meet outside the private sphere," have tea, eat, and socialize, if not mingle for long periods (Direnberger, 2011, p. 3).

The hang out places teemed with adolescent boys and girls who scrutinized one another; then, if the attraction proved mutual, they exchanged a few words, along with telephone numbers, with a view to meeting at some later date (Rezaei, 2015; Peyghambarzadeh, 2016). So simple an approach to engaging members of the opposite sex appealed especially to youth from families of modest means, unable to host private parties or attend the underground concerts that mushroomed during this period and were the preserve of more affluent youth (Peyghambarzadeh, 2016). In political terms these hang out places, for youth the principal sites of bodily presentation, represented nodes of defiance, contesting the administration's efforts to control conduct in public spaces and segregate the sexes along gender lines.

Along with new ways of socializing, there emerged new forms of dating that more often than not succeeded in frustrating law enforcement efforts to scrutinize and control bodies in public spaces. One of the most popular of these involved an amorous couple driving about town in a taxi, most often in the evening hours when darkness made detection more difficult (Rezaei, 2015). Should their taxi be pulled over for inspection by the security forces, the couple could always claim to be sharing a ride. This new mode of dating effectively transformed governmentalized zones into new, and for youth irresistible, pleasure nodes that lay beyond the private sphere of the home.

Public spaces were not the only sites of contention between the authorities and the subjugated masses during Ahmadinejad's first term; cyberspace opened up new and unprecedented opportunities for undermining the administration's neo-Islamist governmentalizing project. With access to the Internet increasing by leaps and bounds during this period,[4] some youth, student and women's movements set themselves the task of combatting the dominant ideology disgorging from *basij* websites, the object of which laid in indoctrinating the masses with establishment values, attitudes, assumptions and norms. At a time when the government was either harassing or banning outright alternative media, members of these movements were stepping up to fill the breach by creating blogs that became the chief means of voicing dissent (Peyghambarzadeh, 2016; Amir-Ebrahimi, 2008).

Denied a "public forum [or any] opportunity to express themselves [publicly]" (Amir-Ebrahimi, 2008, p. 93), these bloggers risked circumventing government censorship in order to inform on-line audiences of their personal experiences as dissidents speaking truth to power, even if they had to do so "under a pseudonym or a constructed identity" (Amir-Ebrahimi, 2008, p. 102). Young female bloggers, Zeynab Peyghambarzadeh (2016) reports, proved particularly adept at reaching out to adolescent girls and young women, the most likely targets for moral indoctrination and disciplinary measures, making a case for their entitlement to social, political and economic rights; debunking patriarchal notions of masculinity, sexuality and virginity; disseminating information relating to sex education, and in particular safe-sex practices; and even going so far as to "write [of] their erotic and sexual experiences in personal but subtle and non-pornographic terms" (Amir-Ebrahimi, 2008, p. 103). As Masserat Amir-Ebrahimi contends, "th[is] feminine narration" challenged entrenched rules and norms by naturalizing and normalizing the debate on matters too sensitive, too delicate, too unmentionable, too long hidden, too private to discuss in a public venue, in the process opening "new window[s] on [youth and female sub-] culture[s]" (2008, p. 105). For adolescent girls and young women, such revelations worked to counter the government's patriarchal project of creating invisible, cloistered and duty-bound women, while also developing among them a sense of confidence and empowerment as rights-bearing and demand-making citizens.

Student movements also discovered in the blogosphere the means to make themselves visible and their issues, concerns and demands public. As Zeynab Peyghambarzadeh (2016) noted during an interview with the author, with the closure of so many student newspapers and journals, blogging came to be seen as the sole remaining means of reaching large audiences. Those logging onto any of the scores of student blogs up and running on any given day could expect to be assailed by oppositional views on everything from securitizing universities in the name of Islamization to reintroducing curricula embodying Western thought, particularly as manifest in the arts, humanities and social sciences—all banned as a sop to the spirit of nativism promoted by the government. Also to be found online were comparative analyses of works by Western and Islamic/Iranian philosophers, including Friedrich Nietzsche, Emmanuel Kant, Ibn Khaldun and Al-Farabi, that worked to counter the exclusivist and nativist project that the government was so keen to promote within the universities (Rezaei, 2015;

Peyghambarzadeh, 2016). In articulating their demands, concerns and aspirations within the confines of the blogosphere, student movements, like their youth counterparts, worked to de-authenticate power, thereby reasserting themselves on the social scene as bearers of alternative knowledges.

Many student groups, in particular the OCU, sought outlets for their energies other than the blogosphere. After the Ministry of Science pronounced the OCU illegal and closed its offices in 2008, for example, its members, in conjunction with their counterparts in various student movements, adopted a counter-strategy that involved holding informal meetings in the playing fields and other open spaces of university campuses, well within sight and earshot of security officials (Peyghambarzadeh, 2016; Afshari, 2016). The latter were unable to disrupt or disperse these gatherings because they were never held under the auspices of the OCU, even though many of those assembled were, in fact, members (Peyghambarzadeh, 2016).

The strategy of creating an informal presence on university campuses was to prove highly effective in educating students and engaging them in oppositional activities. To take but one example, in the summer of 2008, OCU members "initiate[d] a series of public meetings" to discuss the government's new Public Safety Plan for Tehran and other major cities (Khatam, 2009, para. 26). During the course of these gatherings, there was much debate over how the plan violated human rights and what its implications were for politically active groups in general and students in particular (Khatam, 2009). These meetings were often followed by the release of public statements calling for greater engagement in the political affairs of the country on the part of both students and the broader public (Peyghambarzadeh, 2016; Afshari, 2016). In consequence, though the OCU was officially disbanded and outlawed its members, in conjunction with rank-and-file students, succeeded not only in reasserting themselves on the social and political scene, but also in subverting power by applying pressure on the government and advocating for a public debate on individual rights and freedoms.

Like the youth bloggers, students actively opposed the status quo at considerable risk to themselves; their métier, however, laid in creating nodes of defiance within the public spaces of university campuses. In doing so, Farzaneh Sadeghi (2010, p. 1) notes, "the university... bec[ame one of] the main space[s] for socializing [among the] young" during the period 2005–2009. As former student and feminist activist Zeynab Peyghambarzadeh (2015) recalled in an interview with the author, it was common during this time for students attending universities in the Tehran metro area to gather on the open and often green spaces of campus peripheries where they scrutinized one another, then mingle, socialize, exchange telephone numbers and arrange dates; some students, male and female, smoked and consumed alcohol, in flagrant violation of the rules and norms.

For many students, these activities were simply part of everyday existence; for others, as Peyghambarzadeh (2016) recalls, they were a means of exercising their rights—something "they were entitled to do." So densely packed were these so-called informal public spaces that the *basiji* campus watchdogs had no option, according to one the interviewee, but to ignore the proceedings. Once transposed to the public sphere, behaviours and pleasures formerly confined to the private sphere of the home spelled resistance to the official programme of neo-Islamist governmentalization. And while transgressing such norms and taboos can to some extent be attributed to youthful exuberance; there was also afoot a new consciousness impelling many students to exercise their rights as both individuals and citizens.

Defiance of the status quo on the part of women was to be no less bold or, for that matter, public. One of the principal ways the activists made their presence felt lay in challenging both the patriarchal order and the governmentalization of public spaces. The strategy of choice laid in appropriating a practice traditionally the preserve of men: cycling (Green Path, 2010; The National, 2010). The latter had been employed on a modest scale against the Khatami administration (1997–2005); now, in Ahmadinejad's first term, on any given day hundreds of female cyclists could be seen riding through the parks, streets and alleyways of major cities, their very visibility an act of defiance (Green Path, 2010; The National, 2010). Such was the establishment's anxiety over what was clearly intended as a blow aimed at patriarchy that conservative clerics were driven to denounce the malefactors in sermons, thereby obliging law enforcement officials to take action against the code violators (Radio Zamaaneh, 2010).

A simple, everyday act, transposed from the private sphere of the home to public arenas, was enough to alarm the conservative establishment. It is "worrisome" lamented Tehran's Friday prayer leader Ayatollah Ahmad Khatami on December 17, 2010, to observe women cycling in public spaces, immediately prior to requesting that law enforcement agencies deal with these code disobeyers (The National, 2010). Yet despite clerical disapproval and repeated threats of arrest and prosecution, the code/norm violators persisted in these "small transgressions" that signified a determination to participate on an equal footing with men in the public life of the country (Amir-Ebrahimi, 2008, p. 98). In effect, cycling proved one of the most effective means of defying and countering the state-sponsored project of subordinating and marginalizing women by making them visible in public. Despite official warnings that are routinely issued, this practice remains as popular today as ever.[5]

Women were soon to engage in much more than cycling. On February 17, 2008, *Khabarkhodro*, the Islamic Republic's official news website, reported the number of female drivers in urban areas to be growing by leaps and bounds. While, according to this source, the precise number remained unknown, "a simple survey of driving schools ... reveal[ed] a new reality," namely that "most of the new clients [we]re women" (Khabarkhodro, 2010). This phenomenon may be viewed as yet another tactic on the part of women to "gain more visibility and mobility in physical space through their increasing presence" (Amir-Ebrahimi, 2008, p. 98). It also signalled the novel ways in which women were coming to see themselves as active and rights-bearing citizens willing to engage in everyday, public acts of defiance in defence of those rights. In inundating the streets and boulevards of major cities, hundreds of thousands of female drivers blatantly transgressed patriarchal norms, impelled by a new consciousness that worked to de-naturalize, de-normalize and de-authenticate what had so long been viewed as the given or natural or normal status of women in post-revolutionary Iran.

The mobility afforded by car ownership was itself a major spur to change in that it "provide[d] [women] with new [ways to socialize], outside the ... family, new relations with men, access to information, to training, to work and to citizenship," among other opportunities (Saidi, cited in Direnberger, 2011, p. 2). As Lucia Direnberger notes: "[w]omen of different economic and social backgrounds [began moving] around to meet friends or family, to go to school or college, to shop or go sight-seeing, to go to places of worship, or to work" (2011, p. 2). The neoconservative project of restricting women to the private sphere of the home where they remained invisible, duty-bound subjects had gone seriously awry owing, in large measure, to the everyday presence of women in public arenas—a presence enabled, in this case, by access to motor vehicles.

With car ownership becoming increasingly common among women, many began seeking employment as taxi drivers, which raised the prospect of creating a new front for the transgression of patriarchal norms. As early as 2006, they began pressuring the authorities to open to women an occupation that was traditionally the preserve of men (The Guardian, 2007; Shafaf News, 2014). Given this occupation lacked government licensing, regulations requiring some visual means of identifying cabs, women seeking entry had only to press their private cars into service as taxis. No official figures exist as to the number of women who seized this opportunity; however, one thing is clear, so great was the flood of female entrants that officials, however reluctant, had no choice but to acquiesce, albeit on condition that female drivers cater exclusively to same-sex customers. In Tehran alone, as reported in Chapter 3, nearly 700 women were employed as taxicab drivers in 2008, serving 60,000 to 70,000 female passengers annually (Asr Iran, 2008; Guardian, 2007). While the same-sex passenger rule did maintain the gender divide, female cabbies were at least able to negotiate public spaces where they would be both visible and to a large extent masters of their economic fate.

And though the authorities later introduced new regulations—most notably a standardized means of identifying taxicabs—the new female cabbies were allowed, by and large, to set their own working hours and conditions. As might be expected, given an average annual income exceeding $12,000 (US), twice the median figure, many women were attracted to the business (Time Magazine, 2008). In this way, they succeeded in subverting the hegemonic order by way of circumventing gender rules and norms in the workplace, an important milestone in their quest to realize "independent lifestyle[s]" (Bahramitash, cited in Time Magazine, 2008, para. 5).

The months and weeks preceding the 2009 presidential election

The foregoing discussion chronicled how, during the period 2005–2009, all three youth, student and women's movements challenged, defied and at times even negated the neo-absolutist order by conducting everyday life practices in public spaces. What has been referred to here as presence-as-resistance worked to transform public spaces during this time into sites of discontent and contestation where the politics of everyday life collided head-on with the rules, regulations and norms of the dominant order. It was this everyday politics of resistance, enabled by an everyday solidarity binding together the disparate social movements, that fostered a determination to secure fundamental rights, even if this meant taking on what Noushin Ahmadi Khorasani describes as the "most reactionary and repressive elements of the Islamic Republic" (2009, p. 43). Thus, resistance in all of its manifold dimensions—forms, goals, objectives, strategies, tactics, mentalities—cannot be properly understood in isolation from the increasingly reactionary and disciplinized political environment of the time, which by 2009 had made presence-as-resistance the hallmark of a peoples everyday struggle with power.

By the summer of 2009, popular resistance, fuelled by growing alienation from neoconservative rule, was gathering momentum. This explains why in the months immediately preceding the June 2009 election Iran "bec[ame] a highly politicized [society]" (Pourmokhtari, 2014, p. 160), a development Nayereh Tohidi singles out as the "distinguish[ing] factor that set the 2009 presidential election [apart] from previous races" (2009, para. 15).

Not only did the everyday politics of subversion set in motion by the disparate movements succeed in de-legitimizing the political status quo; it also contributed in no small measure to creating among the legions of the disaffected a new consciousness of their political and social rights. This development inspired everyday contentious acts, carried out in public spaces on an enormous scale, thereby "transform[ing] everyday life into a movement for rights," much to the discomfort of the authorities (Yaghmaian, 2012, p. 24). Such a politics of subversion proved to be the harbinger of an alternative kind of politics—grassroots and inclusive, democratic and rights-based, and above all home-grown. In June 2009 its disparate adherents, with the women's movement in the vanguard, made "the air ring with their demands" after a fashion, as will be seen shortly, unprecedented in the history of the Islamic Republic (Boroumand, 2009, p. 19).

The 2009 presidential campaign

In May 2009, just as the presidential campaign was getting underway, rather than accept empty promises, the women's groups demanded from all candidates firm policy measures in return for their support. Of the four conservatives in the race, Mohsen Rezaei and Mahmood Ahmadinejad were non-committal; on the other hand, Mir-Hossein Mousavi and Mehdi Karoubi, sensing perhaps that four years of ill-designed policies and misrule had culminated in a crisis that had to be addressed, were more favourably disposed. This explains why these two figures emerged as the symbolic leaders of what came to be known as the Green Movement.

On May 30, 2009, Mousavi published "Five Goals and Forty-five Strategies for Solving Women's Problems," a manifesto promoting social, political and economic equality for women. Regarded as one of the most "remarkable [policy documents] [of] the post-revolutionary [period]" (Sadeghi, 2012, p. 123), it called for a mix of economic, legal, social, and political reforms aimed at ending gender discrimination, including those government policies directed at promoting polygyny and regulating the public conduct of women under the banner of Islam (Mousavi, 2009). Sensitive to the demands for change issuing from so broad a spectrum of women's groups, the Mousavi campaign took on a decidedly feminist tone—"something unprecedented in Iranian politics" (Pourmokhtari, 2014, p. 163). This owed in large part to the active involvement in the campaign of his wife, Zahra Rahnavard, a Muslim feminist as well as an intellectual and scholar in her own right. As Ziba Mir-Husseini notes, there transpired something unique in the history of the Islamic Republic: "a woman appearing as an equal partner [beside] her man" (2010, p. 129). It was soon discovered that this equal partner was not one to mince words. Responding to "women's ... demands ... for financial independence," a precondition for escaping the private sphere of homemaking and childrearing, Rahnavard, her husband by her side, declared that "[g]etting rid of discrimination and demanding equal rights with men is the number one priority for women in Iran" (NBC News, 2009).

Karoubi (2009) was no less responsive to demands by women for gender equality and full participation in the social and political life of the country. As early as May 19, he issued the Women's Rights Manifesto that laid out a comprehensive strategy for promoting gender equality. Included among its chief components were legal prohibitions on any action or statement meant to threaten or intimidate any woman in any public place and salaries and insurance plans for housewives. In particular, the manifesto underscored the need for women to be included in key government institutions, including the Assembly of the Experts, the Expediency Discernment Council and the Guardian Council (Karoubi, 2009).

The women's groups were also aware that their best hope for success laid in forming a united front. Notes Victoria Tahmasebi Birjani:

> [I]n April 2009, nearly two months prior the election,] for the first time in Iranian history, women formed a broad coalition which brought together civil rights advocates, NGOs, political activists, and women who were active in presidential campaigns, the media and trade unions under one banner ... The coalition presented their [demands] to all four [candidates] and [insisted on] a response from each ... [It further demanded] ... Iran ... [sign] the Convention on the Elimination of All Forms of Discrimination against Women (CEDAW) and ... eliminate all discriminatory laws against women.
> (2010, p. 84)

Asserts Zeynab Peyghambarzadeh (2016), women of all social and political stripes, from Islamists and post-Islamists to secularists and members of the One Million Signature Campaign, merged in a unified front to reclaim what they viewed to be their legitimate rights and to have those rights formalized and guaranteed under law—hence the importance of having CEDAW ratified.[6]

The coalition proceeded to organize conferences and seminars and to "[distribute] brochures, sponsor petitions, and recruit new members" (Boroumand, 2009, p. 18), chiefly from the ranks of student groups and youth. In marked contrast to Mousavi and Karoubi, Ahmadinejad pointedly ignored its demands—indeed, his representative went so far as to criticize the latter for contravening Islamist principles—as did his conservative rival Mohsen Rezaie, a former IRGC commander (Pourmokhtari, 2014). Among the leading presidential candidates, only Mousavi and Karoubi responded positively to the coalition agenda, both "vow[ing] to pursue Iran's adherence ... to the CEDAW" and "pledg[ing] to nominate women to important decision-making posts" within the government (Boroumand, 2009, p. 18).

The student groups also presented candidates with demands and insisted upon unequivocal responses. For example, on May 1 the Office for Consolidating Unity (OCU), though officially banned, issued a list that included the immediate removal of all restrictions on freedom of thought, expression, and association imposed by the government as part of a program to securitize the universities. Ladan Boroumand notes that "the demands ... included ... academic freedom [and] an end to gender discrimination on campus[es], admissions based on political and religious opinions, and ... rules that allow administrators to suspend student dissidents" (2009, p. 18).

The general programme endorsed by the students far exceeded even these demands, in calling for democratic elections, judicial reform, gender equality, and a full slate of rights—social and human, religious and minority, civil, economic and labour (Boroumand, 2009). This programme was to be the centrepiece of a student-sponsored seminar entitled Civil Society, Agenda-Based Action, and Accountable Government held on the 14th and 15th of May. As it turned out, of the full slate of candidates invited, only Mousavi and Karoubi responded positively, albeit by dispatching aides to represent their respective positions. Also in attendance, reports Ladan Boroumand (2009), were representatives from the women's and youth groups who urged all candidates to adopt pro-civil-rights society platforms. The May seminar proved to be a seminal moment in the fight to secure political and social reforms, given that the presence of Mousavi and Karoubi's spokesmen ensured that the demands of the dissident groups received national media coverage and were thus articulated before a nationwide audience.

Owing largely to the momentum imparted by national media coverage, in the weeks prior the June 12th election, Mousavi and Karoubi came to represent for the majority of dissatisfied groups "symbol[s] of resistance to the status quo" and thus "the best [bet to] toppl[e a] polarizing incumbent" (Harris, 2012, p. 439). This lionizing of the two candidates was understandable given that, as Navid Nazifkar argues, "four years of Ahmadinejad's governance" had turned Iran, in large part, into a "frustrated society," one "carrying [the] heavy baggage of ... unfulfilled promises" (2011. p. 8).

These unfulfilled promises, more than anything else, dogged the administration during the run-up to the election. Upon assuming office in 2005, Ahmadinejad had pledged to deliver on his campaign promise of social and economic reform aimed at creating a more just and egalitarian society. Honoring this pledge, however, "proved very difficult and in many respects impossible" (Hunter, 2014, p. 196). The fundamental reason, argues Shirin Hunter, had to do with the "mismanagement of the economy" and even more broadly "the neglect of economic questions altogether," which "greatly contributed to the Ahmadinejad administration's failure to improve ... economic conditions and to fulfill its promises to the people," in particular the urban poor (2014, p. 197). One factor more than any other was responsible for the government's failure in this area: "the expulsion of experts from various economic institutions and the[ir] ... [replacement with] ... [those] less-qualified [or] incompetent" (Hunter, 2014, p. 197). It was also the case that cabinet appointees were often of low calibre. All this combined with other ill-conceived moves—most noteworthy, the dismantling of the Management and Planning Organization that long before the revolution had been responsible for long-term economic planning—spelled economic disaster (Mirtaheri, 2013; Sadeghi, 2012).

Even the administration's initial successes on the economic front ultimately proved hollow. The measures aimed at benefitting workers—raising wages and pensions and loans to low-income families and small businesses—did little more than create a short-lived "superficial boom" that contributed to "inflationary pressures [owing to] the lack of [a] commensurate increase in productive capacity" (Hunter, 2014, p. 197). These measures did the opposite of what was intended; they "hurt the very people—the disadvantaged—that Ahmadinejad wanted to help" (Hunter, 2014, p. 197).

Worse was yet to come. In an effort to maintain the purchasing power of the masses, in particular the poor, the government, rather than addressing systematically the structural problems plaguing the economy, resorted to revving up the Central Bank's printing presses and easing restrictions on credit. With each round of inflation, wages and salaries increased, resulting in a vicious inflationary cycle. By 2009, Iran was suffering, Ahmad Mirtaheri notes, "from high inflation and an unemployment rate ... top[ping] 30 percent" (2013, p. 6). And ironically, all this was unfolding as oil hovered about $60 (US) per barrel, the peak price for the entire post-revolutionary period, and a sixfold increase over the $10 figure prevailing during the previous Khatami administration (Amouzegar, 2013). Ultimately, argues Jahangir Amouzegar, by 2009, "there [wa]s no analyst inside or outside of Iran who d[id] not believe that the Iranian economy [had been] grossly mismanaged, if not permanently damaged, during [the Ahmadinejad] administration," with the urban poor, the very class he had pledged to help, bearing the brunt of the cost (2013, p. 126). For all these reasons, as June drew ever closer, the administration's electoral prospects appeared dim indeed.

The Green Movement as a movement of movements

As the June 12th election approached, the country remained in the grip of massive unemployment and plagued by economic mismanagement. Moreover, as was shown, the incumbent government had succeeded in alienating whole segments of society—women, students, youth, intellectuals, even most among the urban poor, who were now determined to end the nightmare that had been the Ahmadinejad administration. Moreover, in the run-up to the election, many of these dissatisfied groups supported one another in presenting the presidential candidates with demands for wholesale change and insisting that they respond with concrete policy proposals. As the campaigns gathered steam, it soon became apparent that of the slate of four presidential candidates only Mousavi and Karoubi were committed to the cause of fundamental social, political and economic reform. Only if one or the other prevailed on June 12 would there exist any real possibility of oppositional groups reasserting themselves on the political scene and reclaiming their rights. It was very much a case of now or never.

And so with all hope of reform dashed by Ahmadinejad's re-election, and rumours of election fraud circulating, lent credence by an over-hasty announcement that the incumbent had secured an astonishing 63% of the popular vote,[7] the disaffected groups and movements poured onto the streets in vast numbers. On June 13, the day following the election, spontaneous demonstrations erupted in all the major cities—soon to be awash with the color green, Mousavi's official campaign color, and resounding with cries of "Where is my vote?" June 15 would witness the largest and most prolonged demonstrations in the history of the Islamic Republic, wherein women, students, youth and intellectuals, joined by *bazaaris*, the urban poor and workers, delivered a mighty blow that threatened, at least for a time, to overthrow the established order (Abrahamian, cited in Hashemi & Postel, 2010). This outpouring of frustration and rage would only subside in March of the following year—a full nine months on.

Given its diverse composition, the historical context within which it emerged, and the semi-authoritarian political environment in which it developed and conducted operations, the Green Movement might be best described as a movement of movement that can be thought of, variously, as an amalgam of smaller oppositional movements, a coalition of smaller movements of counterconduct or a resistance of resistances arrayed against the Islamic Republic. However one wishes to view it, it was the Green Movement that on June 13th refused with one voice to accept the election results, which it deemed to be fraudulent. Thus did it manifest a defiance of specific modalities of governmental conduct and, more generally, neo-Islamist governmentality.

Independently of one another, the disparate groups constituting the Green Movement would have had little, if any, hope of mobilizing the masses against the conservative establishment, at least not in such great numbers and over so protracted a period, as evinced by the fate of earlier post-revolutionary cases of counterconduct that were either crushed in their infancy or forced underground (e.g., the 1999 student movement). Accordingly, as will be seen shortly, the concept of a movement of movements offers a framework for understanding the Green Movement, not simply as a response to election fraud, but something of far greater substance, namely a fluid, open-ended rainbow collectivity, whose efficacy lay in mounting unsurpassed street demonstrations of a scale and duration that would rock the Islamic Republic to its foundations.

It may be gathered from the above discussion that as a movement of movements, the Green Movement possessed five distinct, albeit interrelated, features. First, its very heterogeneity implies an inclusivity that set it apart from earlier post-revolutionary oppositional groups focused on single issues, such as the rights of women, students and workers, respectively. This inclusivity was both a by-product and manifestation of a new historical phase in post-revolutionary Iranian society, one marked by a burgeoning demand for fundamental rights, which galvanized the demonstrators in resisting the neo-Islamist conduct of conduct. It was this inclusivity that represented a precondition for pursuing a far broader and more ambitious reform agenda, one aimed at institutionalizing political accountability and transparency, the rule of law, citizenship rights, economic and social equality, and civic freedoms, in the process transcending the aims of earlier issue-specific oppositional groups.

From these common demands for broad democratic rights sprang the second characteristic of a movement of movements, namely, political convergence of a radical bent. Key to this development was the strategic sidestepping of group-specific grievances and issues in favour of a much broader, and hence more inclusive, reform agenda that would provide political cohesion during the demonstrations to come. It was this political cohesion, predicated on the common demand for democratic reforms and forged in the crucible of the shared experience of having resisted a governmentalizing order, that united a heterogeneous multitude under a single banner, thereby fashioning a spectral collectivity out of disparate groups that heretofore had pursued very different agendas. This development is clearly evident, as Shadi Sadr (2012, p. 212) shows, in the case of dissident women:

> [During the events of 2009, women] were no longer [pursuing] the right to divorce, equality for blood money, or elimination of the stoning law; rather, they demanded the right to vote, to assemble peacefully, and to [reclaim their citizenship rights].

This willingness on the part of disparate groups to set aside their narrow interests in order to pursue a common, and hence broader, agenda is the hallmark of a politics of convergence. The latter embodies that Foucauldian moment of singularity when a people unite to defy power; it is that juncture when social life can no longer sustain itself, when the rule of the state is perceived to be illegitimate.

This historic and singular moment of political convergence was enabled by the shared experience of having lived within the same zone of governmental conduct, of having been marginalized, disciplined and rendered docile in the same political domain. It was within these public spaces that a solidarity was forged among disparate oppositional groups engaged in everyday resistance; fittingly, it was here that the masses converged to defy and subvert those diverse modalities of power/conduct that had deprived them of fundamental rights; and herein was developed the requisite political cohesion to resist and negate the conduct of conduct. That in 2009 the demonstrators succeeded in this regard may be attributed to the foregrounding of "democratic demands as their first and foremost goal" (Tahmasebi-Birjani, 2010, p. 80). Perhaps nothing illustrates more vividly the power derived from political convergence on this scale than the sight of vast numbers of demonstrators congregating about Tehran's Azadi monument and chanting *Ma Bishomarim*, "We are Countless," *Ey Rahbar-e Bi Gheirat, Beshno Sedaye Mellat*, "Oh Our Nerveless Leader: Listen to the Masses," *Irani Mimirad Zellat Nemipazirad*, "Iranians Would Die But Won't Accept Disgrace," and *Ra'aye Man Kojast?*, "Where is my Vote?" (Faryaade Mardom, 2009; Rahe Sabz, 2010).

The Green Movement's inclusive character, manifest in the way in which its constituents merged politically to form a united front against the conservative establishment, speaks to a third characteristic of a movement of movements: its activists' unshakable will to build an elusive movement capable of winning and securing democratic rights. It was this more than any other attribute of a movement of movements, that lent the Green Movement the requisite dynamism to reinvent and renew itself in its quest to achieve an alternative kind of society and politics, thus investing it with a heterodynamic quality whereby "... no effort [was to be spared] in pursuing the justice [and rights,] ... denied ... [its members]" (Pourmokhtari, 2014, p. 169). Thus, for example, in response to the government's refusal to call fresh elections and subsequent crackdown on the demonstrators, Green Movement activists set about reimagining what had been a mere assumption of election fraud as a "social fact," meaning that it was "no longer relevant whether or not the election [had been] rigged" (Dabashi, 2011b, p. 24).

This act of reimagining plunged the Islamic Republic into an "unprecedented crisis of ... legitimacy," shaking it to its very foundations (Bashiriyeh, 2010: 62). Indeed, from November 2009 on—and most notably 13 Aban Student Day (November 4) and the Shiite holy day of Ashura (December 26)—certain groups of activists targeted Iran's head of state and official face of the Islamic Republic with chants of *Marg Bar Khamenei*, "Death to Khamenei," *Khamenei Ghatele Vilayatesh Batele*, "Khamenei is a Murderer, His Leadership is Invalid," *Irani Mimirad Zellat Nemipazirad*, "Iranians Would Rather Die Before Accepting Disgrace" that resounded throughout the streets and squares of the major urban centres (BBC News, 2009). The slogans were accompanied by calls on the part of some groups to dissolve the Islamic Republic, now perceived as lacking legitimacy. A movement born of mere suspicion of election fraud had become radicalized to the point where some activists were now challenging the very legitimacy of the system itself—a testimony to its ability to reinvent and renew itself.

The Green Movement's heterodynamic character was complemented by a fourth attribute: adaptability and, by implication, resilience. It was this feature that enabled it to survive for so long in so hostile a political environment. It particular, and by virtue of its heterogeneous composition, it was able to function in ways that were conventional or unorthodox, making it possible to respond rapidly and effectively to government efforts aimed at suppressing it. For example, at the beginning of the 2009 June uprising and continuing over the course of the next two months, demonstrators occupied the streets of major urban centres to protest what was generally seen as election fraud. The crowds, while enormous by any standards, were organized for the most part on an *ad hoc* basis. However, the increasingly repressive government measures implemented during this period, including acts of homicide, prompted a shift in "strategy [whereby] smaller and more dispersed demonstrations ... were organized to minimize the threat from security forces" (Eli, 2009, para. 1). When these were suppressed in late 2009, the activists resorted to disrupting state-orchestrated rallies, demonstrations and other official events, however small or large, by appearing in small numbers and chanting anti-establishment slogans.

As government repression peaked following the arrest of Green Movement leaders in the winter of 2010, the majority of its footsoldiers went underground, albeit continuing to offer token of resistance in the form of disrupting high-profile state-sponsored events that were likely to draw large crowds and provide opportunities to stage what might best be called a theatre of defiance, a formula that since 2010 had proved successful in voicing discontent while avoiding, or at least minimizing, retaliation by the security forces. To cite but one example, immediately following Hassan Rouhani's back-to-back victories in the 2013 and 2017 presidential races, his supporters, many of whom were associated with the Green Movement, occupied public spaces in Tehran and other urban centres and began chanting *Sabzo Banafsh Nadare Jonbesh Edameh Dareh*, "This is not About the Color Green or Purple; It is About a Movement that will Continue to Thrive"[8] and *Jonbeshe Sabz Namorde Rouhaniro Avorde*, "The Green Movement has Not Died; It Has Instead Brought to the Fore Rouhani" (Kaleme, 2013; Aparat, 2017).

Such oppositional moments were in no way restricted to presidential elections. On January 10, 2017, on the occasion of the state funeral of Ayatollah Hashemi Rafsanjani, a former president,[9] Green Movement activists and their supporters once again took to the streets. Reminiscent of June 2013 and 2017, the demonstrators chanted anti-establishment slogans such as *Ya Hossein, Mir Hossein*, "Oh Hossen-Mir Hossein," *Marg Bar Diktator*, "Death to the Dictator," *Payame Ma Roshane, Hasr Bayad Beshkane*, "Our Message is Clear, The House Arrest Must End," and *Zendanie Siasi Azaad Bayad Gardad*, "Political Prisoners Must be Freed" (BBC, 2017; Radio Farda, 2017a).[10]

These examples clearly demonstrate a movement of movement's flexibility, as evinced in its capacity to operate in a multimode fashion—organized or disorganized, conventional or unorthodox, above ground or underground, at times continuous over long periods, at times episodic. It is precisely this flexibility, coupled with a dynamism, that accounts for a movement of movements' fifth and final attribute, namely survivability. Despite the overwhelming forces arrayed against it, the Green Movement would survive in one form or another, awaiting only the right moment to make its presence felt, much to the discomfort of the authorities. It is this attribute, more so than any other, that has enabled it to survive, even thrive at times, in a hostile political environment, thus remaining a perpetual thorn in the side of the established order.

A home-grown, rights-based society: Reformism-reconfigured and the rise of a new counterdiscourse in post-revolutionary Iran

The demands made by the heterogeneous groups constituting the Green Movement, particularly with regard to individual rights and freedoms and justice and equality, raise the question of how those who risked everything in challenging a governmentalizing order envisioned themselves. More precisely, how did they come to perceive themselves as empowered to do so?

The first step in addressing this question lies in revisiting Foucault's view of power in relation to resisting bodies: "the individual is not a pre-given entity," writes the great French luminary, "which is seized on by the exercise of power [but rather] the product of relations of power exercised over bodies, multiplicities, movements, desires, [and] forces" (1980a, p. 74). This means that while "power," ultimately, "passes through individuals, [i]t is not applied to them [per se]" (Foucault, 2003, p. 29). To clarify this point, he notes that "we are not trapped [in power relations;] we cannot jump outside [them, but rather we] can always change

[them]," invert them, subvert them, indeed utilize them "in a strategic situation towards [others]," in this case those who wield governmental power (Foucault, 1996a, p. 386). The reader is left in no doubt regarding the implication of the latter claim: "[a] movement through which [a] people say, 'I will no longer obey' [is authentic, if not] irreducible. This is because no power is capable of [rendering resistance to] it absolutely impossible" (Foucault, cited in Afary & Anderson, 2005, p. 263).

Once these connections are made, it may be discerned that the mass "demonstrations of 2009 were not simply a reaction to ... election [fraud,] but ... [in part the result of] years of built-up frustration, dissatisfaction and anger at the ... rule of the Islamic Republic" (Jahanbegloo, 2012, para. 1). Seen in this light, the Green Movement embodied "... a coherent and self-conscious politics," in this case the politics of everyday life practices exercised by grassroots and heterogeneous post-revolutionary movements of counterconduct, one "that evolved within the Iranian public sphere over a long time" (Mirsepassi, 2010, p. ix). In this way, the Green Movement embodied a resistance of resistances on the part of subjugated bodies that in 2009 stylized themselves in relation to a dogmatic neo-Islamist governmentalized order by way of "consider[ing] themselves as bearers of rights" (Vahdat, 2012, p. 31)—as citizens determined at any cost to participate democratically, and by implication meaningfully, in the social and political affairs of the country. Asef Bayat best captures a sense of this rights-based dimension by describing the Green Movement as "a post-Islamist democracy movement to reclaim citizenship [rights]" (2013, p. 296). In other words, it is to be seen as an "attempt to transcend the duty-centred and exclusive Islamist politics [and move] towards a more rights-centred and [inclusive] outlook" (Bayat, 2013, p. 307). In 2009 it was a desperate yearning for political/civic rights that motivated its activists to launch a movement of movements in the teeth of an established order bent on reducing the populous to the status of subjects duty-bound by ties of religion.

Hence, it was the quest for political/civic rights that provided Green Movement activists the requisite motivation and vocabulary to challenge the status quo—political, social, economic, legal and otherwise. As a consequence, the events of 2009 may be seen, in both an existential and symbolic sense, to have opened up a rights-based dimension in Iranian politics, one grounded in an understanding on the part of the demonstrators that to change society, they had first to change themselves—and by way of transforming their very existence through collective action in the form of demonstrations and protestations aimed at expressing the will to realize a more just, in this case rights-based, political order.

Above all, this new political order was to be grounded in a home-grown, rights-based society—home-grown because, as will be seen shortly, developed in relation to a discursive and grassroots everyday politics of resistance to the status quo, rights-based because founded upon the conviction that the conduct of conduct ought to be predicated on the will of the people, and precisely because they had come to see themselves as rights-based agents as opposed to the subordinated, marginalized and disciplined masses that various administrations had to varying degrees hoped to produce.

The emergence of a home-grown rights-based society inaugurated a new phase in the history of post-revolutionary Iran, wherein in response to an Islamist conduct of conduct, implemented, for the most part, by the conservative establishment in a piecemeal fashion over the course of three decades, and in conjunction with the paradoxical and unintended consequences of certain policies and events—the 1979 revolution itself, the Iran-Iraq War, the biopolitical Family Plan of the 1980s—the disparate oppressed and marginalized converged to form a radical front that gave far greater voice to their grievances.

The home-grown rights-based society, moreover, can be viewed as a kind of framework within which Iranians renewed themselves in 2009 in that it provided the conceptual tools, along with the requisite vocabulary, with which to redefine and express themselves; and for this reason, its emergence signals a new phase in the recurrent struggle waged by disparate and dispossessed movements and groups to reclaim their fundamental rights. For all these reasons, it is to be seen and interrogated as a feature of a particular phase creating a rule-bound and pluralistic order capable of sustaining a home-grown democracy.

This home-grown rights-based society stood in stark relief to a conservative-establishment-sponsored Islamist society embodying a totalizing social, political, economic and moral system that was universal and thus intolerant of dissent—a society "which [in practice] denie[d] to both [men and women] their rudimentary rights in the name of the pre-eminence of the Islamic ruler (*valiy-e faqih*)" (Khosrokhavar, 2012, p. 65).

As discussed earlier with reference to the day-to-day struggle against the status quo waged by diverse oppositional groups, the home-grown rights-based society emerged as a "consequence of years of [public] presence and ... active participation" in the social and political life of the country on the part of citizens groups (Bashi, cited in Hashemi & Postel, 2010, p. 39; emphasis added), deeply consciousness of their rights and committed to reclaiming them at any cost. As such, when demonstrators in their hundreds of thousands poured onto the streets chanting their signature refrain "Where is my vote?," what they were demanding was that the state "respect ... the citizen's vote and [adhere to] the moral obligation ... to abide by the *vox populi*" (Khosrokhavar, 2012, p. 57).

Reformism-reconfigured and the green movement symbolic leaders

It is also evident that this rights-based society gave rise in 2009 to a counterdiscourse, specifically a discourse on resistance that I call reformism-reconfigured. The latter contested both the classical reformist and neo-absolutist discourses that had underwritten the Khatami and Ahmadinejad administrations, respectively.

Perhaps the best approach to interrogating this counterdiscourse lies in analyzing the public statements issued by the Green Movement's symbolic leaders, Mir-Hossein Mousavi and Mehdi Karoubi, during the long post-election crisis, extending from June 2009 to April 2010. This line of enquiry is likely to prove fruitful because, as Hamid Dabashi notes, it was the "people [who in 2009] came to the streets, and it was [they] who pushed Mousavi and Karoubi to the streets," in the process moving them in a more radical direction (cited in Hashemi &

Postel, 2010, p. 265). The kind of power exercised by activists as well as ordinary people during this critical juncture is viewed by Ali Assareh and Mahmood Monshipouri as an "original [feature] of the [Green] Movement," precisely because the two oppositional "figures [were] responding to the sentiment on the street rather than directing it" (2009, p. 55); indeed, it would be more accurate to say they were directed by it, thereby reducing them to the status of symbolic leaders of a movement of movements, a label that captures a sense of the Green Movement's unorthodox leadership style—symbolic in character, horizontal and diffuse in its command structure, and by and large reactive to events unfolding in the streets.

Far from constituting a weakness as some have argued (Aghai Diba, 2012; Mahtafar, 2011), these attributes made for greater operational flexibility, which proved crucial to ensuring the Green Movement's survival. In the absence of a formal leadership and hierarchal command structure, it was the Green Movement activists that were left to address the demands of its various constituencies, as well as respond to events unfolding on the streets in real time, thus allowing for rapid and timely decision making on the part of those at the centre of a highly dynamic situation, one wherein awaiting instructions from leaders often far removed from the scene may have proven fatal. For this reason, the house arrest of Mousavi and Karoubi in the winter of 2010, while a serious blow to morale, patently failed to produce the results the authorities had anticipated: the demise of the Green Movement and the dispersal of its footsoldiers. Instead, the latter, operating in an *ad hoc* fashion, renewed their demands and more importantly survived to fight another day. In this way, far from constituting a flaw or inherent weakness, its symbolic, unstructured leadership may more properly be viewed as an attribute of a movement of movements.

Understanding the phenomenon that was the Green Movement's symbolic leadership is important in a second respect: it offers insight into the kind of governmentalizing polity and political order for which the disparate movements of counterconduct as well as their non-affiliated allies were prepared to risk all. Interrogating the public statements and writings of Mousavi and Karoubi, for example, reveals a strategic blueprint for establishing a new governmentalizing order; it further reveals how what I have called the discourse on reformism-reconfigured departs from earlier post-revolutionary discourses on governing everyday life.

Of the numerous post-election writings and public statements by these two figures, perhaps none is more important in respect to elucidating the rise of the new discourse than the Green Movement Charter, issued by Mousavi on June 16, 2010 on the occasion of the second anniversary of the birth of the Green Movement. This document stands as the ultimate expression of the discourse on reformism-reconfigured; it also delineates its relation to both the neo-absolutist and classical reformist discourses. Hailed by Mohammad Sahimi (2010, para. 1) as "historic," the Charter outlines the Green Movement's chief tenants as well as providing strategies for realizing them.

On one level, the Charter/discourse on reformism-reconfigured promotes certain knowledges that run counter to those embedded in the state-sponsored neo-absolutist discourse. It succeeds in this respect by underscoring the importance of rights—social, economic, political, civil—the prerequisites for a just, and by implication home-grown and democratically rule-bound, society. Whereas the neo-absolutist discourse makes "no mention of the people's political and civil rights," and by implication the "the need for political and civil institution building" (Hunter, 2014, p. 196), the Green Movement Charter promotes a kind of knowledge building grounded in "human rights, regardless of ideology, religion, gender, ethnicity, and social position," while advocating the kind of institution building capable of underwriting "the establishment [of] and guarantee[ing] ... human rights ... that no ruler, government, parliament, or power can annul or unjustifiably limit" (The Charter, 2010). In both content and aspirations, then, the discourse on reformism-reconfigured stands in stark contrast to its neo-absolutist counterpart, and particularly with respect to the role civil society groups are expected to play and the scope of individual rights and freedoms.

Interestingly, there is little to distinguish either discourse regarding the preconditions for achieving and guaranteeing freedom, justice and equality or, for that matter, the slogans and catchwords used to promote so grand a project. The neo-absolutist discourse asserts that freedom, equality and human dignity are contingent upon "establish[ing] justice, peace and brotherhood" and that "economic growth" must be managed so as to promote all three (Amanat, 2009, p. 241). In a strikingly similar vein, reformism-reconfigured cites "justice, freedom [and] human dignity ... [as principal] goals" and "economic development and advancement of the country" as a precondition for achieving a "just society" (The Charter, 2010). However, the manner in which social and economic justice is to be achieved and respect for human dignity realized is a world apart in the two discourses.

In the neo-absolutist discourse, and Ahmadinejad's manufactured populism in particular, it is only by establishing a society where all laws emanate from Islam that these absolute goods can exist. Thus, for example, economic justice and "justice [in a broader sense, along with] compassion, fairness and integrity," could only be achieved, Ahmadinejad contended (cited in Amouzegar, 2013, p. 127), within the context of "an Islamic economy," a totalizing project, predicated upon an all-encompassing notion of "human progress" (Ahmadinejad, cited in Takeyh, 2009, p. 235).

In contrast, the discourse on reformism-reconfigured promotes the view that "justice, freedom ... human dignity, and morality are universal values," rather than the exclusive precepts of any religious or ideological sect (The Charter, 2010). It then follows that

> [t]he fair distribution of all resources, whether social, political, economic, or otherwise [as well as the meting out of] ... justice ... is possible only if the political system acts independently, both internally and externally, without any kind of servitude to or reliance on political, economic, and social organizations and power centers, and can guarantee the economic development and advancement of the country in such a way that there is social justice *for all* regardless of ideology, religion, gender, ethnicity, [or] social position.
> (The Charter, 2010; emphasis added)

Moreover, whereas the neo-absolutist discourse, and particularly its classification of the citizenry into *khodis* (us), those who conform to the state ideology and the governmentalizing order it promotes, and *gheir-e khordis* (them), all those in opposition, the new counterdiscourse promoted the view that "[w]e are all Iranians and Iran belongs to all [Iranians]" (The Charter, 2010). This sense of inclusivity carried with it the implication that the state is obligated to "address[] the needs and demands of all … [social] strata and classes" (The Charter, 2010). What is authentic here vis-à-vis Ahmadinejad's manufactured populism is the "emphasis [on] the links between the middle and lower classes of society" and the state's obligation to safeguard the social, political, and economic interests of those "most vulnerable" (The Charter, 2010). In this way, buzzwords such as "[j]ustice, freedom … and human dignity [are elevated to the level of] universal values" (The Charter, 2010).

The pluralistic order promoted by the new discourse posed a direct challenge to the religio-governmentalized order grounded in an exclusivist understanding of neo-Islamist governmentality—a form of governance dedicated to the proposition that religion is capable of resolving every issue and addressing every concern, however trivial or serious. The new discourse fostered a "[re]distribut[ive view of] the role of religion and politics" by emphasizing "the necessity of a faith that is about kindness, morality, and respect for human dignity and rights" (The Charter, 2010). This in turn could be achieved only by establishing a new order predicated upon "preserving the independence of … clerical and religious organizations [vis-à-vis] government" (The Charter, 2010). For its part, the latter constituted "the only means [of] protect[ing] the high moral position of religion and the continuation of its distinguished role in [a rights-based] society" (The Charter, 2010). It was religion that had to occupy a domain separate from the state and eschew instrumentalization in the service of a political agenda.

Not only did the new discourse challenge its neo-absolutist counterpart; it also reconfigured, and by reconfiguring transcended, the classical reformist discourse. The latter was originally developed and promoted by grassroots movements, as was evident on the eve of Khatami's taking office. Later, as was shown, it was appropriated by Islamic Republic elites who, in focusing primarily on achieving and maintaining political rights, overlooked the social and economic rights of the urban and rural poor.

The new discourse reconfigured certain tenants of its classical reformist counterpart that were problematic with respect to promoting social, political and economic rights of an inclusive character upon which a democratic order might be based, in the process transcending the latter with its emphasis on political rights to be achieved at the cost of marginalizing social and economic rights. Indeed, the Green Movement Charter stipulates that "[dispersing] justice in society is possible only [when the system] can guarantee the economic development and advancement of the country in such a way that there is social justice for all" (The Charter, 2010).

At the same time, the discourse on reformism-reconfigured also transcended the classical reformist discourse. As Shabnam Holliday and Paola Rivetti opine, a major limitation of the latter lay in "its limited scope in terms of political aspirations for change" (2016, p. 29), as evinced by the endless compromises and "negotiat[ions] at the top," with the Supreme Leader, the official face of the Islamic Republic, among those most complicit (Hajjarian, cited in Mahdi, 2000, para. 43). To this end, while one can argue, on the basis of the reformist blueprint, that there existed the political will to "rationalize the office of the *vilayat-e faqih*" (Mahdavi, 2006, p. 151), thereby institutionalizing it and, by implication, making it accountable to the *Majlis*, there was a "[genuine] confidence in the ability of existing laws [and institutions]," including that of the Office of the Supreme Leader, "to bring about the needed political changes" (Nabavi, 2012, p. 43).

The new discourse transcended its classical reformist counterpart in two respects. First, while emphasizing that "[e]xecuting all Articles of the Constitution, particularly those that govern the rights of the people … is a primary goal" embedded in the new discourse (The Charter, 2010), it also stipulates that:

> [the] laws of the country, including the Constitution, are not permanent and unchangeable written documents and [that e]very nation has the right to correct its course by correcting and modifying its laws … through the participation of every strata of society and all social groups.
>
> (The Charter, 2010)

One can clearly discern from this that reformism-reconfigured transcended the classical reformist discourse by debunking the divinely-inspired blueprint for the governmentalizing rule so ardently promoted by the state. And one of the chief casualties of this new spirit abroad in the land was the *vilayat-e faqih*, the Rule/Guardianship of the Supreme Jurist, which in both theory and practice constituted the system's chief source of legitimacy. The new discourse promoted the view that it is "[t]he people's will and vote," and no one else's, that "are the source of legitimacy for political power," thereby "reject[ing] any sort of absolut[ism]" (The Charter, 2010). On June 16, 2010, on the occasion of the second anniversary of the Green Movement, Karoubi left no doubt as to his position on the matter:

> I doubt that so much authority and power were given to the Prophets themselves, or the infallible [Shi'a] Imams. I even doubt that God considers himself to have the right to deal with his servants in the same way.
>
> (2010, para. 10)

De-legitimizing the office and persona of the Supreme Jurist in so unprecedented a fashion was contingent upon, and must be understood in reference to, the broader meaning ascribed to the term "rights" in the new discourse, i.e., nothing less than the "first [and foremost] social value" (The Charter, 2010). It is in light of the latter that Karoubi (2010) proclaimed "blood [has been] spilled so that [the mass of the people] may gain rights" (para. 14).

And precisely herein lies yet the second manner in which the new discourse was transcendent, one that may be viewed as its most singular and important feature: it promoted a governmental polity committed to "defending human dignity and human rights, regardless of ideology, religion, gender, ethnicity, [or] social position" (The Charter, 2010). In this and other respects, opines Farhad Khosrokhavar, the new discourse "[went] far beyond [the agenda of classical] reform[ism]" in that "for the first time in Iran's history," at least on so unprecedented a scale, a view of governance was advanced wherein institutionalizing "democracy and the rights of ... citizens" would trump all other social and political imperatives (2012, p. 57). Herein lay the precondition for establishing a rights-based and rule-bound governmentalizing order.

Lastly, in transcending the classical reformist discourse, reformism-reconfigured redefined the role of religion in state and political life. Whereas some religious intellectuals, among them those who had inspired and promoted classical reformism, defied the status quo while seeking to democratize it "in the name of Islam" (Rahimi, 2012, p. 64), the architects of the new discourse, though not necessarily anti-religious, aimed at, in the language of the Charter, "preserv[ing] the independence of ... clerical and religious organizations from the government [as] the only means [of] protect[ing] the high moral position of religion" (The Charter, 2010). According to this view, religion had to be saved from itself by undergoing a process of de-governmentalization, which was essential if the "political system [was to function] independently" of religious institutions (The Charter, 2010).

Thus, in all these different ways, the discourse on reformism, as enshrined in the provisions of the Green Movement Charter, simultaneously reconfigured and transcended "the boundaries of what c[ould] be thought ... and communicated" in post-2009 Iranian society (Baumgarten & Ullrich, 2012, p. 2). Above all, and most clearly, it promoted those knowledges essential to establishing a home-grown democracy in a rights-based society whose foremost political goal laid in guaranteeing every citizen all-inclusive rights.

Conclusion

This chapter has analyzed the 2009 Iranian Green Movement, described variously as a mega oppositional movement, a movement of movements, resistance of resistances, and localized movements of counterconduct—all predicated upon the Foucauldian concept of counterconduct. This historical phenomenon was shown to be, first and foremost, the product of a particular historical phase in the development of a home-grown democracy within post-revolutionary Iran. By interrogating the disparate histories, experiences and trajectories of the women's, student and youth movements that constituted the Green Movement, I have shown it to be inclusive, ultra-flexible and open-ended. It is precisely owing to these attributes, moreover, that its diverse constituencies succeeded in 2009 in remaking and reasserting themselves on the social and political landscape, and for so long a period.

It has also been shown that the Green Movement was above all else a collective response on the part of the heterogeneous oppositional movements and non-affiliated allies, namely ordinary people, that constituted its vanguard, to specific religio-governmentalized exercises of power conducted by a neoconservative administration that by June 2009 had succeeded in subordinating, marginalizing and alienating them beyond endurance. Setting aside their strategic and interest-specific differences, these groups coalesced for the express purpose of negating and rejecting state power bent on controlling every aspect—social, political, economic, moral—of everyday life.

Lastly, as has been shown, it was in response to sustained efforts by the state to transmute the masses into subjects duty-bound by religious ties that those who took part in the June demonstrations consciously sought to preserve their rights as citizens by forging a new subjectivity, one that made it possible to renew themselves and their day-to-day lives. It was this rebirth as rights-bearing citizens from whence sprang the will to open up a home-grown rights-based dimension in politics, hence the slogans of the day: "Where is my vote?," "Give Me Back My Vote," "In My Green Vote There is no Mention of your Black Name"—each signifying not just defiance and contestation of the rules of conduct, but a new historical phase in the development of a home-grown democracy. This new phase was the outgrowth of a historical struggle that manifested itself in almost daily confrontations with governmental power, which in 2009 took on the form of a radical, broadly based and multilayered defiance of specific technologies of power orchestrated by the most reactionary elements of the Islamic Republic.

Notes

1 This strategic alliance would later be dismantled, in particular during Ahmadinejad's second term in office (2009-2013), owing, in part, to his, i.e., Ahmadinejad's, belief that he no longer required the support of the Supreme Leader and the latter's conservative backers to move his governmentalizing mission forward.
2 Such statements must be understood in the context of the politics of the day. As was shown in Chapters 3 and 4, Khamenei and his conservative backers were keen to advocate the participation of women in the public sphere as a means of integrating them into the larger society and moulding a generation of 'revolutionary women.' During this period, and *perhaps* owing to memories of both the prominent role women had played in the 1997 reform movement and their sustained efforts during Khatami's reformist administration (1997-2005) to win social and political rights, conservatives sought to consign them to the margins of social and political life. The point is that such statements must be contextualized vis-à-vis the political imperatives of the day, which required the 'instrumentalization' of women's rights' in the service of power politics.
3 In July 2007, Khamenei criticized Iranian women's rights activists and their efforts to have CEDAW ratified. "In our country," he proclaimed, "some activist women, and some men, have been trying to play with Islamic rules in order to [adopt] international conventions related to women," something he denounced "[a]s wrong." Thus, Nouri's remarks must be understood in relation to Khamenei's stance on women's issues during this period (cited in Radio Farda, 2007).
4 Over the period 2000–2007, the number of Internet users grew at an astonishing 7,100% annually. In 2009, Iran had 32 million Internet users, 56% of all Internet users in the Middle East. For a discussion on why the Internet spread so rapidly during this period, see Amir-Ebrahimi (2008) "Transgression in narration: The lives of Iranian women in cyberspace."
5 It remains one of the most protracted of the everyday strategies adopted by women movements to negate the status quo. Official statistics notwithstanding, the number of female cyclists would grow at so rapid a pace that in September 2016, the Ayatollah Khamenei issued a *fatwa*, or religious ruling, declaring the practice unlawful (Shia News, 2016). Despite Khamenei's censure, however, it is likely, judging by

the countless photographs of women and their bicycles uploaded daily on the social media, that the legions of women determined to cycle continue to grow in number.

6 Note that efforts by women's groups to have CEDAW ratified date back to the Rafsanjani presidency (1989-1997). For a discussion of this point, see Alikarimi (2014) "CEDAW and the quest of Iranian: Women for gender equality."

7 Note that Ahmadinejad was declared the winner less than twenty-four hours after the polls had officially closed on June 12, 2009, leaving insufficient time for all the votes to be counted (Nazifkar, 2011). According to official reports, moreover, Mousavi received fewer votes than Ahmadinejad even in his hometown of Tabriz, one of his strongest power bases, and a city that traditionally "voted disproportionately [in favor] [of] even minor presidential candidates who hailed from [it]" (Cole, 2009). The same fate befell Karoubi in his home province of Luristan where he had a strong power base. As Alizadeh reports, Karoubi's total vote numbered a mere 320, 000, a figure that was lower "than the number of people active in his campaign" (Alizadeh, cited in Hashemi & Postel, 2010, p. 3).

8 Taking a cue from the Green Movement campaign of 2009, Rouhani chose the colour purple to represent his campaign.

9 Following Hashemi's death, the state declared three days of national mourning. It was during this period that anti-establishment slogans were chanted.

10 Note that the first two slogans were among the signature refrains of the Green Movement when it first surfaced in June 2009; the third and fourth pertain to the house arrest of Karoubi and Mousavi.

Conclusion
What were the Iranians dreaming about in 2009? The Green Movement of counterconduct: A history of the past, the present and the future

While witnessing first-hand the 1979 revolution unfold in the streets of Tehran, Foucault was led to wonder what hopes and aspirations had compelled Iranians in their millions to challenge the Pahlavi monarchy. "What are the Iranians dreaming about?" he mused. Thirty years on, and following a second tumultuous uprising in Iran, Foucault's query would inspire this writer to pose another: *What set of conditions—historical, economic, social and political—gave rise to the 2009 Green Movement?* Three others follow logically from such a query: What ends did the Green Movement seek to achieve? To what extent were they realized? And to what degree, if any, does the Green Movement represent a paradigm shift in Iran's social and political landscape?

To address the above questions, I have drawn upon a Foucauldian-inspired model of collective action, which, as was shown, provides a much-needed and timely corrective to dominant social movement theories, with their totalizing accounts that are often West-centric in their orientation and modernist in their assumptions. I have argued on these grounds that they are inadequate for explicating oppositional movements in the Middle East and North Africa or for interrogating the conditions giving rise to the historical factors that led their actors to negate or reject semiauthoritarian regimes.

My analysis suggests the 2009 Green Movement may be viewed more profitably as a movement of movements, by which I mean an amalgam of oppositional movements or coalition of smaller movements of counterconduct. This approach enables an understanding of the Green Movement as a dynamic and open-ended process whereby smaller oppositional movements coalesced into a single mega-oppositional movement of counterconduct. In June 2009, the latter began targeting hierarchies of power that had been rationalized and perpetuated by a neoconservative establishment bent on advancing a religio-governmentalized agenda aimed at both micro and macro-managing the lives of ordinary Iranians.

Chapter 1, "Critical Literature Review," situated the Green Movement within the broader purview of a Social Movement Studies. After surveying some of the dominant theories pertaining to social movements in general, and by way of examining some that reduce MENA oppositional movements to grand causal categories, I concluded that by virtue of having been developed within Western polities, and thus invested with West-centric orientation, modernist assumptions and, in some cases, totalizing accounts of social movements, they are ultimately incapable of accounting for the specificities, and by implication complexities, of oppositional movements operating in the Middle East and North Africa.[1]

Referencing the above critique, Chapter 2, "Theorizing the Green Movement: A Foucauldian Model," drew on Foucault's analytic of power–knowledge–governmentality–resistance nexus, in addition to his work on the French and Iranian revolutions, to develop a theoretical framework—one sensitive to the social, political and geographical context within which oppositional movements emerge and capable of taking into account their histories, trajectories and day-to-day experiences—for historicizing and delineating the conditions of possibility for the emergence of these movements, the processes of solidarity building at work and the techniques and acts of resistance and defiance employed. I believe the theoretical approach employed here serves as a timely and much-needed corrective to the mainstream, hegemonic theories underpinning social movement studies.

Chapter 3, "The Coming of a Disciplinary Society to Post-Revolutionary Iran: Ordinary Iranians and Everyday Resistance," applied to the Iranian case a Foucauldian theoretical model for examining, on the one hand, the twin phenomena of power and knowledge and their role in creating an Islamist governmentality in the context of post-revolutionary Iran and, on the other, grassroots resistance to the processes of governmentality and its implications for social and political change. It was shown that to understand collective action, or counterconduct as Foucault calls it, requires interrogating the day-to-day trajectories and experiences of ordinary people during the course of their day-to-day struggle with governmental power, or, more specifically, in the daily process of resisting efforts on the part of the authorities to discipline the masses with a view to controlling certain aspects of their conduct. In this way, one can map out how that Foucauldian moment of singularity, when great crowds pour onto the streets to resist and negate a governmental system, materializes.

Chapter 4, "Social Mobilization and Political Contestation in Iran at the Turn of the Millennium: The 1999 Student Movement and the 2006 Women's One Million Signature Campaign," interrogated the two outstanding cases of collective action in the post-revolutionary period with a view to shedding light on the experiences and trajectories of the actors, principally women, students and youth. As was shown, the fate of these Green Movement precursors offers a number of critical insights into how the dominant discourse(s) can work to create the conditions of possibility for a counterdiscourse(s) to emerge, one capable of undermining the former's totalizing vision of the world, and hence its legitimacy. I demonstrated, moreover, how the techniques and tactics of resistance—presence-as-resistance and the everyday practices that are its lifeblood—developed and how, in a semi-authoritarian setting, solidarities emerged among oppositional elements. Lastly, it was shown that the very same interests, identities, subjectivities and social cohesion, forged during the events of 1999 and 2006, inspired Green Movement activists in 2009 to defy governmental power regardless of the personal risk to themselves.

Finally, in Chapter 5, "The Green Movement as a Movement of Movements and the Rise of a Homegrown Rights-based Society in Post-Revolutionary Iran," I mapped out the emergence in the late 1990s of a powerful conservative, or more accurately neoconservative, faction bent on promoting a new governmental order. It was shown how this bloc went about imposing a neo-Islamist governmentality after seizing control of the executive branch in 2005, and the profound effect this had on the lives of ordinary Iranians. Moreover, in delineating the history of the activists—women, students and youth—who made up the various oppositional groups during Ahmadinejad's first term in office (2005–2009), I was able to shed light on what it was they experienced during the course of day-to-day confrontations with governmental power in the form of the state security apparatus and its various techniques and practices for monitoring, disciplining and controlling the populace. In particular, I focused on how that power was subverted and negated by means of a grassroots resistance, the hallmark of which was everyday practices—in the case of women, bicycling, driving motor vehicles, wearing diminutive *hijabs* or make-up in public spaces—which, by way of transgressing the established rules, codes and norms of conduct, worked to undermine and delegitimize power, in the process politicizing large segments of the population prior the 2009 election.

This investigation also revealed that the host of government policies aimed at subordinating and controlling the masses had the reverse effect of inculcating a sense of subjectivity as rights-bearing citizens. This awakening marked the emergence of a new historical phase in the development of democracy and civil society within Iran. The crowning achievement of the smaller movements of counterconduct, many operating under the umbrella of the Green Movement, was the creation of a home-grown rights-based society, inherently opposed to the neoconservative establishment's religio-governmentalized project. In arguing that the Green Movement is most profitably viewed as a movement of movements, each bent on reinventing itself and the whole of Iranian society, I emphasized how, via a politics of convergence, these disparate movements coalesced in 2009 into a single immense bloc. Viewed in this light, the Green Movement is, on one hand, the predictable consequence of years of misrule on the part of the conservative establishment and manifestation of a new homegrown rights-based society in the throes of being created, and on the other, the product of the paradoxical effect of policies aimed at advancing a theocratic agenda by managing the lives of Iranians in the most minute detail.

The Green Movement: History, presence and future

The Green Movement has been on the defensive since the winter of 2010. It no longer has any real presence in the streets and its symbolic leaders, Mir-Hossein Mousavi and Mehdi Karoubi, remain under house arrest. Unknown numbers of its members have been executed or tortured or have simply disappeared; others are serving long prison terms. State propaganda either signifies the Green Movement as a phenomenon that was doomed to fail, and thus never a real threat to the established order, or dismisses it as a case of *fitnah*, or sedition, that was dealt with severely, albeit justly (BF News, 2016; Fars News, 2016a).

Paradoxically, more than a decade after the events of June 2009, the state-controlled media still warn of an imminent threat posed by the Green Movement and spare no effort in discrediting it in the eyes of the public, even going so far as to accuse its leaders of being puppets of foreign enemies (Dana News, 2015; Taraz News, 2016; Tabnak News, 2017). The hardliners have circulated a *daayerat-ol moaref-e fintnah*, or Encyclopedia of Sedition, the purpose of which lies in promoting conspiracy theories and disseminating misinformation about the Green Movement, in particular its constituencies and leadership (Tasnim News, 2013; Mehr News, 2013). All its spurious claims are variations on a common theme, namely that the 2009 demonstrations were funded and orchestrated by US and/or Zionist agents, who are still active in the country. This same theme is the staple of state-sponsored films and documentaries (Fars News, 2012; Fars News, 2015). Thus, the Green Movement is signified as both spent force and insidious threat to be resisted by every means available.

The conservative establishment's paradoxical view of the Green Movement amounts to an admission that although its activists have retreated underground, they are alive and well, their demands for political rights and individual freedoms undiminished. And while no longer capable of mounting massive street demonstrations, they remain united and defiant by virtue of a dream born of the collective experience of having been ruled under an Islamist governmentality. But what, precisely, were these activists, and the heterogeneous multitudes they led, dreaming about in 2009?

Addressing this question requires recognizing that theirs was no isolated historical struggle. Indeed, even the most cursory survey of Iran's recent history reveals, as I have sought to demonstrate, a long tradition of resistance to oppression of which the Bábí movement of 1844, the 1906 constitutional revolution, the 1953 nationalist movement, the 1979 revolution, the 1997 reform movement and 1999 student movement represent milestones—each in its own way aiming to establish a democratic, and by implication transparent and rule-bound, polity. Put differently, each constituted a case of localized resistance(s) directed at making Iran democratic or, to be more precise, foregrounding a homegrown rights-based democratic order.

The revolution of 1979 and the 2009 Green Movement: What were in 2009 Iranians dreaming, again?

For those interested in the Green Movement, and particularly its genesis and evolution, what is of special importance is the historical connection to these earlier cases of political contention and collective action, and in particular the 1979 revolution. One especially germane issue in this regard relates to whether the events of June 2009 signify a reprise of earlier oppositional movements, in particular, as Slavoj Žižek (2009, para. 7) argues, "the 'return of the repressed' of the [1979] revolution." Comparing the Green Movement and the 1979 revolution in terms of content and the aspirations of the actors may be instructive here.

Most importantly, in both cases, through radical collective action "subjectivity (not that of great men, but that of everyone) [was] introduce[d] into history and [gave] it its life" (Foucault, cited in Afary & Anderson, 2005, p. 266). Yet the Green Movement cannot be reduced to a mere iteration of 1979, given the very different dynamics, processes, historical/factual specificities and relations at work that postdate that great convulsion.

The revolution of 1979 represented a mass rejection of the autocratic misrule of Mohammad Reza Shah, the second, and as it turned out last, scion of the Pahlavi dynasty, and in particular of what Michel Foucault (2005c) calls the "Shah's [program of] archaic modernization" (p. 196), a grand utopian project directed at resurrecting the glories of ancient Persia while at the same time introducing social and economic policies intended to bring Iran into the 20th century, albeit without extending to the mass of the people democracy and political rights and freedoms. For Foucault (2005c), both the Shah and his approach to modernization were inherently archaic:

> What is old here in Iran is the Shah. He is fifty years old and a hundred years behind the times. He is of the age of predatory monarchs. He has the old fashioned dream of opening his country through secularization and industrialization. Today, it is his project of modernization, his despotic weapon, and his system of corruption that are archaic. It is "the regime" that is the archaism. (p. 198)

That the *Shahanshah*, or King of Kings,[2] one of the Shah's pet sobriquets, was "a hundred years behind the times" speaks to a reality the historian Abbas Milani showcases in a highly acclaimed biography entitled, aptly enough, *The Shah* (2011). The author succeeds in steering a middle course between "the excesses of the [monarch's] overzealous defenders and [those of his most fierce] detractors" (p. v). In his estimation the Shah "loved Iran, [but] not wisely" (Milani, 2011, p. 434), for he was "a ruler [keen on] promot[ing] social and economic [reforms] that hurled Iran into the modern age," while at the same time "in[tent] on ruling the country like a nineteenth-century Oriental Despot" (Milani, 2011, p. 280). This explains why the second Pahlavi to occupy the Peacock Throne, though deeply attached to his native land, chose to drag it into the 20th century by means of a modernization programme viewed by the author as paradoxical, by Foucault as archaic.

This archaic, and hence paradoxical, socio-economic programme of modernization found its ultimate expression in the White Revolution of 1963, underwritten by Iran's considerable oil revenues. So bold and sweeping an initiative was doomed to fail, however, owing to the Shah's antipathy towards democracy and his archaic notion of what constituted progress (Pahlavi, 1961, 1994). According to Milani, "[the Shah] dismissed democracy" because in his view it "only befit[ed] the blue-eyed world" (2011, p. 4).[3]

That the Shah viewed democracy with the inmost suspicion, if not repugnance, speaks to a deeply rooted conviction that it was entirely superfluous to the life of the modern state. It is hardly surprising, then, that in 1979 "nearly all advocates of modernity," so Milani notes, "formed an alliance against [him]" (2011, p. 436). Numbered among these were many alienated by the Shah's paternalism, which in the economic sphere translated into state control of prices, in addition to rampant inflation:

> [What accelerated the Shah's downfall was his] eclectic paradigm of modernization [, according to which, there existed an] urgent need to end feudalism and create a market economy ... linked to Western Capital markets. But he also had a [top-down and paternalistic] vision wherein the state would dominate key sectors of the economy and use all tools, including the military, to control prices and inflation.
>
> (Milani, 2011, p. 436)

This "paradox-[driven]" (Milani, 2011, p. 436) mode of modernization triggered a tidal wave of migration from rural to urban areas which replaced the traditional "village-based economy [with] a rapidly industrializing, increasingly urban, capitalist system" (Milani, 2011, pp. 436–437). This, in turn, created large urban slums, among the chief breeding grounds of discontent. All this gave rise to massive economic inequality during the closing years of the Shah's reign, thereby alienating broad segments of Iranian society.

The *Aryamehr*, or Light of the Aryans,[4] yet another of the Shah's pet sobriquets, envisioned modernization in terms of a messianic self-fulfilling prophecy foretelling the rise of a modern, and hence progressive, state (Pahlavi, 1961, 1994). According to this calculus, the country was to be remade by a Kemalist-inspired programme of archaic modernization enforced by the SAVAK, a brutal secret police force charged with overseeing the Pahlavi's disciplinary mode of governance.

Beyond all this, there existed yet a more formidable problem: the legacy of the 1953 *coup d'état* orchestrated, as is now commonly known, by Britain's M16 and the US Central Intelligence Agency. In a matter of days, the nationalist-democratic government of Mohammad Mossadegh, the first of its kind to emerge in the Middle East and North Africa, was overthrown by the Shah, with the aid of his British and American backers, who proceeded to govern after the fashion of an absolute monarch, and an unenlightened one at that. These measures, along with the Shah's contempt for individual rights and freedoms and rule of law, instilled in Iranians of virtually all stripes, and particularly women, students, intellectuals and *bazaaris*, a profound distrust of monarchical rule, in addition to creating for the Peacock Throne a crisis of legitimacy, which in the winter of 1979 spilled over into revolution (Parsa, 1989; Mahdavi, 2015). Argues Ervand Abrahamian, "[i]n an age of republicanism, radicalism and nationalism," the "Pahlavi regime [could only be viewed by the mass of the people as a bulwark of] monarchism, conservativism, and Western imperialism" (1989, p. 17). It was this crisis of legitimacy, in tandem with the Shah's oxymoronic programme of archaic modernization, that was in part responsible for creating "an immense movement from below" (Foucault, cited in Afary & Anderson, 2005, p. 87).

Foucault (2005c, p. 195), who personally witnessed this epic scene unfolding, was quick to grasp its significance: "I had understood that recent events did not signify a shrinking back in the face of modernization by extremely retrograde elements, but the rejection, by a whole culture and a whole people, of a modernization that is itself an archaism[:]"

... I do not mean that mere mistakes and failures have doomed the recent forms that the Shah wanted to give to modernization. [However, i]t is true that all the great efforts undertaken by the regime since 1963 [, the year the so-called White Revolution was inaugurated,] are now rejected, by all social classes.

(Foucault, 2005c, p. 196)

More specifically, Foucault saw in this historical struggle "a possible source of creativity and inspiration rather than an expression of backwardness finally unleashed forward toward progress" (Ghamari-Tabrizi, 2016, p. 3). His observation speaks to the individuality of this movement, lending it its singular character and context-based dimensions as a "movement [that] ha[d] no counterpart and no expression in the political order," and precisely because of the "political will" galvanizing it (Foucault, 2005d, p. 221). It was this will, according to Foucault (2005, p. 208), that had the effect of opening "a spiritual dimension in politics," what he calls a "political spirituality[:]"

> [I understand] spirituality [as] that which precisely refers to a subject acceding to a certain mode of being and to the transformations which the subject must make of himself in order to accede to this mode of being.
> (Foucault, cited in Carrette, 1999, p. 1)

Thus, political spirituality "impressed" precisely because it was employed by revolutionary cadres "as a form of 'political will;'" it also intrigued because it "politiciz[ed] structures that were inseparably social and religious [and above all because, it bears repeating,] it ... attempt[ed] to open a spiritual dimension in politics" (Foucault, 2005, p. 208).

But what of political spirituality in this localized power–governmentality–resistance nexus? Perhaps the best way to address this question, which is central to understanding the specificities of the '79 revolution and their historical contingency, is first to examine Foucault's views on religion:

> So what role has religion [played in the uprising? Certainly] not that of an ideology... it really has been the vocabulary, the ceremonial, the timeless drama into which one could fit the historical drama of a people that pitted its very existence against that of its sovereign.
> (Foucault, cited in Afary & Anderson, 2005, pp. 122–123)

Religion, in this case Shiite Islam, which for Foucault constituted "the source of ... political spirituality" (Ghamari-Tabrizi, 2016, p. 63), worked to "wed[] the state (as the instrument of coercion), religion (as the instrument of legitimation), and the individual (as the protagonist of self-governing technologies)" (Ghamari-Tabrizi, 2016, p. 64), thereby "collapsing the boundaries between politics, religion and the ethics of the self" (Carrette, 1999, p. 42). Hence, Foucault's references to religion when writing on the Iranian revolution had "not[hing] to [do with] anything spoken by the mullahs or articulated by any other exponent of the divine text;" on the contrary, religion "constituted[, for him] a force that perpetuated the hermeneutics of the subject on the streets of revolutionary Iran" (Ghamari-Tabrizi, 2016, p. 65):

> [Religion] transforms thousands of forms of discontent, hatred, misery and despair into a force. It transforms them into a force because it is a form of expression, a mode of social relations, a supply and widely accepted elemental organization, a way of being together, a way of speaking and listening, something that allows one to be listened to by others.
> (Foucault, 2005a, p. 252)

More specifically, Foucault elaborates on the analytical category of spirituality in relation to that of religion in his formulation of political spirituality, which he elaborates thus:

> When I talk about spirituality, I'm not talking about religion; that is, spirituality and religion need to be appropriately distinguished. I'm stupefied to see that spirituality, spiritualism, and religion comprise a remarkable jumble, a mishmash, an impossible confusion in people's minds! Spirituality is something that can be found in religion, but also outside of religion; that can be found in Buddhism, a religion without theology, in monotheisms, but that can also be found in Greek civilization. Thus, spirituality isn't necessarily bound to religion, even though most religions comprise a dimension of spirituality. What is spirituality? I think it's a certain practice by which the individual is displaced, transformed, disrupted, to the point of renouncing [his] own individuality, [his] own subject position. It's no longer being the subject that one had been up to that point, a subject in relation to a political power, but also the subject of a certain mode of knowledge [savoir], subject of an experience, or subject of a belief. It seems to me that that possibility of rising up from the subject position that had been fixed for you by a political power, a religious power, a dogma, a belief, a habit, a social structure, and so on— that's spirituality, that is, becoming other than what one is, other than oneself.
> (cited in Vaccarino Bremner, 2020, p. 128)

For Foucault, a political spirituality grounded in Shiism was most conducive to creating the kind of hermeneutics essential to transforming the self (Ghamari-Tabrizi, 2016). It was this phenomenon that "transform[ed] [Iranians] into new subject[s]—subject[s] that one could never imagine [them] capable of becoming," subjects possessing a collective will sufficient to reject Pahlavi rule (Foucault, 2005, p. 209).

In this formulation, political spirituality is conceived as a blueprint for "an alternative to historical determinism" (Ghamari-Tabrizi, 2016, p. 62)— that linear, universalist and developmentalist Western paradigm of revolutionary politics, social change and progress, as represented, for example, by Marxism. What it alludes to exclusively is a kind of corporeal spirituality understood "as a desire to liberate the [political] body," or historical subject, in this case the disciplined and governed subject, "from the prison house of the soul" (Ghamari-Tabrizi, 2016, p. 63).

Put differently, the distinguishing feature of political spirituality lies, it bears repeating, in "perpetuat[ing] the hermeneutics of the subject on the streets of revolutionary Iran" (Ghamari-Tabrizi, 2016, p. 65), for it had the dual effect of intensifying "a collective will that ha[d] been very strongly expressed politically" and heightening "the desire for a radical change in [the] ordinary life [of Iranians]," which translated into the political will to topple the Peacock Throne (Foucault, cited in Afary & Anderson, 2005, pp. 124–125). Asserts Foucault:

> The political will yearns for the end of dependency, the disappearance of the police, the redistribution of oil revenue, an attack on corruption, the reactivation of Islam, another way of life, and new relations with the West, with the Arab countries, with Asia and so forth.
>
> (2005d, p. 221)

Thus, most certainly for Foucault—and crucial to understanding the historically-contingent and singular character of the revolution—this political spirituality must be understood primarily as the by-product as well as the effect of a history of governmentalization, what Foucault calls the "governmentalization of the state" by the Pahlavi dynasty (cited in Ghamari-Tabrizi. 2016, p. 63).

By contrast, the Green Movement was a response to a very different form of semi-authoritarian misrule, one characterized by the militarization and securitization of the universities, state-sponsored patriarchy, the enforcement of strict disciplinary codes of conduct, and the instrumentalization and governmentalization, of religion, in this case Shi'a Islam—all justified under the rubric of Islamizing society. One can add to this imposing list economic mismanagement, evinced by mass unemployment among women, especially those under 30, students and youth, which at its peak in 2014 stood at a staggering 28%, according to official estimates (Mehr News, 2015; Ilna News, 2015; Farda News, 2016).

Moreover, while the Green Movement was triggered by the allegedly fraudulent re-election in 2009 of the presidential incumbent Mahmood Ahmadinejad, at its core laid a deeply rooted commitment to radical political reform aimed at creating a polity capable of building a homegrown rights-based society, one whose chief lineaments were formed, as was shown in earlier chapters, in the crucible of political contestation and resistance that was post-revolutionary Iran, and above all under the aegis of the Islamic Republic's programme of state-led Islamization or "Islamization from ... above," which was "often [conducted by means of] coercion and compulsion" (Bayat, 2013, p. 284).

That radical reform supplanted full-fledged revolution as the focus of oppositional movements in 2009 may be attributed, at least in part, to their recognition that the revolution of 1979 had, notwithstanding its democratic genesis and orientation, ultimately gave rise to a "failed and repressive [political order]" (Bayat, 2013, p. 285). Asef Bayat contends that the experience of a failed revolution led the demonstrators of 2009 to "long [not] for a revolution, but for meaningful reforms" (2013, p. 285). So sober and pragmatic a programme speaks to an assessment of the political situation that was informed by a clear understanding of the power relations and historical specificities extant in post-revolutionary Iranian society, which in large part were responsible for creating the requisite political will to contest the established order.

The latter point is an acknowledgment that the political will to contest the post-revolutionary political and social order was a function and by-product of Iran's post-revolutionary history of governmentalization.[5] This means that in 2009, in response to a project of Islamist governmentality that had become unendurable, a people transformed themselves into subjects intent on radically reforming the post-revolutionary order. In this way, the Green Movement of counterconduct "embodied the culmination of a collective sentiment to reclaim ... violated civil and political rights" (Bayat, 2013, p. 285) from a governmentalized clerical faction that had ignored "long-standing yearnings for a dignified life free from fear, moral surveillance, corruption and arbitrary rule" (Bayat, 2013, p. 296).

Put differently, in 2009, it was a yearning for the political rights denied them by a conservative establishment that once again galvanized Iranians into stylizing, reimagining and reasserting themselves against a power regime bent on reducing them to duty-bound citizens. It was this aspiration to reclaim fundamental rights that emerged as the chief dynamic, or compulsory response, driving the 2009 demonstrations, providing the participants with a lexicon of defiance and, what was to prove even more decisive, the political will to resist, contest and negate the status quo.

This yearning for rights, understood in an inclusive sense, became in Foucauldian parlance the soul of the uprising, meaning that in June and the months to follow, the demonstrators saw in the principle of civil rights the basis upon which to change themselves and their society. This is clearly revealed in the slogans chanted during the demonstrations: "Where is my vote?," "A fresh round of elections equals an end to street demonstrations," "If there was no election fraud, we would not be here," and "Give me back my vote" (Faryaade Mardom, 2009)—the cries of a people longing for democratic rights.

Thus, far from constituting a coincidental convergence of disparate groups with little, if anything, in common, the Green Movement came to represent a case of localized resistances from a power regime that had instrumentalized, and hence normalized and naturalized, and ultimately governmentalized, religion for the purpose of securing its legitimacy, advancing exclusivist and discriminatory political and social agendas, macro and micro-managing every aspect of social and political life and, and more than anything else, surviving.

It inevitably came to challenge the existing order because over the better part of a decade of conducting a grassroots struggle against the status quo, its followers had come to imagine themselves, indeed believed themselves to be, rights-bearing citizens entitled to be treated as such. This collective political will to reclaim rights thus represents the dynamic driving efforts to secure social and political justice. In this way, the Green Movement proved to be the product of a democratically-oriented, rights-based politics, one born of and sustained by grassroots movements pushing back at the repressive policies and practices that were the hallmark of a religio-governmentalizing order.

The post-revolutionary movements of counterconduct: The social as political

As was shown earlier, Iranians had endured misrule and misconduct by successive administrations, only to reimagine themselves as rights-bearing citizens determined to shape the country's social and political landscape in their own image. This is clearly evident in the 1999 Student Movement and 2006 Women's One Million Signature Campaign, which, while focused on achieving limited ends, nonetheless prepared the ground for the emergence in 2009 of the Green Movement, thereby succeeded in creating a united front out of what had been a collection of disparate oppositional groups. Put differently, in the years leading up to 2009 the latter's specific grievances were subsumed in the broader struggle for civic rights and freedoms, the rule of law, and transparency and accountability on the part of state. This marks a paradigmatic shift in the aspirations, and hence demands, of citizens' groups in the sense that "for the first time in Iranian history ... democracy [wa]s both the goal and the process" (Khosrokhavar, 2012, p. 57).

In 2009 various Green Movement constituencies sought, each in its own way, to defy and negate the hierarchies of political power perpetuated by the state and promoted justice, equality and freedom, along with transparency and accountability within government, in the process transforming and renewing themselves and the larger society by taking on new dimensions, incorporating new experiences, adopting a new lexicon, posing new questions, and raising new concerns.

Retreat is not defeat; rather, it is a sign of flexibility, vitality and maturity, attributes that will ensure that for the foreseeable future the prospect of radical social and political reform remains a reality that the forces of reaction might ignore only at their peril. This is inevitably so given that, as was shown, the Islamic Republic's Achilles' heel—what Foucault calls "the weak points [or effects] of power" (cited in Afary & Anderson, 2005, p. 189)—lies in governmentalizing the masses in public spaces wherein everyday life practices are fused with everyday contentious politics to challenge and negate the dominant order. The authorities are acutely aware that their regime of conduct, underwritten by various apparatuses of power, can only survive by creating innovative ways and means for scrutinizing and controlling individuals in public spaces. Paradoxically, and most vexing for the authorities, it is these very public spaces where the status quo continues to be contested and de-legitimized.

This means that in the Iranian context the democratization process manifests itself, as was shown, in the day-to-day struggle with power, waged to a large extent over how people live their lives—how they earn a living, socialize, spend leisure time—in the minutes and hours that make up a lifetime. This was necessarily so given that the authorities have historically politicized and delegitimized the most mundane of everyday life practices, including, but not limited to, singing, bicycling, driving motor vehicles, and attending university. Put differently, in the Iranian case the social was almost always political. Once this connection is made, one may clearly discern that members of post-revolutionary movements of counterconduct—particularly those representing women, that most socio-economically marginalized and deprived of groups[6]—are not only agents of social change but the very harbingers of a new political order.

This explains why I have been at pains to show that in order to understand contention and collective action in the Iranian context, it is essential to take into account, beyond interrogating the activities and trajectories of activists, the public lives of ordinary people and their aspirations for fundamental change. This is because in the public spaces of everyday life one can bear witness to the politics of grassroots empowerment being played out in the form of ubiquitous and cunning counter-governmentalizing strategies directed at negating and rejecting power. These strategies represent both a mode, and at the same time a politics, of counterpower that strike Foucault as one of the most dramatic manifestations of what he calls "critique," in this context radical resistance, subversion, and defiance of the rules, codes and norms, enabled by "the art of voluntary inservitude, of reflective indocility" (1996, p. 386)—a mode and politics of contestation that Iranians set in motion, as was documented in earlier chapters, for the express purpose of bringing about social and political change, notwithstanding the factional politics of the post-revolutionary period.

This mode or politics of critique, and hence counterpower, was possible because, as was shown, while the state clearly possessed the requisite means to crush any oppositional movement, its governmentalizing rule was limited in its capacity to control the normal flow of everyday life; moreover, any effort to do so might end in exposing its disciplinary project for all to see. By analyzing and scrutinizing the Islamic Republic's conduct of conduct, and in particular by exposing its disciplinary project, I have sought to reveal "the weak points of power, from which we can attack it" (Foucault, cited in Afary & Anderson, 2005, p. 189). This is essential, for, as Foucault (1978, p. 86) tells us, "[p]ower is tolerable only on condition that it mask[s] a substantial part of itself. Its success is proportional to its ability to hide its own mechanisms." And even if absolute control were possible, it could only be purchased at the cost of converting every public space into a militarized zone, something the authorities, as documented throughout this work, were unwilling to do. This is because, as Thomas Osborne opines, "[even the] most malign ... the most well-armed brutal power [can] be resisted [and/or inverted] by the force of [a people's] will" (1999, p. 206).

The power underpinning the Islamic Republic of Iran's system of governance—this thing enabled by an Islamist governmentality—is predicated on the instrumentalization and politicization of Islam. The latter is responsible for decades of disastrous social, political, religious and economic policies conceived and carried out in the name of Islam. Herein lies a pernicious mode of governance wherein the high priests are the politicians; the repressed multitude their sacrificial lambs; the anguish of the masses of unemployed and homeless their incense; the insidious and irrelevant formulae for ruling in the name of god their stock in trade. It is this Islamist governmentality that has deprived women, workers, students, youth and religious minorities of fundamental human rights. So unsound, it is this mode of governance that Iranians will, sooner or later, consign to the dustbin of history.

Notes

1 Certainly, it goes with out saying that such assertions do not apply to all accounts of social movement theories.
2 The title *Shahanshah*, literally meaning King of Kings, was bestowed upon the Shah by the *Majlis* in 1967 to commemorate his ascension to the Peacock Throne and to underscore his connection to the great Persian rulers of the past, in particular those of the Achaemenid and Sassanid kingdoms, which at their zenith controlled much of present day Iran, in addition to large swaths of central Asia, the Arab Middle East and North Africa. These grand potentates adopted the title King of Kings as an expression of their power. For more on this point, see Houshang Nahavandi (2014), *Mohammad Reza Pahlavi: The Last Shahanshah*.
3 Milani notes this was particularly the case during the last decade of his rule.
4 The title *Aryamehr* was bestowed upon the Shah by a joint session of both houses of the Iranian Parliament on 15 September 1965, some two years prior to his coronation. The intention was to foreground the Shah as a symbol of Pahlavi nationalism. The term Iran is derived from *Airya*, meaning Iranian. The term Aryan, or people of the Aryan race, refers to the Indo-Iranian people believed to have resided in Central Asia circa 1500 BCE and to have migrated to present-day Iran circa 1800 BCE. According to the Pahlavi mythology, the Aryans founded the great Persian kingdoms of Achaemenid and Sassanid. This mythology would underwrite the Shah's modernization program aimed at recapturing the grandeur and glory of the Persian Empire. In recent years this mythological construct has been rejected by historians. For a further discussion, see Houshang Nahavandi (2014), *Mohammad Reza Pahlavi: The Last Shahanshah*; see also Reza Zia-Ebrahimi (2010) "Iranian Identity, the 'Aryan Race,' and Jake Gyllenhaal."
5 As inferred above, this is not to suggest that pre-revolutionary history and politics played no role in shaping the Green Movement or informing the aspirations of its cadres; indeed, as discussed above, there had been numerous cases of radical resistance and defiance of the state, going as far back as the early 1800s. Rather, it is to argue that understanding the history of the post-revolutionary period is key to elucidating the Green Movement's genesis and the conditions for its emergence.
6 To cite but one example, according to official statistics, in 2015 the participation rate for women in the job market stood at 10%. For a discussion re this matter, see Radio Farda (2017).

Bibliography

List of Interviews

Abdi, A. (2015). Interview with Ali Abdi, former student activist, former member of the One Million Signature Campaign, and former political prisoner.

Afshari, A. (2015, 2016). Interview with Ali Afshari, former member of the Office for Consolidating Unity, or *daftar-e tahkim-e vahdat*, and former political prisoner.

McCall, C. (2015). Interview with Dr. Corey McCall, Elmira College.

Rezaei, S. (2015). Interview with Sabra Rezaei, former member of the One Million Signature Campaign and Green Movement Activist.

Safshekan, R. (2015, 2016). Interview with Rouzbeh Safshekan, former student activist and political prisoner.

Walters, W. (2015). Interview with Dr. William Walters, Carleton University.

Farsi References

Aftab News. (2016). *Gasht-e ershad kei va chegoone aghaz shod?* Retrieved from http://aftabnews.ir/fa/news/362295/.

Aftab News. (2017). *Boodjeye nahadhaye nezami cheghadr ast? Aastaneh ghods belakhare maliyat midahad.* Retrieved from http://aftabnews.ir/fa/news/494727/بودجه-نهادهای-نظامی-چقدر-است-آستان-قدس-بالاخره-مالیات-میدهد-۹۷.

Ahkam TV. (2016). *The official page of zolal-e ahkam.* Retrieved from http://ahkam.tv3.ir/.

Akhbar Rooz. (2009). *Tahkim-e vahdat koshte shodan-e 5 daneshjoo ra ta'id kard.* Retrieved from http://www.akhbar-rooz.com/news.jsp?essayId=21594.

Akhbar Rooz. (2015). *Ansa-re hezbollah mojri-e amr-e be marouf va ahye az monkar.* Retrieved from http://www.akhbar-rooz.com/article.jsp?essayId=65179.

Alef News. (2012). *Laghv-e jamavariy-e mahvareh ().* Retrieved from http://alef.ir/vdce-vw8zpjh8nni.b9bj.html?152586

Alvadossadegh. (2011). *Nezame siasiye eslam dar asr-e gheibat az manzare ayatollah javadi amoli.* Retrieved from http://www.alvadossadegh.com/fa/article/61-zohoor-a-gheybat/7980--7980.html

Andisheh Siasi. (2017). *Nezaarat bar valiye faqih.* Retrieved from http://siasi.porsemani.ir/node/2049.

Asoo. (2017). *Dieh be bahaiyat ta'allogh nemigirad.* Retrieved from http://www.aasoo.org/fa/documents/1057.

Asr Iran. (2008). *Gozaresh-e bbc az taxihay-e zananeh dar khiaban-hay-e tehran.* Retrieved from http://www.asriran.com/fa/news/57888/گزارش-bbc-از-تاکسی-های-زنانه-در-خیابان-های-تهران.

Asr Iran. (2013). *gasht-e ershad; Be naf-e hejab ya be ziyan-e Nezam.* Retrieved from http://www.asriran.com/fa/news/293487/.

Bibliography 203

Asr Iran. (2016). *Moze'giriye rouhani darbaareye gashte namahsoose polis: Keraamate ensani moghaddam bar din ast*. Retrieved from http://www.asriran.com/fa/news/463296/.

Asr Khabar. (2015). *Chera serialhay-e mahvareh hamchenan mahboob hastand?* Retrieved from http://www.asrkhabar.com/fa/news/70790/.

Aviny. (2009). *Bayanat [rahbar] dar didar ba asatid-e daneshgaha*. Retrieved from http://www.aviny.com/bayanat/88/06_08.aspx.

Bahai News. (2006). *Sazemane melal-e motahed migooyad Iran anvaal va daaraaihaaye bahaiha ra mosadere mikonad*. Retrieved from http://news.persian-bahai.org/story/7.

Bahejab. (2015). *Takrim az hejab-e bartar dar khiabanhaye shahr*. Retrieved from http://bahejab.com/.

Balatarin. (2016). *Ba aghab neshinie nirooye entezaqmi, "gashte ershad-e namahsoos" motevaghef shod*. Retrieved from https://www.balatarin.com/topic/2016/5/3/1016611.

BBC. (2007). *Bar khord ba bad hejabi az avale ordibehesht dar Tehran*. Retrieved from http://www.bbc.com/persian/iran/story/2007/04/070408_shr-dress-code.shtml.

BBC. (2013). *Rahbar-e Iran: Hozoore zanan dar manaasebe ejrai eftekhar nadarad*. Retrieved from http://www.bbc.com/persian/iran/2013/05/130511_145_khamenei_women.shtml.

BBC. (2017). *Sho'aarhaye hamiyan-e joneshe sabz dar maraseme tashi jenaz-eye akbar hashemi rafsanjani*. Retrieved from http://www.bbc.com/persian/interactivity-38571377?SThisFB.

BBC News. (2008). *Karmandan-e 'bad hejab' ekhraj mishavand?* Retrieved from http://www.bbc.com/persian/iran/story/2008/04/printable/080430_ka_hejab.shtml.

BF News. (2016). *Mardom dar 9 dey fitneh ra dar notfeh khafeh kardand*. Retrieved from http://www.bfnews.ir/vdcb98b0.rhb0gpiuur.html.

Bultan News. (2014). *Payamadhay-e eghtesadi laghv-e tahrim bar bazare naft*. Retrieved from http://www.bultannews.com/fa/news/284903/.

Cyber.police.ir. (2017). *FATA's Official Website*. Retrieved from http://cyber.police.ir/.

Dana News. (2015). *Taharokate 16 azar neshan dad ke khate nofooze fetneh hanooz zende ast*. Retrieved from http://www.dana.ir/news/598883.

Daneshjoo News. (2015). *Bazkhani-e hamle be kouye daneshgah Tehran dar 18 tir 1378*. Retrieved from http://www.daneshjoonews.com/archives/18484.

Dolate Bahar (2014). *Taeb: Eghdam-e amali gorouhay-e ansar-e hezbollah bedoun-e mojavez haram ast*. Retrieved from http://www.dolatebahar.com/print-18825.html.

Ebtekar News. (2008). *Zanan posht-e farman-e ranandegi*. Retrieved from http://old.ebtekarnews.com/Ebtekar/News.aspx?NID=40905.

Eghtesad Iran Online. (2014). *Afzayesh-e estefadeh az mahvareh dar Tehran*. Retrieved from http://eghtesadeiranonline.com/vdca0unei49nwm1.k5k4.html.

Esra News. (2012). *Payam-e hazrat-e ayatollah javadi amoli be dovvomin hamayeshe "honar-e velaei."* Retrieved from http://www.portal.esra.ir/Pages/Index.aspx?kind=1&lang=fa&id=MTc3Ng%3D%3D-QMFDZYnDd18%3D.

Etemadi, N. (2009). *Jomhoorie irani mote'alegh be mossadeq ast*. Retrieved from http://www1.rfi.fr/actufa/articles/120/article_10015.asp.

Fararu. (2008). *Jannati: Daneshgah raftane dokhtaran moshkel saaz shode ast*. Retrieved from http://fararu.com/fa/news/17682/جنتی-دانشگاه-رفتن-دختران-مشکل-ساز-شده-است.

Fararu Daily. (2013). *Vahede zanan-e yegan-e vije polis tashkil mishavad*. Retrieved from http://fararu.com/fa/news/138408/واحد-زنان-یگان-ویژه-پلیس-تشکیل-می-شود.

Farda News. (2016). *Bikari 50 darsadie daneshgahian dar rah ast*. Retrieved from http://www.fardanews.com/fa/news/479644/.

Bibliography

Fars News. (2010). *Tazakore emam jom-e tehran be afrad-e bihejab*. Retrieved from http://www.farsnews.com/newstext.php?nn=8901270510.

Fars News. (2012). *Foroushe 3.5 miliardie ghaladehaye tala*. Retrieved from http://www.farsnews.com/newstext.php?nn=13910524000945.

Fars News. (2015). *Agar fetneh 88 be piroozi miresid amrica niazi be rah andaziye daesh nadasht*. Retrieved from http://www.farsnews.com/printable.php?nn=13941001000983.

Fars News. (2016a). *Shiveye jaded-e bad hijabi dar Tehran*. Retrieved from http://www.farsnews.com/newstext.php?nn=13950121000721.

Fars News. (2016b). *Aghaze be kare 7000 irooye namahsoose gashte amniat-e akhlaqi*. Retrieved from http://www.farsnews.com/printable.php?nn=13950130000601.

Fars News. (2016c). *Modiriyat-e rahbar-e moazzam inqelab-e fitne ra khafe kard*. Retrieved from http://mazandaran.farsnews.com/news/13951008001522.

Fars News. (2017). *Nazar-e ghat'eie foghahay-e shoraye negahban darbareye montakhabe zartoshtie shoraye shahre yazd e'elam shod*. Retrieved from http://www.farsnews.com/13960802001335

Faryaade Mardom. (2009). *Shoaarhaye mardome iran dar eteraz be taghalobe gostarde dar entekhabat va rooydadhaye pas az aan*. Retrieved from http://faryade-mardome-iran.blogspot.ca/2010/02/blog-post.html.

Ghatreh. (2013a). *Enteghad-e shadide ayatollah makareme shirzai be mas'aleye badhijabi*. Retrieved from http://www.ghatreh.com/news/nn14776191/.

——— (2013b). *Ayatollah safi golpayegani: Badhijabi mohemtarin rahe gomrah kardan-e jaame'e ast*. Retrieved from http://www.ghatreh.com/news/nn15761162/.

Goftegoo News. (2014). *Hameye rooznamehaye toghif shode az sale 76 ta konoon*. Retrieved from http://www.goftogoonews.com/Pages/News.

Gooya News. (2013). Retrieved from http://news.gooya.com/politics/archives/2013/06/162059print.php.

Gooya New. (2016). *Kaf zadan az jaheliyat-e ghabl az eslam ast*. Retrieved form http://news.gooya.com/politics/archives/2015/11/204593.php.

Green Path. (2010). *Hokoumati ke z docharkhe savari-ye zanan negaraan ast az sambol shodan-e neda khab be cheshm nadarad*. Retrieved from https://greennpath.wordpress.com/2010/08/06/.

Hamshahri Online. (2010). *Ashnai ba markaze omoore zanan va khanevade rais jomhoori*. Retrieved from http://hamshahrionline.ir/details/105479.

Hawzah Net. (2004). *Hokm-e dast zadan*. Retrieved from http://www.hawzah.net/fa/Magazine/View/6023/6812/81809/.

Hawzah News. (2009). *Zan dar bayane rahbare enghelab*. Retrieved from http://www.hawzah.net/fa/Article/View/82887/.

Hawzah News. (2010). *Jame-e madani dar nazariyehay-e velayat-e faqih*. Retrieved from http://www.hawzah.net/fa/Article/View/89692/.

Hosseini, N. (2012). *Hadaf az sahmiebandihaye jensiati va boomi gozini dar daneshgahhaye iran chist? Iran Global*. Retrieved from http://www.iranglobal.info/node/8656.

Iran Briefing. (2012). *Ansar-e hezbollah sanbol-e vahshigari va kharabkari dar iran*. Retrieved from http://farsi.iranbriefing.net/.

Iran Eslami News. (2015). *Eslahat; Doran'e talaiye hejab setizan*. Retrieved from http://www.iraneslaminews.com/fa/doc/article/42592/.

Iran Press Watch. (2010). *Mosadereyeh zaminhaye keshavarzie bahaian-e roostaye eival*. Retrieved from http://fa.iranpresswatch.org/post/1610/.

Iran Wire (2015a). *Moghabeleh ba nofouz-e doshman az tarigh-e gasht-e ershad*. Retrieved from https://iranwire.com/features/8333/

Iran Wire. (2015b). *Majaray-e niloofar ardalan*. Retrieved from https://iranwire.com/features/8077/

Iran Wire. (2016a). *Be monasebat-e yek miliooni shodane safheye azaadihaye yavashaki*. Retrieved from http://iranwire.com/blogs/8356/8278/.

Iran Wire. (2016b). *Tipeh maa pesaraaneh nist, alayhei hejaba-e ejbaari ast*. Retrieved from https://www.iranwire.com/features/9149/

IlnaNews.(2015).*Jamiat-ezanan-ebikar100ta150darsadafzayeshmiyabad*.Retrievedfrom http://www.ilna.ir/%D8%A8%D8%AE%D8%B4-%D8%A7%D8%AE%D8%A8%D8%A7%D8%B1-50/32637-%D8%AC%D9%85%D8%B9%DB%8C%D8%AA-%D8%B2%D9%86%D8%A7%D9%86-%D8%A8%DB%8C%DA%A9%D8%A7%D8%B1.

ISNA News. (2013). *Shenasaai-e hofrehaye sazmaanhaye dolatiye be komake polise fata*. Retrieved from http://www.isna.ir/news/92072816972/.

ISNA News. (2016a). *Jannati: Ghanoone mamnooiate mahvare bayad eslah shaved*. Retrieved from http://www.isna.ir/news/95040112168/.

ISNA News. (2016b). *Payamak-e rouhani hamzaman ba emzaye manshoore hoqoughe shahrvandi be mardom*. Retrieved from http://www.isna.ir/news/95092918048/.

Jahan News. (2013a). *Eterafat-e montasher nashodeye abtahi darbareh hashemi, mousavi va khatami ()*. Retrieved from http://www.jahannews.com/fa/doc/news/320742/.

Jahan News. (2013b). *Pak kardane soorat-e mas'ale az lavaazeme arayeshi-eh taghalobi*. Retrieved from http://jahannews.com/prtdoo0fnyt0f56.2a2y.html.

Jalalipour, H. (2003). *Jameshenasi-e jonbeshhay-e ejtemaei: Ba takid bar jonbesh-e eslahieh dovome khordad*. Tehran: Tarheno.

Jonoub News. (2014). *Ansar-e hezbollah: Motor savaran-e amre be marouf bar migardand*. Retrieve from http://www.jonoubnews.ir/showpage.aspx?id=135829.

Kar, M. (2006). *Shuresh: Yek ravayat-e zananeh as enghelab-e Iran (Rebellion: A feminine narration of the Iranian revolution)*. Stockholm: Baran.

Karoubi, M (2009). *Manshour-e hoquq-e zanan*, Available from http://www.magiran.com/npview.asp?ID=1862444.

Khabar Online. (2013a). *Aya khanandegiye zanan haram ast? Nazar-e ayatollah Khamenei va ayatollah makaarem*. Retrieved from http://www.khabaronline.ir/detail/320418/culture/religion

Khabar Online. (2013b). *Barkhord ba bad hejabi ba dadan-e shakhe gol be bahejabha shourou shod*. Retrieved from http://khabaronline.ir/detail/290188/society/Police.

Khabarkhodro. (2010). *Gozareshi az ranandegie zanan dar khiabanhaye shahr*. Retrieved from http://www.khabarkhodro.com/detail.asp?id=37946.

Khamenei, A. (1994). *Bayanaat dar salgard-e ertehale hazrateh emam khomeini*. Retrieved from http://farsi.khamenei.ir/speech-content?id=2717.

Khamenei, A. (1998). *Bayanat dar jaleseye porsesh va pasokhe daneshgahe tehran*. Retrieved from http://farsi.khamenei.ir/speech-content?id=2887.

Khamenei, A. (2000a). *Bayanat dar didare azaaye heiyate elmie kongereye emam Khomeini*. Retrieved from http://farsi.khamenei.ir/speech-content?id=2988.

Khamenei, A. (2000b). *Bayanat dar didare ba javanan dar mosallaye bozorg-e tehran*. Retirieved from http://farsi.khamenei.ir/speech-content?id=3003.

Khamenei, A. (2010). *Porsesh va pasokh-e daneshjooyan ba rahbar-e enghelab darbareye vazayefe daneshjoo*. Retrieved from http://farsi.khamenei.ir/speech-content?id=10683.

Khamenei, A. (2013). *Chera modaeian-e taghalob dar entekhabate 88 ordookeshi kardand? Chera ozrkhahi nemikonand?* Retrieved from http://www.farsnews.com/news-text.php?nn=13920506001276.

Khamenei, A. (2014a). *Azemat-e zan dar hefze efaf va amikhtan-e hijab ba ezzat-e moemenane ast.* Retrieved from http://www.irna.ir/fa/NewsPrint.aspx?ID=80983243.

Khamenei, A. (2014b). *Bayaanat dar didare jami az maddahan.* Retrieved from http://farsi.khamenei.ir/speech-content?id=22443.

Khamenei, A. (2014c). *Didare jami az banoovane bargozideye keshvar ba rahbar-e enghelab.* Retrieved from http://farsi.khamenei.ir/news-content?id=26147.

Khamenei.ir. (2016a). *Dast zadan (Clapping).* Retrieved from http://farsi.khamenei.ir/treatise-content?id=101&pid=101&tid=-1.

———. (2016b). *Mousighi va ghena.* Retrieved from http://farsi.khamenei.ir/treatise-content?id=99#1128.

———. (2016c). *Ahkam-e poushes.* Retrieved from http://farsi.khamenei.ir/treatise-content?id=123&pid=123&tid=-1.

Khamenei. Ir. (2017). *The Official Website of Ayatollah Khamenei.* Retrieved from http://www.khamenei.ir/.

Khatami, M. (2008). *Gozaresh-e kamel-e sokhanranie khatami dar daneshgahe Tehran.* Retrieved from http://alef.ir/vdci3qap.t1aqw2bcct.html?36659.

——— (2013). *Khatami: Nemishavad nazar-e anhai ke hasr shodeand ra nadideh gereft.* Retrieved from http://www.mashreghnews.ir/fa/news/200708/.

——— (2015). *Seyyed mohammad khatami: Daneshgah va daneshjooi ke natavanad naghd konad morde ast.* Retrieved from http://kaleme.com/1394/07/05/klm-225544/.

Kheybar Online. (2014). *Barrasie ahkam-e kaf zadan dar marasem-e shadiye ahle beit.* Retrieved from http://kheybaronline.ir/fa/news/30280/.

Khodnevis. (2010). *Ahmadinejad va Khamenei: "Doshman-e azadie matbooat."* Retrieved from https://khodnevis.org/article/42033.

Mahdavi Kani, M. R. (2011). *Dar rahe velayat ta payeh shahadat istadeim.* Retrieved from http://www.farsnews.com/newstext.php?nn=8912161071.

Mashregh News. (2013). *Joziaate tarh-e jaded-e gashte ershad.* Retrieved from https://www.mashreghnews.ir/news/211264/.

———. (2014). *Daneshjooyan-e motabartarin daneshgahhaye jahan chegoone lebas mipooshand?* Retrieved from http://www.mashreghnews.ir/fa/news/267266/.

Matin, F. (2014). *Tejarat-e por soud-e rooye poshte bam. Rooz Online.* Retrieved from http://www.roozonline.com/persian/news/newsitem/article/-66c0a103c4.html.

Mehrkhane. (2014) *Valentine; roozi bedoone rishe dar iran.* Retrieved from http://mehrkhane.com/fa/news/10200/.

Mehr News (2013). *Daayertol moarefe fiteneye 88 roonamai shod.* Retrieved from http://www.mehrnews.com/news/2202197/.

———. (2015). *Nerkh-e bikariye javanan record zad.* Retrieved from http://www.mehrnews.com/news/3017104/.

———. (2017). *Markaz-e etelaa resanieh polise paytakh eelam kard: Barpaie kelase amoozeshi varaye kamtavajoha be hijabe eslami.* Retrieved from https://www.mehrnews.com/news/4184959/.

Meidaan. (2015). *Tajrobehay-e zanan az gasht-e ershad.* Retrieved from https://meidaan.com/archive/6373.

Mizan Online. (2015). *Sevomin conger-he beinolmelali-e oloume ensani farda dar Tehran aghaz- e be kar mikonad.* Retrieved from http://www.mizanonline.ir/fa/news/93253/.

Mobarezeh News. (2013). *Jannati dar baraabar-e jannati va ja'ameeyeh daneshgahi!* Retrieved from http://mobareze.ir/news/12259.html.

My Stealthy Freedom. (2017a). *Azadiye yavashaki.* Retrieved from http://mystealthyfreedom.net/fa/campaigns/items/3123/?exclude_id=3123&page=2&campaign=5.

———— (2017b). *I have no fear of you, my camera is my weapon.* Retrieved from https://www.facebook.com/StealthyFreedom/videos/1969307423083342/.

————. (2017c). *Women in Iran are recording men who are harassing them on the street.* Retrieved from https://www.facebook.com/Maher/posts/10155239483532297?comment_id=10155239736442297&comment_tracking=%7B%22tn%22%3A%22R9%22%7D.

————. (2017d). *This is how we should stop the morality police or individuals interfering in our personal choices.* Retrieved from https://www.facebook.com/StealthyFreedom/videos/1984598808220870/.

————. (2017e). *This cleric stopped me in the street using foul language.* Retrieved from https://www.facebook.com/StealthyFreedom/videos/2037593876254696/.

————. (2017f). *Unbelievable, this man is telling me that if you were my daughter I'd kill you for not wearing the hijab.* Retrieved from https://m.facebook.com/story.php?story_fbid=10155489687682740&id=12384827273

————. (2017g). *By declaring that they will no longer arrest "badly-veiled" women in Tehran, the government has taken a step back.* Retrieved from https://www.facebook.com/StealthyFreedom/videos/2040622419285175/.

Navabi, E. (2006). *Chamran, kingkong va goodzila. Rooz Online.* Retrieved from http://www.roozonline.com/persian/news/newsitem/article/-18608206b9.html.

Noghrehkar, M. (2009). *Lebas shakhsiha. Gozaar.* Retrieved from http://www.gozaar.org/persian/articles-fa/3434.htmlpiroozie.

Pars News. (2015). *Nazari be zamineha va peidayesh-e jarian-e [ansar-e] hezbollah pas az enghelab-e eslami.* Retrieved from http://www.parsnews.com/ %D8%A8%D8%AE%D8%B4-%D8%B3%DB%8C%D8%A7%D8%B3%DB%8C-3/308366-%D9%86%D8%B8%D8%B1%DB%8C-%D8%A8%D9%87-%D8%B2%D9%85%DB%8C%D9%86%D9%87-%D9%87%D8%A7-%D9%BE%DB%8C%D8%A7%D9%85%D8%AF%D9%87%D8%A7%DB%8C-%D9%BE%DB%8C%D8%A7%D9%85%D8%AF%D8%A7%DB%8C%D8%B4-%D8%AC%D8%B1%DB%8C%D8%A7%D9%86-%D8%AD%D8%B2%D8%A8-%D8%A7%D9%84%D9%84%D9%87-%D9%BE%D8%B3-%D8%A7%D8%B2-%D9%BE%DB%8C%D8%B1%D9%88%D8%B2%DB%8C-%D8%A7%D9%86%D9%82%D9%84%D8%A7%D8%A8-%D8%A7%D8%B3%D9%84%D8%A7%D9%85%DB%8C-%D8%AD%D8%A7%D9%81%D8%B8-%D8%AD%D8%B1%DB%8C%D9%85-%D8%A7%D8%B1%D8%B2%D8%B4-%D9%87%D8%A7-%D9%85%D8%A8%D8%A7%D9%86%DB%8C-%D8%A7%D9%86%D9%82%D9%84%D8%A7%D8%A8.

Peyk Iran. (2010). *Gozareshgaraane bedoone marz: Toghife matbooat va mahkoomiate sangin baraye rooznamenegaraan eghdami roozmarre dar iran.* Retrieved from http://www.peykeiran.com/Content.aspx?ID=20712.

————. (2014). *Viraj-e motor savarhay-e ansar-e hezbollah baray-e nahy az monkar.* Retrieved from http://www.peykeiran.com/Content.aspx?ID=78178.

Quds Online. (2016). *Sardar aghakhani farmandehe intezami-e bartar-e keshvar shod.* Retrieved from http://qudsonline.ir/news/378052/.

————. (2017). *Farmandehe entezamie ostane Isfahan: sarbaz-e vilayat boodan; bozorgtarin eftekhar-e polis bad az inqelab ast.* Retrieved from http://qudsonline.ir/news/498311/.

Radio Farda. (2007). *Karname 2 saleh Ahmadinejad: Jonbeshe "setaredareh" daneshjooi.* Retrieved from http://www.radiofarda.com/a/f4_student_review/399212.html.

Radio Farda. (2009). *Enteshaar-e fehrest-e 72 nafareye koshteshodegane havaadese entekhabaati.* Retrieved from https://www.radiofarda.com/a/F8_LIST_KILLED_PEOPLE_POST_ELECTION_NOR OUZ/1814704.html.

Radio Farda. (2011). *"Hazf-e" 13 reshteye oloume ensani az reshtehaye daneshgahe allameh tabatabaei.* Retrieved from http://www.radiofarda.com/content/f2_iran_etemaad_daily_13_humanities_disciplines_deleted_from_list_for_students_allameh/24288600.html.

Radio Farda. (2016). *Kaboutaran-e velayat ya peik-e vahshat; lebas shakhsiha kistand?* Retrieved from http://www.radiofarda.com/content/f2_Iran_Revolutionary_Guards_plain_clothes_Ebrahimi/1765957.html.

Radio Farda. (2017a). *Sahme rohaniyat az poole mellat.* Retirved from https://www.radiofarda.com/a/sixth-hour-clerics-share-from-budget/28920792.html.

Radio Farda. (2017b). *Enteghad-e rahbare iran az talash baraye taghire ghavaanine zanan.* Retrieved from https://web.archive.org/web/20071113051113/http://www.radiofarda.com/Article/2007/07/04/o1_khamenei-critisiz.html.

Radio Farda (2017c). *Tanha 10 darsade zanan-e dar senn-e kar dar iran shaqel hastand.* Retrieved from https://www.radiofarda.com/a/f12-women-jobs-problem-iran/28632020.html.

Radio Farda. (2017d). *Shoarha dar hemayat-e az mousavi, karoubi, va khatami dar tashiyeh hashemi.* Retrieved from https://www.radiofarda.com/a/f8--hashemi-farewell/28223307.html.

Rahe Sabz. (2009a). *Bouleten-e vijeye irna: 37 koshteh dar rooze Ashura dar sartaasar-e keshvar.* Retrieved from http://www.rahesabz.net/story/6669/.

Rahe Sabz. (2009b). *Vezarat-e behdasht amaare majroohane ashuraye Tehran ra bish az 60 nafar elaam kard.* Retrirved from http://www.rahesabz.net/story/6516/.

Rahe Sabz. (2010). *Tarhe sabz.* Retrieved from http://www.rahesabz.net/cartoon/18372/87900--/P640/.

Raja News. (2014). *Gozaareshee raja news az roozhaye moltahebe 5 sale ghabl.* Retrieved from http://www.rajanews.com/news/175706#.

Ramezanzadeh, F. (2015). *Nerkh-e balay-e bikari zanan. Rahe Sabz.* Retrieved from http://www.rahesabz.net/story/81704/.

Saremi, N. (2015). *Tashdid-e bohrane bikariye zanan-e iran. Rooz Online.* Retrieved from http://www.roozonline.com/persian/news/newsitem/article/-475839be49.html.

Satrs News. (2014). *Vaakaaviye jarianat-e tondro pas az enghelab.* Retrieved from http://satrnews.ir/content/%D9%88%D8%A7%DA%A9%D8%A7%D9%88%DB%8C-%D8%AC%D8%B1%DB%8C%D8%A7%D9%86%D8%A7%D8%AA-%D8%AA%D9%86%D8%AF%D8%B1%D9%88-%D9%BE%D8%B3-%D8%A7%D8%B2-%D8%A7%D9%86%D9%82%D9%84%D8%A7%D8%A8-1-%DA%AF%D8%B1%D9%88%D9%87%D9%87%D8%A7%DB%8C-%D9%81%D8%B4%D8%A7%D8%B1-%D9%84%D8%A8%D8%A7%D8%B3-%D8%B4%D8%AE%D8%B5%DB%8C-%D9%87%D8%A7-%D9%88-%D8%A7%D9%86%D8%B5%D8%A7%D8%B1%D8%AD%D8%B2%D8%A8-%D8%A7%D9%84%D9%84%D9%87-%D8%B9%D9%84%DB%8C%D9%87-%D8%AF%D9%88%D9%84%D8%AA.

Shabestari, M. M. (1996). *Hermenutik, kitab va sunnat.* Tehran: Tarh-e Naw.

Shabestar News. (2014). *Nopo aamad/otoboushaye jaded-e yegan vije roonamai shod.* Retrieved from http://shabestarnews.ir/13100/%D9%86%D9%88%D9%BE%D9%88-%D8%A2%D9%85%D8%AF-%D8%A7%D8%AA%D9%88%D8%A8%D9%88%D8%B3-%D9%87%D8%A7%DB%8C-%D8%AC%D8%AF%DB%8C%D8%AF-%DB%8C%DA%AF%D8%A7%D9%86-%D9%88%DB%8C%DA%98%D9%87-%D8%B1%D9%88%D9%86%D9%85/.

Shabtab News. (2017). *Padidei mosoom be Zahra ayatollahi.* Retrieved from https://shabtabnews.com/2017/12/26/%D9%BE%D8%AF%DB%8C%D8%AF%D9%87-%D8%

A7%DB%8C-%D9%85%D9%88%D8%B3%D9%88%D9%85-%D8%A8%D9%
87-%D8%B2%D9%87%D8%B1%D8%A7-%D8%A2%DB%8C%D8%AA-
%D8%A7%D9%84%D9%84%D9%87%DB%8C-%D9%84%D8%A7%DB%8C%D8
%AD%D9%87/.

Shafaf News. (2014). *Yek shab ba ranandeh taxiye zan dar Tehran* Retrieved from http://shafaf.ir/fa/news/292555/.

———. (2015). *Nahve barkhord-e badhejaban ba gasht-e ershad*. Retrieved from http://khabarfarsi.com/ext/13733386.

Shia News. (2016). *Hokme docharkhe savarie banoovan az nazare ayatollah Khamenei*. Retrieved from http://www.shia-news.com/fa/news/126733/.

Souroush, A. K. (1994). *Qisse-yi arbab-e ma'rifat*. Tehran: Mu'sssih-yi Farhangi-e Sirat.

Tabnak News. (2017). *Ayatollah Jannati: Risheye fetneh dar iran khoshk nahode*. Retrieved from http://www.tabnak.ir/fa/news/752397/.

Talabegi Blog. (2014). *Ahkam-e hejab bar asas-e fatwaye ayatollah ozma Khamenei*. Retrieved from http://talabegi.blog.ir/post/%D8%A7%D8%AD%DA%A9%D8%A
7%D9%85-%D8%AD%D8%AC%D8%A7%D8%A8-%D8%A8%D8%B1-%D8%A7
%D8%B3%D8%A7%D8%B3-%D9%81%D8%AA%D8%A7%D9%88%D8%A7
%DB%8C-%D8%A7%DB%8C%D8%AA-%D8%A7%D9%84%D9%84%D9%87-
%D8%A7%D9%84%D8%B9%D8%B6%D9%85%DB%8C-%D8%AE%D8%A7%
D9%85%D9%86%D9%87-%D8%A7%DB%8C.

Taraz News. (2016). *Michel Ledin: Saraan-eh jonbesh-e sabz az Obama taghaazaay-e komak kardan*. Retrieved from https://www.taraznews.com/content/146866.

Tasnim News. (2013). *Daayertol moarefe jeldie fitne roonamaei shod*. Retrieved from https://www.tasnimnews.com/fa/news/1392/10/04/230816/.

———. (2015). *Ayatollah mesbah yazdi: Eslami shodan oloum-e ensasi ba tahavol-e amigh dar no-e negah be ensan mohaghagh mishavad*. Retrieved from http://www.tasnimnews.com/fa/news/1394/07/09/876381/.

Tavaana. (2016a). *Jamileh Sadeghi: Zani tavaanmand va moasese avalin tazie sevise zanan*. Retrieved from https://tavaana.org/fa/content/.

———. (2017). *Roya hakkakian darbareye vaziyate yahoodian-e iran migooyad*. Retrieved from https://tavaana.org/fa/content/.

Tejaratemrooz.ir. (2017). *Ris-e polise Tehran: Digar hich badhejabi bazdasht nemishavad*. Retrieved from http://tejaratemrouz.ir/fa/news/28965/.

Tejarat News. (2000). *Baray-e chand nafar ja hast? Control-e jamiat va tanzim khanevade dar iran*. Retrieved from http://www.tejaratnews.com/Pages/Printable-News-3294.aspx.

Telewebion. (2016). *Zolal-e ahkam*. Retrieved from http://www.telewebion.com/en/4448/zolale-ahkam.html.

VOA News. (2016). *Eblaghe siasathaye koliye khanevadeh*. Retrieved from http://ir.voanews.com/a/iran-supreme-leader-women/3492331.html?nocache=1.

Webshad. (2013). *Akshaei az oj-e bad hejabi-e dokhtaran-e support poush*. Retrieved from http://www.webshad.com/.

Welayatnet. (2013). *Morvarid-e jan va sadaf-e bihijab*. Retrieved from http://www.welayatnet.com/fa/news/14796.

Yalsarat News. (2015). *Dolatha az hamegani shodan-e amre be marouf mitarsand*. Retrieved from http://yalasarat.com/vdcc00qsm2bqxo8.ala2.html.

Yazdi, M.. (2017). *Vilayat-e faqih*. Retrieved from http://mesbahyazdi.org/farsi/?../lib/porsesh1/ch04.htm.

YouTube. (2017a). *Gasht-e ershad zanan ra dar khiaban kotak mizanad*. Retrieved from https://www.youtube.com/watch?v=s0Zt91b3JoE.

YouTube. (2017b). *Zir gereftan-e yek dokhtar tavasote mashine gasht-e ershad*. Retrieved from https://www.youtube.com/watch?v=H-n300wRa58.

YouTube. (2017c). *Barkhord-e tahghir amizeh ma'mooran-e entezami ba zanan-e tehranie dakhele van-e gashte ershad*. Retrieved from https://www.youtube.com/watch?v=U33KRGpdq9k.

YouTube. (2017d). *Sar dadan-e sho'areh ya hossein, mir hossein va tashvighe islandi tavassote havadaran-e rouhani dar varzeshgah-e azadi*. Retrieved from https://www.youtube.com/watch?v=DweUjCoDMx4.

YouTube. (2017e). *Sho'are ya hossein, mir hossein, dar hamayeshe entekhabatie rouhani dar qazvin*. Rerieved from https://www.youtube.com/watch?v=GvgfEI_N0hA.

Zanaane Emrooz. (2014). *Tabieeze jensiati dar Nezam-e amouzeshe aali*. Retrieved from http://zananemrooz.com/fa/print.aspx?id=285.

Zistboom News. (2016). *Sokhanaan-e imam jome-h isfahan dar morede khoshk shodaneh zayanderood*. Retrieved from http://zistboom.com/fa/news/32116/.

110nopo. (2013). *Maraseme fareghol tahsiliye faragiriye yegan-e nopo*. Retrieved from http://www.110nopo.blogfa.com/post/40.

English References

Abdi, A. (2001). The reform movement: Background and vulnerability. *Global Dialogue*, 3(2/3), 1–11.

Abdo, G. (2003). Media and information: The case of Iran. *Social Research*, 70(3), 877–886. Abingdon, UK: Routledge.

Abrahamian, E. (1989). *Radical Islam: The Iranian Mojahedin*. Tauris.

Abrahamian, E. (1993). *Khomeinism: Essays on the Islamic Republic*. Berkeley: University of California.

Abrahamian, E. (2008). *A history of modern Iran*. Cambridge: Cambridge University Press.

Abu-Lughod, L. (1990). The romance of resistance: Tracing transformations of power through Bediun women. *American Ethnologist*, 17(1), 41–55.

Adelkhah, F. (2012). The political economy of the Green Movement: Contestation and political mobilization in Iran. In N. Nabavi (Ed.). *Iran: From theocracy to the Green Movement*. (pp. 17–38). New York: Palgrave Macmillan.

Afary, J. (1996). *The Iranian constitutional revolution, 1906–1911: Grassroots democracy, social democracy, & the origins of feminism*. New York: Columbia University Press.

Afary, J. (2009). *Sexual politics in modern Iran*. Cambridge, UK: Cambridge University Press.

Afary, J., & Anderson, K. B. (2005). *Foucault and the Iranian revolution: Gender and the seductions of Islamism*. The University of Chicago Press.

Aghai Diba, B. (2012). Is the Green Movement of Iran dead? *Payvand*. Retrieved from http://www.payvand.com/news/12/apr/1020.html.

Ahmadi Khorasani, N. (2009). *Iranian women's one million signatures campaign for equality: The inside story*. Washington, DC: Women's Learning Partnership.

Akbari, A. (2009). The women's movement: An emerging power. *LSE Research Online*. Retrieved from http://www.lse.ac.uk/IDEAS/publications/reports/pdf/SU002/akbari.pdf.

Al-Ali, N. (2008). Women's movements in the Middle East: Case studies of Egypt and Turkey. *United Nations Research Institute for Social Development*, Retrieved from https://eprints.soas.ac.uk/4889/2/UNRISD_Report_final.pdf.

Al-Haj, M. (2014). Syrian authorities arrest opposition leader. Retrieved from http://www.al-monitor.com/pulse/originals/2014/11/syria-regime-arrest-bss-leader.html.

Alikarimi, L. (2014). CEDAW and the quest of Iranian: Women for gender equality. *Open Democracy*. Retrieved from https://www.opendemocracy.net/5050/leila-alikarami/cedaw-and-quest-of-iranian-women-for-gender-equality.

Alkarama. (2016). Syria: Political activist Faeq Al Mir disappeared for three years. Retrieved from http://www.alkarama.org/en/articles/syria-political-activist-faeq-al-mir-disappeared-three-years.

Allen, A. (1999). *The power of feminist theory: Domination, resistance, solidarity*. Westview Press.

Alvarez, J. (1992). *How the García girls lost their accents*. New York: Plume.

Amanat, A. (2009). *Apocalyptic Islam and Iranian Shi'ism*. New York: I.B. Tauris.

Amir Arjomand, S. (1992). Constitution of the Islamic Republic. *Encyclopaedia Iranica*. Retrieved from http://www.iranicaonline.org/articles/constitution-of-the-islamic-republic.

Amir Arjomand, S. A. (2000). Civil society and the rule of law in the constitutional politics of Iran under Khatami. *Social Research*, 67(2), 283–301.

Amir Arjomand, S. A. (2002). The reform movement and the debate on modernity and tradition in contemporary Iran. *International Journal of Middle East Studies*, 34(4), 719–731.

Amir Arjomand, S. A. (2005). The rise and fall of president Khatami and the reform movement in Iran. *Constellations*, 12(4), 502–520.

Arjomand, S. A. (2009). *After Khomeini: Iran under his successors*. Oxford: Oxford University Press.

Amir-Ebrahimi, M. (2006). Conquering enclosed public spaces. *Cities*, 23(6), 1–7.

―――― (2008). Transgression in narration: The lives of Iranian women in cyberspace. *Journal of Middle East Women's Studies*, 4(3), 89–118.

Amouzegar, J. (2013). Ahmadinejad's legacy. *Middle East Policy Council*, xx(4), 127–132.

Ancelovici, M., Dufour, P., & Nez, H. (Eds.). (2016). *Street politics in the age of austerity: From the indignados to occupy*. Amsterdam University Press.

Anderson, C. (2013). Iranian internet infrastructure and policy report. *Small Media*. Retrieved from https://smallmedia.org.uk/sites/default/files/u8/IIIPSepOct.pdf

Ansari, A. M. (2006). *Iran, Islam and democracy: The politics of managing change*. Chatham House.

Ash, T. (2009). We can't decide Iran's struggle. But we can avoid backing the wrong side. *The Guardian*, Retrieved from http://www.theguardian.com/commentisfree/cifamerica/2009/sep/23/iran-struggle-back-wrong-side.

Ashraf, A., & Banuazizi, A. (2001). Iran's tortuous path toward "Islamic Liberalism". *International Journal of Politics, Culture, and Society*, 15(2), 237–256.

Assareh, A., & Monshipouri, A. (2009). The Islamic Republic and the "Green Movement:" Coming full circle. *Middle East Policy*, XVI(4), 27–46.

Azam, T. (2007). *Performing Islam: Gender and ritual in Iran*. Leiden; Boston: Brill.

Bakan, A.B., & MacDonald, E. (Eds.). (2002). *Critical Political Studies: Debates and Dialogues from the Left*. McGill-Queen's University Press.

Baker, K. M. (1994). A Fouclauldian French revolution? In J. Goldstein, (Ed.). *Foucault and the Writing of History*. Cambridge, MA: Blackwell.

Bakhash, S. (1984). *The reign of the ayatollahs: Iran and the Islamic Revolution*. New York: Basic Books.

Ballvé, T. (2011). Spatiality & power. *Agrarian Political Economy & Ecology*, Retrieved from http://territorialmasquerades.net/spatiality-power/.

Banuazizi, A. (1999). Iran, Islamic state and civil society. *Invited Joseph Sterlitz Annual Lecture in Middle Eastern Studies*. Retrieved from http://dspace.africaportal.org/jspui/bitstream/123456789/22439/1/Islamic%20State%20and%20Civil%20Society%20in%20Iran.pdf?1.

Barnett, C. (1999). Culture, government, and spatiality: Re-assessing the 'Foucault effect' in cultural-policy studies. *International Journal of Cultural Studies*, 2(3), 369–397.

Bartilet, J. (2016). Foucault, discourse and the call for reflexivity. *Centre for Humanities and Philosophy Polytechnic University of the Philippines*. Retrieved from http://theoryworkshop.weebly.com/uploads/9/0/9/1/9091667/foucault_discourse_reflexivity.pdf.

Bashi, G. (2010). Feminist wave in the Iranian green tsunami. In N. Hashemi, & D. Postel (Eds.). *The people reloaded: The green movement and the struggle for Iran's future*. New York: Melville House.

Bashiriyeh, H. (2001). Civil society and democratization during Khatami's first term. *Global Dialogue*, 3(2/3), 1–8.

——— (2010). Counter-revolution and Revolt in Iran: An interview with Iranian Political Scientist Hussein Bahiriyeh. *Constellations*, 17(1), 61–77.

Baumgarten, B., & Ullrich, P. (2012). Discourse, power, and governmentality. Social movement research with and beyond Foucault. *Social Science Research Centre Berlin (WZB)*. Retrieved from https://depositonce.tu-berlin.de/bitstream/11303/4865/1/baumgarten_et-al.pdf.

Bayat, A. (1997). *Street politics: Poor people's movements in Iran*. New York: Columbia University Press.

Bayat, A. (2005). Islamism and social movement theory. *Third World Quarterly*, 26(6), 891–908.

Bayat, A. (2007). *Making Islam democratic: Social movements and the post-Islamist turn*. Stanford, CA: Stanford University Press.

Bayat, A. (2009). No silence, no violence: A post-Islamist trajectory. In M. J. Stephan, (Ed.). *Nonviolent struggle, Democratization, and governance in the Middle East*. The Palgrave Macmillan Series on Civil Resistance.

Bayat, A. (2013). *Life as politics: How ordinary people change the Middle East*. Stanford, CA: Stanford University Press.

Bayatrizi, Z. (2007). From revolution to freedom: The discursive mobilization of civil society in Iran, 1997–2001. *Asia-Japan Journal*, March(2), 21–31.

BBC News. (1998). *World: Middle East arrests made in Iran murder case*. Retrieved from http://news.bbc.co.uk/2/hi/middle_east/234954.stm.

———. (2015). *Why are Iranian husbands standing up for their wives?* Retrieved from http://www.bbc.com/news/blogs-trending-34404030

Beck, G., & Nashat, G. (Eds.). (2004). *Women in Iran from 1800 to the Islamic Republic* Urbana, IL: University of Illinois Press.

Beinin, J., & Vairel, F. (Eds.). (2011). *Social movements, mobilization, and contestation in the Middle East and North Africa*. Stanford, CA: Stanford University Press.

Boghrati, N. (2006). Islamic dress code to be strictly enforced. *World Press*. Retrieved from http://www.worldpress.org/mideast/2334.cfm.

Boroumand, L. (2009). Civil society's choice. *Journal of Democracy* 20(4), 16–20.

Brass, R. P. (2000). Foucault steals Political Science. *Annual Reviews*, 3, pp. 305–330

Braungardt, J. (2017). *Foucault's Philosophical explorations*. Retrieved from http://braungardt.trialectics.com/projects/political-theory/foucault/.

Bröer, C., & Duyvendak, W. (2009). Discourse opportunities, feeling rules, and the rise of protest against aircraft noise. *Mobilization: An international journal*, 14(3), 337–356.

Brumberg, D., & Farhi, F. (Eds.). (2016). *Power and change in Iran: Politics of contention and conciliation*. Indianapolis: Indiana University Press.

Buechler, S. (1995). New social movement theories. *The Sociological Quarterly*, 3(3), 441–464.

Butler, J. (1993). *Bodies that matter: On the discursive limits of "sex."* New York: Routledge.

Butler, J. (1997). *Excitable speech: A Politics of the performative*. New York: Routledge

Butler, J. (2011). Bodies and alliance and the politics of the street. *European Institute for Progressive Cultural Policies*. Retrieved from http://www.eipcp.net/transversal/1011/butler/en.

Carrette, R. J. (1999). *Religion and culture*. New York: Routledge.

Calderon, F. (1986). *Los movimientos sociales ante la crisis*. Buenos Aires: CLASCO/UNU.

Centre for Human Rights in Iran (2015a). *One year after acid attacks against women in Isfahan, no arrests*. Retrieved from https://www.iranhumanrights.org/2015/10/one-year-after-acid-attacks/.

―――― (2015b). *Official statements on women: State-sanctioned discrimination*. Retrieved from https://www.iranhumanrights.org/2015/02/womenreport-official-statements-on-women-state-sanctioned-discrimination/.

Clark, J. A. (2004). *Islam, charity, and activism: Middle-class networks and social welfare in Egypt, Jordan, and Yemen*. Bloomington: Indiana University Press.

Canavez, F., & Miranda, H. (2011). Resistance in Freud and Foucault. *Rexhercnes en psychoanalyse*, 2(12), 150–157.

Chehabi, H. E. (2001). The political regime of the Islamic Republic of Iran in comparative perspective. *Government and Opposition* 36(1), 48–70.

Child, P., & Williams, P. (1996). *An introduction to post-colonial theory*. New York: Prentice Hall.

Cohen, J. (1985). Strategy or identity? New theoretical paradigms and contemporary social movements. *Social Research*, 52(4), 663–716.

Cole, J. (2009). Stealing the Iranian election. *Informed Comment Blog*, available from http://www.juancole.com/2009/06/stealing-iranian-election.html.

Collins, P. (2000). *Black feminist thought: Knowledge, consciousness, and the politics of empowerment*. New York: Routledge.

Cooper, A. S. (2016). *The fall of heaven: The pahlavis and the final days of imperial Iran*. New York: Heny Holt and Co.

Country Meters. (2016). *Iran population clock*. Retrieved from http://countrymeters.info/en/Iran.

Crampton, J. W., & Elden, S. (Eds.). (2007). *Space, knowledge, and power: Foucault and geography*. Burlington: Ashgate.

Dabashi, H. (2006). *Iran: A people interrupted*. New York and London: The New Press.

Dabashi, H. (2009). Iran conflict isn't class warfare. *CNN International*. Retrieved from http://www.cnn.com/2009/WORLD/meast/06/22/dabashi.iran.myths/index.html?iref=24 hours.

Dabashi, H. (Eds.). (2010). The real revolution is that people are entering the society as agents. In N. Hashemi, & Postel, D. *The people reloaded: The green movement and the struggle for Iran's future*. New York: Melville House.

Dabashi, H. (2011a). *Shi'ism: A religion of protest*. Cambridge: The Belknap Press of Harvard University.

―――― (2011b). *The Green Movement in Iran*. New Brunswick, NJ: Transaction Publishers.

Davidson, A. I. (2001). *The emergence of sexuality: Historical epistemology and the formation of concepts*. Cambridge, MA: Harvard University Press.

Davis, D. (1999). The power of distance: Re-theorizing social movements in Latin America. *Theory and Society*, 28(4), 585–638.

Dean, M., & Hindess, B. (1998). Introduction: Government, liberalism, society. In M. Dean and B. Hindess. (Eds.). *Governing Australia: Studies in Contemporary Rationalities of Government*. Cambridge University Press. 1–19.

Death, C. (2010). Counter-conducts: A Foucauldian analytics of protest. *Social Movement Studies*, 2(3), 235–251.

Death, C. (2011). Counter-conducts in South Africa: Power, government and dissent at the world summit. *Globalizations*, 8(4), 425–438.

Death, C. (2015). Ungoverned spaces, heterotopia, and counter-conducts. Unpublished Manuscript. In BISA 40th annual conference, London.

Direnberger, L. (2011). From the street to the internet: Feminine and feminist contestation in Tehran. Moving gender in the post-electoral demonstrations in Iran in 2009. *JS*. Retrieved from https://www.jssj.org/wp-content/uploads/2012/12/JSSJ3-12en.pdf.

Dreyfus, H. L., & Rainbow, P. (1982). *Michel Foucault: Beyond structuralism and hermeneutics*. Chicago: University of Chicago Press.

Ebadi, S. H.. (2006). *Iran awakening: From prison to Peace Prize: One woman's struggle at the crossroads of history*. Toronto: A.A. Knopf Canada.

Eli, L. (2009). Iran protestors alter tactics to avoid death. *The Washington Times*. Reprieved from http://www.washingtontimes.com/news/2009/jun/25/opposition-alters-tactics-to-avoid- protest-deaths/?page=all.

Ensor, J. (2017). *Iran and Saudi Arabia race to pass gender reforms as Tehran relaxes headscarf arrests*. Retrieved from http://www.telegraph.co.uk/news/2017/12/29/iran-saudi-arabia-race-pass-gender-reforms-tehran-relaxes-headscarf/.

Escobar, A. (1992). Imagining a post-development era? Critical thought, development and social movements. *Social Text*, 31(32), 20–56.

Esfandiari, H. (2010). The women's movement. *The Iran Primer*. Retrieved from http://iranprimer.usip.org/resource/womens-movement.

Fadaee, S. (2012). *Social movements in Iran: Environmentalism and civil society*. Netherlands, Cambridge University Press.

Fairclough, N. (2001). *Language and power*. 2nd edition. London and New York: Longman.

Farhi, N. (2015). An 'Iranian Spring': How Iran's youth are seeking reform in a new way. *Huffington Post*. Retrieved from http://www.huffingtonpost.com/nazila-fathi/iranian-spring-irans-youth_b_6664786.html.

Fassihi, F. (2009). Regime wages a quiet war on 'star students' of Iran. *The Wall Street Journal*. Retrieved from http://online.wsj.com/news/articles/SB126222013953111071.

Feminist News. (2013). *CEDAW rejected in Iran*. Retrieved from http://www.feminist.org/news/newsbyte/uswirestory.asp?id=7996.

Ffrench, P. (2004). A different life? Barthes, Foucault and everyday life. *Cultural Studies*, 18(2–3), 290–305.

Fimyar, O. (2008). Using governmentality as a conceptual tool in education policy research, *Critical Review*, 3–18.

Fischer, M. (2010). The rhythmic beat of the revolution in Iran. *Cultural Anthropology*, 25(3), 497–543.

Fisk, R. (2009). Symbols are not enough to win this battle. *The Independent*. Retrieved from http://www.independent.co.uk/voices/commentators/fisk/robert-fisk-symbols-are-not-enough-to-win-this-battle-1714153.html.

Foran, J. (1993). Theories of revolution revisited: Toward a fourth generation. *Sociological Theory*, 11(1), 1–20.
Foucault, M. (1970): *The Order of Things*. New York: Routledge.
Foucault, M. (1972). *The archaeology of knowledge*. Translated from the French by Sheridan Smith. New York: Pantheon.
Foucault, M. (1974). *Dits et Ecrits t. ll*. Paris: Gallimard.
Foucault, M. (1977a). Intellectuals and Foucault. In D. Bouchard, (Ed.). *Language, Counter-memory, Practice: Selected Essays*. Ithaca: Cornell University Press.
Foucault, M. (1977b). *Language, counter-memory, practice: Selected essays and interviews*. In D. F. Bouchard (Ed.), translated from the French by D. F. Bouchard and S. Simon. New York: Cornell University Press.
Foucault, M. (1979). Interview with Lucette Finas. In M. Morris and P. Patton, (Eds.). *Michel Foucault: Power, Truth, Strategy*. Sydney: Feral Publications.
Foucault, M. (1980a). In *Power/knowledge: Selected interviews and other writings, 1972–1977* C. Gordon (Ed.). New York: Pantheon.
Foucault, M. (1980b). Questions on geography. In C. Gordon, *Power/knowledge: Selected interviews and other writings, 1972–1977*. New York: Pantheon
Foucault, M. (1982). The subject and power. *Critical Inquiry* 8(4), 777–795.
Foucault, M. (1984a). Docile bodies. In P. Rainbow, (Ed.). *The Foucault Reader*. New York: Pantheon Books.
Foucault, M. (1984b). Nietzsche, genealogy, history. In P. Rainbow, (Ed.). *The Foucault Reader*. New York: Pantheon Books.
Foucault, M. (1984c). So is it important to think? In *Power: Essential works of Foucault 1954–1984* (Ed.). Translated from the French by R. Hurley. New York: New York Press.
Foucault, M. (1988). *Madness & Civilization. A history of insanity in the age of reason*. Vintage Books.
Foucault, M. (1989). *Resume des cours, 1970–1982*. Paris: Julliard.
Foucault, M. (1991). Questions of method. In G. Burchell, C. Gordon, & P. Miller, (Eds.). *The Foucault Effect: Studies in Governmentality*. Chicago: University of Chicago Press.
Foucault, M., & Trombadori, D. (1991). *Remarks on Marx*. Translated from the French by R. James Goldstein and James Cascaito. New York: Semiotext(e).
Foucault, M. (1995). *Discipline and punish: The birth of the prison*. Translated from the French by Alan Sheridan. New York: Vintage Books.
Foucault, M. (1996a). What is Critique? In J. Schmidt, (Ed.). *What is Enlightenment? Eighteenth Century Answers and Twentieth Century Questions*. Berkeley: University of California Press.
Foucault, M. (1996b). *Foucault live: (interviews, 1961–1984)*. New York: Semiotext(e).
Foucault, M. (1997a). Technologies of the self. In P. Rainbow, (Ed.). *Ethics: Subjectivity and Truth. Volume 1, The Essential Works of Foucault 1954–1984* New York: The New Press.
Foucault, M. (1997b). The ethics of the modern concern for self as practice of freedom. In P. Rainbow, *Ethics, Subjectivity and Truth*. (Ed.). Translated from the French by R. Hurley et al., New York: New York Press.
Foucault, M. (1997c). Sex, power and the politics of identity. In P. Rainbow (Ed.). *Ethics, Subjectivity and Truth*, trans., R. Hurley et al., New York: New York Press.
Foucault, M. (2000). Is it useless to revolt? In James D. Faubion, *Essential Works of Foucault: Volume 3*. (Ed.). New York: New York Press.
Foucault, M. (2003a). *Society must be defended*. New York: Picador.
——— (2003b). The lives of infamous men. In P. Rainbow & N. Rose, (Eds.). *The Essential Foucault*. New York: New Press.

——— (2005a). The mythical leader of the Iranian revolt. In J. Afary, & K. B. Anderson, (Eds.). *Foucault and the Iranian Revolution: Gender and the Seductions of Islamism.* The University of Chicago Press.

——— (2005b). The Shah is a hundred years behind the times. In J. Afary, & K. B. Anderson, (Eds.). *Foucault and the Iranian Revolution: Gender and the Seductions of Islamism.* The University of Chicago Press.

Foucault, M. (2005c). What are the Iranians dreaming about? In J. Afary, & K. B. Anderson, (Eds.). *Foucault and the Iranian Revolution: Gender and the Seductions of Islamism.* The University of Chicago Press.

Foucault, M. (2005d). Iran: The spirit of a world without spirit. In J. Afary, & K. B. Anderson, (Eds.). *Foucault and the Iranian Revolution: Gender and the Seductions of Islamism.* The University of Chicago Press.

Foucault, M. (2005e). What are the Iranians dreaming about? In J. Afary, & K. B. Anderson, (Eds.). *Foucault and the Iranian Revolution: Gender and the Seductions of Islamism.* The University of Chicago Press.

Foucault, M. (2005f). The revolt in Iran spreads on cassette tapes. In J. Afary, & K. B. Anderson, (Eds.). *Foucault and the Iranian Revolution: Gender and the Seductions of Islamism.* The University of Chicago Press.

Foucault, M. (2005g). The Shah is a hundred years behind the times. In J. Afary, & K. B. Anderson, (Eds.). *Foucault and the Iranian Revolution: Gender and the Seductions of Islamism.* The University of Chicago Press.

Foucault, M. (2005h). The mythical leader of the Iranian revolt. In J. Afary, & K. B. Anderson, (Eds.). *Foucault and the Iranian Revolution: Gender and the Seductions of Islamism.* The University of Chicago Press.

Foucault, M., & Chomsky, N. (2006). *The Chomsky-Foucault debate: On human nature.* New York: New Press.

Foucault, M. (2007). *Security, Territory, Population: Lectures at the Collège de France, 1977–1978*, Michael Senellart. (Ed.). New York: Palgrave Macmillan.

——— (2008). *The birth of biopolitics: Lectures at the College de France 1978–1979.* Translated from the French by G. Burchell. New York: Palgrave Macmillan.

——— (2012). The mesh of power. *Viewpoint Magazine.* Retrieved from https://viewpointmag.com/2012/09/12/the-mesh-of-power/.

Foucault, M., & Deleuze. (1977). Intellectuals and power. In D.F. Bouchard, (Ed.). *Language, Counter-memory, Practice: Selected Essays and Interviews.* Ithaca: Cornell University Press.

Foucault, M. (1978). *The history of sexuality: Volume 1.* Translated from the French by Robert Hurley. New York: Pantheon Books.

Fraser, N. (1989). *Unruly practices: Power, discourse and gender in contemporary social theory.* Minneapolis: University of Minnesota Press.

Gallagher, M. (2008). Foucault, power and participation. *International Journal of Children's Rights,* 16 (3), 395–406.

Garland, D. (1997). "Governmentality' and the problem of crime: Foucault, criminology, sociology" in theoretical criminology, *Theoretical Criminology* 2(1), 173–214.

——— (2014). What is a "history of the present"? On Foucault's genealogies and their critical preconditions. *Punishment & Society,* 16(4), 365–384.

Garner, R., & Tenuto, J. (1997). *Social movement theory and research.* London, MD: The Scarecrow Press.

Ghaedrahmati, S., & Rezaei, M. R. (2012). An analysis of Iran's cities distributions in related to earthquake hazard. *International Conference on Applied Life Sciences.* Retrieved from http://cdn.intechopen.com/pdfs-wm/39871.pdf.

Ghaemi, H. (2010). The Islamic judiciary. *The Iran Premier*. Retrieved from http://iran-primer.usip.org/resource/islamic-judiciary.

Ghamari-Tabrizi, B. (2004). Contentious public religion: Two conceptions of Islam in Revolutionary Iran. Ali Shariàti and Abdolkarim Soroush. *International Sociology*, 19(4), 504–523.

——— (2016). *Foucault in Iran: Islamic Revolution after the Enlightenment*. Minneapolis: University of Minnesota Press.

Gibbs, L. (2015). Female soccer captain gets one-time exemption to leave Iran against her husband's wishes. *Think Progress News*. Retrieved from http://thinkprogress.org/sports/2015/11/24/3725423/iran-overrules-husband-of-football-captain/.

Gilroy, P. (1991). *There ain't no black in the union jack: The cultural politics of race and nation*. The University of Chicago Press.

Goldstone, J. (1980). Theories of revolutions: The third generation. *World Politics*, 32(3), 425–453.

Golkar, S. (2015). *Captive society: The Basij Militia and social control in Iran*. New York: Columbia University Press.

Goodwin, J. (2001). *No other way out*. Cambridge: Cambridge University Press.

Goodwin, J., & Jasper, M. J. (Eds.). (2004). *Rethinking social movements: Structure, meaning, and emotions*. New York: Littlefield Publishers.

Goodwin, J., & Jasper, M. J. (2012). *Contention in context: Political opportunities and the emergence of protest*. Stanford, CA: Stanford University Press.

Gordon, N. (2002). On visibility and power: An Arendtian corrective of Foucault. *Human Studies*, 25(2), 125–145.

——— (2008). *Israel's occupation*. Berkeley: University of California Press.

Gorgin, I. (2002). *Radio Farda's program will soon be modified*. Retrieved from https://www.radiofarda.com/a/1139106.html.

Habermas, J. (1975). *Legitimation crisis*. Boston: Beacon Press.

Hafez, M. (2003). *Why Muslims rebel: Repression and resistance in the Islamic world*. Boulder, CO: Lynne Reiner.

Hakimian, H. (2012). How sanctions affect Iran's economy. *Council on Foreign Relations*. Retrieved from http://www.cfr.org/iran/sanctions-affect-irans-economy/p28329.

Haller, M. (2002). Theory and method in the comparative study of values. Critique and Alternative to Inglehart. *European Sociological Review*, 18(2), 139–158.

Halliday, F. (2005). Iran's revolutionary spasm. *Open Democracy*. Retrieved from https://www.opendemocracy.net/globalization/iran_2642.jsp.

——— (2010). Iran's tide of history: Counter-revolution and after. In N. Hashemi, & D. Postel. (Eds.). *The people reloaded: The Green Movement and the struggle for Iran's future*. New York: Melville House.

Halper, L. (2005). Laws and women's agency in post-revolutionary Iran. *Harvard Journal of Law & Gender*, 28(1), 85–106.

Harraway, D. (1988). Situated knowledges: The science question in feminism and the privilege of partial perspective. *Feminist Studies*, 14(3), 575–597.

Harris, K. (2012). The brokered exuberance of the middle class. *Mobilization*, 17(4), 435–455.

Hashemi, N., & Postel, D. (2010). Introduction. In N. Hashemi, & D. Postel. (Eds.). *The people reloaded: The Green Movement and the struggle for Iran's future*. New York: Melville House.

Holliday, J. S. (2011). *Defining Iran: Politics of resistance*. Burlington, VT: Ashgate.

Holliday, S., & Rivetti, P. (2016). Divided we stand? The heterogeneous political identities of Iran's 2009–2010 uprisings. In S. Holliday & P. Leech, (Eds.). *Political identities and popular uprisings in the Middle East*. Rowman & Littlefield International Ltd.

Hook, D. (2007). *Foucault, psychology and the analytics of power*. New York: Palgrave Macmillan.

Howarth, D. (2000). *Discourse*. Buckingham & Philadelphia: Open University Press.

Human Rights & Democracy for Iran. (2017). *Mahshid Nirumand*. Retrieved from https://www.iranrights.org/memorial/story/-3089/mahshid-nirumand.

Hunter, S.H. (2014). *Iran divided: The historical roots of Iranian debates on identity, culture, and governance in the twenty-first century*. Lanham: Rowman & Littlefield.

Idlenomore. (2017). *Idlenomore Official Website*. Retrieved from http://www.idlenomore.ca/.

Independent News. (2015). French journalist confronts President Rouhani with picture of an Iranian woman without a hijab. Retrieved from http://www.independent.co.uk/news/people/french-journalist-confronts-president-rouhani-with-picture-of-an-iranian-woman-without-a-hijab-from-a6732001.html.

———. (2016). *Nimr Baqir al-Nimr: Saudi Arabian Shia cleric who denounced the kingdom's rulers and called for religious freedom*. Retrieved from http://www.independent.co.uk/news/obituaries/nimr-baqir-al-nimr-saudi-arabian-shia-cleric-who-denounced-the-kingdoms-rulers-and-called-for-a6798061.html.

Inglehart, R. (1997). *Modernization and postmodernization: Cultural, economic, and political change in 43 societies*. Princeton, NJ: Princeton University Press.

Inglehart, R., & Baker, W. E. (2000). Modernization, cultural change, and the persistence of traditional values. *American Sociological Review*, 65, 19–51.

Inglehart, R., & Norris, P. (2003). The true clash of civilizations. *Foreign Policy* 135, 62–70.

Inglehart, R. (2008). Changing values and Western publics from 1970 to 2006. *West European Politics*, 31(1), 130–146.

International Campaign for Human Rights in Iran. (2014). *Security agencies and the prosecution of online activists*. Retrieved from https://www.iranhumanrights.org/2014/11/internet-report-security-agencies-and-the-prosecution-of-online-activists-2/.

Internet World Stats. (2015). *Internet users in the Middle East*. Retrieved from http://www.internetworldstats.com/stats5.htm

Iran Press Service (2000). *Ganji identified Fallahian as the "master key" in chain murders*. Retrieved from https://web.archive.org/web/20130510193711/http://www.iran-press-service.com/articles_2000/dec_2000/ganji_named_fallahian_11200.htm.

Jahanbegloo, R. (2010). The Gandhian moment. In N. Hashemi, & D. Postel, (Eds.). *The People reloaded: The Green Movement and the struggle for Iran's future*. New York: Melville House.

Jahanbegloo, R., & Soroush, A. (2010). Why a manifesto? Iran on the edge. *New Perspectives Quarterly*, 27(2), 31–34.

Jahanbegloo, R. (2012). The Green Movement and non-violent struggle in Iran. *Eurozine*, Retrieved from http://www.eurozine.com/the-green-movement-and-nonviolent-struggle-in-iran/

Jenkins, J. C. (1983). Resource mobilization theory and the study of social movements. *Annual Review of Sociology*, 9(1), 527–553.

Jerusalem Post. (2015). *Iranian police arrested 50 women for 'un-Islamic' dress*. Retrieved from http://www.jpost.com/Middle-East/Iranian-police-arrested-50-women-for-un-Islamic-dress-386335.

Kadivar, M. (2011). *Biography*. Retrieved from http://en.kadivar.com/sample-page-2/.

Kamali, M. (1998). *Revolutionary Iran: Civil society and state in the modernization process*. Brookfield, VT: Ashgate.

Kamrava, M. (2008). *Iran's intellectual revolution*. Cambridge, UK: Cambridge University Press.

Karami, A. (2016). Will house arrests of Green Movement leaders come to an end? *Al-Monitor*, Retrieved from http://www.al-monitor.com/pulse/originals/2016/03/rouhani-entezami- house-arrests-green-movement-leaders.html.

Karbassian, A. (2000). Islamic revolution and the management of the Iranian economy. *Social Research*, 67(2), 621–640.

Karoubi, M. (2010). Mahdi Karoubi: Complete statement for the anniversary of the birth of the Green Movement. *Khordad88*. Retrieved from http://khordaad88.com/?p=1696#more-1696.

Kaulingfreks, F. (2015). *Uncivil engagement and unruly politics: Disruptive interventions of urban youth*. Palgrave MacMillan.

Khamenei, A. (2015). Ayatollah Sayyid Ali Khamenei: Miscellaneous Fatwas. *Islamic Mobility*. Retrieved from http://www.islamicmobility.com//pdf/Miscellaneous%20 Fatwas.pdf.

Khatam, A. (2009). The Islamic Republic's failed quest for the spotless city. *Middle East Research and Information Project*. Retrieved from http://www.merip.org/mer/mer250/islamic-republics-failed-quest-spotless-city.

Khomeini, R. (1979). *Islamic government: Governance of the Jurist*. Translated by Joint Publications Research Service. New York: U.S. Joint Publications Research Service.

Khosrokhavar, F. (2012). The Green Movement in Iran: Democratization and secularization from below. In R. Jahanbegloo, (Ed.). *Civil society and democracy in Iran*. Lanham, MD: Lexington Books.

Kian-Thiébaut, A. (2002). Women and the making of civil society in post-Islamist Iran. In Eric J. Hooglund, (Ed.). *Twenty years of Islamic revolution: Political and social transformation in Iran*. (pp. 56–73). Syracuse, NY: Syracuse University Press.

Kitschelt, H. (1986). Political opportunity structures and political protest: Anti-nuclear movements in four democracies. *British Journal of Political Science* 16(1), 57–85.

Klandermans, B. (1991). New social movements and resource mobilization: The European and American approaches revisited. In D. Rucht, (Ed.). *Research on Social Movements: The State of the Art in Western Europe and the USA*. Frankfurt am Main: Campus Verlag; Boulder, CO: Westview Press.

Kurzman, C. (1996). Structural opportunity and perceived opportunity in social movement theory: The Iranian revolution of 1979. *American Sociological Review*, 61(1), 153–170.

─────── (2004a). The Poststructuralist Consensus in Social Movement Theory. In J. Goodwin, & J. Jasper, (Eds.). *Rethinking social movements: structure, meaning, and emotion*. Lanham, MD: Rowman & Littlefield Publishers.

─────── (2004b). Conclusion: Social Movement theory and Islamic studies. In Q. Wiktorowicz, (Ed.). *Islamic activism: A social movement theory approach*. Bloomington, Indiana: Indiana University Press.

─────── (2012).The Arab Spring: Ideas of the Iranian Green Movement, Methods of the Iranian Revolution. *International Journal of Middle East Studies*, 44(1), 162–165.

Larana, E., Johnston, H., & Gusfield, J. R. (Eds.). (1997). *New social movements: From ideology to identity*. Philadelphia: Temple University Press.

L'Eplattenier, B. (2009). An argument for archival research methods: Thinking beyond methodology. *College English*, 72(1), 67–79.

The Library of Congress (2009). *Global legal monitor*. Retrieved from http://www.loc.gov/law/foreign-news/article/iran-new-womens-inheritance-law-is- enforced/.

Lundskow, G. (2012). Authoritarianism and destructiveness in the Tea Party Movement. *Critical Scoiology*, 38(4) 529–547.

Mahdavi, M. (2008). Rethinking Structure and Agency in Democratization: Iranian Lessons. *International Journal of Criminology & Sociological Theory*, 1(2), 142–160.

——— (2011). Post-Islamic trends in post-revolutionary Iran. *Comparative Studies of South Asia, Africa and the Middle East*, 31(1), 94–109.

——— (2015). The rise of Khomeinism: Problematizing the politics of resistance in post-revolutionary Iran. In A. Adib-Moghaddam, (Ed.). *A Critical Introduction to Khomeini*. Cambridge University Press.

Mahdi, A. A. (2000). Wake-up call: The student protests of July 1999. *The Iranian*. Retrieved from https://iranian.com/Opinion/2000/July/Students/index2.html.

Mahmood, S. (2005). *Politics of piety: The Islamic revival and the feminist subject*. Princeton, NJ: Princeton University Press.

Mahtafar, T. (2011). The Green Movement could fail for lack of leadership and organization. In D. A. Miller, (Ed.). *Iran*. Detroit: Greenhaven Press.

Majd, H. (2010). *The Ayatollah's democracy: An Iranian challenge*. New York: W. W. Norton & Co.

Makarem.ir (2017). *The official website of Ayatollah Makarem Shirazi*. Retrieved from http://makarem.ir/index.aspx?lid=1.

Maloney, S. (2013). The legacy of reform in Iran. Sixteen years later. *Middle East Politics & Policy*. Retrieved from http://www.brookings.edu/blogs/markaz/posts/2013/05/23-khatami-anniversary.

Markoff, J. (2012). Response to Jack Goldstone. In J. Goodwin & J. Jasper, (Eds.). *Contention in context*. (pp. 52–58).

Mashayekhi, M. (2011). The revival of the student movement in post-revolutionary Iran. *International Journal of Politics, Culture and Society*, 15(2), 283–313.

Matini, J. (2003). *Democracy? I meant theocracy: The most truthful individual in recent history*. Retrieved from https://www.iranian.com/Opinion/2003/August/Khomeini/.

May, T. (1993). *Between genealogy and epistemology: Psychology, politics and knowledge in the thought of Michel Foucault*. The Pennsylvania State University Press.

McAdam, D., McCarthy, J., & Zald, M. (1996). *Comparative perspectives on social movements: Political opportunities, mobilizing structures, and cultural framings*. (Eds.).Cambridge: Cambridge University Press.

McAdam, D. (1996). Conceptual origins, current problems, future directions. In D. McAdam, J. McCarthy, & M. Zald, (Eds.). *Comparative perspectives on social movements: Political opportunities, mobilizing structures, and cultural framings*. Cambridge: Cambridge University Press.

McAdam, D., Tarrow, S., & Tilly, C. (2001). *Dynamics of contention*. New York: Cambridge University Press.

McCall, C. (2004). Autonomy, religion, & revolt in Foucault. *Journal of Philosophy & Scripture*, 2(1), 7–14.

——— (2013). Ambivalent modernities: Foucault's Iranian writings reconsidered. *Foucault Studies*, 15, 27–51.

——— (2014). Conduct. In L. Lawlor and J. Nale, (Eds.). *The Cambridge Foucault lexicon* New York: Cambridge University Press.

——— (2017). Risking Prophecy in the Modern State: Foucault, Iran, and the Conduct of the Intellectual. (Unpublished Manuscript).

McCarthy, D. J., & Zald, N. M. (1973). *The trends of social movements in America: Professionalization and resource mobilization*. Morristown, NJ: General Learning Corporation.

——— (1977). Resource mobilization and social movements: A partial theory. *American Journal of Sociology*, 82(2), 1212–1240.

McLaren, M. (2002). *Feminism, Foucault, and embodied subjectivity*. State University of New York Press.

Meade, R. (2014). Foucault's concept of counter-conduct and the politics of anti-austerity in Ireland. *Concept: The Journal of Contemporary Community Education Practice Theory*, 5(3), 1–13.

Medina, J. (2011). Toward a Foucauldian epistemology of resistance: Counter-memory, epistemologic fiction, and guerilla pluralism. *Foucault Studies*, 12, 9–35.

Mehran, G. (2010). Khatami, political reform and education in Iran. *Comparative Education*, 39(3), 311–329.

Melucci, A. (1989). *Nomads of the present: Social movements and individual needs in contemporary society*. London: Hutchinson Radius.

――― (1996). *Challenging codes: Collective action in the information age*. Cambridge: Cambridge University Press.

Meyer, D. (2001). Protest and political process. In K. Nash & A. Scott, (Eds.). *The Blackwell companion to political sociology* Malden, MA: Blackwell Publishers.

Meyer, S. D. (2004). Protest and political opportunities. *Annual Review of Sociology*, 30(1), 125–145.

Milani, A. (2011). *The Shah*. New York: Palgrave Macmillan.

Miller, P., & Rose, N. (1992). *Governing the present: Administering economic, social and personal life*. Cambridge: Polity.

Mir-Hosseini, Z. (1999). *Islam and gender: The religious debate in contemporary Iran*. Princeton, NJ: Princeton University Press.

――― (2002a) Debating women: Gender and the public sphere in post-revolutionary Iran. In A. Sajoo, (Ed.). *Civil society in comparative Muslim contexts*. London: I.B Tauris & Institute of Ismaili Studies.

――― (2002b). The conservative-reformist conflict over women's rights in Iran. *International Journal of Politics, Culture and Society*, 16(1), 37–53.

――― (2003). The construction of gender in Islamic legal thought and strategies for reform. *Hawwa: Journal of Women in the Middle East and the Islamic World*, 1(1), 1–28.

――― (2006). Muslim women's quest for equality: Between Islamic law and feminism. *Critical Inquiry*, 32(4), 629–645.

Mir-Husseini, Z. (2010). Multiplied, not humiliated: Broken taboos in post-election Iran. In N. Hashemi & D. Postel. (Eds.). *The people reloaded: The green movement and the struggle for Iran's future*. New York: Melville House.

Mirsepassi, A. (2010). *Democracy in modern Iran*. New York: New York University Press.

Mirtaheri, S. A. (2013). The politics of Ahmadinejad and Chavez: A misplaced comparison. *Class, Race and Corporate Power*, 1(1), 1–6.

Moghisi, H. (2004). Troubled relationships: Women, nationalism and the left movement in Iran. In S. Cronin, *Reformers and revolutionaries in modern Iran: New perspective on the Iranian left*. (Ed.). London: RoutledgeCurzon.

――― (2011). Islamic feminism revisited. *Comparative Studies of South Asia, Africa and the Middle East*, 31(1), 76–84.

Moslem, M. (2002). *Factional politics in post-Khomeini Iran*. Syracuse: Syracuse University Press.

Mostaghim, R., & Daraghi, B. (2009). Iranian cleric raises to become the voice of opposition. *Los Angeles Times*. Retrieved from http://articles.latimes.com/2009/sep/09/world/fg-iran-karroubi9.

Motlagh, A. (2012). *Burying the beloved: Marriage, realism, and reform in modern Iran*. Stanford, CA: Stanford University Press.

222   Bibliography

Mousavi, M. (2009). Five Goals and Forty-Five Strategies for Solving Women's Problems. *Kalameh-ye Sabz* 1(11).

Nabavi, N. (2012). From "reform" to "rights": Mapping a changing discourse in Iran, 1997–2009. In N. Nabavi, (Ed.). *Iran: From theocracy to the Green Movement.* (pp. 39–54). New York: Palgrave Macmillan.

Nahavandi, H. (2014*). Mohamad Reza Pahlavi: The Last Shahanshah.* Ketab Corp.

Nasri, R. (2009). Iran's green revolution: Rethinking old paradigms. Interview with Reza Nasri. *International Foundation for Peace.* Retrieved from http://www.roadstopeace.com/articles/irans-green-revolution-rethinking-old-paradigms- interview-with-reza-nasri.

Nazifkar, N. (2011). Introduction. In H. Dabashi, (Ed.). *The Green Movement in Iran.* New Brunswick, NJ: Transaction Publishers.

NBC News. (2009). *Candidate's wife a new political star in Iran.* Retrieved from http://www.nbcnews.com/id/30968206/ns/world_news-mideast_n_africa/t/candidates-wife-new-political-star-iran/#.WJN_hXkzWUk.

Nealon, J. (2008). *Foucault beyond Foucault: Power and its intensifications.* Stanford, CA: Stanford University Press.

New York Times. (2009). *Latest Iran protests reverberate online.* Retrieved from https://thelede.blogs.nytimes.com/2009/07/31/latest-iran-protests-reverberate-online/?r=0.

Newman, S. (2015). 'Critique will be the art of voluntary inservitude': Foucault, La Boétie and the problem of freedom. In S. Fuggle, Y. Lanci, & M. Tazzioli, *Foucault and the history of present.* (Eds.). (pp. 58–74). Palgrave Macmillan.

Niakooee, A., & Ejazee, E. (2014). Foreign policy and economic development: Iran under Rafsanjani. *Iranian Review of Foreign Affairs*, 5(3), 179–203.

Nomani, F., & Behdad, S. (2012). Labor rights and the democracy movement in Iran: Building a social democracy. *Northwestern Journal of International Human Rights*, 10(4), 212–230.

O'Farrell, C. (2005). *Michel Foucault.* London: SAGE Publications.

Oberschall, A. (1973). *Social conflict and social Movements.* Englewood Cliffs, NJ: Prentice-Hall.

Offe, C. (1985). New social movements: Challenging the boundaries of institutional politics. *Social Research*, 52(4), 817–868.

Oliver, E. P., Cadena-Rao, J., & Strawn, D. K. (2003). Emerging trends in the study of protest and social movements. *Research in Political Sociology*, 12(1), 213–244.

Osanloo, A. (2009). *The politics of women's rights in Iran.* Princeton, NJ: Princeton University Press.

Osborne, T. (1999). Critical spirituality: On ethics and politics in the later Foucault. In S. Ashenden, & D. Owen, (Eds.). *Foucault Contra Habermas: Recasting the Dialogue between Genealogy and Critical Theory.* Sage Publications.

Pahlavi, M. R. (1961). *Mission for my country.* Hutchinson.

——— (1994). *Toward the Great Civilization: A dream revisited.* Satrap Publishing.

Pahlavi, F. (2004). *An enduring love: My life with the Shah. A Memoir.* New York: Miramax Books.

Parsa, M. (1989). *Social origins of the Iranian revolution.* New Brunswick: Rutgers University Press.

Pourmokhtari, N. (2013). A postcolonial critique of state sovereignty in IR: The contradictory legacy of a 'west-centric' discipline. *Third World Quarterly*, 34(10), 1767–1793.

Pourmokhtari, N. (2014). Understanding Iran's Green Movement as a 'movement of movements'. *Sociology of Islam*, 2(3), 144–177.

Pourmokhtari, N. (2017a). Protestation and mobilization in the Middle East and North Africa: A Foucauldian Model. *Foucault Studies*, 22, 177–207.

Pourmokhtari, N. (2017b). Foucault, the Iranian revolution and the politics of collective action. "Behrooz Ghamari-Tabrizi, Foucault in Iran: Islamic Revolution after the Enlightenment. SCTIW Review Book Symposium on Behrooz Ghamari-Tabrizi's Foucault in Iran." *SCTIW Review/Jadaliyya*.

Povey, T. (2016). *Social movements in Iran and Egypt*. Hampshire: Palgrave Macmillan.

Powers, P. (2007). The philosophical foundations of Foucauldian discourse analysis. *Critical Approaches to Discourse Analysis across Disciplines*, 1(2), 18–31.

Purewal, N. (2014). Disciplining the sex ratio: exploring the governmentality of female foeticide in India, *Global Studies in Culture and Power* 21(5), 466–480.

Qhaneei Fard, E. (2013). *Nightmare of Evin - Memoirs of a political prisoner at Evin*. Ketab Corp.

Radio Zamaaneh. (2010). *Islamic Republic hardliner criticizes women's cycling*. Retrieved from http://www.zamaaneh.com/enzam/2010/08/islamic-republic-hardline.html.

Radio Zamaneh. (2017). *Polompe mahalle kasb-e bahaiyan edameh darad*. Retrieved from https://www.radiozamaneh.com/350918.

Rafizadeh, M. (2011). The unrecognized social movements: One million signature campaign and the Islamist state of Iran. *Middle East Studies*, 3(6), 47–78.

Rahimi, B. (2012). The sacred in fragments: Shi'i Iran since the 1979 revolution. In N. Nabavi, (Ed.). *Iran: From theocracy to the Green Movement*. (pp. 39–54). New York: Palgrave Macmillan.

Rahnema, S. (1992). Work councils in Iran: The illusion of worker control. *Economic and Industrial Democracy*, 13(1), 69–84.

Razavi, R. (2009). The cultural revolution in Iran, with close regard to the universities, and its impact on the student movement. *Middle Eastern Studies*, 45(1), 1–17.

Refworld, (2006). *Routine abuse, routine denial: Civil rights and the political crisis in Bahrain*. Retrieved from http://www.refworld.org/docid/45cafc9e2.html.

Reisinezhad, A., & Farhadi, P. (2016). Cultural opportunity and social movements. The Iranian Green Movement and the Egyptian Tahrir Revolution. *Sociology of Islam*, 4(3), 236–260.

Rejali, D. (1994). *Torture & modernity: self, society, and state in modern Iran*. Boulder: Westview Press.

Rhoads, C., & Fassihi, F. (2011). *Iran vows to unplug internet*. Retrieved from http://halalfocus.net/iran-vows-to-unplug-internet/

Rivetti, P., & Cavatorta, F. (2013). 'The importance of being civil society': Student politics and the reformist movement in Khatami's Iran. *Middle Eastern Studies*, 49(4), 645–660.

Sadeghi, F. (2009). Foot Soldiers of the Islamic Republic's "Culture of Modesty". *Middle East Research and Information Project*. Retrieved from http://www.merip.org/mer/mer250/foot-soldiers-islamic-republic%E2%80%99s-%E2%80%9Cculture-modesty%E2%80%9D#_4.

——— (2010). *Negotiating with Modernity: Younger Generations and Sexuality in Iran*. Retrieved from http://www.ascleiden.nl/Pdf/youthconfsadeghi.pdf.

——— (2012). The green movement: A struggle against Islamic patriarchy? In N. Nabavi, (Ed.). *Iran: From Theocracy to the Green Movement*. New York: Palgrave Macmillan.

Sadr, S. (2012). Women and for women's movement in post-elections: Double females. In R. Jahanbegloo, *Civil society and democracy in Iran*. (Ed.). Lanham, MD: Lexington Books.

Safshekan, R. & Sabet, F. (2010). The Ayatollah's praetorians: The Islamic revolutionary guard corps and the 2009 election crisis. *Middle East Journal*, 64(4), 543–558.

Sahimi, M. (2010). *The green movement Charter*. PBS. Retrieved from http://www.pbs.org/wgbh/pages/frontline/tehranbureau/2010/06/the-green-movement-charter.html.

Samimi, M. (2013). *Cosmetics boom in Iran*. Retrieved from http://www.al-monitor.com/pulse/originals/2013/12/makeup-iran-women-boom-counterfeit-plastic-surgery.html.

Sandberg, S. (2006) Fighting neo-liberalism with neo-liberal discourse. *Social Movement Studies*, 5(3), pp. 209–228.

Schwerin, U. V. (2015). *The dissident mullah*. London: I.B. Tauris.

Shabani, O. P. (2013). The green's non-violent ethos: The roots of non-violence in the Iranian democratic movement. *Constellations*, 20(2), pp. 347–360.

Shilandari, F. (2010). *Iranian women: Veil and identity*. Gozaar: A Forum on Human Rights and Democracy in Iran. Retrieved from http://www.gozaar.org/english/articles-en/Iranian-Woman-Veil-and-Identity.html.

Simons, J. (2013). Power, resistance, and freedom. In C. Falzon, T. Oleary, & J. Sawicki, (Eds.). *A Companion to Foucault*. (Eds.). Malden, MA: Wiley-Blackwell.

Skocpol, T., & Williamson, V. (2016). *The Tea Party and the remaking of republican conservatism*. Oxfor University Press.

Sreberny, A., & Torfeh, M. (2013). *Cultural Revolution in Iran: contemporary popular culture in the Islamic Republic*. London: I.B. Tauris.

Tahmasebi-Birjani, V. (2010). Green women of Iran: The role of the women's movement during and after Iran's presidential election of 2009. *Constellations: An International Journal of Critical & Democratic Theory*, 17(1): 78–86.

Tahmasebi, S. (2012). The One Million Signatures Campaign: An effort born on the streets. *Amnesty International, Middle East and North Africa Regional Office*. Retrieved from http://amnestymena.org/en/Magazine/Issue20/TheOneMillionSignatureCampaigninIran.aspx?articleID=1101.

Takeyh, R. (2009). *Guardians of the revolution: Iran and the world in the age of the Ayatollahs*. Oxford; New York: Oxford University Press.

Tarrow, S. (1998). *Power in movement: Social movements and contentious politics*. Cambridge: Cambridge University Press.

Tavaana. (2016b). *One million signatures: The battle for gender equality in Iran*. Retrieved from https://tavaana.org/en/content/one-million-signatures-battle-gender-equality-iran

Taylor, D. (2011). Introduction: Power, freedom, and subjectivity. In D. Taylor, (Ed.). *Michel Foucault: Key Concepts*. Acumen.

Tazmini, G. (2009). *Khatami's Iran: The Islamic Republic and the turbulent path to reform*. New York: Tauris Academic Studies.

Tazzioli, S., Fuggle, S., & Lanci, Y. (2015) Introduction. In M. Tazzioli, S. Fuggle, & Y. Lanci, (Eds.). *Foucault and the history of our present*. New York: Palgrave Macmillan.

The Atlantic. (2012). *'Murder': Some accountability in Iranian blogger Sattar Beheshti's death*. Retrieved from https://www.theatlantic.com/international/archive/2012/11/murder-some-accountability-in-iranian-blogger-sattar-beheshtis-death/265203/.

The Charter. (2010). The Green Movement Charter. *PBS*. Retrieved from http://www.pbs.org/wgbh/pages/frontline/tehranbureau/2010/06/the-green-movement-charter.html.

The Guardian. (2007). *Iranian taxi company breaks ranks to enlist women cabbies*. Retrieved from http://www.theguardian.com/world/2007/feb/02/iran.roberttait.

———. (2009). *Iran election protests: The dead, jailed, and missing*. Retrieved from https://www.theguardian.com/world/blog/2009/jul/29/iran-election-protest-dead-missing.

The National. (2010). *Women cyclists face jail, warns Iranian police chief*. Retrieved from http://www.thenational.ae/news/world/middle-east/women-cyclists-face-jail-warns-iranian-police-chief.

The World Bank. (2016). *Iran: Overview*. Retrieved from http://www.worldbank.org/en/country/iran/overview.

Thomassen, T. (2001). A first introduction to archival science. *Archival Science*, 1(4), 373–385.

Tilly, C. (1978). *From mobilization to revolution*. Addison-Wesley Pub. Co.

——— (1984). Social movements and national politics. In C. Bright, & S. Harding. (Eds.). *State- making and social Movements: Essays in history and theory* Ann Arbor: University of Michigan Press.

——— (1997). History and sociological imagining. In K. Erikson, *Sociological Visions: With Essays from Leading Thinkers of Our Time*. Lanham, MD: Rowman & Littlefield.

——— (2004). *Social movements, 1768-2004*. Boulder, CO: Paradigm Publishers.

Time Magazine. (2008). *The Islamic Republic's women at the wheel*. Retrieved from http://content.time.com/time/world/article/0,8599,1847151,00.html

Time. (2009). *Iran's show trials: The hard-liners build their case*. Retrieved from http://content.time.com/time/world/article/0,8599,1914294,00.html

Tohidi, N. (1999). Student movement: The harbinger of a new era in Iran. *ISIM (International Institiue for the Study of Islam in the Modern World Newsletter)*, 4(1). Available from https://openaccess.leidenuniv.nl/bitstream/handle/1887/17356/ISIM_4_Student_Movement-The_Harbinger_of_a_New_Era_in_Iran.pdf?sequence=1.

——— (2006). "Islamic feminism": Negotiating patriarchy and modernity in Iran. In I. M. Abu-Rabi, (Ed.). *The Blackwell companion to contemporary Islamic thought*. Oxford, UK: Blackwell Publishing, pp. 624–643.

——— 2009. Women and the presidential elections: Iran's new political culture. *Informed Comment Blog*. Available from http://www.juancole.com/2009/09/tohidi-women-and-presidential-elections.html.

Topinka, J. R. (2016). Terrorism, governmentality and the simulated city: the Boston Marathon bombing and the search for suspect two, *Visual Communication* 15(3), 351–370.

Touraine, A. (1977). *The self-production of society*. University of Chicago Press.

——— (1981). *The voice and the eye. An analysis of social movements*. Cambridge: Cambridge University Press.

——— (1988). *The Return of the actor: Social theory in postindustrial society*. Minneapolis: University of Minnesota Press.

Tripp, C. (2012). Acting and acting out: Conceptions of political participation in the Middle East. In M. Freeden & A. Vincent, . (Eds.) *Comparative Political Thought: Theorizing Practices*. New York: Routledge.

Vaccarino Bremner, S. (2020). Introduction to Michel Foucault's "political spirituality as the will for alterity". *Critical Inquiry*, 47(1):115–134.

Vahdat, F. (2004). Modernity in Iran: The intersubjective hermeneutics of Mohammad Mojtahed Shabestari. In S. Taji-Farouki, (Ed.). *Modern Muslim intellectuals and the Qur'an*. (pp. 193–224). Oxford: Oxford University Press.

——— (2009). The challenges and opportunities facing the green movement. *Gozaar: A Forum on Human Rights and Democracy in Iran*, available from http://www.gozaar.org/english/articles-en/The-Challenges-and-Opportunities-Facing-the-Green-Movement.html.

——— (2010). Iran's civic movement one year on. *Gozaar: A Forum on Human Rights and Democracy in Iran*. Retrieved from http://www.gozaar.org/english/articles-en/Iran-s-Civic-Movement-One-Year-On.html.

——— (2012). Theorizing civil society in contemporary Iran. In R. Jahanbegloo, (Ed.). *Civil society and democracy in Iran*. Lanham, MD: Lexington Books.

Vinthagen, S., & Johansson, A. (2013). "Everyday resistance": Exploration of concepts and its theories. *Resistance Studies Magazine*, 1, 1–46.

Vucetic, S. (2011). Genealogy as a research tool in international relations. *Review of International Studies*, 37, 1295–1312

Walters, W. (2012). *Governmentality critical encounters: Critical issues in global politics*. Abingdon, UK: Routledge.

West-Pavlov, R. (1999). *Space in theory: Kristeva, Foucault, Deleuze*. New York: Rodopi.

WFSCC. (2017). *Description of duties*. Retrieved from http://en.zn.farhangoelm.ir/Home/Description-of-Duties.

Wiktorowicz, Q. (2004). *Islamic activism: A social movement theory approach*. Bloomington, Indiana: Indiana University Press.

Wilson, C. (2009). Beyond state politics: Subjectivities and techniques of government in contemporary neoliberal social movements. In S. Binkley, & J. Capetillo, (Eds.). *A Foucault for the 21st Century: Governmentality, Biopolitics and Discipline in the New Millennium* Cambridge Scholars Publishing.

World Education News & Review. (2013). *Education in Iran*. Retrieved from http://wenr.wes.org/2013/04/wenr-april-2013-an-overview-of-education-in-iran/

———. (2014). *Iranian student mobility on growth path*. Retrieved from http://wenr.wes.org/2014/05/iranian-student-mobility-on-growth-path/.

Worldometers. (2016). *Iran population*. Retrieved from http://www.worldometers.info/world-population/iran-population/

Yaghmaian, B. (2002). *Social change in Iran: An eyewitness account of dissent, defiance, and new movements for rights*. Albany, NY: State University of New York Press.

Yazdan Panah, H. (2015). *Iran's labor movement: Interview with labor activist Mansour Osanlou*. Retrieved from https://medium.com/middle-east-news/iran-s-labor-movement-interview-with-labor-activist-mansour-osanlou-78e7e7e3ac91.

YouTube. (2013). *Debate Noam Chomsky & Michel Foucault - On human nature*. Retrieved from https://www.youtube.com/watch?v=3wfNl2L0Gf8&t=643s.

Zia-Ebrahimi, R. (2010). Iranian identity, the 'Aryan Race,' and Jake Gyllenhaal. *PBS*. Retrieved from http://www.pbs.org/wgbh/pages/frontline/tehranbureau/2010/08/post-2.html.

Žižek, S. (2009). Berlusconi in Tehran. *London Review of Books*, available from http://www.lrb.co.uk/v31/n14/zize01_.html.

Zubaida, S. (1997). Is Iran an Islamic state? In J. Beinin, & J. Stork, (Eds.). *Political Islam: Essays from Middle East Report*. Berkeley: University of California Press.

Index

Ahmadinejad, Mahmoud 3, 7–8, 15, 21, 57–58, 83, 140, 146, 148, 153–161, 165–166, 168, 170, 172–176, 181, 183–184, 187–188, 191, 197
Arab Spring 2, 21
Art of repression 20, 80, 82
Al-Nimr, Nimr Baqir 16

Bahrain 15–17, 19, 31–32
Basij 77, 82–84, 91, 94, 122, 124, 127, 137, 162, 165, 168
Bayat, Asef 10, 15, 17–18, 25–29, 32, 40, 41, 64, 72, 81, 87–88, 90, 92, 95, 97, 105, 106, 109, 112–115, 120, 123, 125–126, 131–132, 134, 136–139, 167, 180, 197
Bicycling 150, 191, 199
Biopower 44, 46–47, 54
Bou'azizi, Mohammad 21

Civic movement 10
Civil rights 2–3, 12, 173–174, 183, 198
Constellational governmentality 41, 43, 44
Counterdiscourse 7, 26, 47, 99, 102–103, 106, 143, 146, 152–153, 179, 181, 184, 190

Dabashi, Hamid 1, 3, 9, 28, 31, 64, 106, 178, 181
Disciplinary power 46, 75–76, 106, 147, 150–151, 165
Discourse analysis 4, 57
Dominant discourse 7, 47, 52, 99, 102–103, 146, 148, 152–153, 190

Egypt 17, 23
Everyday resistance 6, 54, 61, 85–87, 96, 143, 166, 177, 190

Foucauldian model 5, 33, 59, 148, 190
Foucault, Michel 3, 33, 193

Goodwin, Jeff 32, 34–35, 41
Governmentality 4, 6–7, 34, 40–44, 48, 54–56, 60–64, 67–68, 95, 97–100, 103, 105–107, 110, 115–116, 118, 124, 128–130, 135, 142–144, 146, 148–150, 156–157, 176, 184, 190–192, 195, 198
Governmentalization of joy 75
Green Movement 1–11, 18, 20–21, 27–33, 41, 54, 56–60, 71, 79, 81–83, 86, 131, 143, 146–148, 153, 172, 175–186, 188–192, 197–199, 201
Guardian Council 1, 16, 27, 66–67, 109, 115, 138, 155, 162, 173

Hussein, Louay 16

Iran's green movement 11, 27–29, 33, 41, 54, 56
Iranian revolution 17, 25–26, 31, 50, 149, 156, 190, 195
Islamism 25–28, 160
Islamist governmentality 6–7, 44, 54–56, 61–62, 64–65, 67–68, 72, 85, 95, 97, 99, 105–107, 110, 115, 118, 124, 128–130, 135, 143, 146, 190, 192, 198, 200

Jackson, Michael 113

Karoubi, Mehdi 1–2, 7, 10, 16, 108, 138, 172–175, 181–182, 185, 188, 191
Khamenei, Ali 74, 104

Index

Khatami, Mohammad 15, 16, 20, 82, 92, 107–108, 111, 114–118, 121, 123–124, 126–127, 135, 137–138, 140, 144–145, 154–158, 161, 166, 170, 175, 181, 184, 187
Khomeini, Ayatollah 7, 26, 32, 64, 66–67, 70, 72–73, 99, 103–104, 106, 108, 120, 125, 132

Mainstream social movement theories 3, 5, 9, 11, 27, 32
Majlis 16, 66–67, 78, 84, 104, 107, 109, 114, 116, 121, 127, 130, 137–140, 143, 145, 154–155, 160–162, 185, 201
McAdam, Dough 9, 12–13, 32
MENA 17–19, 21
Mousavi, Mir-Hossein 1–2, 7, 10, 16, 60, 172–176, 181–182, 188, 191
Movement of movements 5, 7–9, 29–32, 56–57, 146, 148, 175–180, 182, 186, 189–191
Movements of counterconduct 5–6, 29, 48–50, 54, 86–92, 95–98, 100–101, 112, 114, 148–151, 176, 180, 182, 186, 189, 191, 199–200
Mosaddegh, Mohammad 16, 194

Neo-absolutist discourse 153, 156–157, 159–160, 181–184
Neo-Islamist governmentality 7, 146, 156–157, 159, 168, 170, 176, 180, 184, 191
New social movements 13–15

Presence-as-resistance 44, 138–139, 166–167, 172, 190
Political contestation 6–7, 18, 56, 62, 98–100, 103, 118, 190, 197
Political opportunities 12–13, 20, 28, 69
Political process theory 12, 19
Post-Islamism 26–27
Post-Islamist feminists 133–135
Post-Revolutionary Iran 1–2, 5–8, 56–58, 61–62, 68, 70, 85, 103, 125, 133, 142, 146, 148, 170, 176, 179, 181, 186, 190, 197–198

Refolution 10
Reformism 106, 110, 123, 125–126, 186
Reformism-reconfigured 179, 182–186
Reformists 9, 67, 109–110, 114, 118, 120–123, 125–126, 138, 139, 154–156
Resource mobilization theory 12
Revolutionary Guard 1, 71, 74, 82, 84, 122, 126, 129, 156
Rights-based society 7, 146, 179–181, 184, 186, 190–191, 197

Salman, Ali 16
Saudi Arabia 15–16
Shi'a Islam 1, 79–80, 197
Shari'a law 16, 67, 72, 131–134, 137–138, 142, 155
Sharif, Ibrahim 16
Social mobilization 6–7, 11–12, 25, 27–28, 33, 41, 56–57, 62, 98, 100, 103, 190
Social movements 3, 5–6, 8, 9, 11–13, 15, 20, 22–25, 27–29, 31–33, 40–41, 48–49, 53, 56, 59, 102, 172, 189
Sovereign power 44–45, 47, 55
Supreme Leader 1, 2, 27, 32, 55, 64–68, 71, 73–74, 80–82, 97, 104–106, 109, 115, 119, 121–123, 129, 154, 158–159, 185, 187
Syria 15–16, 26

Tilly, Charles 11–12, 15, 17, 31–32, 41
Tunisia 17, 21, 28

Uprising of Dignity 17

Valiy-e faqih 64–67, 118, 158, 181

Women's One Million Signature Campaign 4–6, 18–19, 31, 57–58, 98, 103, 131, 140–142, 144, 166, 190, 199

Yemen 17

Žižek, Slavoj 3, 192